THE BRITISH
ADMIRALTY

THE BRITISH ADMIRALTY

LESLIE GARDINER

WILLIAM BLACKWOOD & SONS LTD
EDINBURGH AND LONDON
1968

Printed at the Press of the Publisher
William Blackwood & Sons Ltd, Edinburgh
SBN: 85158 001 7

Introduction and Acknowledgments

When dealing with a subject so rich and complex as the British Admiralty, one cannot allow more than a passing reference to some of the important events of naval history. They deserve, and in many cases have, whole books devoted to them. Readers who want to brush up on the development of the Royal Navy might consult some of the books listed in the bibliography at the end of this work. That is what the author did, and for background material on the story of the Royal Navy's ruling body through the ages he found the works of Sir Geoffrey Callender and F. H. Hinsley, Christopher Lloyd, David Hannay, Sir Julian Corbett and Professor Michael Lewis most useful. They are standard literature on the British sea service and are found in every self-respecting public library.

Naval administration has been a rather neglected branch of naval studies. From among the few published records on the subject the author has relied heavily in their periods on the histories of Professor M. Oppenheim (1509 to 1660) and of Sir John Briggs (1827 to 1892).

The spate of reminiscences by, and lives of, the renowned admirals and political personalities which begin towards the end of the nineteenth century has happily never subsided. Once again, considerations of space prevented some fascinating tales of Admiralty from being more than hinted at in this work. For the full flavour, the reader must go to those twentieth-century volumes of memoirs and biographies which are acknowledged in the bibliography on pages 400 and 401.

Among the naval officers who gave him valuable information about Admiralty history and organisation from personal experience, the author wishes especially to thank Admiral of the Fleet Earl Mountbatten of Burma, Admiral of the Fleet Sir William James and Admiral Sir Peter Reid.

He also expresses his gratitude to Captain David Wilson, Royal Navy (Retired), who read the typescript and made numerous important corrections and suggestions; the staff of the Accommodation and Messenger Branch (Royal Navy) of the Ministry of Defence; the staff of the Naval Library, Fulham; and the Librarian and staff of the County Library in Haddington, East Lothian.

Contents

Illustrations

1 Stately Home of Admiralty

' 'Twas by Saint Martin's half-past four
As from the Adm'ralty I started;
The First Lord's levée was just o'er,
And many left him broken-hearted. . . .'

—but we shall not accompany the half-pay lieutenant down Whitehall, or listen to the rest of his twenty-odd stanza complaint. He will be back to-morrow, and the next day, to kick his heels in that so aptly-named 'waiting' room. The junior officer who holds the record for assiduous daily attendance on Their Lordships, a midshipman upon whom Interest never smiled, 'waited' there for three years.

Instead we shall approach the foliated stone screen on the Whitehall front, put up in 1760 to protect the Lords of the Admiralty from the indiscretions of desperate unpaid seamen. We shall squeeze through the arch—it is soon to meet the risk of destruction, when the organisers of Nelson's funeral, on a wintry morning in 1806, suddenly realise the gun-carriage is too wide to go through, and thirty admirals and a hundred captains are waiting outside to escort the body to Saint Paul's—but they carry the hero out in the end; another twenty years, and it actually is knocked down, to let the Duke of Clarence's carriage through. We shall cross the cobbled courtyard on which the London mob, having broken the main gates off their hinges, built a bonfire of sedan chairs to the first-floor windows on the night of the Keppel-Palliser riots in 1779.

All this in our imagination, of course. There is not much about

A

the outside of the Old Admiralty Building today to help us recapitulate its old glories and old woes. A plain stone wall, like the high wall which originally protected the frontage and was surrendered for street-widening in Whitehall, has replaced most of the ornamental screen of 1760. The cobbled courtyard lies under three inches of tarmac, and the black limousines of Cabinet ministers and secretaries gleam in the parking bays. It must be years since a disgruntled sailor flung a half-brick through the Old Admiralty windows.

Going south from Admiralty Arch, a keen eye detects symbols of Admiralty here and there on grimy, starling-infested granite: anchors or tritons in the stonework of buildings long converted to other uses, all the way down Spring Gardens, across the Mall and past the stage-door of the Whitehall Theatre. Spring Gardens: they really were gardens once, one of them the First Lord's, with chapel and summer-house, bowling-green and sundial, a country plot in the slum-heart of Westminster. Into an upper room came a Treasury official to meet Admiral Sir George Tryon. He was hypochondriacal, and the Admiral knew it and had all the windows open ready for him. " How cold it is, Sir George "—" Yes, it's better to have cold rooms than to catch typhoid fever. The smells in this neighbourhood are so awful " —and the man from the Treasury quickly agreed to the Navy's demands and fled, handkerchief to mouth.

Step into the Old Admiralty Building—nowadays called the Ripley Block in memory of an architect who, architects say, would be better forgotten—and you step into the past. Open-work brass candle lanterns surmounted by royal crowns festoon the entrance hall—they belonged to the Navy Board residences in Seething Lane, and Pepys may have written his diary by their light. Flimsy black-oak chairs with a slanting foul-anchor device on their backs are ranged underneath; they came ashore when the fourth *Enchantress*, last of the Admiralty yachts, was broken up. (The entrance hall, like *Enchantress's* saloon, is picked out in the Admiralty's favourite colour scheme of white, gold and duck-egg blue.) The pair of hooded blue chairs (a third has been 'borrowed' by the Minister of Defence next door) came from a Dutch admiral's flagship. They remind you of old-fashioned basketwork seaside chairs, the kind you still see on the beach at Zandvoort and Scheveningen. A deep drawer pulls out under their seats, full of cleaning rags and metal-polish tins, but once packed with blankets to keep the night-porter's feet warm. A door in the entrance hall—at least, the commissionaire is positive of it—contains wood from a Spanish galleon of 1588.

Those commissionaires, walking manifestations of the in-flexible Navy Rules, a surer defence than iron gates and stone screens, apply the same dispassionate scrutiny to Sea Lords and junior typists, to sailors, soldiers, airmen and civilians. Mankind for them has only two distinctions: those with an admittance pass and those without. They are the spiritual descendants of Admiralty servants down the ages, beginning with that first Navy Board porter who, twenty-four hours a day for £25 a year, suffered 'no Beggar to infest the Houses, nor the Children to play about the Grounds, nor any Suspicious Person to lurk, nor any Horse to water'.

In 1967 they have taken to wearing a new lapel-badge, rejecting the combined-operations theme of the Ministry of Defence. It is the historic 'tri-anchor' of Henry VIII's Navy Board. The more we haul our Admiralty into the future, the deeper it plunges its roots into the past.

The commissionaires scrutinise arrivals and departures; and Admiral Viscount Nelson keeps a cold eye on them too—E. H. Baily's more-than-lifesize plaster model, the original of the Trafalgar Square monument. Round the corner the Admiral, naturally, has a room all to himself, the room in which his corpse rested when it was brought home from Trafalgar, although for years there were arguments as to precisely which room that was.

The Nelson Room is along the corridor, next to the old captains' waiting room. A plaque determines the exact spot on which the coffin rested. Coloured engravings, portraying like stations of the cross the hero's progress to his tomb in Saint Paul's, look down on various personal relics. There is a 'God Bless You' on worn parchment, scrawled with a spluttering pen: Nelson's first essay in left-handed writing after he lost his arm. (The story goes that a gunner slipped the paper in his pocket, kept it for years and traded it to Their Lordships for a job— a nice example of Interest earned on faith in his young captain's future, for Nelson's career prospects looked gloomy at the time.)

Junior naval officers of the eighteenth and nineteenth centuries could have drawn you every cobweb and furniture scratch in the waiting room. The ancient globe they idly spun is defaced with their finger-marks. The rhyme attributed to Captain Marryat—considered the wittiest of squibs by simple-minded midshipmen and lieutenants of his day—is scribbled on a water-colour on the wall:

'In sore affliction tried, by God's commands,
Of patience, Job the great example stands.
But in these days a trial more severe
Had been Job's lot, if God had sent him here.'

The original went to surroundings the growth of the Fleet made more appropriate, the office of the Drafting Commander in the Royal Naval Barracks at Portsmouth.

Having brushed up on their world geography and English literature, unemployed officers could study the peculiar tele-graphic code which the Admiralty devised for the Napoleonic wars and by which a transmission time of twelve minutes was claimed for London-Portsmouth messages in clear weather. It is all set out on a chart in the waiting room, with a diagram of the shutter telegraph once mounted on the Admiralty roof, with repeating structures on hill-tops and church towers at intervals of about ten miles, all the way to Portsmouth in the south-west, Chatham in the south-east and, later on, Harwich in the north-east.

It worked on a kind of blackboard divided into six 'ports'. Combinations of ports, opened or closed, denoted the letters of the alphabet. When all the ports were open the blackboard looked like a blank square frame and that meant the telegraph (like the occupants of the room below) was 'Not Working': a fairly common situation. Even when the south of England was at its unindustrialised fairest, operators on the Admiralty telegraph must have spent many hours huddled on their draughty perches waiting for the weather to clear. London fog and drizzle was the system's worst enemy. Here is Marryat's Captain O'Brien dashing to Portsmouth to 'read himself in' aboard his new ship before some rival captain brings Interest to bear and changes the First Lord's mind:

'I looked up at the sky as I left the Admiralty portico and was glad to see that the weather was so thick and the telegraph not at work, or I might have been too late.'

Bits of wood and ironmongery from the telegraph, and sockets and stanchions, are still rotting and rusting about the stations in the southern counties. Details of the Harwich link seem to be lost, but the 'Chatham line' went: (1) the roof of Admiralty House, the First Lord's residence; (2) Number 36, West Square, Southwark; (3) New Cross Gate, Nunhead (now called Telegraph Hill); (4) Shooter's Hill; (5) Swanscombe; (6) Gad's Hill, Shorne; (7) Chatham Dockyard.

And to Portsmouth: (1) Admiralty House; (2) Royal

Hospital, Chelsea; (3) 'The Highland', Putney; (4) Netley Heath; (5) Hascombe; (6) Blackdown; (7) Beacon Hill, Harting; (8) Portsdown Hill; (9) The Glacis, Portsmouth.

In the seventeen-nineties metropolitan citizens and sleepy-hollow rustics alike gaped at the telegraph and speculated on the nature of the message its twinkling ports was conveying to the Fleet; took comfort, perhaps, from the thought that at least one Government department remained abreast of science and alive to the perils of invasion. The telegraph helped to make the name of Admiralty more familiar and impressive than that of any other Government department. A famous express stage-coach, the London-Nottingham flyer, was christened 'Telegraph'; ships, balloons, race-horses, even furniture and new styles in hats, used the exotic word. It signified everything that was new, startling, efficient or supernaturally swift; by association, the British public got it into its head that the Admiralty was all of these things.

Note the dark-oak wall-clock at the foot of the staircase in the main building; another memento of Napoleonic days, one of the public timepieces called 'Parliamentary clocks', installed in all the Government offices to mitigate the effect on private timepieces of Billy Pitt's clock tax. Enter, at the top of the stairs, the central attraction of Old Admiralty, an apartment not large but full of character, modestly furnished but infused with all the authority and dignity of the Royal Navy's ruling house.

Two portraits glare at each other from opposite ends. You recognise Nelson—Guzzardi's Nelson of 1799, not a flattering likeness but they say the Admiral was sick at the time. Whoever can the other be? You have to be acquainted with the Georgian monarchs, their pendulous chops and celebrated 'slouching eyelids' to identify Admiral of the Fleet His Royal Highness Prince William, Duke of Clarence, in the gorgeous purple and gold of the Lord High Admiral.

The Duke, one of the briefest and least happy Lords High Admiral in history, presided over the council of admirals for less than a year, but he left his mark on the Board Room. He designed the big armchair with the curved back, they say, and the long mahogany table, though he never meant it to have that bay cut out at the end—that was done for George Ward Hunt's benefit, a First Lord of Disraelian times who, at twenty-four stone, had difficulty getting near his papers. The Duke presented the great silver inkstand too—showing the Lords that, although they sacked him, he bore them no ill-will—and members to this day, whenever they meet in the Board Room (which is not often), can sign the minutes with its silver quill pen.

The room looks unlived in, is getting the air of a small museum. Members of the Admiralty Board, since they lost the fine ringing title of Lords Commissioners for Executing the Office of the Lord High Admiral, generally assemble in the main Defence Building farther down Whitehall. They have left their Admiralty-pattern blotting pads behind: all except one decorated with a golden foul anchor, and that one the Deputy Secretary's pad—he was never a full member of the Board.

You stumble over a grey wooden box made, it says in silver on the blue velvet lining, from timber of H.M.S. *Victory*. This is where the flag of the Lord High Admiral reposes, when the civilian clerk in charge of it has remembered to bundle it up and put it away properly: the flag of crimson silk, with golden anchor twice fouled, fourteen feet long and six feet wide (the only naval flag, ensign or standard so shaped), which flew above the Admiralty Building and in ships in which the Lords of the Admiralty were embarked, and also in warships at their launchings.

It flew its last full day on 31st March 1964 and—in the words of the silver inscription on the box—was 'lowered with due ceremony on that evening in the presence of the Board of

Admiralty '.

Next day the Board of Admiralty became the Admiralty Board (after a fight: Whitehall wanted to call it the Navy Board). The Queen assumed the ancient office of Lord High Admiral—someone had to; for the Board, for the first time in more than a hundred years, was ' out of commission '. Her Majesty was the first Lord High Admiral since her great-great-great-granduncle Clarence.

She received the flag and returned it to the Board Room for safe keeping. You still see it floating above Whitehall on occasions, and that means that the Queen is in the Old Admiralty Building, probably watching the Retreat beaten, or some similar military ceremony performed, from a window overlooking the Horse Guards Parade.

The Queen returned the flag, but kept the ' verge ' at Buckingham Palace—the Lord High Admiral's staff of office, a decorated silver stick half as tall again as its bearer. The Board Room holds the second-best verge instead—the staff which once belonged, like the brasswork in the entrance hall, to the Principal Officers of the old Navy Board, at one time the executive directors of the Royal Navy under Their Lordships' administration. Another Navy Board trophy catching the sunlight under the window takes you back to those days of a dual-control Admiralty. It is the huge breastplate badge, silver on scarlet, of the Navy Board coxswain of 1736. One of the major ceremonial sights of London for four centuries was the Principal Officers afloat in their barge, when a barge was as good a means of transport as any for getting them between their offices in Seething Lane and their masters in Whitehall.

The coxswains and their crews lingered on into the nineteenth century and some of the badges they surrendered when they retired were melted down and made into Naval Long Service medals.

First Lords of recent years avoided the bay of George Ward Hunt and settled themselves halfway down the table. Their colleagues, whose number varied between four and fourteen, some naval and some civilian, some very senior and others not, sat on their straight-backed armless ' board room ' chairs in no special order; but over the centuries a custom evolved for the professional Lords to cluster on the First Lord's right, and the lay and secretarial Lords on his left.

The First Lord's empty place faces the Board Room show-piece: the fireplace with the black-leaded arms of Charles II going up the chimney, surrounded by intricate light-oak carvings of astrolabes, sextants, bearing-rings, all manner of old-fashioned nautical instruments and symbols, with parts which actually work, attributed to Grinling Gibbons. Above hung a fitting from which charts could be pulled down, but it is many a long year since charts were there. A big disc covers it. This is the wind-indicator often depicted in naval histories—a circular map of the British Isles and their western approaches, dated about 1750, and a three-foot brass pointer to swing across it, geared to the weather-vane on the Admiralty roof for at-a-glance appreciation of the vital element in sailing-ship tactics. Modern orthography has left the spelling far behind on the map, but the indicator seems to work all right. So does the grandfather clock in the corner (a Bradley clock), and if it is out of step with the date, that is because date-recorders were exciting novelties on clocks of Bradley's period, and not expected to be foolproof.

Crowning the fireplace display, a symbolic assemblage of gilded carvings, trumpets of victory, swords of fame, the all-seeing eye, keeps the room in mind of Stuart conceptions of the divine rights of kings.

Sit in the First Lord's chair and let the all-seeing eye pick out the bits we have missed. Two barely discernible battle-scenes cover the wall's highest panels. A mark is cut in the woodwork lower down—often pointed out to visitors as a measurement of Nelson's height, but actually the standard applied at one time to young gentlemen who appeared before Admiralty Selection Boards for cadetships in the Navy. A side table is allocated for the framed Letters Patent appointing the last Lords Commissioners; the name of Jellicoe leads them— the last First Lord, son of Admiral Jellicoe. A white ceiling, inscribed with interlocking circles of golden emblems, canopies the Royal Navy's most important chamber afloat or ashore.

It was not true, incidentally, though widely rumoured in the Fleet at the time, that the Germans knew better than to drop bombs on the Admiralty and wreck the fount of naval confusion. The old Board Room suffered two hits, one on either side, in the raids of 1941.

Like most old Whitehall strongholds—more than most—the Admiralty's ground and middle floors were divided into moderately spacious suites and apartments, reserved to the use of the Lords and their senior colleagues. The clerks fitted in where they could, even in recent times, in breezy attics and damp windowless basements, courting pneumonia, eye-strain and rheumatoid arthritis. Secretive and anonymous, they inked in names on commissions and warrants, sending the Navy's officers and men with a stroke of a quill to death, glory or oblivion.

Working conditions at the Admiralty at any given period were always regarded as about a hundred years behind every other Government department's. There are old-timers who claim to remember perfectly the uproar over the first fountainpens and typewriters.

Through some of those attic rooms and Defence Ministry stationery barricades we can climb to the roof of the Ripley Block and, on a day of telegraphic visibility, gaze over the spires and ragged rooftops of the City. Down there on Horse

Guards Parade is the building's back entrance, at one time its front entrance. The Duke of Clarence had an eye on that too: he planned an arch and gatehouse, but Croker conveniently mislaid the plans until he was out of the way—Croker the Admiralty secretary, fuming at not having been consulted.

Down there too, under the windows of the junior Lords' residences, a pillory used to stand. Admiral Lord Cochrane very nearly came to it, although it was so infrequently used in his day that any occupant got his name in the papers:

' Mr Cock, a purser of the Navy, stood in the pillory yesterday opposite the Admiralty for defrauding His Majesty of naval stores.' (*The Times*, May 1802.)

First Lords had suites of rooms in the main building, known in Admiralty jargon as the ' Private Office'. But they lived at Admiralty House, part of a new wing (new in 1786) added to the Old Building on the Horse Guards Parade side. From where we stand you can see its entrance in the courtyard, with brass knocker, oak door and plain portico; see someone patrolling the roof, too, or perhaps just inspecting the guttering. Cabinet ministers live in the 'new' wing.

There is an Admiralty House for every naval outpost in the world and every home port in the British Isles—residence of commander-in-chief or admiral superintendent. Most are gracious stone mansions of the best period, early Georgian, with elegant balconies and flights of steps flanked with lions and unicorns in mellowed stone, sometimes with exophthalmic figureheads of painted oak from the old ships. Admiralty House in London went in for no such frills. To Sir Samuel Hoare, First Lord in 1936, it resembled ' some great magnate's residence in town or country '—north-country. It was he, or Lady Hoare, who tore down the pitch-pine portico which a predecessor had put up one night for a party and no one had thought to take away again; who pulled up the dirty messdeck

corticine and disclosed a handsome stone-blocked pavement on
the ground floor, rejuvenated the fine old paintings of Cook's
voyages and Samuel Pepys and First Lords dead and gone, and
restored the ferocious array of pikes and grappling irons which
have ever since adorned the hallway.

Since Admiralty House became the residence of the Defence
Minister there have been changes. But the naval pictures remain
and so does some of the ' Fish ' furniture—so called not because
it is decorated with dolphins but because a Mrs Fish presented it
in memory of Nelson.

First Lords traditionally paid £500 a year rental for their
official home—a figure supposed to be nominal but by some
considered excessive. Yet, with its living quarters much reduced
and whole tiers of apartments gone for offices, it remains not a
bad figure for a city-centre mansion.

The Old Admiralty Building originated as a group of
residences for the Naval Lords and Secretaries, centred round
the Board Room. The Admiralty's working strength in 1694,
when the place was planned, was one secretary, two chief clerks,
six other clerks, a messenger, two servants, one porter, one
watchman and a woman cleaner. From the time William and
Mary came to the throne the Board had met in a house belonging
to Judge Jeffries in Duke Street, Westminster. Before the new
house could be started, Wallingford House had to be cleared
from the site and by that time the Admiralty needed more
space for a growing staff. It acquired two houses next door,
the property of King George I, and Mr Ripley, with the practical
help of Thomas Churchill, Master Bricklayer of the Office of
Works and Buildings, was commissioned to construct the block.
The Board first met in the famous Board Room on 30th
September 1725.

Early occupants besieged the Office with complaints. Cracks
developed in the stonework, the cellars got waterlogged every

time the Thames rose to flood level, the Principal Officers of the Navy Board carried out survey after survey and each report made more pessimistic reading than the preceding one. The clerks, Parliament was told in 1786, 'sit at their desks in damp cellars where the water frequently rushes in '.

Throughout the nineteenth century some surveyors were advising demolition of the Old Admiralty Building. In 1892, when extensions rose to west and north (Admiralty Arch was built at the end of the century, part of the Mall improvement scheme), the architects scheduled the Old Building again for destruction. But it had become a sort of national monument and surveyors reprieved it with a report that it was good for another seventy-five years, with care. ' The hideous wing of the Old Admiralty,' said Sir John Briggs, ' which, as reported, cannot last . . . and has its foundations upon the mud of the Thames, is to have an addition made to it in flaring red brick, quite out of keeping with its character.' Those new offices of the eighteen-nineties are stone-faced and suitably venerable-looking, now that three-quarters of a century have gone by. The rough red railway-cottage brick is decently clothed.

Underground, in two World Wars, they dug the cellars deeper and spread them wider, waterproofing and insulating as they went. The mysterious, concrete-bound warren of ' Lenin's Tomb '—so mysterious that one worked there for months before finding one's way about—became the headquarters of the Royal Navy's most secret communications systems, employing hundreds of sailors, Wrens, cypher experts and clerks. The Admiralty telegraph, twentieth-century style, was lifted off the rooftops and hidden in the depths of the earth.

' Long before that date,' says an old *Mariner's Mirror*, referring to 1967, ' the traffic problems will, we may predict, have become so acute as to force the Government to intervene and pull down the whole range of buildings flanking Admiralty Arch.' But

they still stand. No one in 1967 talks of re-condemning the
Ripley Block. The other great dread of its inhabitants in the
nineties—that they might have to share their quarters with the
Army—has been realised; their successors are sharing with, and
outnumbered by, representatives of both Army and another
Service undreamed of in 1892. The Defence Council has sup-
planted the individual naval, military and aviation administrators.
These days, if you want an Air Board official, you go to the Old
Admiralty Building for him; and if you are looking for an
Admiralty department you may well find it in the War Office
across the road.

The government of the Navy goes back, of course, much
farther than the Ripley Block. Their Lordships of the Admiralty,
the superintending council of admirals, enter history in comparatively recent times and, as a Government department, the
Admiralty in the sense in which most people understand it is
quite a modern creation. But a naval administration is obviously
about as old as the Navy itself and, before we gaze farther afield
from our rooftop vantage-point in Whitehall, it will be as well
to distinguish broadly between the twin systems of old-time
naval administration; although the distinction is to become clear
in more detail as this history progresses.

The Admiralty proper, the dignified part of the establishment, derives from the venerable office of Lord High Admiral.
In the pages which follow, any institution or office which has
an ' Admiralty ' or ' Lord ' in its title may be taken to belong
to this branch; what might be considered the Royal Navy's
Upper House.

The Lower House, the effective part of the establishment,
senior to the Admiralty in age but no other respect, was (until
1832, when it was swallowed by the Admiralty) the Navy
Board. In the offices we shall deal with, the word ' Navy ' is

the clue.

Many designations, especially in eras of rampant bureaucracy, seem to have been invented expressly to confuse the layman; but remembering 'Lords' and 'Admiralty' for the one branch and 'Navy' for the other avoids the worst confusions. For example, it places 'Lord Commissioner' where he belongs, at the Admiralty; and 'Navy Commissioner' where *he* belongs, at the Navy Board.

'Naval officer', even, as long as the Navy Board existed, meant officer of the Navy Board. What we call a naval officer today used until well into the nineteenth century to be a sea officer, and as such he will be normally described in this work.

The earliest known Admiralty headquarters was the Gun tavern, now pulled down, on the Green at Deptford, which Lord Howard of Effingham inhabited as Lord High Admiral in Queen Elizabeth's reign. A writer of the last century recalls that Lord Howard's coat-of-arms was engraved on the stone chimney-breast, but remembers nothing else remarkable about it. Tradition says the original Admiralty Board Room was upstairs, overlooking the sweep of the Thames. This, historians think, is the place afterwards called 'Her Majesty's House at Greenwich' from which at times the Treasurer of the Navy— a Navy Board official—addressed his letters.

After the execution of Charles I, the so-called Admiralty Committee met in Whitehall Palace and then at Derby House, home of the Duke of Ormond who happened to be a Lord Commissioner.

When Samuel Pepys took over the Admiralty at the end of his memorable career on the Navy Board, he meant to establish it in York Buildings at the foot of Buckingham Street, off the Strand. (The Buildings replaced York House, London residence of the Archbishop of York, demolished in 1675. It had passed fifty years earlier into the hands of the Duke of Buckingham and you can still see the Villiers crest, oyster-shell decorations and Navy Office anchor on the riverside watergate, only surviving relic of the mansion.)

On York Buildings, at the present Number 12, Buckingham Street, Pepys erected a shield with the imperial crown and anchor, eight feet wide and six feet high. He also put in an order for a giant-sized King's Arms, fifteen feet by nine, but left his job before it was finished, when the arrival of a new king had in any case made the design obsolete. Pepys left Number 12 to go to prison; left it for good on his retirement in 1688; and lived next door (site of the present Number 14) until 1701—just before his death.

By that time his colleagues and successors had settled temporarily in Judge Jeffries' house and were shortly to enter the new Admiralty Building which would outlast the Admiralty itself.

Thus the Admiralty at a very early stage established itself, as was proper, in Westminster, close to the seat of Government. The Navy Board, appropriately again, clung to the City. At first it worked in the Consultation House on Tower Hill, with dumps of stores and victuals for the Fleet all round it. In 1654, reputedly because the Principal Officers could no longer stand the flies and smells from the Navy Victualler's slaughter-yard, it went to the address which Pepys's Diary has made famous, Seething Lane. Sometimes it is called Crutched Friars, a street on which the residences abutted. The row of Navy Board houses included Muscovy House, where the Muscovy Company originated and where Peter the Great lodged when he first came to London to study dockyard management.

This area suffered heavily in World War II and still more heavily—from the sentimental historian's point of view—from the enthusiastic building spate of later years. Crutched Friars

House remains—Number 4 in the street—but none of the gracious Navy Board dwellings with their balustrades and pediments and stone ornamentation. Saint Olave's Church in Hart Street, restored after partial destruction in 1941, looks up wonderingly at a skyline a couple of hundred feet higher than of old, in the complex of office blocks round Fenchurch Street station. It was the Principal Officers' place of worship. But broad new roads and bits of public gardens, the consolation prize of the bombing which swept away a mass of untidy old properties, have opened vistas on the Tower and the Thames which Pepys and his associates never knew.

Different Navy Board officers settled at different times in a neighbouring quarter, never far from the river or from the Navy Pay Office on Tower Hill. In 1786 they all came together again to a headquarters of real splendour, in Somerset House in the Strand. When the Inland Revenue department began to move in, the Navy Board began to move out. Both Navy Board and Admiralty bitterly opposed a move to perpetuate their term of gracious living by putting them in the Old Admiralty Building, to which a new floor would have been added; it was like expecting the ship's officers to take up residence in the Captain's cabin.

Room was eventually found for the Principal Officers in the Admiralty annexe by persuading the junior Lords to go and live elsewhere. The Controller and other Principal Officers went first into a temporary refuge in Spring Gardens, from where they watched the chaotic transfer take four years to complete. Most of the files and historical documents had mercifully been rescued beforehand and deposited in the Public Record Office in Chancery Lane. Even so, miscalculations of staff requirements and the subsequent wrangles kept the Admiralty disorganised for a generation; and from the hopeless mix-up of its records and the inadequacy of the accommodation the Navy

Board never recovered.

Parts of Somerset House are mementoes still of the Navy Office's short tenure. Here and there a cupola'd roof, a spiral staircase, a curved door and the blue, white and gold décor are unquestionably Navy Board style of the Age of Elegance. There is even a Nelson Room—opinions differ why it is so named; the man on the gate tells you confidentially that that was where the Admiral had his private rendezvous with Lady Hamilton. These days they use it for interviewing prospective inspectors of income tax.

On the Embankment front of Somerset House, blocked up and high and dry above the river's present-day level, you can inspect the broad-arched watergate under which Middleton and Byam Martin were rowed daily. Is it Neptune's head, or the head of some superannuated Principal Officer which, with flowing white beard of granite, surmounts the river entrance? No, it is Father Thames, the guide-book says—the London river, for so long the physical link and separation between Navy Board and Admiralty. That wind-vane in the Board Room in Whitehall must often have served a more immediate purpose than to influence the strategy of the Fleet. *The Military and Naval Gazette*, 1863, was announcing the final phase in the Navy Board take-over and mid-century modernisation when it reported:

'Directions have been received at Chatham for the State barges, shallops, gigs, luggage boats, etc., formerly used by the Lords of the Admiralty on State occasions, to be removed from Somerset House and placed in store at Sheerness, the Board of Admiralty having discontinued their use.'

But, on this very spot, a white ensign preserves the old administration's rights on the river. It flies from H.M.S. *President*, a training ship alongside the Embankment. The Navy has a rule that every shore establishment shall be named for a ship, and have a ship of that name in commission afloat. The Admiralty or, as current terminology has it, the Ministry of Defence (Royal Navy), is no exception. Those who actually serve on board this vessel are not Admiralty staff; but every officer and man who comes from the Fleet to serve in the Admiralty departments ashore, whether in London or elsewhere, is appointed on paper to H.M.S. *President*. On paper she has a crew of thousands, including hundreds of Wrens.

2 Before the Dawn

The splendid and evocative word Admiralty, a word of wide meaning, appears from the distant past and confers a spurious antiquity on a Government department which in fact is not so old. The word looks like going on, too, while the institution disappears.

For the Admiralty's physical abolition, a date is soon given: 31st March, 1964. The date of its beginnings is not so easily arrived at.

A naked savage in a coracle grins from the chapter-heading of a nineteenth-century book on naval history. This is travelling rather a long way back in search of an Admiralty. At what point did the fighting sailors acquire governors, a control centre and a headquarters ashore ? Who was responsible for the war-like and organised deployment of the rafts and barges which so impressed Julius Caesar, and whose was the brain behind Constantine the Great's coastal defence system? Can the Count of the Saxon Shore, a Roman colonial officer who exacted the price of Admiralty from the inhabitants of the Channel ports be called a prototype First Lord? Is it fair to trace the modern Admiralty Board's ancestry as far back as the Lord Warden of the Cinque Ports? He certainly dresses like an admiral and at coronations holds the protective canopy, symbol of the sea shield, over the sovereign's head.

King Alfred, says Asser the Welsh monk, ' commanded boats and galleys to be built throughout the kingdom to offer battle to the enemy as they were coming. On board these he placed sailors, whom he commanded to keep watch on the seas. . . .

He also gave orders to his sailors to prevent the enemy from obtaining any supplies by sea.' He inaugurated building, operations, blockade (though of his own coastline)—they are the functions of an Admiralty in an up-to-date conflict. But one must come down the years to pick up the first strands of the complicated organisational network the British Admiralty became—down past 1360 and the reign of Edward III, which saw the High Court of Admiralty established under one head, not to fight wars at sea but to enforce the law of the land in coastal waters. The first warship, if it could be so described, was a kind of fishery protection cruiser.

But this was Admiralty in a different sense of the word, and 1360 will therefore not do. Neither will the next administrative datemark, 1546, when Henry VIII gave the clerks of his ships extra status by appointing them Principal Officers and getting them to consult with each other: it paved the way for the Navy Board, but the Navy Board was not the Admiralty. Something might be said for 1618 (clean sweep of the Navy Board and first appointment of Navy Commissioners, by Charles I); or 1628 (when the Lords Commissioners appeared); and something for 1649 (Parliamentary Commissioners appointed to carry out the duties of Lord High Admiral). They were years of a tangling bureaucracy. The hint of a genuine Admiralty system gleams a moment and is extinguished.

Such a gleam appeared in the golden summer of 1660, when Charles II came home, Pepys joined the Navy Board, the fighting fleets were for the first time designated Royal Navy and the title of Admiral came into common use; again in 1675, when a grateful monarch allowed his faithful servant *carte blanche* to put the Navy on a proper administrative footing and Pepys took the modern title of Secretary of the Admiralty; and again —a more powerful gleam—when Pepys in 1688, upon the fall of the House of Stuart, ' laid down his office and would serve no more'; and a council of which the modern Board of Admiralty was a more or less direct development arose in his place.

Yet the final fitting together of the elements which produced the Admiralty of 1964 and which gave it the character, the standing and the relationship to Crown, Cabinet, Government, Parliament, public and Fleet understood by most people today could not occur before 1832, year of the Admiralty Act, when old Admiralty and old Navy Board united to form one powerful —and expensive—administrative body.

If, on the tombstone of the Board of Admiralty, we inscribe '(1832-1964)' we shall not be far out.

Its history began in the beginning, long before the dawn: when naval operations came under the general heading of war, the strategy was entirely military, the word 'warship' not understood, and movements of fleets and coastal defence arrangements not ordered by a naval staff. It is an interesting thought that a Naval Operations Division of south-country sea-dogs and warrior earls as full of bright advanced ideas as their monarch might have organised King Alfred's campaigns at sea—but it is no more than a thought. Schemes of an exceptional unorthodoxy, suggestions of an enlightenment ages ahead of its times—these indicate the genius of one man. You do not associate them with the actions of a Government department.

William the Conqueror would have seen little need for a controlling body for an Anglo-Norman fleet. He attached little importance to command of the seas. He burned his ships on arrival, allegedly some nine hundred vessels—the way invading princes inclined to do, to deter his soldiers from too many backward glances towards home.

Nor did the 'wooden walls' concept appeal to his successors over the next century or so. In those days the Cinque Ports squadron was England's Navy and the Lord Warden probably came as close to being a little local First Lord of the Admiralty as anyone in medieval times: a First Lord who represented all the maritime interests that mattered and who could exact privileges from the monarch in exchange for a promise to mobilise his ships in an emergency. (Even today the Royal Navy salutes the Lord Warden with nineteen guns, two more than the First Lord would ever be entitled to. In the seventeenth and eighteenth centuries his job would often be combined with that of Lord High Admiral.)

Early English kings called up ships and led them to sea on purely military operations. They were troop transports and nothing more. Throughout the Middle Ages, when the Army had to launch an assault or repel an attack, we find the Lord Warden, or the merchants of London or the Governor of Dover Castle, in the King's absence, laying hands on ships and sending them out. There was no one to store and victual the King's Navy, appoint sea officers, recruit crews and issue the operational orders—no one to perform the duties of an Admiralty. There was not, in fact, until the reign of the Stuarts, a real King's Navy.

A piece of sabre-rattling by King John first created the demand for something on the lines of a permanent patrol force of warships, although it did not create the force. John threatened to make a prize of every foreign vessel which failed to dip its colours to the English sovereign's at sea: an affirmation of a principle recognised as long as the King of England ruled France, that the narrow seas of the Channel were English territorial waters; a principle which, too stubbornly insisted on, kept later Navy Boards and Privy Councils busy smoothing out diplomatic arguments and disciplining English commanders who neglected to enforce it.

John is the first since Alfred to qualify for the title of ' sailor king '. Among his court appointments appears a germ of

Admiralty in the person of William of Wrotham, a priest, as were most of the court officials of the age. William, Archdeacon of Taunton, was made Keeper of the King's Ships. For the casual part-time Plantagenet fleets, the Keeper of the King's Ships did what a Board of Admiralty, half a millennium later, would do for the fleets of Howe, Hawke and Saint Vincent. Down a genealogical line never very straight and sometimes lost sight of for a generation or two, the Keeper descended to Clerk of the Ships, Clerk of Marine Causes, Clerk of the Navy and Clerk of the Acts—and Samuel Pepys, under its last title, carried the post across the gap between the executive and the administrative, to the dignified style of Secretary of the Admiralty.

Fleets were bigger in those days. It is nothing for the old chroniclers to muster an armada of four hundred sail to carry the King to France, or to sink five hundred French ships on passage. One would load those ships by the hundred on the flight deck of a modern aircraft-carrier, and all were begged, borrowed or stolen for the job in hand.

Henry the Fifth indulged an eccentricity by building ships for himself, with his own money. The skeleton ' King's Navy ' was so little regarded as a part of the national defence plan that it was auctioned off under the terms of his will. The few ships the Crown had owned—flatteringly or facetiously referred to as the King's Navy Royal—lay most of their life in the Thames or Hamble River, looking picturesque and providing subsistence for a few shipkeepers and a host of teredo worms. The Clerk's job included hiring them out from time to time to merchants and giving the monarch a small return on his capital investment. They were not meant to win, or even fight, a war. In time of crisis they formed small exclusive rallying-points in the fleets at sea, not to be sacrificed except as a last resort. Hard-working craft of the fishing communities, or merchant vessels hired and commandeered with crews complete, did the serious fighting.

The typical naval adventure of Plantagenet times might be visualised as a kind of Dunkirk affair—a cluster of private owners, traders and enthusiasts setting off in a totally unorganised fashion, vaguely bound for the nearest trouble-spot; among them, crewed by civilians and packed with soldiers, the splendid banners, outrageously top-heavy gilding and spit-and-polish of the useless Navy Royal.

Thus equipped, England and the Continental seafaring nations won and lost their sea-fights well into the reign of Elizabeth I. Thus protected, the Navy Royal evolved into the Royal Navy and behind it, on shore, the seed of Admiralty germinated.

The King's ships carried their care-and-maintenance men to sea with them: carpenter, sailmaker, boatswain, perhaps even a gunner. They assumed a certain dignity in war-time, being then formally engaged by Royal Warrant.

At such a time a captain would be installed. He would be both courtier and soldier perhaps, but rarely a seaman. When he arrived the ship was ' in commission '. Later—Elizabethan times—he would sometimes bring a young man known as a lieutenant, who was ' commissioned ' to deputise for the captain and bring the ship home when the latter died in action.

The traditional barrier between 'commissioned' and 'warrant' officer began to be eroded only in the middle of the nineteenth century. The term ' warrant officer ' vanished from the Navy as recently as 1948 and to the present day the Admiralty office which handles the appointments of naval officers to their ships and establishments is called the C.W. (Commissions and Warrants) Branch.

Admiralty in those ancient days meant, not the governing body of the Navy but the conduct of nautical affairs in the widest sense. To the pre-Elizabethen era belongs the old courtly nomenclature of rank and office which have bequeathed a touch of quaint chivalry on the modern Navy.

'Admiral', for instance, applied to a commander of ships but in no sense a rank, is at least as old as 1297, in which year a State document describes Sir William de Leybourne, a favourite of King Edward I, as Admiral of the Sea of the King of England (short title: Sea Viceroy). The first admirals in Europe were those of Alfonso X of Castile, from whom England's Richard I borrowed the word, along with some rules for the behaviour of mariners.

Soon there were three English admirals, one for the north coast (Dover to Berwick-upon-Tweed), one for the south (Dover to Cornwall) and one for the west (Irish Sea). They had civil and military powers. Edward III merged these appointments into one in 1360 and gave it to a knight of his court, Sir John Beauchamp, for an experimental period of one year.

Sir John drew the fees and commissions formerly taken by the lesser admirals, and presided over the High Court of Admiralty into which the three courts of the north, west and south had been combined. (This is the Court which corresponds to the British Prize Court of today, where in wartime contraband is condemned, prize money allocated for the capture or destruction of enemy ships and salvage claims debated.) When Edward III regularised the Admiral's powers and enlarged his sphere of jurisdiction the High Court of Admiralty became a part of the civil legal system. To complete its tale—for it has little to do with the history of *the* Admiralty—the High Court was removed to the Central Criminal Court in 1834 and to the Assize Courts ten years later; under the Judicature Act of 1873 it formed with two other minor courts—Probate and Divorce—a three-apartment independent house of law.

The first Admiral of all England had legal control, not physical dominion, over the seas. His day-to-day tasks were to keep the peace between seamen—mediating when rival fishing fleets brawled over territorial rights, for example—and to repress piracy, handle disputed contracts between builders, buyers and charterers of ships and adjudicate on questions of prize. But his importance increased with the increase in sea trade and the maritime industries, and he progressed to the position of Great Admiral of England, Ireland and Aquitaine. By the fourteen hundreds he was ranked ninth among the nine ' Great Officers of the Crown '—just like a First Lord of the Admiralty at the height of Britain's naval prestige, with his important place in the Cabinet.

He was the obvious choice for supreme commander, when English forces were at sea—on paper, at least, for the actual operation would probably be carried out by his nominee. The Great Admiral's deputy is almost as venerable as the Great Admiral himself and, what is more, exists at the present day. He is the Lieutenant-Admiral, otherwise known as the Lieutenant of the Admiralty. At first, he presided on behalf of his master at the High Court; for long periods he had a merely decorative function and at times the post disappeared for years; at other times he held down vitally important jobs. The histories of the Lieutenant of the Admiralty, and of the other archaic survival of pre-Admiralty naval administrations—the Vice-Admiral of England and Rear-Admiral of England—are told in the next chapter.

Great Admirals, strictly men about court, were apparently not much missed either in the early days, when appointments were casual and whimsical and the duties nebulous. A tradition grew up of bestowing the post on a relative of the sovereign, rather in the manner of modern royalty with their personal naval aides-de-camp. Some of the noblemen whose names appear in the roll of Admirals of England played serious politics in their day, regarding the maritime office as a profitable sinecure to be obtained for services rendered and aghast at any suggestion that they might sometimes take a trip to sea, or at least to a shipyard. They included John Beaufort, Earl of Somerset (1406), Edmund Holland, Earl of Kent (1407), Thomas Beaufort (1408), John, Duke of Bedford (1426), John Holland, Duke of Exeter (1435), William de la Pole, Duke of Suffolk (1447), Henry Holland, Duke of Exeter (1450), Richard, Duke of Gloucester (1462), Richard Neville, Earl of Warwick ('king-making Warwick') (1471), John Howard, Duke of Norfolk (1483) and John de Vere, Earl of Oxford (1485).

While the Great Admiral, or Lord Admiral, or Admiral of England (the Latin of the original is variously rendered) dabbled in everything except seamanship and drew his £1000 a year plus perquisites, there lived on the banks of the Hamble River in Hampshire a person to whom all questions about building, refitting, manning and hiring out of the King's Navy Royal were referred. He was William Soper, merchant and sometime mayor and collector of customs at the port of Southampton, the first full-time Keeper and Governor of the King's Ships. He watched over the top-heavy craft with trivial armament, museum-pieces even in Henry V's reign, which bore names to match their gaudy sails and timbers and bunting: *Holigost of the Tower, Marie Spayne of the Tower, Cracchere of the Tower, Red Cog of the Tower*—' of the Tower ' being the fifteenth-century equivalent of ' H.M.S.'

Soper got £40 a year from the King, but some of the ships he saw towed away to pay royal debts (merchants of the southern ports paying anything from £80 to £200 apiece for them) belonged more to him than to His Majesty, because he had spent much of his own money on them. Seaport trade and local government being what they were, no doubt Soper had opportunities of feathering his nest at someone else's expense.

One Richard Clyveden succeeded Soper and after him

there is a break in the continuity of the office until it reappears in 1480 as the Clerk of the Ships, with Thomas Rogers, ' citizen and fishmonger', in charge. Rogers followed an increasing trickle of instructions from the King (Edward IV) about providing stores and crews (there is a reference to payment for winter comforts for the sailors) and with royal approval he bought and sold various craft among the civilian shipowners of the region. He lived into the reign of another ' sailor king '— Henry VII, who enacted the first Navigation Laws to ' increase the Navy of England, which is now greatly diminished'. Navy still meant merchant navy. It was laid down that England's principal import, Bordeaux wine, must be carried in English ships; from their storage capacity, measured in ' tuns', derive the complicated ' tonnage' standards which determine the official displacement of ships the world over.

Rogers saw an age dawn in which ships were to be built for purely warlike purposes, not just to carry troops abroad. He was still alive when the 180-gun *Regent*, first major war vessel in British history, had her keel laid. He died, in spite of that ludicrous salary, a wealthy landowner.

He was the last of the fishmonger amateurs. Clerks of Ships were to be more and more technical after him—seamen and boat-builders, like the aptly-named William Cumbresale and Robert Brygandine towards the end of Henry VII's reign. The latter built the first dry dock, at Portsmouth, for £193, specifically to accommodate the *Regent*, which was too big to lie alongside in any English harbour.

Brygandine made himself indispensable in a new century and under a new king—Henry VIII—he rode a mounting wave of sea enthusiasm. The Clerk's increasing responsibilities were soon to be acknowledged with a new title, Clerk of the Acts; but Brygandine in practice was secretary, controller, paymaster, chief constructor and director of supplies rolled into one, with an influence and freedom of manœuvre not to be attained by any subsequent individual or Board of Admiralty. England's naval administration, as long as he lived, was medieval in character. The gap he left, not easily filled by one man, brought into focus the need for a Department, prompted King Henry VIII to start juggling with names and offices, and established the idea of having a group of professionals to run the royal ships. It was the start of a slow process which would end by putting the definite article in front of 'Admiralty'.

3 The Naval Reformation

For a convincing representation of a dressy, rumbustious, damn-your-eyes shipmaster of the first half of the sixteenth century, see Holbein's portrait of Henry VIII. 'Bluff' goes with sea-dog as it goes with King Hal and the King allowed himself to become as much of one as duty and pleasure permitted. A picked crew in livery would pull him down the Thames and he piped his orders to them on a jewelled bo'sun's call ' as loudly as upon a trumpet '. (The story is often told how his Great Admiral, Sir Edward Howard, before being cut to pieces on the deck of a Breton galley, tossed his golden whistle, a replica of the King's, into the sea. Sailors had risen, hauled on ropes, hove round the capstan, trimmed sails and gone to bed to the tune of that instrument since Richard the Lionheart crossed the Channel. The French used a similar shrill pipe, and Bourbon monarchs conferred the Order of the Whistle of Honour on captains who beat the British. It was the badge of Great Admirals and it survives in scarcely-altered shape as the modern bo'sun's call, a penny-whistle anachronism which holds its own in the face of competition from bugles, loud hailers, broadcast systems and all the marvels of twentieth-century warships' internal communications.)

In the first five years of his reign, Henry VIII collected the nucleus of a proper navy. The names of some of the ships read as quaintly as ever: *Peter Pomegranate*, *Kateryn Fortileza*, the *Less Bark*, the *Great Bark* and the *Black Bark*. Later came the *Struse of Dawske*, whatever that meant, the *Galley Subtille*, the *Brigandine* and *Falcon-in-the-Fetterlock*. The pride of the

fleet, the *Henry Grâce à Dieu*, a 1000-ton leviathan, is supposed
to have been designed and built by Robert Brygandine, Clerk
of the Ships.

Their decoration, if not their gunnery, must have made
them awesome sights at sea. It was a College of Heralds, not
an Admiralty, they needed to look after them. Among the *Peter
Pomegranate's* flags, above many square yards of paintwork,
crochet work and carving, floated banners of Saint Katherine,
Saint Edward and Saint Peter; of a Red Lion; two flags of
the Castle, eight streamers of Saint George and four standards
with the Rose and Pomegranate emblem. The pomegranate,
Granada apple, complimented the homeland of Katherine of
Aragon.

The distinguishing mark ' of the Tower ' had gone. It was
hard for an onlooker to see the ships for flags and impossible
still to determine which were the King's own and which on
charter from British or foreign merchants—until the Admiral
of England went to sea and hoisted the royal arms in the maintop
of the chief ship of the King, twice the size of any other flag in
the squadron.

Admirals of England, in Henry's time, were expected to go
to sea. The post was becoming one of direct executive command and, saving the monarch's presence, of administrative
power. Some admirals entered into the spirit of the game
and were keen, or prudent, enough to contribute little fleets of
their own: the Earl of Southampton on his death in 1542 bequeathed his ' gret schippe ' to the King. This was the age
when the naval administration, in the persons of a Great Admiral
and a Clerk of Ships, began the long series of negotiations and
profiteering with the owners of the oak forests then covering
much of Kent, Sussex and Hampshire—negotiations which would
keep Navy Board and Admiralty in perennial states of anxiety
as long as wooden ships lasted.

There is no suggestion so far, of course, that lack of skill in handling ships and men or of dedication to the naval principle is a bar to appointment. More than one Great Admiral has his greatness thrust upon him and staggers under the burden of it—like John Dudley, a powerful schemer ashore but a shrinking violet afloat, who tells the King after a miserable effort to raid the French coast:

'I do thynck I shuld have doon his Maiestie better service in some meaner office wherein to be directed and not be a director.'

The Great Admirals of the reign were: Sir Edward Howard (1512), his brother Lord Thomas Howard (1513), Henry, Duke of Richmond (1525), Sir William Fitzwilliam, afterwards Earl of Southampton (1536), John, Lord Russell (1540) and John Dudley, Lord Lisle, afterwards Duke of Northumberland (1543).

Sir Edward Howard, a genuine fighting admiral, is described as ' an able statesman, a faithful counsellor and a free speaker '—just the qualities a First Lord needed. His term of office, brief but full of incident, ended with his death in action while annoying the French.

His brother Thomas, while Great Admiral, abandoned his ships in time of war and went to command the English Army at Flodden. Faced with a choice between naval and military commands, a Tudor courtier hesitated not a moment.

There began to crop up, from 1520 onwards, a kind of Great Admiral-designate, when the post of Vice-Admiral of England was instituted. Its first holder, William Fitzwilliam, was also the first professional sailor to be raised to the peerage—a precedent which upset the Rip Van Winkles of the time much as the appearance of athletic personalities in modern Honours Lists has done within our own era.

The naval service was becoming a career for landsmen. More and more civilians found steady employment as the reign

B

progressed and Henry VIII added Woolwich and Deptford to the royal dockyard his father had established at Portsmouth. His daughter Elizabeth founded Chatham, completing the original quartet of English navy yards with their little world of superintendents, overseers and labour force, traditionally overstaffed and underpaid. The King enlarged Portsmouth in 1527; selected Woolwich as the cradle of the *Henry Grâce à Dieu* in 1512 and took Deptford five years later, and improved them step by step until they ranked among the most impressive dockyard ports in Europe.

Maritime activity of the purely naval kind, it seemed, would be concentrated on the Thames, where His Majesty could keep a personal eye on his ships. The Clerk of the Ships had lived at Portsmouth from the date the new yard was opened, but there was a case for transferring the administrative headquarters, such as it was, to Westminster or the City. The year old Robert Brygandine retired (it is fixed by the usual document acquitting him of any undetected crimes which might come to light after he had gone, in 1523), John Hopton brought up to London his pens, parchments, measuring instruments and resounding new title, ' Clerk Comptroller of the Ships '.

Henry planned no merely ornamental Navy. He encouraged his ships to go to sea, showing the flag and embarking on little adventures on foreign coasts. One war scare followed another, mobilisation and demobilisation kept the clerks and the sailors up to scratch, the sixteenth-century equivalent of the Naval Estimates rose from half a million to nearly a million and a half pounds. Someone in Whitehall was experimenting with a naval bureaucracy, of which the prime duty had to be keeping track of expenditure. Curious functionaries move like birds of passage across the State Papers of the reign and are never heard of again. Once the Treasurer of the Sea is mentioned, and here are hints of a Treasurer of the Admiralty, Paymaster of

the Sea, Treasurer of the Sea Marine Causes—but whether these
are four different officials or the same official one cannot tell.
On the tombstone of Sir Thomas Spert the title ' Comptroller
of the Navy ' is inscribed, centuries before its time.

Corruption may be as old as the dockyards, but Henry VIII's
Privy Council maintained a grip on book-keeping which Pepys,
long afterwards, would have regarded with envy. The Great
Admiral himself was not exempt from investigation or responsibility for his subordinates. John Dudley, reluctant hero at sea,
a clever intriguer on land who over-reached himself when he
tried to put his daughter-in-law Lady Jane Grey on the throne
and went with her to the scaffold, plaintively addressed the
Secretary of State:

' You write unto me that the Tresawrer of thadmiralltie
being called to accompt his reckoning is so ill-favoridly mad
that there semith a want of £2000 which you cannot well se
what is become of hit.'

Only thirty years earlier, Sir Edward Howard had been able
to administer the Fleet from his own sea cabin—clothing, food
and pay; had even managed to get all his men dressed in the
same colours, Tudor green-and-white. The idea caught on and
the forerunner of the Admiralty's Victualling department (which
has always handled clothing as well as food) wrestled for a
while with the costs, supply, damage to and disappearance of,
green-and-white uniform jackets. After Henry's death everyone
agreed that uniform for sailors was an unnecessary extravagance.
The complications of Dress Regulations and Clothing Allowances
were not to bother the Admiralty seriously for another two
hundred years.

British institutions having always been addicted to rules and
regulations, it is not surprising to find King Henry laying down
the law for sailors before he had an executive to enforce it.
He established discipline on paper, between squadrons and ships

and between captains and their men, by a code drawn up by
Sir Thomas Audley, a courtier unconnected with the sea, and
based, for want of other authority, on the thirteenth-century
book of the Castilian admirals. In it were enshrined K.R. & A.I.
(the *King's Regulations and Admiralty Instructions*), the Navy's
standing orders by which naval officers and men live, die and
are buried; also the framework of the Naval Discipline Acts
and the Fighting Instructions, the rules by which admirals and
captains conduct their fleets and their ships in action.

Covering instructions to Audley's *Book of Orders for the War
by Sea and Land* decreed that they were to be set in the mainmast
in parchment, to be read as occasion should serve. Gathered
off duty round the mainmast, the sailors could hear a literate
messmate declaim such feudal rules as Number 1 ('No captain
shall go to windward of his admiral'—something a midshipman
in charge of a boat must bear in mind in 1968), and such seemingly
democratic ones as Number 8 ('The admiral shall not enter an
enemy's harbour, nor land men, without first calling a council'
—presumably to remind the flag officer that he was on the
King's service and not in business for himself).

The domestic side of discipline carried punishments for the
common offences, from thieving (the culprit to be ducked two
fathoms under water, towed ashore at the stern of a boat and,
if he was still alive, dismissed the Service) to sleeping on watch
(first offenders to be mastheaded and doused with water, repeated
offenders to be 'armed'—their hands stretched by ropes and
cold water poured down their sleeves—then bound to the mainmast and loaded with as many gun-chambers as their bodies
could stand, afterwards suspended from the bowsprit-end in a
basket with the choice of starving to death or cutting themselves
into the sea).

Supplements to the *Book of Orders* came out from time to
time, like the modern Navy's current publication *Admiralty*

Fleet Orders. One addendum of 1545 must have fallen into the hands of our national anthem's composer: 'The watchword at night is to be "God Save King Henry", when the other shall answer "Long to reign over us".'

Twentieth-century commanding officers have no room on their mainmasts to display the Articles of War, logical continuation of the *Book of Orders.* But the Admiralty still requires them to be displayed ' in an accessible part of the ship ' and to be read to the assembled ship's company once every quarter. Sailors who commit crimes not provided for in the book can be put ashore to face the civil power, and this happened in Henry VIII's time too. When Edward Foster in 1539 argued on the messdeck that if his blood and His Majesty's were both in the same dish there would be nothing to choose between them, he had to go and explain to the mayor of Portsmouth what he meant by such scandalous revolutionary talk.

The untidy scattering of bureaucrats who controlled the Navy Royal—part-time feudal superiors handsomely remunerated and more-than-full-time workers badly paid—came dramatically together when, without much warning or fanfare, Henry VIII announced the creation of a Navy Board. The royal Letters Patent, issued on 24th April 1546, established an official naval administration which continued without fundamental reform for close on three centuries. The last Tudor sovereign's so-called ' Principal Officers'—Treasurer, Surveyor, Comptroller and Clerk —bore styles and performed duties much as did those of the last Hanoverian king. A sea captain or dockyard clerk of Bluff King Hal's day would have felt himself on reasonably familiar ground in the Navy Office of 1832, if nowhere else.

That courtly layabout, the Lieutenant of the Admiralty, comes into his own in 1546. He becomes head of the Navy

Board, with a salary of £100 a year; although he resigns the
chair to the Admiral of England, John Dudley, Lord Lisle,
whenever the latter feels like presiding, which is but rarely.

Sir Thomas Clere, first Lieutenant with a definite administrative job to do, lasts until 1552, and after the death of his successor,
Sir William Woodhouse, the office falls vacant and the next
senior Navy Board official, who is called Treasurer of the Navy,
steps into the chair.

King James has to revive the Lieutenantcy in 1604 to pay a
debt to an adherent, Sir Richard Leveson. It passes, as a consolation prize for a middle-aged officer with a good war record,
to Robert Mansel, the courtier who makes money faster and
more blatantly out of the Navy (against formidable competition)
than anyone in his century. Mansel never presides at a Board
meeting, though Sir Robert Slingsby ' heard him say he would
do so '. He survives at least two attempts to turn the job over
to a man with fewer pre-occupations and he draws his £100
(for a rough approximation to present-day values, multiply by
twelve) a year until his death at a great age in 1656.

During the Restoration distribution of honours, Sir Edward
Montagu, who brought the King home, who was cousin and
protector of Samuel Pepys and who became Earl of Sandwich,
is appointed Lieutenant of the Admiralty with pay and allowances amounting to about £450 a year. Prince Rupert succeeds
him, in whose person the office of Vice-Admiral of England is
joined with that of Lieutenant of the Admiralty and never again
separated from it.

Next appears a Rear-Admiral of England, to look after the
Vice-Admiral, who is an inexperienced child (the Duke of
Grafton, natural son of James II). The King chooses a favourite
sailor, Arthur Herbert, but Herbert offends his master in 1687
and is deprived of his office.

On and off down the years, made and broken at the sovereign's whim, the appointments are taken up and laid down by various historic figures, admirals all: Sir Cloudesley Shovel, Sir George Rooke (who is the first Vice-Admiral of Great Britain, upon England's union with Scotland and the disbanding of the Scottish Navy), Lords Anson, Hawke, Rodney, Howe and Exmouth, Admirals Byam Martin and Provo Wallis.

Queen Victoria abolishes the salaries and then drops both offices. Her son Edward VII re-establishes them as honorary posts, making Sir Michael Culme-Seymour the Vice-Admiral of the United Kingdom (as it had become in 1801) and Sir Edmund Fremantle the Rear-Admiral (still, by what can only be a clerical oversight, ' of England ') in 1901.

There existed at one period seven Vice-Admirals of the United Kingdom and four of Ireland, relics of the archaic Admiralty Court procedure which had allocated sections of coastline to local dignitaries. In a Navy List of 1819 there is a Vice-Admiral of Great Britain, an honorary post, for every maritime county. Current reminders of these offices are the magistrates of maritime towns who still administer fishing rights in certain harbours, as the Court of the Lieutenant of the Admiralty formerly did; and the ' Admirals ' of London, Southampton, Leith and other seaports, usually the first citizens of those towns who, when visiting a warship of the Royal Navy, are still received on board with the honours traditionally attributed to their office.

' Vice-Admiral of the United Kingdom and Lieutenant of the Admiralty ' heads the list of the Royal Navy's officers even today—followed immediately by the Rear-Admiral of England and a third strange survival, the Vice-Admiral of the Province of Ulster. The last-named is normally a civilian retired from some prominent position in Northern Ireland; the ex-Governor General for instance. The other two are nowadays retired admirals of exceptional distinction who have usually served as

Sea Lords at the Board of Admiralty. They represent the sovereign at naval ceremonies and attend royalty on naval occasions; they are the sea-going equivalents of Gold Stick-in-Waiting and Silver Stick.

Their huge parchment commissions, splashed with the Great Seal of the Virgin Queen, award them command under the Lord High Admiral of all the 'mariners, soldiers, gunners etc.' in the land—a picturesque hyperbole, like the extensive references on the same documents to their 'fees, pay, salaries, wages, emoluments, remunerations and rewards'. There is not a penny to be made out of succeeding to the last of the early Tudor titles.

Many tides have flowed and ebbed in the narrow seas since these officers had anything directly to do with the history of the Admiralty. In 1546, however, the Lieutenantcy was very much involved in the administration of the Navy.

One plain oak table in a simple brick-and-timber house on Tower Hill accommodates all the Navy Board in this last year of Henry VIII's reign. Below the Lieutenant, in descending order of importance which their official salaries confirm, sit Robert Legge, 'Treasurer of Our Maryne Causes' at a hundred merks a year; William Broke, 'Comptroller of All Our Ships' (£50 a year); Benjamin Gonson, son of a former Clerk of the Ships, himself 'Surveyor of All Our Ships' (£40 a year); and Richard Howlett, 'Clerk of All Our Ships' (£33. 6s. 8d.).

As time goes on the Admiral of England's attendance becomes more regular, his attitude less dictatorial and his contributions to debate more informed and realistic. Departmental responsibility is transforming him from society fop and flamboyant amateur-at-sea to a serious student of naval affairs.

The Clerk of the Ships has shifted status too. The Navy's oldest executive is relegated to fourth position on the council. Richard Howlett and his successors, if they are not careful, will find their time taken up with scribbling minutes and recording resolutions, losing themselves in paperwork about decisions their colleagues will have taken without them.

His Majesty has ordered the Navy Board to meet at least once a week and to present a report of its meeting to the Lord High Admiral (a title newly-invented) or to the Lieutenant of the Admiralty. The Treasurer is to submit his accounts once a month to the Lord High Admiral; and once a month the Surveyor, the Comptroller and the Clerk are to hand in a report showing which ships are being careened or docked. The Clerk has a special duty—perhaps a sop, but if so a practical one, because there is money to be made out of it—to arrange the supplies of timber for shipbuilding and repair. On this he, too, submits a monthly report.

Each officer—and this is an arrangement which persists throughout Admiralty history—is head of a department, each is directly responsible to the Lord High Admiral. They are under the general supervision of the Lieutenant of the Admiralty, who occupies the position of something resembling that of a Chief of the Naval Staff.

To discover where the King got his ideas for a Navy Board it is probably not necessary to look further than next door on Tower Hill, to the Ordnance Office at the Tower of London itself. That institution had functioned with a similar spread of duties from far back in history: from long before the *Christopher of the Tower* mounted her tubes of leather-coated wood and iron and fired a ball of about eight ounces through them.

Gunnery had been for soldiers until the King started fitting Mechlin cannon to his *Mary Rose*, the first big-gun warship. In the year following the establishment of the Navy Board the King had a fleet of eighty ships, and more coming forward which he would never see launched. The Principal Officers of the Navy Board made the Ordnance Office the target of one of their first concerted attacks. It was high time, they complained, that the Master-General of the Ordnance—a soldier—handed the Navy's powder and shot to the Navy.

The day the Board came into existence His Majesty had shown that he was thinking along the same lines by announcing the appointment of Sir William Woodhouse as Master of the Ordnance of the Ships; but all the Navy's ammunition, though stowed in separate magazines, must still be kept at the Tower, under the Master-General's care. It was the beginning of a long fight by the Navy to free itself from Army control.

Successive strokes of the royal pen, all through Henry's long reign, stripped the naval chiefs of their feudal robes. Every one of thirty-eight years had marked some advance in naval construction or administration. The King had trodden a path, as Professor Oppenheim has said, which some of his predecessors had indicated but none had followed. He ' revolutionised [the Navy's] armament and improved its fighting and sailing qualities, he himself inventing or adapting a type thought fit for the narrow seas. He enlarged the one dockyard he found existing and formed two others in positions so suitable for their purpose that they remained in use as long as the wooden ships they were built in connection with. Regulations for the manœuvring of fleets and discipline of their crews were due to him. He discarded the one medieval officer of the Crown and organised an administration so broadly planned that, in an extended form, it remains in existence today '.

4 Admiralty and the Armada

The medieval officer of the Crown whom Henry VIII discarded was the Admiral of England, controller of commerce, customs and coastguards, judge of maritime causes in the courts. ' Supremos ' after him were to be almost invariably sea officers with combat experience, professional administrators, men whom both sea captains and Navy Board officers could look to with respect, who could make the Navy their chief concern and to whom the sovereign could safely entrust all nautical matters; wielders of the whip or the rubber stamp, according to temperament, over the Navy Office on Tower Hill.

The new style of Lord High Admiral (new, but borrowed from a name by which the Admiral of England had occasionally been known) suggested no epochal transformation for the holder; but Sir Edward Howard's conception of his duties at the beginning of the reign must have borne little resemblance to Lord Seymour's terms of reference at the end.

Lord High Admiral is one of the last of the old State offices with the sonorous titles: created 1547, and Thomas, Lord Seymour of Sudeley its first holder. There have been no more than seventeen of them in British history. They include the sea-minded royalty, Charles II, James II, Prince George of Denmark (husband of Queen Anne, first Lord High Admiral of the United Kingdom in 1707), Queen Anne herself and Prince William, afterwards William IV (appointed 2nd May 1827 and resigned 12th August 1828). The latest is Queen Elizabeth II.

The Lord High Admiral, when not the monarch himself, is the personification of supreme naval power under the monarch.

Twentieth-century King's Regulations continue to define 'Admiralty' as 'The Lord High Admiral for the time being of the United Kingdom and, when there shall be no such Lord High Admiral in office, any two or more of the Commissioners for executing the office of Lord High Admiral'. And saluting regulations still advise that this sometimes mythical personage is entitled to a nineteen-gun salute and that he will return salutes gun for gun to foreign warships but not to British.

'A man of much wit but very little judgment' was Queen Elizabeth I's verdict on Lord Seymour, the first Lord High Admiral. He was hand in glove with pirates and buccaneers, encouraged shady adventurers on the French coast and was rather too close to the Court for the Navy's peace of mind. On Henry VIII's death he had married the widow, Catherine Parr, and rumour went that he was only waiting to get rid of her to make an offer for the hand of fourteen-year-old Elizabeth who would soon be Queen. 'His relations with her had already been unduly familiar.' (Agnes Strickland, *Life of Queen Elizabeth*.) Lord Seymour lost his head for treason after being Lord High Admiral for only eighteen months, but it was considered that his brother the Duke of Somerset had trumped up the charges. Somerset, intrigued against by the former Great Admiral, John Dudley, suffered the same fate for 'an offence against the Queen's person' and Dudley in his turn went the same way. The early Lords High Admiral set an ominous precedent with their journeys one after the other to the execution block.

Bitter power struggles round the throne among its principals should have slowed down, halted and put into reverse the naval administrative machine; especially while the new King was a minor and an invalid, and the Navy Office remained locked up for weeks on end because the four chiefs were away commanding ships or squadrons; arranging little get-rich-quick expeditions with the royal fleet was one of the advantages of being a Principal

Officer, and around the fifteen-fifties there were opportunities on the coasts of Holland and France not to be missed.

But Edward VI had a youthful fondness for ships, and the progress his father had made towards building a proper fleet was not altogether thrown away. Among Benjamin Gonson's accounts (he had moved up to Treasurer in 1548 on the death of Robert Legge) is a claim for improvements to Deptford High Street, to make a passage to the dockyard fit for a king. Edward approved—may even have suggested—an expansion of naval interest towards Chatham, and the earmarking of a fleet anchorage in ' Jillingham water ', as the lower reaches of the Medway were called.

Side by side with the new Navy Office he established a Victualling Office, appointing Edward Baeshe and Richard Watts joint surveyors of the fleet's victuals, with a contract to provide food for sailors at a fixed rate per man. Previously the feeding of ship's companies had been a matter for individual arrangement between captains and land-sharks—both sides hard-bargaining and full of clever ruses. Small fortunes had been made but the seamen went hungry. At first the Victualling Office was independent of the Navy Board. Inevitably the Board strengthened its hold on the general administration of the Navy, and victuals gradually fell under its direction.

The second Lord High Admiral (1550 or 1552) has been called ' a true naval officer who had seen active service in the French and Scottish wars '. He was Edward Fiennes, Lord Clinton and Saye, and he suffered from the occupational hazard of Tudor courtiers but, unlike his predecessor, he only lost his job. And that was restored to him after it had been in the hands for four years of a young nobleman whose name would ring down the centuries: Howard of Effingham.

Clinton took a fleet to sea for Queen Mary and successfully irritated the French. On his restoration he steered a careful course through political shoals and hung on to his Lord High Admiralship for thirty years. It was the pattern: the first few months made or marred. Naval chiefs of the old days lasted either a few months, or for life.

On the executive level, important comings and goings occurred remarkably infrequently, considering the unsettled state of the times. Sir William Woodhouse followed Sir Thomas Clere as Lieutenant-Admiral and was ordered to take all Navy Board minutes and resolutions to Lord Clinton for approval— a habit which, persisting long after it had ceased to be practical, slowed down the running of the naval machinery.

Thomas Windham became Ordnance chief in Sir William's place. The Board settled down for a spell of undisturbed concentration. Its key figure, Treasurer Benjamin Gonson, lasted until 1577, completing thirty years of service. He superintended work in the shipyards, designated ships' moorings, organised recruitment and took a hand in the routine business of Ordnance and Victualling Offices—an accountant with fingers in many pies, not all legitimate ones. Himself the son of a long-serving Clerk of Ships, he got his son-in-law John Hawkins to succeed him as Navy Treasurer. Among the three of them, the family put in not far short of a hundred years of service in naval government.

Running down the roll of Tudor navy officials, the eye catches the same names again and again. Patronage and nepotism controlled the succession. It did not necessarily make for inefficiency, although it may have encouraged corruption. Family traditions have always been strong in the naval service: it is good for a newcomer to have the example of a celebrated ancestor to emulate. Appointees are extra-keen, because of the ease with which the job comes to them, to make good in the eyes of jealous and critical subordinates—something Lord Fisher had at the back of his mind, perhaps, when he announced that favouritism was the keynote of efficiency.

While the Gonson-Hawkins trio held the summit of the administrative pyramid, an interesting dynasty had begun to flower much lower down. The Pett family, most famous among dockyard names, had moved up to Chatham from Portsmouth. Peter, the first Pett (according to some, the second, but his relationship with an earlier builder of that name has not been determined) was made Chief Shipwright to the Navy Board at Portsmouth.

Mary Tudor inherited thirty-two major vessels and to Elizabeth she bequeathed twenty-two. The run-down was less serious than it sounds, and her reign was conspicuous for an all-round tightening up of naval affairs, a consolidation of Lord High Admiral's and Navy Board's powers, and a flexing of their pinions with a few bureaucratic take-overs in view.

Naval stores and victuals increasingly aggravated the headaches of a government committed to an economy drive. Some attempt was made to standardise the different scales of issues to the different categories of ship—a fairly ambitious idea, for the age. In 1557 the Privy Council took the Navy Board by surprise and offered it a fixed annual sum for all naval expenditure: the Principal Officers felt themselves in Utopia. Nor was this primitive Navy Vote a cheese-paring one, although the Board concealed its delight with the restraint the spending departments have always shown.

There was £2000 for stores, £1000 for rigging, £6000 for dockyard wages and victualling ashore, £5000 for repairs and new construction. The total was a good deal more than Elizabeth, history's favourite 'sailor queen', would ever be persuaded to allocate to the Navy of Drake and Frobisher, and it did not include fairly substantial expenditure on capital projects in three and a half dockyards and pay and provisions for ships at sea.

For the time being, the fixed annual sum arrangement linked policy firmly with finance and stressed the superiority of the Navy Treasurer over his three associates. Naval matters were more the province of Mary's Lord Treasurer and the Treasurer of the Navy than of any other officers. Control of the cash and the works slipped from the hands of the Lord High Admiral himself: he became a cipher in the administration, hanging about on call to go to sea some time and defeat England's enemies. It sounds as though the Privy Council was hard put to it to find Lord Howard of Effingham a job, during his first administration (1553 to 1557), when it peremptorily instructed him to 'repayre himself forthwith' on board selected ships in the dockyards and make a spot check of the books: a come-down for a Lord High Admiral who, three years before, while commanding in chief at the welcoming ceremonies for Philip of Spain, had told that king to take in his colours on entering the narrow seas and fired on his admiral for not obeying fast enough.

When the Crown agents bought up the marshland round 'Jillingham water' and acquired the house called Chatham for the Navy Board, it was Treasurer Gonson who negotiated the deal, not the Lord High Admiral. When in 1585 the Board accepted Sir John Hawkins's proposal to run a chain across the Medway at Upnor to protect the new anchorage it was he, as Navy Treasurer, who arranged all the details in consultation with, not the Lord High Admiral, but the senior purse-bearer in Elizabeth's Privy Council, Lord Burghley.

A chilling wind of economy sighed throughout the reign of a queen obsessed with delusions of poverty. The Navy Board felt it, like every government department. Elizabeth, whose name is so readily identified with the rise of British sea-power, increased her fleet by seven ships in forty-five years. Some of the evil communications and sordid scandals which blossomed in the following century were sown on Tower Hill in the consulting rooms of a Navy Board which attempted impossible tasks without financial support.

The ship names of Elizabethan days began at least to have an up-to-date ring: *Bonaventure, Speedwell, Swiftsure, Dreadnought, Tiger, Revenge*; also *Ark Royal*, originally christened *Ark Raleigh* after Sir Walter; and the first *Victory*, a giant of about seven hundred tons. (The biggest ship afloat was said to be the Portuguese carrack *Madre de Dios*, 165 feet long—the length of a small modern minesweeper.)

Throughout the period there was still no distinct difference between naval and merchant craft. The term Royal Navy, like the Admiral and Admiralty, had no meaning for Elizabethan Englishmen. A century ahead, fleet commanders were being styled ' generals-at-sea ' and were soldiers first and mariners a poor second.

Some merchants built ships to a sort of Navy Board specification and the port authorities periodically published lists of them, to let the Board know their numbers and location in case of emergency. On the Queen's behalf they hired out the royal ships to traders for long voyages. Even foreigners could apply for them. William Borough, Navy Comptroller in the latter part of the reign, drew up a rough classification between ships intended primarily for war and others designed chiefly for trade —one group fast sailers with shipside protection against cannon shot, the other mere cargo-carriers—and slowly the separate categories, warship and merchant ship, began to emerge.

Elizabeth's was a rainbow fleet, with her favourite green and white predominating. A parsimonious Treasury saw no economy in cutting down on the decoration, and the carving of ' great personages in timber ' remained among the costliest parts of the fitting-out bill. *Bonaventure* sported a dragon figurehead, the royal arms across the stern and two lions and two dragons on her galleries—and would not have captured the limelight along-side, say, the *White Bear*, who carried Jupiter sitting on a huge eagle among clouds, a ' great piece ' of Neptune and the Nymphs round her stern and many cubic feet of carvings on her sides, all expensively painted and gilded.

On such extravaganzas, reminiscent of the painted junks of the heathen Chinese, the Navy Board with its sea captains and officers spent anxious hours of discussion; on flags, too, although these were more a matter for a captain's individual taste. All ships wore the green-and-white Tudor ensign while acting as units of a squadron. On detached service, or in harbour, a Queen's ship might hoist the Saint George's Cross—there would be no precise rule about it until the next reign, when James I and VI ordered the double cross, Saint George and Saint Andrew, to fly from the main—an order which produced some weird combinations of national insignia. A fleet commander at sea always told his ships what flags to wear, if he told them nothing else.

The old coloured trappings of the warships—the silken banners and golden tableaux—were to fade as the years rolled by, but Salutes, Ceremonies and Distinctions, to which the sixteenth-century Navy Board paid scarcely any attention, were to preoccupy the authorities more and more and even today fill a good slice—the first in the book—of the *Queen's Regulations and Admiralty Instructions*.

Adornment made the ships, and also the men. While the gentlemen-officers competed with each other in exuberance of ruff and doublet, the common sailors went in rags. Clothing for seaman never interested Elizabeth as it had done her father. Occasionally a clerk in the Navy Office or dockyard would sign a contract with the Navy Treasurer and undertake to clothe the Fleet at so much a head; most contractors were soon pleading to be released from a highly speculative bargain.

The most splendid apparel of all, the gold and purple robes of the Lord High Admiral, passed from Lord Clinton to Lord Howard of Effingham in 1585. One of the historic partnerships of Admiralty was formed: the partnership between Effingham and his Navy Treasurer, Sir John Hawkins. A powerful Board supported them, every member a sea officer with fighting experience and a sensible committee man: Sir William Winter, Surveyor of the Ships (his Ordnance appointment was combined with it); William Borough, Clerk and afterwards Comptroller of the Ships; and Benjamin Gonson, brother-in-law to Hawkins, third of the Gonsons to administer the Navy, as Clerk of the Ships after Borough.

There might have been an extra Principal Officer. The Queen proposed in 1564 to instal a Chief Pilot of England at the Navy Office. His job would have been to examine masters, mates and bo'suns, award them certificates and generally improve the professional standards of the sea; to take charge of lighthouses, buoys and beacons. For another thirty years the Navy Board was to keep responsibility for the latter task; then it went to a semi-official body which Henry VIII had set up, called the Guild of the Holy Trinity and Saint Clement. The Guild, popularly known as Trinity House, would be one more monument to the King's determination to make England the first ship-trading and deep-sea fishing nation in Europe.

The Chief Pilot never materialised, but an official with the confusing title of Master of the Navy creeps into the old documents about this time. He had no Principal Officer status—when the Board was spreading its tentacles and pulling in more strands of the nautical network, it was sometimes argued that he should have. He was the official in charge of docking and 'grounding' warships, and of security in the yards. Up to 1588 there were four Masters, one for each naval base. That year the Queen increased the number to six. They were sights for men to marvel at in their ferociously-braided cloaks and elaborately-plumed hats; but only part-timers, on pitiful salaries. At a much later date they were to become fully established Navy Board officials, called Masters Attendant. In the late nineteenth century naval personnel assumed the duties; the experienced officers who act as Captains of Dockyards and their assistants the Queen's Harbourmasters are the old-time Master Attendants' legitimate successors.

The new Lord High Admiral not only planned the strategy which humiliated Spain but also commanded English naval forces at sea in 1588. His second-in-command, Sir Francis Drake, was one of the few prominent seamen of his day who, although a member of a royal commission on the Navy, never held a Navy Board post. Treasurer Hawkins, son of a merchant adventurer, himself a deepwater captain of repute, ranked third when England's sailors engaged the Armada.

Elizabethans saw nothing incongruous in top-flight shore-bound executives leading ships to sea in wartime. The Principal Officers served as often afloat as ashore, and all were involved in the story-book battles of their times. Fame and fortune were bought with military deeds, not office reputations.

Sir William Winter, Surveyor and Master of Naval Ordnance, hurried off to join a warship and dispute the Channel with the Armada. (At his death next year a soldier took back control of naval armaments. Ordnance on Tower Hill degenerated into a hive of rogues and pilferers who smuggled out powder and shot and sold it at home and abroad; successive public outcries provoked commissions to enquire and reformers to reform, but they nibbled at the corruption without getting near its roots.)

News that a junior admiral had been tried for mutiny and then made a Sea Lord at the Admiralty would make strange reading today, but it happened to Comptroller Borough when he went to Cadiz under Drake in 1587 and sailed away in the middle of the action in protest against his superior's dictatorial attitude. Borough's case made history: it went down as the first naval court martial. His subsequent promotion to Principal Officer suggested that the findings—never published—went in his favour.

One man overshadowed his colleagues in newsworthiness: Sir John Hawkins, Navy Treasurer, fifty-eight in Armada year, veteran of fabulous voyages to the Indies with an obstinate dislike of the Spanish (because they treacherously attacked him before his country was at war) and of the English Privy Council (because they refused to make a diplomatic issue of it). Wealthy enough to indulge personal whims, he led a crusade on behalf of the lower deck and achieved something generally regarded as impossible under Elizabeth: a rise in pay for the common sailor. The approaching conflict with Spain and the need to attract able men helped the argument. It was the first pay increase for forty years and the adjusted rates, ten shillings a month for experienced hands, paved the way to new and more profitable negotiations in the Queen's old age.

In 1590 Hawkins founded the Chatham Chest (on Drake's suggestion, it is said)—something of a sick joke in the Fleet, a bottomless coffer which, no matter how much was poured into it, turned out to be empty when unlocked; but a useful idea in principle. The chest, a plain box with a slot in the lid—it can still be seen in the National Maritime Museum—accepted six-pences, a compulsory deduction from every sailor's monthly pay, intended for a benevolent fund.

Four years later, with a notable contribution from his own fortune (conscience money, his enemies called it), Hawkins established a hospital at Chatham for ten poor sailors and ship-wrights. He had been impressed by the incident off Plymouth, as well remembered as the game of bowls and better vouched-

for, when Lord Howard of Effingham dug into his own pocket
to provide warm clothes and medicines which the authorities
declined to allow its sick and dying heroes.

On return to his office, Hawkins wrote out permits for
disabled seamen who called to see him, authorising them to beg
at church doors on Sundays.

He had what J. A. Williamson has called the ' solid connection of brains, courage and capital ' which enabled the Elizabethan
sailors to go far.   He could act decisively and independently.
Like every Navy Treasurer who ever held office, he dealt in
questionable activities and has been alternately blackguarded and
whitewashed by historians.   Two of his close colleagues, Sir
William Winter and his brother George Winter, who had
three votes between them out of five on the Navy Board, savagely
opposed him and alleged that he never forced through a reform
except ' for the better lining of his pockets '.   But he had the
unqualified support of the Lord Treasurer, Burghley, and the
Lord High Admiral, Effingham: the two who mattered most.

Hawkins and Lord Howard of Effingham held jobs of which
the duties had never been expressly defined, jobs to be made as
insignificant or influential as the holders cared to make them.
Both were enlightened, ambitious men in their youth and
middle age.   Hawkins towered over the Navy Board, making
it understood once and for all that the Treasurer counted for
more than any other two Principal Officers put together.   Virtually single-handed he forced a new class of ship on the Fleet—
its prototype the *Revenge*.   He laid down the first blueprint
for manning, based on a figure of one sailor for every two tons
of displacement.

Howard joined battle with the Privy Council and asserted
the feudal power of the Lord High Admiral.   Armada accounts
reveal that the Crown, to avoid what looked like needless expense, ordered him to return to harbour and send his crews

home when the Spaniards failed to appear at the expected time. The Lord High Admiral paid no attention: it was for him, as supreme naval commander, to decide when to call off the operation. (The Crown as usual had the last word, and told him he must pay the men out of his own pocket.)

When the ships were got together again for the big raid on Cadiz in 1596, Howard and Hawkins drew up new regulations, models for posterity: the ships' companies to unite in prayer twice a day; swearing, dicing and brawling forbidden; a weekly return of provisions to be submitted (thin end of the Admiralty clerk's wedge); ships to be washed down daily; the fleet to close in at dusk; guns to be fired and drums beaten in fog; no man to strike his superior officer; no man to circulate evil rumours adverse to his superior officer's reputation.

Between jaunts to sea, the Principal Officers on Tower Hill deliberated business which had increased enormously since the beginning of the reign, dramatically as the building rate had slowed down. From their windows they looked out over the mud and slime of the slaughter-yards, where their protégés the Victualling Surveyors were floundering in a smaller, but more treacherous, bureaucratic morass. Surveyor Watts had seen the writing on the wall and got out in time. Baeshe remained. He had originally undertaken to victual the Navy for fourpence a day per head—a sum any sailor could reasonably live on, but overheads had reduced the amount which actually reached his plate to about a pennyworth. Pathetic pleas by the Victualler, though countered by Treasury delaying tactics, had increased the figure to fivepence, then sixpence and then sevenpence, but Baeshe complained he was still losing money—a claim Whitehall took with a sack of salt, for even in those days it was understood that victualling officers quietly erected rows of houses on their illicit profits. Baeshe eventually secured his release and handed over the job to James Quarles, a clerk from the royal kitchens.

The newcomer was soon begging to be sacked—a request warmly supported throughout the Fleet, for food had never been so scanty, poor in quality and unfairly distributed: clear proof, according to everyone from the Lord High Admiral downward, that Quarles was coining money even faster than Baeshe had done. In the Elizabethan view, navy contractors had to be either knaves or fools. No actual proof was brought against either man. To the astonishment of envious officials in other departments, both died practically penniless.

Schemes for taking on navy work by contract always stank in the Navy Board's nostrils. A proposal loaded with fraudulent possibilities reached them, in the guise of a suggestion to stream-line the Comptroller's department, when a consortium of ship-wrights led by Pett offered to build the Queen's ships for her at an all-in bargain price. Peter Pett and Matthew Baker, famous constructors both, were then at Chatham, the dockyard of the future, and on intimate terms with the Comptroller of the Ships. The contract-built vessels made neither man rich and ruined some of their colleagues—but none of this exempted Pett or the whole breed of shipwrights from charges of abuse and misappropriation. Few of Queen Elizabeth's servants made money out of her, or got it when it was due. It was the same at sea: adventurers sailed with her blessing and came home the envy of the nation, having allegedly cleaned up vast sums on the Spanish Main. Most Elizabethan explorers in fact ended up penniless, and from the minority who made spectacular hauls the Queen took the lion's share into her Treasury.

Records of the reign contain many accounts of investigations into the conduct of Government officials, down to the meanest clerk. Few charges stuck and a high percentage were made by hopefuls who naïvely offered themselves in the same breath for the ' criminals' ' posts. Treasurer Gonson's supposed mis-

demeanours, like Hawkins's after him, are still a controversial
subject among historians. All the Principal Officers were close
to, if not actually involved in, dubious deeds. Hawkins's brother
William was tried and found guilty of piracy—along with
William Winter, the Surveyor's near relative, and Richard
Grenville, captain of the *Revenge*. Admiralty agents in the
western ports blatantly assisted pirates to escape gaol.

Sir John Hawkins sank under the strain of his job, disgusted
with the gossip and overwhelmed with complaints, petitions and
ever-increasing labours. The work, he told Lord Burghley,
was too much for one man; there ought to be a separate office
for the Navy Treasurer, like the Victual. He died at Puerto
Rico in 1595, having a final tilt at the Spanish. He was apt,
said an obituarist, ' to differ from the opinions of others and
yet was reserved in discovering his own. He was slow, jealous
and somewhat irresolute . . . and now that we are making a
catalogue of his faults, let us not forget the greatest, which was
love of money '. The Navy Office expanded after he had gone,
and corruption entered on a grand scale. His old associates
constantly murmured their own threnody: " It would never
have done for Sir John."

Up to 1546, throughout the impressive building programme
of the first two Tudors, all the civil work of the Navy had been
done by one Clerk of Ships, with a small staff of subordinate
clerks and labourers at the ports. In that year the Navy Board
came in, the Principal Officers went up to four and a Victualler
was soon added. The fleet grew no bigger, or not much bigger,
but ships, stores and seamen became more of a permanent care
in Elizabeth's time and a nucleus of dockyard personnel formed
at the royal ports. Near the end of Elizabeth's reign, the Navy
Office had the elements of a widespread oligarchy:

Lord High Admiral (in Whitehall, or at his home)

Lieutenant of the Admiralty (vacant)

Treasurer, Comptroller, Surveyor and Clerk of the Navy (Principal Officers of the Navy Board, Tower Hill, London)

Assistants to the Principal Officers (three in number)

Surveyor of Victuals (Victualling Office, Tower Hill)

Keeper of the Stores-General (Navy Office)

Keeper of Stores (Portsmouth)

Master for grounding the Great Ships (Deptford)

Master Shipwrights (one at Deptford, one at Woolwich and one at Chatham)

Pilot for the Black Deeps (Woolwich).

Posterity saw the Elizabethan Navy Board as an outstandingly simple and efficient form of Admiralty, more advanced than anything then found in Europe. Large credit for the Armada victory belongs to its members—those who fought and those who stayed at their desks. Allowing that the Lord High Admiral and Principal Officers were expected to spend months on end at sea, that Victualler and Storekeeper had to pay their own staffs and therefore kept them to a minimum, that dockyard officials found it hard to recruit or retain labour for an employer as mean and difficult as the Queen, that transport was slow and uncertain and the keeping of naval records a new and imperfectly understood art—allowing all this, it is hardly surprising that foreign military authorities trembled in 1599 when their spies reported that a squadron of twenty English ships had been 'rigged, victualled and furnished to sea' in a mere twelve days.

5 Death of a Lord High Admiral

Calling up the Principal Officers of the Navy from their temporary quarters in Saint Martin's Lane (the Tower Hill consultation house having become an island in an abattoir), King James I and VI told them he attached paramount importance to co-ordination and co-operation. In future they must meet twice a week instead of once, must live as near each other as possible and, apart from their official meetings, must take every opportunity of consulting together 'by common council and argument of most voices'.

For the Navy a golden era was dawning; marked by a substantial increase in pay for everyone, screwed out of a dying queen. The new pay code included for the first time something for officers, who had formerly relied on their private fortunes, the rewards of piracy or prize and their 'dead shares'. (A captain was entitled to so many servants; if he dispensed with some of them he claimed the pay they would have drawn—these were 'dead shares'.)

James intended, predictably, to build better and bigger than his predecessors. The *Prince Royal*, laid down in 1608 and launched in 1610, was the greatest ship ever seen in a British dockyard. Her architect had found a way to the King's heart by making model ships for the royal children: Captain Phineas Pett, greatest of the shipwright dynasty. A thousand pounds went on decoration alone, and was probably worth it: the public travelled miles to watch the *Prince Royal* fitting out; her gorgeous bulwarks were identified with the splendour of the

Crown and, if scarcely one act of James's reign endeared him to the nation, this prestige project came nearest to it.

The Navy Board had more than the *Prince Royal* to worry about. An energetic building programme was getting under way, for both France and Holland were re-arming. One by one the stately ships of Phineas Pett slid into Medway and Thames, swung in the tides before huge crowds of onlookers, like mannequins displaying handsome coats, were towed back into the yards—and left to decay.

After all, the Golden Age was not to be. The King took a keen, an embarrassing interest in naval affairs, but a childish one. Lack of professional knowledge, a conviction that a Stuart could do no wrong (it was nothing for him to double the number of cannon on a ship specification, with a sublime disregard for little technicalities like topweight and stability), a muddled brain and an advisory service of corrupt courtiers—these helped to degrade and undermine the powerful institution the Principal Officers of sixty years had begun creating.

Oppenheim lumps together the naval papers of the reign as a 'sorry collection of frauds, embezzlements, commissions of enquiry and feeble palliatives'. Among those papers occurs the often-quoted testimony of an expert: 'The Navy is for the greatest part manned with aged, impotent, vagrant, lewd and disorderly companions; it is become a ragged regiment of common rogues': an opinion of 1608, only six years after real inducements had at last been offered to seamen, though not necessarily honoured.

Expenses mounted, the naval strength declined, the machinations of the Board grew more complicated, less effective and more open to abuse. King James could not be blamed for everything; but his was the prime error of placing and keeping unsuitable persons in office.

Lord Howard of Effingham, created Earl of Nottingham

after the Armada, still governed the Navy as Lord High Admiral. For a spell, in 1599, when a Spanish invasion threatened again, he had actually been Lord Lieutenant-General of all England, supreme commander of the armed forces on land and sea, and at James's coronation he had officiated as Lord High Steward. Queen Elizabeth had given him what she gave rarely and with tremendous reluctance: a pension for life. But the last twenty years of his glorious career (he died, aged eighty-eight, in 1624) were clouded by greed, obstinacy and participation in ignoble deals with his cousin Sir Robert Mansel.

Appointed Treasurer of the Navy in 1604, Mansel was an Armada veteran too—if one who had strutted the poops of 1588 as a fifteen-year-old could be termed a veteran—and no Navy official turned his authority and seniority to more profit. He had the Surveyor, Sir John Trevor, and the principal architect, Phineas Pett, under his thumb; ordered stores three or four times over for the same job, bought materials privately and resold them to himself as representative of the Crown at twice their price. He profiteered on a scale that compels admiration. He built himself a ship at Deptford, with naval labour and naval materials, then hired it to the King for Lord Nottingham's embassy to Spain. With the Lord High Admiral's connivance he sold appointments to admirals who went to sea only on paper, and he took a percentage of their imaginary allowances and expenses.

The Chatham Chest, which had begun to derive no trivial income from the sixpences of sailors whose numbers had greatly increased, became Mansel's own petty-cash box. He was in the happy position, when he himself went sailing, of having to approve his own lavish expense claims. He kept ships on the books which had long before been burned, or sold, or broken up, and charged the King for their maintenance. When some of his crimes came to light during the investigations of the

Royal Commission on the Navy in 1618 and pressure was brought on him to resign, he prudently did so; but cut himself a handsome slice of compensation and then—making the most of a confused set of accounts for which he alone was responsible —sent in a claim for ten thousand pounds in respect of travelling expenses he had 'overlooked'.

'The chief Officers of the Navy bear themselves insolently, depending on powerful friends at court,' said a witness before the Commission. Requests for an enquiry into the state of the Navy had been loftily turned aside by Nottingham, although in 1608 and again in 1613 two boards of enquiry had made an effort to frighten his Lordship into going straight, without actually threatening sensational disclosures.

The Lord High Admiral was not, says David Hannay (*A Short History of the Royal Navy*), an evil man. 'He looked upon the minute examination of accounts as work beneath his dignity and fit only for subordinate officials, whom he regarded as his servants. He managed the Navy, in fact, very much as a profuse, easy-going nobleman would have conducted the affairs of his own house. Of course he was robbed . . . so fraud and peculation flourished under the protection of his honourable name.'

Twice King James had to have the Principal Officers up before him, but each time they got off with a caution. His was the family failing of the Stuarts: they were, as Lord Dartmouth was one day to tell Mr Pepys, 'good at giving orders and encouragement to their servants in office to be strict in keeping order, but were never found stable enough to support officers in the performance of their orders'. They were inclined to rely on a 'Make sure this doesn't happen again' without taking steps to see that it did not, or to remove the causes of its happening.

Admiralties and War Cabinets of every land and period have been cursed with leaders who—as an officer on the spot at

Gallipoli was to complain, three centuries after James's day—
'think they merely have to say "Do this" and it is done—
but done in such a manner that it would be better left
undone '.

The investigation for which Nottingham's critics had grown
tired of clamouring, the need for which was evident to any
casual stroller in the royal dockyards, might not have taken
place in the reign of King James, had not George Villiers, afterwards Duke of Buckingham, risen to power; not that Buckingham could afford to rebuke sin, in general matters, but that he
was hostile to the old Earl and wanted his job.

Under his guidance the King appointed a high-powered
commission—what in twentieth-century parlance would have
been called the Cranfield Commission or the Coke Commission,
Sir Lionel Cranfield and Sir John Coke, incorruptible and industrious civil servants, being its leading members. It started
collecting evidence in 1618 and within the year had retired the
Lord High Admiral (comforting him with an annuity on top
of his life-pension), persuaded Mansel to go (no price was too
high, to get rid of him) and swept the Navy Board clean.

'We find the chief and inward causes of all disorder,'
declared the Commission, 'to be the multitude of officers and
poverty of wages, and the Chief Officers commit all the trust
and business to their inferiors and clerks. . . . Neither due
survey is taken of ought that cometh in, nor orderly warrant
given for most that goeth out, nor any particular account made,
nor now possible to be made, of any one main work of service
that is done.'

What it did not find was twenty-one of the forty-three
ships supposed to constitute the active fleet. All but the latest
vessels were hulks past mending. 'Naked backs and empty
bellies' summed up the sailors' situation. Pay for the lower
deck had fallen in arrears and the Surveyor of Victualling, for

the first time since the post was created, seemed to be making a significant profit. Carrying more men on his books than actually existed in the Navy was only one source of it.

As for the ' multitude of officers ', it appeared that every branch of the naval dockyards and outlying establishments, left to carry on by itself, had spawned a gang of useless minor functionaries, who in turn had collected parties of hangers-on to help them do nothing. The Commission was sympathetic towards one aspect of overmanning; who would not be, when ' aged and blind ' was the notation against the names of so many? They were old-timers who had been round the world with Drake, or gone treasure-hunting with Raleigh, or had fought under Hawkins in '88 and had been eased into quiet dockyard jobs to totter out their lives. It would have done the Navy more good to have pensioned them off decently, instead of letting them drag out their days in a dangerous charade, filling sometimes responsible positions.

The Commission found the dockyards lying open to all, paradises for scroungers. Deptford rigging lofts and timber yards were scrap-heaps of ' rotten wood and bad cordage '. Anything worth stealing had been stolen. So-called storekeepers drew salaries for looking after mounds of rubbish. Scales were light, yardsticks short, canvas inferior to the standards laid down. Upnor Castle above the new dockyard at Chatham, a royal fort whose garrison came under the Navy Board's orders, was stated to be ' a staple of stolen goods, a den of thieves, a vent for the transport of ordnance '. The Medway had indeed been an excellent strategical choice—for gun-runners to the Continent. One always imagines that things moved more slowly, towards good or evil, in the olden times. But twenty years had seen a galloping cancer pervade the Navy's affairs.

The Commission criticised the Lord High Admiral, the Treasurer and Surveyor, for allowing extravagant expense claims

From a commemorative tapestry of 1588: two Elizabethan Sea Lords

Street Plan, 1654: purlieus of the Navy Office

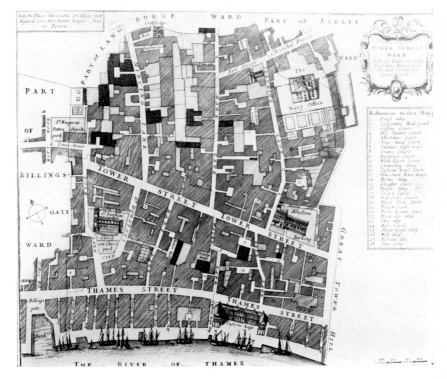

Thomas, Lord Seymour of Sudeley

Sir Thomas Audley

—especially their own: Sir John Trevor was asked to explain how a journey from London to Chatham and back could cost him nineteen pounds sixteen shillings. It criticised Phineas Pett for lack of supervision in the yards and was deterred from attacking his personal character by a hint that he was Britain's one naval architect of genius. It criticised the habit retiring officials had got into of selling their places—the newcomers would hardly have been human if they had not tried to recoup the purchase-money; but the lowly clerks and storekeepers were only aping their betters: the Lord High Admiral charged his successor £3000 for the post when he retired in 1619.

The Cranfield-Coke 'axe' was not the end of the Earl of Nottingham, nor of his naval life. Five years after resignation (when 'aged and blind' might have been noted against his name, too), he took a squadron to sea to convoy the Princess Elizabeth across the North Sea to her wedding. He died untouched by public scandal, loaded with honours and awards.

Nor was Mansel permanently crushed by the Commission's report. Both James I and Charles I thought highly of him. He had been a gallant fighter in his youth—perhaps he had been told too often how much England owed him. He emerged as Lieutenant of the Admiralty, which, after he had made it a sinecure, would never again be the dignified administrative position it had been intended for. He commanded an expedition to Algiers in 1620, the first of a series of discreditable demonstrations abroad—Cadiz, 1625; Ile de Rhé, 1627; Rochelle, 1629 —which announced to the world the decline of British shipbuilding and naval *esprit*.

Almost on the eve of the Civil War in 1642, King Charles would have passed over a dozen ambitious commanders to appoint Mansel head of the royalist fleet, had the old rogue, in his seventieth year, not looked and acted more like a man of ninety. The Government dismissed its Navy Board because the

C

members had failed to carry out their duties. The definitions of those duties have survived. They might have been more comprehensive, one feels—but the Commission, probably wisely, refrained from comment. Put briefly, the Treasurer's job was to supervise all payments and to co-ordinate the activities of the Board as a whole; the Comptroller's, to check the Treasurer's accounts; the Surveyor's, to inspect ships, wharves and buildings and prepare stores' inventories; the Victualling Surveyor's, to inspect victualling stores and accounts; and the Clerk's, to keep minutes of meetings and attend the annual survey of the Fleet.

The Principal Officers, all friends and close neighbours, 'consulting frequently together', must have found their responsibilities neatly dovetailing in. They had inhabited an office insulated from the world of landsmen, had been interdependent on each other and had had to make reciprocal checks on each other's honesty. They went, but their official duties went on. Throughout Navy Office history, each Principal Officer was to vouch for the integrity and efficiency of his fellow. Where one was corrupt, he soon corrupted the rest. And where all were corrupt, the opportunities for personal enrichment bloomed all round them.

George Villiers, Duke of Buckingham, had not always seen himself clad in the mantle of Admiralty. It was said that Robert Mansel, shifting his allegiance in good time, first suggested to Villiers that he was the man for the job—as a stepping stone, it was understood, to higher offices of State. The Duke could not, or would not, take Mansel with him; the Lieutenantcy fell into abeyance once more. Nor could he, at first, select his own Navy Board. He had to accept Sir William Russell as Treasurer—a Treasurer whose powers were confined to the letter of his instructions, so that in effect he was paymaster of the Fleet and nothing more; Sir John Coke as his 'principal commissioner', at a salary of £300 a year; Thomas Norreys as Surveyor (£200 a year). A dockyard commissioner from Chatham and another from Deptford—both practical men who were expected to spend most of their time in their ports—made up the five-strong Board—no longer a Board, officially, but a 'Navy Commission'. Each had, as of old, a direct responsibility to the Lord High Admiral and the term of each appointment was fixed at five years.

Phineas Pett, uncrowned king of dockyards, was passed over for the Chatham post and bided his time. His name had been mentioned in connection with a ship-trading swindle involving Mansel and Nottingham, and was being whispered in connection with another involving Mansel and Buckingham. Letters came in accusing him of incompetence and indifference; from an enquiry about misappropriation at Woolwich he was lucky to escape with a 'not proven' verdict.

The Navy Commissioners recommended a thirty-ship fleet—a smaller one than Elizabeth's, but of greater total tonnage. They prepared a building programme, to replace the impulsive extravagances of the past, basing their calculations on two new royal ships a year, a number which they judged would keep the total steady. They selected Deptford to be the sole building yard, to simplify the system.

There the King launched his *Happy Return* and *Constant Reformation*—ship-names which the Commissioners might have taken for a compliment and a warning.

The Principal Commissioner soon made his presence felt. He achieved a drastic reduction in expenditure—the first year. In 1620 costs soared again and the Commissioners ceased boasting about producing better results for less money. Sir John thought he knew where most of the trouble lay; he openly warned his colleagues that he had his eye on them.

Kept in line by their Principal and cordially supported by Buckingham, who had turned out a more able and accessible Lord High Admiral than anyone had believed possible, the Commissioners were able to report favourably on themselves at the end of their five-year term, and to show records to prove it.

They had enlarged and repaired the dockyards, and increased the number of serviceable King's ships from a doubtful twenty-three to a positive thirty-five. Unlike their predecessors they had taken the trouble to go out and investigate complaints for themselves. From Plymouth, during a plague of Turkish pirates (all the swarthy foreigners who cruised in the Channel were 'Turks'), they informed the Lords of the Council that the weeping of the robbed and bereaved women and children was 'so grievous that we know if your Lordships heard it as we do we are assured that it would move the same passion and grief in your noble hearts as it does in ours'.

Reappointed for a second term, they started looking at the broader aspects of the safety of the realm and the reserve of British shipping. After 1625, no shipowner could sell a vessel abroad without their authority, or that of the Lord High Admiral himself, or of the Judge of the Admiralty Court. Even the Chatham Chest came in for reform: the Commissioners made it an iron box with five locks, the keys to be kept by named officials in each of the five naval departments, the locks to be changed every year. Well into the early years of Charles I's reign the Commissioners took the motto 'Constant Reformation' and tried to live up to it.

And yet they failed. The Navy lacked heart and purpose, the country had lost its interest in sea adventures, no national hero had arisen since Howard of Effingham to capture the enthusiasm of the mob. King Charles craved glory, naval and military, but, persistently at odds with his parliament and chronically short of money, lacked the means to gain it.

The seamanship traditions of the island race had taken firm root in Tudor times; under the Stuarts they withered and almost died. Fortunately for Britain, the Navy Board of James I was never tested in war. The Navy Commissioners were, and were found, hopelessly wanting. Of the criminally-organised and incompetently-led Cadiz expedition, Oppenheim has written: ' The shameful picture of that confused mass of ships crowded together helplessly without order or plan, colliding with each other, chasing or deserting at their own will, the officers losing spars and sails from ignorance of elementary principles of their art, is the indictment against the Government of James I which had allowed the seamanship of Elizabeth to die out in a generation.'

In defence of the Commissioners, it could be said they started off as honest, well-meaning, industrious men of affairs, as men of affairs went. But neither they, nor apparently the Government, remembered the lessons their forebears had painfully learned. Admiralty, they had failed to understand—civil servants and politicians were to make the same mistake after them—was a branch of the nation's business with special characteristics of its own. Sailors responded differently from landsmen. The whole organisation bristled with peculiarities which an outsider could pick up in time—but only if he applied himself diligently and sympathetically to a study of the sea, the ships that sailed it, the men who built them and the crews who manned them.

Ignorance of wartime needs—inability to handle storing, personnel and ammunitioning problems—panic reactions to every emergency: such were the Fleet's inevitable strictures on the Commissioners; to which might be added their conviction that nothing must be done without the book of rules, regardless of the realities of the situation. Even King Charles, a notably polite correspondent, drew his Lord High Admiral's attention to what he delicately called ' the slow proceedings of the Commissioners of the Navy (which all Commissioners are liable to) '.

No medicines, clothing, food or stores arrived to comfort ships' companies returning wounded and famished from Cadiz. When mayors of Plymouth, Falmouth, Milford and other western ports refused to let captains land sick men for fear they would spread infection, the Commissioners, finding nothing about it in the regulations, took no action. (Captain Pennington by-passed the Commissioners and told the Lord High Admiral that if nothing were done quickly ' you will break my heart '.)

Several ships' companies mutinied after their homecoming from Cadiz. Several disappeared ashore to live on what they could steal or beg. A commander warned the Duke of Buckingham's secretary that his master would soon have more ships than sailors. But after weeks of it, the Commissioners were sending back the stereotyped answer: ' There are many ships in the same predicament.' And they added that, in any case, they would neither ' meddle nor make ' with any individual who omitted to transmit his request through the proper channels. The administration had come to the end of its tether at about the same time as the Fleet.

A big pay rise, for which the Commissioners had worked hard, ironically came to the Navy at the height of the confusion, when the machinery had all but broken down entirely. Sailors swarmed up to London, to see what this money looked like, of which they had heard so much and seen so little. The Commissioners had to appeal to the Duke of Buckingham for protection: they dared not meet because of angry mobs of seamen and dockyard workers. There were disadvantages no one had thought of, in siting the yards and fleet anchorages so close to the Navy's control centre.

For twenty days the Commissioners lived under siege from the Chatham shipwrights, who had marched up in a body to collect twelve months' back pay. Proclamations warned naval personnel ' not to presume to address the Commissioners '—

but from ships in the Thames they uninhibitedly did so, until the Lieutenant of the Tower of London was ordered to ' repress the insolencies of the mariners [by] shot or other offensive ways '. Most of them would have been happy with a little something on account. One John Wells, giving evidence to a committee set up to look into grievances, claimed to have been unpaid for seven and a half years.

In such an atmosphere, while a half-hearted show of naval force in the Biscayan ports of France petered out, the great Duke himself prepared to take the Fleet to sea. The programme for his embarkation at Portsmouth required abundance of gun salutes, the hoisting of the royal standard in his flagship, the manning of yards in every ship. ' All who carry whistles,' the Commissioners ordered, ' are to whistle his welcome three times and in the intervals the crowds are to cheer.'

This stirring spectacle was not to take place. On the eve of his departure, in an alleyway next door to his lodgings at Portsmouth, by a man named Felton who had followed him down from London, the Lord High Admiral was fatally stabbed ' with a tenpenny knife '. The assassin said he did it to avenge private grievances and to right his country's wrongs.

Buckingham has gone into history as the playboy of West-minster but, considering the Crown's unhealthy financial state, he could not have hoped to achieve much. He at least backed up his Commissioners, never obstructed them. One innovation is ascribed to him personally: he regularised the introduction of lieutenants into the Navy; he was among the first to attempt to breed a corps of professional officers, by offering young men of good family a life at sea. They had to be tempted, unfortunately, with rates of pay out of all proportion to those given to the sailors who taught them the ropes, and so a praiseworthy scheme lent fuel to discontent.

The Lord High Admiral's murder coincided with the end

of the Navy Commissioners' second term of office. They could hardly hope, and after their last rough passage probably did not want, to renew it. One or two, towards the end, had fallen from grace. The ups and downs of the Chatham Chest are a good barometer of naval morals: Treasurer Russell succeeded in ransacking it in spite of its five locks; his successor, Sir Sackville Crowe, emptied it completely, but with laudable motives. He wanted to pay the sailors their wages, he said, but the Privy Council's committee suggested he had paid men and women also who, to put it mildly, would have looked strange in sailors' suits.

6 A Change of Ownership

The reshuffle of court appointments after the Duke of Buckingham's death brought changes in the great Offices of State. Lord Weston became Lord Treasurer—a blessing for the Fleet, because he thought it deserved some money. Sir Sackville and his colleagues, however, had lost their privilege of handling it. Admiralty history passed another milestone in September 1628—or went back to an earlier one. The Navy Commissioners forfeited their important powers and became a Navy Board again—a Board reduced in status, with a stern set of overlords.

The Lord High Admiral's post—this made it a very noticeable milestone—disappeared. It went for a time in name and in essence for ever; sacrificed to a clever idea of the Lord Treasurer's, that the profits of the office would go some way towards paying the Duke of Buckingham's debts. There would be Lords High Admiral again, and some famous ones; but none with the ultimate sway over all things naval that Buckingham had possessed.

Into that office stepped a group of six Lords Commissioners. Members of the Board of Admiralty were called Lords Commissioners after them from 1628 to 1964—as long as the office of Lord High Admiral was 'in commission'; but 'Lord' would be an archaism in future years, a throwback to the days when the Commissioners were actually Lords of the Council as well.

For what some might regard as an infant Board of Admiralty,

C 2

King Charles assembled a formidable team: Lord Weston the
Lord Treasurer; Lord Lindsey the Great Chamberlain; Lord
Pembroke the Lord Steward; Lord Dorset the Queen's Lord
Chamberlain; Lord Dorchester the Vice-Chamberlain of the
Household—and solid John Coke, by that time a Secretary of
State. During the thirties, William Juxon the Bishop of London,
protégé of the all-powerful Archbishop Laud, joined them.
Whether the team could play ninety minutes, as it were, was
another matter. Except for Sir John and the late Duke's secretary,
who continued as secretary to the Lords Commissioners, none
had had previous dealings with the Navy. All had troubles of
their own, and could be expected to devote only a fraction of
their time to the Navy's.

Documents of the period confirm that they usually managed
to meet twice a week, either at Wallingford House (on the site
of the present Old Admiralty Building) or in the Council
Chamber in Whitehall. Sad legacies of Rhé and Rochelle
crowd the early agendas. We hear of ' poor men's petitions
presented above six months and never read '—without much
chance of ever being read, when piles of papers confront Their
Lordships, with tales of mutinies, bad food, no food at all, and
captains pawning their sails and cordage to keep their crews
from starving.

The Lords Commissioners make time nevertheless to issue
a stream of new instructions to the Fleet through the no-longer
' Principal' Officers. Some orders echo those produced for
Cadiz forty years earlier: prayers to be said twice daily, a psalm
sung at the setting of the evening watch, twenty-four hours in
irons for absentees, fighting prohibited, only ' such officers as
are authorised' to strike a man. The King's warships, and no
other craft, by a regulation of 1634, are entitled, but not obliged,
to fly the Union Flag. (Fifteen years later, in the year of King
Charles's execution, warships are told to wear the Saint George's

Cross, which will one day become the distinguishing flag of a British admiral.)

The Principal Officers not only find themselves borne down upon by a rather supercilious committee of court officials, but they have not yet found, as a Board, a permanent meeting-place and rallying-point. From Saint Martin's Lane they have moved in 1630 to Mincing Lane, but one or two have turned their own homes into offices and one or two have a house which goes with the job. Consequently they do not see each other as often as they ought; it further weakens their authority.

Financially they are doing nicely, especially the Treasurer. During the 'Constant Reformation' era, Sir Sackville Crowe did not omit to reform his salary scale, and in 1630 the Navy Treasurership was worth £645 a year, plus poundage (three-pence commission on every payment, and the payments ran into hundreds a week), a villa at Deptford and certain perquisites. Sir Sackville has missed all this: main target of the mob after Rhé and Rochelle, he is serving a long sentence in the Tower for mixing up the Navy's accounts with his own.

The only survivor of the Navy Commissioners of 1618-1628 is the Comptroller, Sir Guildford Slingsby. His new colleagues are even more afraid of him than of the Lords Commissioners in Whitehall, for he is celebrated all over town as a person of warm temperament. He threatened to murder Mansel, some years ago, for keeping him out of a Navy Office job. He threw the Navy Storekeeper out of one of the official residences, with wife, family and furniture, when he took a fancy to it himself. Now the Principal Officers are complaining to the Lords Commissioners that Slingsby has knocked down the Navy Office caretaker with the butt of his pistol, has pushed him out of the building and refused to let him in again.

The Navy officials whom Slingsby keeps daily in a state of alarm include Sir Thomas Aylesbury (Surveyor), Sir Kenelm

Digby—beau, intellectual and man of alchemy—and Phineas Pett: no shortage of talent or personality in this group, but the Principal Officers have lost face since the Lord High Admiral died.

They are humiliated from above and sniped at from below. The storekeeper at Portsmouth, they complain, has called them 'loggerheads'—is this not a case for disciplinary action ? But it is nothing to what Their Lordships call them in reply, in letters which begin on the lines of 'If you were as careful of His Majesty's Service as you are to cast blame on others . . .' and go on to brand them 'foolish and troublesome' and rebuke their 'supine negligence'.

Eastward under the shadow of that Tower which must always be a dark reminder to nervous navy officials of the penalties for being found out, a procession of Victualling Surveyors comes and goes. By 1637 the victualling rate is eightpence-halfpenny per man per day, but John Crane is already petitioning for a compassionate release, after a few months in the job, for the sake of his thirteen children.

How did the Fleet fare under such uneasy government ? Charles's money resources grew more strained as his relations with Parliament moved to a final break. There were no wars to fight, no hopes of profitable voyagings in search of treasure. The Navy was Charles's pride and he was always ready to examine plans for super-ships—although, like his father, he tended to redraw them to suit his own ideas and, when the designer dared to point out the technical impossibility, would minute the objection with an unanswerable 'I am not of your opinion'. The Fleet, in Parliament's eyes, was a part of the Court—a most expensive part. Yet, if members could have been assured that ship-money really was meant to be applied exclusively to ships, John Hampden might not have been heard of and Oliver Cromwell might have lived and died a minor political deputy.

Somehow, fine ships were built, notably the *Charles* and the *Henrietta Maria*. The wonder of the reign, or any contemporary reign in Europe, was the *Sovereign of the Seas*, launched at Woolwich in 1637, *chef d'œuvre* of Phineas Pett who designed her and his son Peter who built her. On the *Sovereign* the exterior decorators surpassed themselves. Part of the specification read: '. . . upon the stem-head a cupid, or child, bridling a lion; upon the bulkhead right forward, six statues in sundry positions; these figures represent Concilium, Cura, Conamen, Vis, Virtus, Victoria; upon the hamers of the water, four figures, Jupiter, Mars, Neptune, Aeolus; on the stern, Victory in the midst of a frontispiece; upon the beakhead sitteth King Edgar on horseback, trampling on seven kings.'

The *Sovereign of the Seas*, the first true three-decker, a long stride forward in naval architecture, earned fame and congratulations for at least one Principal Officer. 'Pallas herself flew into [Pett's] bosom and . . . inspired him in the management of so exquisite and absolute an architecture,' Pym told Parliament.

She cost £40,000. The margin for error in the Service Estimates is not much greater today than it was then: Pett's calculated price had been £13,680 and some shillings and pence. He took the trouble to add his escape clauses and get in a dig at the Lords Commissioners at the same time, when reporting progress on her. Insisting that they must not send down materials or order stores on his behalf, he wrote them: 'Already I find certain extraordinary unnecessary charges of new buildings of dwelling houses bestowed and employed in Woolwich yard, which I doubt not will be brought on the charge of the ship.'

'Is there any other family with such a record of work done for the Royal Navy ?' asks a writer in the *Mariner's Mirror* in 1913. 'The Petts have had their failings, but it does seem hard that there has never been a ship bearing the name—not even a yard craft.' (Yard craft are small tenders employed in the dockyards.) The Royal Navy still awaits H.M.S. *Pett*. He is not the only pioneer the Warship Names Committee have left unhonoured. There is no H.M.S. *Pepys* either, and never has been.

'The Petts have had their failings'—their history is dockyard history in the main, but Phineas and the younger Peter both entered the inner councils of Admiralty in the end, as full-blown Navy Commissioners.

The *Sovereign* and her brilliant consorts made curious sights, jewels on a dustheap, berthed in the ravaged waste of England's pre-Civil-War dockyards. Woolwich seemed an abandoned site, to anyone who had known its state ten years earlier. Part was derelict, part leased out to the East India Company. Portsmouth, just that little bit too far from London, looked a forgotten town, and although Pett surveyed it in 1630 and recommended extending the dockyard, the shipwright colonies massed about Thames and Medway refused to go and bury themselves in lonely Hampshire. To encourage their obstinacy, someone started a rumour that the teredo worm infested Portsmouth harbour. Few ships were based there, and it was another twenty years before the first ship was launched there (called H.M.S. *Portsmouth*) and the outcast of British yards got its first full-size dry dock.

When the Dutch menace hung over England, the Navy Office opened up Harwich and built a house there for a Commissioner; the idea of having a Principal Officer permanently established at each of the major ports had often been urged by the Treasury, face to face with travelling expense claims like Sir John Trevor's.

Pett's own preserves at Chatham had become the one great fully-employed dockyard in England—first in size, in turnover and in corruption. What it lacked, he hinted to the Lords Commissioners, was 'some able understanding man to regulate the inferiors, as it was while the Commissioners [the old Commissioners, 1618-1628] had the government'. Pett was happier at Chatham than in London, and he was allowed to take up residence there again, with special responsibilities, while keeping his Navy Office seat.

Indeed the inferiors needed regulating. Orders from Their Lordships after annual dockyard inspections tell their own tales: thefts too common for particular mention, stores accounts in a mess or simply given up in despair, flagrant instances of criminal collusion between shipkeepers and wharf watchmen. An order to the Chatham superintendent in 1631, telling him to provide a separate room for each ship's sailing gear, reveals that up to then the canvas and rigging for the whole Fleet was kept 'in one confused heap'.

The saga of the Chips was as good as a play to anyone but a Commissioner. Chips were odds and ends of wood which shipwrights could traditionally take home with them: a harmless perquisite which, since the time of King James, had somehow swollen into a riotous racket. A participant in an economy drive in the sixteen-thirties told Their Lordships : " A great quantity of wood is carried away by workmen when they go to breakfast, and at dinner-time and at night, under colour of chips. They cut up good timber and call it chips."

With disarming impudence, dockyard workmen built themselves fashionable little cabins on the docksides out of chips—for keeping chips in. After 1642, one of the Parliamentary Committees found whole families squatting in these desirable chip-furnished modern residences—clothed and fed by ships' pursers and discharging their obligations in chips.

Local pursers, tarred with the same brush as the Victualling chief above them, had long been bywords for dishonesty on the grand scale. Some abuses were hallowed by ancient precedent, and eradicated only to peevish complaints of injustice: 'We know not how to subsist in our places without the continuance of what has ever been tolerated, or else the grant of a competent salary,' wailed a round-robin to the Surveyor of Victuals in 1639.

The birth of the great ticket-forging swindle crowned a decade of uncontrollable Navy corruption: simplest and least easily detected of crooked conspiracies. It was a mystery that it had never been thought of earlier, and it persisted for two centuries. Any number could play, provided they knew some scholar who could write. Captains, pursers, lodging-house keepers and dockyard storemen plied a brisk trade in it and made a steady income. It merely involved writing out certificates for imaginary sailors, encashable for wages due. The Navy Treasurer was the last person to know whether they were genuine or not.

Under the Lords Commissioners, from 1628 to 1638, the naval administration vaguely resembled the eighteenth-century system, at least on paper. The 'Admiralty', emblem of dignity, supervised the 'Navy Board', emblem of executive control, which in turn supervised the Fleet and the civil works. But, when scandal followed scandal and crisis succeeded crisis, King Charles decided the Navy was due for another new broom and he put it in the hands of a five-year-old boy. He made his little son the Duke of York Lord High Admiral for life, taking the office 'out of commission' and handing over the actual power to a kind of regent, the Earl of Northumberland.

Back came the Navy Board to almost its former status and independence. (There were resignations and re-appointments:

Northumberland told a crony who applied for the Surveyorship that there was ' much striving for the place ' but that he
would be better off without it because the work was ' full of
trouble and but of small profit '.)

In the Earl it had only a probationary chief, appointed
' during His Majesty's pleasure ', but one who had done his
sea time, cruising in the Channel and forcing foreign shipping
to dip their ensigns to him. He lasted three years (1639-1642)
and during that time presided over the one genuine test of
British narrow-seas supremacy in Charles's reign—perhaps the
saddest humiliation a British squadron ever suffered. He was
obliged to watch Van Tromp destroy the Spaniards, practically
within sight of the Sussex coast. No foreigners saluted the
Union Flag that day; no one took any notice of England's
battle-line, for all its banners and figureheads and frontispieces.
On his sovereign's instructions, Northumberland offered to join
in first on one side and then the other, and touched the nadir
of British naval prestige.

Whitehall looked ready for another round of naval musical
chairs when the King stripped Northumberland of his office.
But a more general explosion was imminent. Near the cul-
minating point of unrest in the Fleet and unhappiness at the
Navy Office, King and Parliament began issuing contradictory
instructions. Before Northumberland delivered up his seals,
Charles ordered him to appoint a royalist commander-in-chief;
Parliament told him to instal someone else.

The Navy Board, loyal to the King, was sending despatches
to outlying establishments and ships reminding them of their
duty to the Crown; but the Lord High Admiral was declaring
for Parliament, and the King's ships went Roundhead, on the
principle that any change of ownership must be a change for
the better.

7   Roundhead Admiralty

Parliamentary committees ruled the Navy for eighteen years, through Civil War and Commonwealth. They were replicas of the Lords Commissioners, though of a more military colour; an insignificant Lord High Admiral headed them nominally but was in effect their errand-boy. He was Northumberland's Parliamentary nominee, the Earl of Warwick, and he served a first term of three years. Three years after that, in 1648, when some of the Fleet changed sides, put their admiral, Colonel Rainsborough, ashore for his ' insufferable pride, ignorance and insolvency ' and sailed off to Holland to join the Prince of Wales, Warwick returned as Lord High Admiral for a second term. His one lasting memorial of nine crowded years in the naval administration is the officer's cap badge of the present day, the design of which is based on his coronet-anchor-and-wreath seal of office.

The Navy Board acquired its own seal, and put it up in the new headquarters in Mincing Lane: three anchors surrounded by a legend. Disturbed astonishingly little by the fluctuations and passions of civil war, the ' working Admiralty ', well clear of Whitehall, ran the ships and the dockyards without much interference. It was quite like old times.

Most of the inferior officers remained at their posts. At least two Navy Treasurers survived for generous periods: Sir William Russell and Sir Henry Vane the younger. (When Vane retired, Parliament awarded him an estate for his conduct of naval finance in difficult circumstances.)

The superior officers, properly known at that time as Navy Commissioners, had to work rather more as a team. Their duties were pooled, they no longer had independent access to the Lord High Admiral, and every move had to be approved in full committee, in regular revolutionary style. Day to day work jogged on as unexcitingly as ever, until one member, temperamentally unsuited to it, succumbed to frustration or another found the taunts and demands of the sea officers or the Parliamentary Committee more than he could bear.

Five Navy Commissioners settled down to see the war out: Messrs Cranley, Norris, Tweedy, Batten and Pett. All were seafaring men, or at least dockyard men. Four have been described as 'obscure fellows'—but William Batten, a puritanical ex-merchant skipper who had become Surveyor in 1638, had his moment of glory when he bombarded Bridlington in 1643 and forced Queen Henrietta Maria to fly 'bare-legged' from her lodging. He, for one, had the Elizabethan horror of being caught hiding behind a desk when fighting had to be done.

Pett was Phineas Pett, a stubborn old man whose reputation through two reigns many had assailed but few dented. He brought his son Peter on to the Board of Navy Commissioners in 1646; the Petts had climbed a few rungs of the ladder in fifty years. (Phineas died in 1647, but left plenty of Petts behind to keep a firm grip on the naval yards: Peter a commissioner at Chatham, nephew Joseph the master-shipwright, nephew Peter master-shipwright at Deptford, younger son Christopher assistant master-shipwright at Woolwich and another son Phineas clerk of the check at Chatham.)

The ramifications in the hierarchy, which only a few legalistic brains bothered to try and follow, and the absorbing game of referring back and forth for action between the different committees could not but slow down the democratic process. Yet, in the early stages of the Civil War, the Navy did appear to be entering its promised land. Sailors' pay went up to nineteen shillings a month (deductions went up too, for Chest, chaplain and surgeon)—and was moreover paid when due. Able seamen on hazardous operations could earn as much as twenty-five shillings a month.

The framing of 'Articles of War' represented a big administrative advance: a code of conduct and discipline for the Fleet, which puts the fear of Admiralty into sailors even today, but which was cleverly designed to protect as well as control them. Unsolicited testimonials informed the Navy Commissioners that publication of those Articles was bringing in recruits ' cheerfully and in great numbers ', and Peter Pett reported from Chatham that the disgruntled ships' companies down there had begun to ' attend to their duties handsomely '. That there could have been no serious manning or victualling problem is suggested by a Navy Commission edict that any man who refused to eat meat during Lent (Lent having been done away with) might be dismissed as ' refractory '.

In the iron grip of the Protector, England's older order began to shake. Cromwell had abolished the monarchy, threatened to abolish the House of Lords and saw no need to keep a Lord High Admiral. The naval command underwent a series of complex reorganisations. Parliamentary Navy Committees gave place first to an Admiralty Committee of the Council of State; then, for a short time, to a Committee of Commissioners of Navy and Customs, concerned primarily with finance; then, when the Lord High Admiral lost his job in 1654, to a Commission of the Army and Navy, an inter-service group of twelve to fifteen members which included Robert Blake, George Monk and William Penn.

The Commission had wide administrative and strategical powers. It met once a week in Whitehall (once a day during Dutch scares) until 1655, and thereafter at Derby House.

One step beneath, unaffected by refinement and upheaval in the policy-making councils, the Navy Commissioners retained their name and responsibilities. The last order they issued from Mincing Lane was a warning to commanding officers to keep an eye on right-wing romantics, four days before Charles I went to the scaffold. Then they were on the move again, back to Tower Hill and a consultation chamber in the Victualling Office and in 1654 they took over a lovely old house which had belonged to Sir John Wolstenholme, in Seething Lane. This, and the neighbouring buildings acquired over the next few years, was the address to which Samuel Pepys was shortly to report for duty; the address to be identified with so many of the annals of the executive half of Admiralty.

Admiralty and Navy Office came to friendlier terms after the Royalist surrender. Staunch committee men and officers described as ' honest, virtuous and enthusiastic ', who knew their way about a ship, served both bodies. The Navy Commissioners, for so long on the defensive, began probing into lost territory.

They demanded Naval Ordnance—and got it, but only for a few years as things turned out. The Ordnance Office, they found, had muddled along in its typical way; the official who went to look it over reported ' the Surveyor sick, the clerk restrained of his liberty, one of his clerks absent, the Master Gunner dead, the yeoman of the ordnance never present, nor any of the gunners attendant, and the stores for ordnance empty '.

The Victualling fortress, too, surrendered its independence at last to a Navy Office campaign, after Colonel Pride himself had failed to purge it of old abuses or to make it show a profit. The Navy Commissioners, energetically supported in the Admiralty Committee, got approval to set up a large department under Captain Thomas Alderne and to build storehouses for provisions in the principal dockyards. Alderne was no Navy

Commissioner, but after his death three Navy Commissioners offered to combine victualling with their other duties, and the second phase of the take-over was completed, amid forecasts of three hearty meals a day for every man-jack in the Fleet.

Among the dozens of new and re-grouped civil servants in the Commonwealth administration, an authority on the period singles out the Navy Commissioners for especial praise, for working ' with an attention to the minutest details of their daily duties, a personal eagerness to ensure perfection, and a broad sense of their ethical relation towards the seamen and workmen of whom they were at once the employers and protectors, with a success the Admiralty never attained before and has never equalled since ' (Oppenheim, *Administration of the Royal Navy, 1509-1660*).

They handled matters which no group of five Principal Officers had hitherto dreamed of. For the first time in history, they had overseas fleets to supervise. They dealt with every submission from captains at sea—only questions of State security were passed on to the Admiralty Committee; they collected ships' logs and vetted them—for the first time in history; they set up courts to investigate collisions and groundings of ships— again for the first time; they studied and confirmed courts-martial proceedings (much increased, since drunkenness, embezzlement and cruelty had been added to the black list of maritime offences); led a crusade to clean up pursers (' They forge the Captain's signature, make false entries of men, falsify the time men have served, charge men with clothes not sold to them, sign receipts for full consignments of stores when only part have been received ')—but resisted a proposal to erect a pillory for errant pursers outside their office; wrestled continually with the ticket-forgery nuisance and at length got Admiralty approval to commit offenders to prison, which was something but not much; administered new and highly involved

Prize Regulations; and ruled the dockyards with a firm hand. (From the day the *Happy Entrance* was burned to the waterline at Chatham, no senior official was permitted to leave the yard without the Commissioners' express permission. And they stamped out an indiscretion fashionable among naval shipwrights —the Petts had started it—of taking shares in private yards.)

The Navy Commissioners informed ships' captains that they, too, must get permission if they intended to stay away from their ships for more than six hours, and that in their absence the lieutenant should always remain on board (a rule which still holds good). They appointed lieutenants, the first wardroom officers, to all big ships; created ' able ' seamen; produced, in addition to the Articles of War, the first *Fighting Instructions*, battle orders devised partly by sea-generals Blake and Penn on the Admiralty Committee, by which and in spite of which British admirals were to win actions at sea for the next hundred years.

In their spare time, three of these Commissioners victualled the Navy and the other two tackled the new Navigation Acts which Blake's victories had made possible, enforcing the carriage of British imports in either British ships or ships of the country of origin. Very occasionally they are found admitting their limitations and candidly declining to lay down the law at sea. This was to the Admiralty Committee, on a proposal by Blake, Deane and Popham that admirals should adopt a special code of flags:

' As to the distinguishment of wearing flags, pendants and ensigns, we are not capable to give our advice therein; but to leave it to those commanders at sea (who best know the causes of such kinds of distinctions) to advise; and we shall attend the significance of your pleasure, what shall be provided. All of which we leave to your wisdom. Resting at Your Honours' commands.'

Oppenheim cites the case of Susan Crane as an instance of the efficiency of their information services and their infinite capacity for taking pains even over little matters like widows' pensions: when she complained that five pounds a year was not a lot, they sharply reminded her that she had never lived with her husband, that she led a loose life and in any case was a skilled stocking-maker.

In obedience to a Protectorial *diktat*, the Commissioners were faced with the problem of finding a Bible for every sailor in the Fleet. To satisfy the Puritans they were put to the extreme bother of investigating hundreds of allegations of moral turpitude in the Navy and the dockyards, current and retrospective. (They had to examine one of the Petts on suspicion of scandalous behaviour with an unmarried girl at Chatham.)

On the victualling side, the Commissioners cleaned up an ancient wrong in the clothing branch by establishing a fixed retail price for every garment sold in ships; and went beyond what some considered the humanitarian limits by paying out two pounds a head to survivors who had lost their kit—more than the Admiralty was paying to survivors three centuries later.

But the promised improvement in deliveries of provisions to the Fleet never came. Born to a tradition of sharp practice, brought up on the principle that nothing could poison a sailor, meat purveyors sent off cargoes as rotting and short-weight as ever, then hurried to the Victualling Office brandishing their exorbitant accounts. The cash which had seemed so plentiful during the honeymoon phase of Commonwealth suddenly ran out. The old plaintive tales poured in, of captains providing out of their own pockets and men let loose ashore to forage for themselves. Harassed Principal Officers addressed letter after letter to the Admiralty Committee, pleading for money and begging to be acquitted of blame when, as looked inevitable, the whole victualling system for the Navy should break down.

Ships' companies at Deptford and Woolwich refused to prepare for sea, disgusted with bad food and stale beer. Those eager volunteers quickly found that the New Model Navy was not much different materially from the old. When the Dutch war broke out recruiting had dropped alarmingly and the Navy Commissioners, combating trickery with treachery, tried to halt the re-enlistment slump by carrying men's pay forward from an old ship to a new. The scheme, in the Commissioners' own words, caused ' so much clamour and discontent that we are scarcely able to stay in office '.

Such alarms would send a Commissioner, equally at home with sword or pen, skulking up to Whitehall to beg for a job at sea. On such a journey he took his life in his hands, for the mob had learned violence and lost its respect for authority over the past few years. The officers attached to the dockyards journeyed in disguise and in terror whenever they had to visit Seething Lane for a conference. Petitioners and delegations of workers, sailors in full cry after the money they had been cheated of, gathered under the Navy Office windows and bellowed insults. Peter Pett in 1658 had to leave Chatham and go into hiding to escape the pensioners, after word had gone round that he was robbing the Chest—a rumour not without foundation. He never did satisfactorily explain its deficiencies, nor convince a humourless Admiralty Committee that fifty-two pounds was a reasonable sum for a governors' annual dinner, and the Chatham Chest a reasonable source of funds for it.

All but one of the Principal Officers might have felt entitled to pick up a little bonus here and there. All but one drew moderate salaries: £400 a year, with an additional £250 a year for those who had taken on victualling. The exception was Mr Richard Hutchinson, who had replaced Vane as Treasurer.

The Navy Treasurer was beginning to set a pattern for his

successors by holding himself aloof from his fellows. Instead
of following them to Seething Lane, he had set up in comfortable official quarters in Leadenhall Street, surrounded by a
suitable staff of clerks and accountants, clear of the mob. In
pre-banking days, when treasurers great and small had the
anxiety of responsibility for hoards of coin, there was some
justification for locking themselves away in a safe place.
Hutchinson, 'a glorified clerk whose work demanded neither
energy, foresight or talent', could consider himself well-paid
for his worries. He earned £2500 a year, nearly as much as
all the other Commissioners put together, and looked on himself more as a financial adviser to the Treasury than as a higher-
grade servant of the Navy.

The rest of the Commissioners kept not even a secretary.
They wrote their own letters and recorded their own minutes,
sometimes had to deliver their own mail. The first result of
their plea for extra staff was the removal of a small corner of
their empire: battle casualties. A curious organisation sprang
up, popularly known as the 'Sick and Wounded' or 'Sick
and Hurt'; officially the Commissioners of Sick, Wounded and
Prisoners at Little Britain. They looked after the health of
sailors ashore—the way diseased and mutilated men were being
left to lie about the streets of Chatham and Portsmouth was
becoming a scandal—and, as if that were not enough for four
men to be going on with, they were given custody of the
Chatham Chest.

The first quartet of Sick and Hurt Commissioners included
the diarist John Evelyn. The organisation was going strong as
recently as 1832, a fairly large department by then, still an
autonomous branch of the Navy Office, carrying out for sailors
in peace and war some of the duties which the British Red Cross
does today.

In the middle of the seventeenth century it took very little weight off the Navy Commissioners' shoulders. They still sent up piteous cries for help. A last despairing petition to the Admiralty Committee pleaded for ' a timely remedy ' for their troubles or ' dismissal from our employment '. The Navy Commissioners had achieved another ' first ' in history: they were the first Principal Officers to threaten resignation *en masse*. At that, Parliament increased their number from five to seven.

Commonwealth bureaucrats consumed much time and parchment recommending economy. Parliament slashed expenditure on gilding and carving in ships, fixing eighty pounds' worth as the maximum. (The florid piece representing King Edgar trampling on seven kings was carried over to the flagship *Naseby* and touched up to depict Oliver Cromwell trampling on six nations.) Policy decreed a general run-down of shipping and naval establishments, but for one reason and another the Navy increased and managed to operate squadrons in the Mediterranean and West Indies. The Navy Commissioners entered cautiously on a new world, full of insoluble problems of repairs, provisioning, accounting, appointments and replacements in faraway places.

The Commonwealth spent four times as much on the Navy every year as Charles had done and, on the whole, got better value for it, launching ships in tens where the King had launched in ones or twos. Except in the first years, expenditure vastly outstripped estimates. At one point the Army Treasurer was ordered to subsidise his naval colleague to the amount of £60,000. Another time, it is said, Cromwell gave the Navy £10,000 of his own fortune.

At the last, messages from the Fleet were recapitulating the sailor's ancient moans: pay in arrears, stores and provisions withheld. Reliable sources affirmed in 1660 that wages had not been sent to some ships for more than four years, and that the

Navy Treasurer owed the Navy half a million pounds.

Financed for twelve years on a scale Sir John Coke would have wept tears of gratitude over, the Navy ran true to form and ran into bankruptcy. As far as the fighting Fleet could see, the much-advertised square deal for seamen was never coming. Things were no better than in 1642. Old sailors grew openly sentimental about good King Charles's golden days. When the nation chose Restoration, a thousand disillusioned deckhands were ready for it.

8   And so to Pepys

The Civil War had been an Army affair in the main, as Civil Wars generally are. No great popular naval story came out of it, only vignettes like Commissioner Batten's ungallant chase of the Queen of England. And throughout the Commonwealth, the nation's leaders tended to treat the Navy as an arm of the Army. The naval commanders, from Blake downwards, were nearly all soldiers afloat.

But the Navy accomplished the Restoration from start to finish—the start being the Channel Squadron desertions to Holland in 1648, the finish the arrival of King Charles II in the *Royal Charles*, ex-*Naseby*, flagship of Sir Edward Montagu. We are not told what modification her impressive Cromwellian figurehead underwent for the occasion; Pleasure perhaps, trampling on six Duties. She also brought home the prince of Admiralty clerks, Samuel Pepys. In company, in the *London*, sailed James, Duke of York, Lord High Admiral in exile, returning to claim his naval empire for the first time in his adult life.

Third of three 'bad kings' to whom the Navy owes much (John and Henry VIII were the other two), Charles advanced both Service and administration by important steps. From the earliest days of his reign dates the third Navigation Act, putting stiffer prohibitions on foreign merchant shipping and needing an organised preventive fleet to enforce them. Then comes a new Naval Discipline Act, giving commanders-in-chief afloat almost imperial powers, based on Puritan articles of 1652 but embracing most of the old ' Custom of the Sea ' by which rough-

and-ready mercantile skippers had always imposed their will. (Flogging round the fleet, unknown before 1653, becomes a recognised punishment for insubordination and desertion.) The old sonorous phraseology of the King's lawyers—'death or such other punishment'—'prejudice of good order and naval discipline'—'derogation of God's honour and corruption of manners'—echoes down the years. It can be heard still on the quarter-decks of Her Majesty's ships.

Although King Charles gave an attention to naval matters which some of his counsellors would have liked to see him devote to even more necessary affairs of state, although he has been portrayed as presiding in person at Admiralty meetings 'with the punctuality of a paid Commissioner', it was upon his brother James, Duke of York—'Squire James', the Fleet called him—that the burden devolved of transforming an unsettled collection of warships and a ragged regiment of officers and sailors still unsure where their duty lay into the reliable naval shield of a first-class island power.

James, Duke of York, virtually a Lord High Admiral born, was not a brilliant personality nor very ready with his tongue, but court circles pronounced him handsome and a good deal pleasanter to work with than his brother the King. Bishop Burnet recalled that he 'was very brave in his youth . . . naturally candid and sincere; but he had no true judgment, was soon determined by those whom he trusted and was obstinate against all other advice'.

At the Restoration, Sir Oswyn Murray has said, 'the Navy emerged into the full sunlight of royal favour'. Clouds considerably bigger than a man's hand were already massing on the horizon, but that sun continued shining intermittently through two reigns, and at times it positively blazed.

In the two young men (Charles was just out of his twenties, James still in his), the fortunes of British politics had thrown up an oddly irresponsible couple to guide the Navy's destinies. What was more, they were on bad terms with each other all their lives. Parties and pleasures had less appeal for James than for his brother. He liked being among men of action and of his personal courage there had never been doubt. He yearned to command an English fleet at sea, and was soon to do so: off Lowestoft on 3rd June 1665, in the *Royal Charles*, three members of his staff fell to Dutch chain-shot, drenching him in their blood, and James himself got a wound from a flying piece of human skull. His heart was truly in the Navy, as never Lord Admiral's before him. He pushed through some important administrative reforms at a particularly difficult time. He inevitably meant well, and the pity was that he lacked a head for large affairs. They said at the Admiralty that ' the King could see things if he would, and the Duke would see them if he could '.

The Admiralty: it is almost time to start using that word in an official sense—meaning the Duke's chambers in Whitehall Palace where, when he was at sea, the acting Lord High Admiral, the Duke of Albemarle (*né* George Monk), presided. The sumptuous quarters of the great Officers of State ringed it; they have all gone now. The Admiralty outlasted them and, if it can be accepted as a distinct office in 1660, it must be among the first of modern government departments.

Turning up Whitehall and entering the quagmire alleyway of the Strand or, which was usual, going down to the stairs and getting into a boat bound downriver, you left the city of Westminster and arrived half an hour later in the city of London, just below the Tower. Off Great Tower Street you found the peaceful residential backwater of Seething Lane—found it as a rule by the landmarks of its two churches, one at either end, Saint Olave's and All Hallows. They were among the most fashionable in London; the famous Earl of Essex had been christened in one of them, and London's Lord Mayors had once lived next to the other.

Though far from 'society' London, Seething Lane had a serene, modish air all its own. Its solid brick houses were mostly fairly new and mostly belonged to the Commissioners of the Navy (civil servants were having to get used to calling them the Navy Board again), or were branches of the Navy Office itself. The document exists which appoints a porter to the main office at about Restoration date. For £25 a year he must be on call day and night, and up and about for fourteen hours. It warns him 'not to permit the Beggars to infest the Houses, nor the Children to play about the Grounds, nor any Suspicious Person to lurk thereabouts'. And he is not to 'suffer any Horses to water here, but such as belong to our own Stables'.

Thus from the dignified heights of Admiralty, which was concerned with politics, you descended to the homelier but still dignified surroundings of Navy Board, which was concerned with the Fleet. You could go down a step farther, without leaving the naval administration altogether—to the Navy Pay Office in Broad Street, just north of the Royal Exchange, or on to Tower Hill to find the Ordnance Office, the Victualling Office and the Sick and Hurt Office. Clerks in those offices liked to think themselves independent of the Principal Officers, and rather resented being sent for by Seething Lane. The Navy Board patronised and bullied them, they claimed, when things were going smoothly, and left them to face the music when trouble was brewing.

The Broad Street contingent especially resented it. Pay Office clerks affected a superiority which even Seething Lane envied. Were they not the associates of the great Sir George Carteret, Treasurer of the Navy, who spent so much of his time up at Whitehall, conferring with 'Squire James' and

Buckingham Street, London: the Watergate

Navy Office, 1714

Mr Samuel Pepys

Albemarle and their secretary Sir William Coventry, and helping to get money out of the Government and directing naval policy ? The humdrum details of building and repairs of ships, recruiting and paying-off of ships, appointments of subordinate officers to ships—surgeons, carpenters, chaplains, bo'suns and such-like—were on a lower plane altogether, Navy Board business.

Sir George Carteret had the best of the attractive two-storied houses with the big topiary and rose gardens in Seething Lane. Sir William Batten the Surveyor lived next door—that tough tarpaulin Batten who had held office under Charles I and Cromwell, had been a Parliamentary commander at sea, had changed sides just before the Restoration and got back his old job on the Board, with a knighthood to go with it.

Next along the row came Samuel Pepys, the new Clerk of Ships. He had won his first battle with fellow Principal Officers who feared that the Clerk did not seem to know his place, and his prize was an official residence in the Lane. There were never enough to go round. The Victualler had to look for lodgings elsewhere.

Fourth member of the Board, Pepys's neighbour in the Lane, was Colonel Sir Robert Slingsby, the Comptroller, another newcomer to the naval administration. They were all new to their jobs, new to and slightly sensitive about their titles; but they filled the shoes of the Principal Officers of old, the original quartet of Treasurer, Surveyor, Comptroller and Clerk.

Three of them began by ' consulting together with equal voice', reaching their decision and then telling the Clerk to see to it. That was not, Pepys decided, what King Henry VIII had had in mind. Armed with his precedents, he fought to get the Clerk of Ships restored to his ancient status. He was odd man out on the Board, an upstart, unpopular member. Unfortunately for his colleagues, he studied harder, knew more

D

about their jobs than they bothered to find out for themselves, and had to be recognised as indispensable. " Ask Pepys," was the Principal Officers' ready answer to an awkward question. A disinclination on the part of active and self-important men to get themselves mixed up with tedious administrative details helped him into an impregnable position at the Navy Office.

Three ' extra Commissioners ' sat with the Principal Officers whenever they could spare themselves from more exciting occupations, to balance the voting and bring a breath of practical air into the discussions. In the first years they were Peter Pett, at that time Master of Chatham Dockyard in succession to his uncle Phineas; Lord Berkeley, naval officer, member of a distinguished seafaring family; and Sir William Penn, Vice-Admiral in the Fleet, a youngish but gouty and battle-scarred warrior who, like Batten, owed his knighthood to having reached Holland in time to help King Charles home.

Another ' extra Commissioner ' joined the Board in 1662. He was the Lord High Admiral's private secretary, Sir William Coventry—an intelligent and industrious civil servant who, with a foot in both camps, might have gone down in history as the right hand of the Navy, had his achievements not been eclipsed by the contemporaneous deeds of Samuel Pepys. Sir William gave half a lifetime to the study and care of the King's Navy. Pepys owed much to his wisdom and tact.

Two years later a fifth ' extra ' came to the Navy Board. Lord Brouncker was not a Navy man by training or, initially, inclination, but the King, who thought him the foremost scientist and scholar of the age and had made him first president of the Royal Society he had founded, decided he would be an asset to Seething Lane.

Brouncker had a proper sense of his own value. Like so many of the prominent civilians for whom the Admiralty always finds a job in difficult times, he began by telling the ' tarry-breeks' what was wrong with the Navy. From the beginning he claimed the chairmanship of the Board, pointing out that a nobleman could not possibly sit under a commoner. While Pepys and his colleagues were content to share a carriage down to Deptford and go round the dockyards on horseback, Lord Brouncker 'would not move except in a coach and six'. He brought back a breath of the ostentatious old courtier days of the King's grandfather, and Navy Office opinion held that he would be the ruin of the Board. In a sense they were right, because a fire which broke out in his mistress's boudoir in the official residences in 1672 destroyed the whole main building and those on each side of it; buildings which had escaped, as though by a miracle, the Great Fire a few years earlier. Pepys managed to get his minute-books out, but lost a lot of important papers.

In a little volume published for James, Duke of York, the Principal Officers' duties are again laid down and brought up to date—although they have a suspiciously old-fashioned look. The Treasurer is re-appointed chief of naval finance, drawer of funds from the Lord Treasurer, witness to all payments and inspector of the other departments of the Navy Office. The Surveyor must estimate annual stores requirements, inspect ships' stores and keep the Fleet's store-books and repair bills. The Comptroller witnesses all payments and is present at all stores transactions, and he audits the Pay Office's books. The Clerk heads the secretariat, such as it is, keeps the official records, and arranges the contracts for naval and civil works—with orders to ensure a 'plurality' of contractors; that is, to spread the work around among different firms.

As of old, the Surveyor surveys the Treasurer, the Comptroller controls the Surveyor, the Clerk watches the Comptroller and the Treasurer accounts for everyone; all the Principal

Officers must keep a check on each other. James copied most of his *Oeconomy of the Navy* verbatim from older regulations, forgetting that a steady increase in Navy business over a long period had made impossible tasks of what had always been difficult ones. It was plainly out of the question that two great heads of departments should personally attend every pay-table in the Fleet and the dockyards. (James relaxed this rule for his Surveyor, in the light of his far-flung commitments. He could be represented by a Clerk of Survey in distant establishments, but it had to be understood that any mismanagement would be his, the Surveyor's, responsibility.)

The extra Commissioners had their watchdog duties too, and separate instructions for administering each of the main dockyards—in the Dutch wars, these were Chatham, Portsmouth and Harwich. Then the *Oeconomy* listed the principal subordinates: Storekeeper-General; Clerk of the Check at each dockyard (he was time-and-wages supervisor); Master Attendant, for berthing and docking duties; Master Shipwright; Clerk of the Ropeyard; Bo'sun of the Yard; down to the many minor clerical and overseer appointments whose incumbents were charged, in general terms, with certifying the honesty and efficiency of their colleagues.

The Lord High Admiral excelled, like his ancestors, in getting rogueproof orders down in black and white. Like them he lacked the machinery to enforce the rules. Forbidden officially to delegate their duties, the Principal Officers had to leave things undone or take the risk of having them done by subordinates who, acting without personal responsibilities, had nothing to lose by leaving them undone. The spirit of the times was carefree. England expected a man to look after himself. Stealing from the Crown was no robbery.

The high command too, highly centralised on paper, suffered from regular interruptions and dispersions. The Duke of York

liked going to sea, and would then put his naval affairs in the
hands of two senior officers whose views on policy often conflicted.
Sir Edward Montagu, afterwards Lord Sandwich, cousin and
former employer of Samuel Pepys, who had brought the royal
brothers over from Scheveningen and commanded fleets in two
Dutch wars, took up between sea appointments the duties of
Lieutenant of the Admiralty and Vice-Admiral of England and
displaced Brouncker as chairman of the Navy Board. In James's
absence on active service, the post of Lord High Admiral passed
to George Monk, Duke of Albemarle, the fighting ex-Crom-
wellian before whom England and Scotland had trembled. He
was another firebrand who, as soon as he heard the Dutch were
at sea, pushed his Admiralty files aside and buckled on his
armour. ' When the sailors cried larboard and starboard, Monk
shouted "Ay, boys, we'll board 'em"'—but the Fleet was
resigned after all those years to having a landlubber in charge.

He made the Navy tremble too: ' The seamen came to the
Navy Office in crowds to demand pay. He [Albemarle] told
them there were fifteen hundred ships to be sold and that as
soon as they were sold they should have their money, with
which they seemed to be satisfied. But in the afternoon there
came four or five thousand of them towards Whitehall which,
Monk hearing, met them at Charing Cross where, without
much expostulation, he drew his sword and wounded several of
them, upbraiding them with not depending on his word, who
never broke it. Which had such an effect that they tamely
retired.'

An able seaman's condition in mid-seventeenth century much
resembled that of his equivalent rank two or four centuries before.
' Breeding men to the sea ' was a phrase some times used in
Navy Board debates—it was not the ordinary sailor the Principal
Officers were thinking of; such men were supposed to be bred

already, from their peacetime occupations of fishing, or crewing England's trading vessels. To provide naval training for a common sailor would have been like opening the doors of an agricultural college to carthorses.

Long-serving Navy Board employees had, however, through the years, noticed a change of attitude towards the men who commanded the ships. James, Duke of York, crystallised the aspirations of the progressives when he spoke of forming a nucleus of a permanent officer corps, to look after what everyone at the Admiralty hoped would become a standing Navy. Professional ability, to James, had always ranked higher than political colour or court interest; faced with the choice of putting ' rebels ' in command of his ships or seeing the Navy drastically reduced, he had opted without hesitation for the ' rebels '—even for one who sturdily said that ' unless the King minded his manners he would not last long '.

James launched the campaign which, many years after he was gone, rid the Service of its rough-and-tumble shellback captains and put men of birth and education in their places; which made the naval officer a distinctly polite person. He got Secretary Coventry to write to selected ships' captains, asking them each to take one volunteer ' young gentleman ' aboard, with a view to teaching him navigation and seamanship and allowing him after a mere seven years of it to become a midshipman. Promotion thereafter, it was explained, would depend on ability, in direct competition with others who might have spent twenty-seven, or thirty-seven, years achieving the same position.

It was the historic King's Letter scheme and, although it staggered under the abuses all such experimental innovations were heir to (it became the accepted thing to put a lad's name down at birth, to give him maximum seniority), it helped to achieve, or at least point a way to, something the Navy could

never be a real Navy without: a framework for the entry,
training, promotion and retirement of a class of regular officers.

Pepys had much to do later on with refining and imple-
menting the scheme. In his time the 'gentlemen probationers'
could go to sea with a captain's nomination at the age of eleven;
or with Admiralty nomination two years later. At twenty
they could sit for a lieutenantcy and, depending on the result,
would go farther ahead by favour and selection or remain midshipmen for the rest of their lives. Pepys noted a satisfactory
decrease in the 'bastard breed pressing for employment' who
had formerly taken up so much of his time, once word had gone
round that they had to pass the examination.

When prospective 'King's Letter Boys' applied for their
Admiralty nominations, the naval administration could take for
the first time a look at its future sea officers. In the twentieth
century, every executive officer of the Royal Navy or Royal
Marines starts his career with an appearance before the Admiralty
Interview Board; up to the seventeenth, the rulers of the King's
Navy could go through life without a clear idea of what the
typical sea officer looked like, for the only ones they saw were
admirals.

Colbert's reforms in the French Navy, which created an
officer corps and a register of seamen, are regarded as James's
inspiration in his moves towards an officer structure. He had
little to build on. The midshipman was the popular manifestation of sea officership—only half an officer, midway between
forecastle and cabin, really the senior non-commissioned officer
of his time. The post of lieutenant meant the post of a second-
in-command, of whatever experience and seniority. The captain
was the commanding officer—if Captain Jones left his small
ship and went as second-in-command to a big one, he became
Lieutenant Jones. Except while serving, he was plain 'Mr'.
Rank had no meaning and seniority no significance, in the

present-day sense of those terms.

The Duke of York's Admiralty achieved a resounding victory over the Treasury when, in 1668, it secured the right to give retaining fees to admirals while they remained on shore. ('Admiral' meant squadron commander; his qualification of Red, White, or Blue was tacked on to distinguish the divisions of the Fleet when the Lord High Admiral or other supreme commander assembled it.) The outlay, though small enough in the sixties and seventies, when admirals were so constantly at sea, established the principle that a naval officer ought to be supported by the Navy even if not actually employed—another feature of the 'permanent corps of professionals' ideal.

Over the next thirty years, when Admiralty, Privy Council and even the monarchy had to accept spectacular changes, the 'half-pay' system for unemployed sea officers made steady ground, until after 1700 one of the most important Admiralty publications of all time, the Sea Officers' List, put admirals, captains and lieutenants on a proper footing. By that date not only were all officers eligible for half-pay, but they could earn long-service increments as well.

It was still—the Merry Monarch would not let it be forgotten—the King's Navy. And, where so much of public affairs was run on the courtier network, side by side with the democratic reforms went the time-honoured practice of giving the best commands to young men whose chief claim to advancement was the possession of a relative or protector whom Government had to woo or placate. The utter dependence of such scented novices on the hard professional core of the Fleet helped in a crude way to narrow social gaps at sea. The same gales swept over all, the same spray wetted them. Until they stepped ashore, there was not that unbridgeable gulf of caste between the well-born and the self-made. The Admiralty recognised it and, in a fashion which would be rare a century later, impossible two centuries later and improbable today, humble sailor-lads rose to be commanders-in-chief. Sir John Leake entered the Navy as a gunner. Sir David Mitchell and Sir John Benbow both began their careers apprenticed to fishing skippers. At a later period when a desperate call went out for more officers—in the Napoleonic wars—it would be hundreds to one against a lower-deck man becoming a commissioned officer, thousands to one against his reaching flag rank.

James, Duke of York, Lord High Admiral for only twelve years (but by sentimental royalist reckoning, thirty-five), managed to wear his great silken red-and-yellow flag several times at sea. In 1665 he flew it as Commander-in-Chief and Admiral of the Red in the summer campaign against the Dutch (with cousin Rupert his ' White ' and Lord Sandwich his ' Blue '). Albemarle took over Whitehall, Penn went as Captain of the Fleet, and Commissioner Batten removed to Harwich as naval officer in charge: almost the routine dispositions, they were getting to be, for hostilities. Pepys's diary tells of panic and dismay in Seething Lane at such an exodus and all it implied.

James returned sooner than expected: Parliament was for ever complaining about the Heir Presumptive risking his neck; put that way it sounded better, but few believed he was the best man for the job in any case. Seven years later he fought his last battle, a messy, indeterminate affair which could have been a victory, strategists were saying, if the Duke had only listened to Sandwich's advice. It was Solebay, where Lord Sandwich lost his life—or threw it away, as Navy Board gossip had it, out of shame for Stuart pig-headedness.

The Lord High Admiral emerged with confidence in his own divinely-inspired wisdom unimpaired, but a few months later the Test Act (to protect the heir to the throne) deprived him of another chance to snatch military glory. His office of Lord High Admiral passed to Prince Rupert.

D 2

The Dutch wars were unhappy ones for the Navy Office. Wars generally had been; especially when royal dukes and princes were commanding the Fleet, personages whom the Principal Officers dared not argue with. Tactical failure in battle, if not ascribed to subordinates on the spot, was inevitably laid at the Navy Board's doorstep: the wrong stores had been sent; the right stores had been sent to the wrong place; no stores at all had been sent; the crews had not turned up; the cordage and timber parted and splintered under stress of the fight. Tactical failures abounded, and the complaints were frequently fully justified. In the darkest days, as Pepys's papers so graphically show, the shadow of the Plague hung over Seething Lane, until the long-delayed message came from a Court which had wisely established itself eighty miles from town and left most of the Government offices to fend for themselves: 'His Majesty's Principal Officers and Commissioners are instructed to establish their office at Greenwich and to conduct all their business from that place until ordered to return'.

Scarcely had the Navy Board re-established itself in Seething Lane than the Great Fire drove it out again. While his colleagues commandeered most of the staff to drag their personal effects to safety, Pepys and his clerk buried the office files in a hole in the garden. The Fire gutted All Hallows at the foot of the street, but the residences escaped—only to be destroyed with most of their contents after Lord Brouncker's little mishap, mentioned above.

The twin Furies, Parliament and the mob, pounced on the Board when the Dutch sailed up the Medway to smash through the Upnor boom defence and burn the English ships at their moorings. Protective measures, too few and too late, had been hampered because a hunger march of dockyard workmen had been up at Seething Lane demonstrating about arrears of pay. The Privy Council selected Pett for their chief victim—

Pett who had dodged many an official arrow in his day—and brought him down. At the climax of England's disgrace he had been seen collecting his precious ship-models together and carrying them away to safety—while the real ships foundered and blew up in the river. The Privy Council could not accept that the Chatham Commissioner had been taking the long view, and it committed him to the Tower.

Old Sir William Batten died shortly afterwards—worn out by the strain of the wars and, it was rumoured, sunk in melancholia at the nation's shame. Sir Thomas Middleton from the Portsmouth yard took his place as Surveyor.

The Commissioners' troubles were only beginning. In October 1667 Parliament sought scapegoats for the naval errors exposed by the wars. It appointed an ominously-named Committee of Miscarriages. The Board had to defend Pett's inadequacies all over again; to explain why the Ordnance had failed to supply ready-use ammunition; to account for the noisy scandals at the Ticket Office (Pay Office) and the misappropriation of prizes. The Duke of Albemarle, as acting Lord High Admiral, had already got in first with voluminous ' reasons in writing' which partly incriminated the Principal Officers.

Six out of seven Principal Officers and Commissioners stood at the bar of the House and made their apprehensive bows to the Speaker: Penn was a member of Parliament himself, and therefore a spectator when his colleagues winced under a tongue-lashing and resigned themselves to impeachment. But this was the Clerk's finest hour. Samuel Pepys, the man with all the answers, spoke for three hours, numbed Parliament's wrath and saved the Board. He so impressed his audience that the Lord Chancellor proposed that he should be given a free hand to reorganise the administration and cut away the dead wood: a vision of power beyond his most optimistic dreams, for one who had made a nuisance of himself for six years, struggling with knights and noblemen for his 'equal voice' in Board counsels.

While the Navy escaped heavy censure, Parliament took advantage of the King's embarrassment to increase its authority over his officials. It voted him £300,000 to repair the State's defences—but insisted on knowing how the money was spent. The principle of appropriation of supplies to particular purposes was established. Parliament would inspect the accounts, and call for explanations. The 'lump sum for the Navy'—which had occasionally been hung round the neck of a royal mistress—was a thing of the past.

Samuel Pepys, a child of his time, never backward when easy money was around, earned such modest spoils as came his way. He joined in as joyfully as any, when the Navy's governors made away with the cargoes of the prize ships anchored off Erith and Chatham. Charged with failing to practise the selfless dedication to the Service he preached, he could give with justification the answer anyone in his position would have given: if he did not fill his pockets, others would fill theirs. The social and political climate of his day was the real villain: relief and relaxation from a Puritan dictatorship. A holiday atmosphere prevailed in Westminster, in the City and all over the country.

Pepys deserved a better Navy than the Navy he toiled for—better than the Navy he retired from. The Fleet and its administrators only began to appreciate his genius long after he was gone. The machine he was building failed, in his lifetime, every time it came to the test.

In the reign of Charles II, the naval administration had little hope of imposing its authority directly on the Fleet, where fraud, drunkenness and cruelty—the sailor's cardinal vices—flourished unchecked. Captains of His Majesty's ships could disappear on private voyages with unofficial passengers and cargoes, without much fear of detection. Some captains remained 'unblushing absentees' unseen by their ships' companies from beginning to end of a commission—like he of the *Lark*, whom Pepys saw lounging in Covent Garden when he was supposed to be with his ship in the Mediterranean, and whose offence has gone down in the Diary for all posterity to read. Sailors and dockyard workmen took their time from their superiors and there were hundreds at Chatham and Deptford who were only in their place of duty at meal-times and on pay-day.

After the great Parliamentary fracas, the Navy tottered from one difficulty to another. The nation still grudged the King his money, and the Principal Officers always seemed to be in the way when another financial blow fell. 'No money, no credit and no stores' was Pepys's perennial cry. Other cries pierced his ears, the 'horrible cries and lamentable moan' of unpaid seamen and their starving families. To Court and to Parliament he bragged of the Navy's grand spirit and instant readiness for any task; but to the Lord High Admiral, in confidential memoranda, he alleged that his brother Commissioners were neglecting their duties and disregarding their instructions; and said that only a new, even more drastic overhaul of the Navy Office could save the Navy.

Principal Officers had always regarded their jobs as might a Town Councillor who attends a couple of meetings a week and devotes the rest of his time to earning a living. Pepys was the first to see his job as a full-time one. That way he could do his colleagues' work as well as his own, and when the day was done he dipped into the history of the department, collecting ammunition for the next tussle with Treasurer, Victualler or Comptroller. No one ever had so complete an understanding of the lumbering mechanics and complicated structure of that remarkable organism on which the very safety of the realm had so often depended.

Most of the naval administration's history towards the end of the reign was made in Pepys's office, and Pepys made most of it against astonishingly little domestic opposition. Some of his reforms were neat and simple: when he took over the Surveyorship of the Victual in 1666 he began by compiling a black list of contractors. Some of his projects were ambitious and costly, and ranged far ahead of their time: he got the building of Greenwich Observatory started, drew up a plan for encouraging southern landowners to plant oaks, and engineered a contract with plantation owners in New England to supply Douglas firs to the English dockyards, in case war in the North Sea should interfere with the provision of warships' masts from the Baltic states.

One wonders what Pepys was using for money. Any day in the life of the Pay Office found Sir George Carteret under pressure. For eighteen months King Charles ruled without a Parliament and ran the country on promises. The goldsmiths of London, Sir George's last hope, turned their backs on him and he resigned; was persuaded to return; and was dismissed by the Parliament the King had had in desperation to recall in 1669. The members put Lord Anglesey in the Treasurership and warned the rest of the Principal Officers that they, too, with the exception of Pepys, could easily be dispensed with.

The rise to power of the Duke of Buckingham and his Cabal blew open a crater in the summit of Navy administration which its hard-pressed senior officials had been gingerly walking over for the past seven years. One of the Duke's first acts when he became Lord Chancellor was to persuade the new Treasurer to resign in favour of a two-man office: Sir Thomas Osborne and Sir Thomas Littleton became joint Navy Treasurers. The Cabal, the power behind the Privy Council, was determined to keep a

Catholic king off the throne, and part of their campaign against
the Duke of York involved putting a fierce spotlight on the
Admiralty and Navy Board. Pepys alone faced it with a more
or less clear conscience. Buckingham invited him to draw up
his own 'Regulations for the Navy Office' and told him he
would be kept on, but the rest must go. Vice-Admiral Penn,
most experienced and most outspoken of British naval officers,
resigned his office and the Navy Board crumbled away.

In Whitehall, 'Squire James' handed his brother the seals
of the Lord High Admiral. It was generally understood that he
would remain active behind the scenes, but the King replaced
him with cousin Rupert, whom he named First Commissioner
of an Admiralty council; and hardly had the nation swallowed
the unfamiliar title when Prince Rupert was out, dismissed for
incompetence, and King Charles himself took the helm.

Had the King thought of delegating the duties, his naval
administration might have struggled on. But decentralisation
was a word Charles was quite unfamiliar with. Disenchant-
ment, on the other hand, his subordinates learned very quickly.
Frustration and uncertainty at the top were reflected in an
accelerated run-down in the condition of the Fleet and what
remained of the morale of its personnel. Panic rumours swept
the Navy, and the truth of some was stranger than fiction. The
Popish Plot scare discovered treasonable elements in Seething
Lane; Pepys himself was caught up in the chase and joined
dozens of respectable civil servants in the Tower. He had, said
his accusers, been a secret Catholic for years, had carried information and sold military secrets to Catholics and had been in
communication with the French.

The panic passed. James came home from Scotland, to be
Lord High Admiral all over again, and old-timers said everything would be well, for he was 'General, soldier, Master,
pilot, seaman: to say all, everything a man can be'. The King's

government returned to the King's own hands and, such was the magic of his personality, it was like the Restoration a second time round.

Pepys went from prison (he had only been remanded in custody, and released after eighteen days) to a brief retirement. Royalty itself commanded his presence: he was to be Secretary for the Affairs of the Admiralty of England, the autocrat of the Board Room table. Ever conscious of the dignity of that new post—he interpreted his responsibilities in the most generous sense—the one-time captain's clerk extracted every ounce of authority from his position. He must have been unbearable to work for. It was common for him to remind the Duke of York that he, Samuel, was answerable to the King alone and he was known, when he saw his master flouting the regulations, to enter a sharp protest to King Charles himself.

Ten years of undiluted Pepys might have restored the Navy to administrative efficiency, if not fighting pre-eminence. But the King's health was failing, the King growing crotchety and falling under the influence of ministers with the wrong ideas. Pepys had reached the top too late.

In 1679, in a fit of pique, Charles suspended his brother from office, deprived his Admiralty Council of its powers, put Sir Henry Capel in charge of a new Navy Board with not a single sailor on it (to 'sport himself with their ignorance', said Pepys) and restored the Commission of 1673, though with a new set of Commissioners: Lord Falkland, Sir John Narborough (famous for his charting voyages in South American waters), Sir Richard Haddock and others, including the spring-loaded Pett, who bounced back into office as Sir Peter.

The number of ships built or building used, in those days, to be the practical measure of Admiralty efficiency. The new Commissioners took over a fleet of about a hundred; they received a generous provision from Parliament, half a million pounds in round figures every year, for maintenance and new construction; whatever they asked, within reason, was granted; they could count on the sympathetic co-operation of King and Lord Treasurer. From the day they entered office, the King decided his Commissioners must be given no excuse for putting blame on anyone outside their own department. If they failed, they and they alone must be dismissed in disgrace.

They did and they were. They lavished money on useless projects, poured good after bad in frantic efforts to save their faces, got their accounts hopelessly entangled. In five years the Navy was reduced from a hundred ships to twenty-five. During the Duke of Monmouth's rebellion the Commissioners succeeded in getting one squadron to sea adequately manned and ammunitioned.

They had no luck with the efforts they made to discourage old abuses. They abolished chips, but could find no buyers for the great heaps of wood and shavings which began to disfigure all the dockyards; they had to back down and, ' by a silent connivance ', agree to the workmen resuming their old disreputable practices.

Like his grandfather seventy years before him, James set up a special commission to find out where all the money had gone. He recalled Pepys who (according to Pepys) chose the members: Sir Anthony Deane, well-known London shipbuilder, wealthy beyond thoughts of corruption or bribery; Sir John Berry, a sea officer; Will Hewer of the Diaries, Pepys's confidential clerk from Restoration days; Sir Peter Pett and Sir Robert Beach of the existing Admiralty Commission and a newcomer, a Mr Saint Michael—these last three went to Chatham, Portsmouth and Woolwich-Deptford respectively, to tidy things up in the yards.

Two members of the old Commission—Narborough and Godfrey—stayed on to guide the newcomers through the labyrinth of precedent and procedure which the ingenuity of clerks and the twists of history had made impenetrable to ordinary mortals entering it for the first time. The disgraced members— Falkland, Tippets, Haddock and Southerne—sat apart, a ghostly tableau of ignominy, condemned to serve until they had reduced their book-keeping to some sort of order.

Pepys entered his kingdom. In about two and a half years he transformed the outlook for the Navy's future, rescued the Fleet from the Thames and Medway mud in which it was decaying, and brought it back to health, paid off half the departmental debt and made ninety-two fighting ships seaworthy.

The nomenclature, like the machinery, began to have an up-to-date business-like ring. From ' First Commissioner ' to ' First Lord ' was a step to be made any year from 1688 onwards; the antecedents of the Sea Lords went into the Admiralty in '82 and '84—Admirals Sir John Chichele and Arthur Herbert— to stiffen the Commissioners and ostensibly provide a professional element (but Pepys said darkly that ' they were not added for the sake of their seamanship ')—and Pepys, restored to his rightful position, was calling himself ' Secretary of the Admiralty '.

Experiment, reorganisation and expansion characterised Admiralty policy in the final years of the Stuart era. The new dockyard laid out in 1665 at Sheerness was put on its feet. The Victualling Board, rejuvenated at the end of Charles's reign, was rejuvenated again at the beginning of James's. Extra departments cropped up. There were Commissioners for Transports, established 1686, abolished 1687 and established again 1688. Some new branches were created, some old ones done away with, but more were created than done away with. The Navy Office in the last year of the reign of James II and VII had fifteen departments attached to it—mostly scattered over and around Tower Hill—and this had come about in a time of financial freeze and serious political disturbances.

History gives Samuel Pepys, Will Hewer and Sir Anthony Deane the credit for creating the second English fleet of post–Restoration days out of a Whitehall shambles. The reformers never saw their work crowned with a sea victory.

Pepys and his clerk had watched the first fleet ruined by the Dutch in the Medway. He saw the second lie impotently by while the 'Protestant wind' wafted William of Orange down the Channel and landed him unopposed in Torbay; and un-smilingly dictated his last operational signal to Lord Dartmouth, who had not fired a shot, to 'refrain from further acts of hostility' and return his squadrons to harbour.

Finally hammered into shape, the reliable naval shield of the first-class island power was turned against its King. The Quiet Revolution sighed itself out, the troops laid down their arms and Pepys laid down his pen.

Surrendering his office in December 1688, aged fifty-six, the Admiralty's first and greatest Secretary told King William frankly he 'would serve no more'. His fidelity to the Stuarts was not too strong to stop him getting his brother John, a Trinity House clerk, appointed to succeed him.

Pepys, reaching high administrative rank at a time when science, seamanship and politics went hand in hand, had also been a member of Parliament and a president of the Royal Society. But on leaving the Admiralty he retired from public life and gave out that he was engaged on a history of the Royal Navy. This important work never appeared: deteriorating eyesight troubled him towards the end.

On 26th May 1703 his fellow-diarist and naval old comrade, John Evelyn, made the following historic entry:

'This day died Mr Samuel Pepys, a very worthy, industrious and curious person, none in England exceeding him in knowledge of the Navy. . . . He was universally beloved, hospitable, generous, learned in many things. . . .'

Pepys lies in the Principal Officers' old church, Saint Olave's, Hart Street, within sight of Seething Lane and the few fragments of the Navy Office fortress that remain.

9 Orange Flavour

The naval administration has fallen clearly into its two main divisions. The golden thread of Admiralty runs through the English tapestry side by side with the blue of Navy Board. Occasionally the two threads touch and intermingle—when a man like Pepys arises, for instance. They move apart again and continue, the gold above the blue.

Up to 1688 the Admiralty is linked with the Sovereign, the Privy Council and all the great offices of state. Its actions are bound with the large events of our island history, the remote control and supreme command of our maritime forces, the operations of the War Staff. Its personnel are royalty and nobles every one.

Up to 1688 it is the Navy Board which plays the departmental part common men can understand—carrying out the plans, trimming the details of naval operations, keeping the ships and the men fit for action—behaving like a modern Admiralty within the framework of the nation's grand defence strategy. Its personnel are Principal Officers, the heads of dockyards and clerical departments and from time to time the senior officers of fighting squadrons. The history of the naval administration, up to 1688, is mostly the history of the Navy Board.

After 1688, the Navy Board plays a less dramatic role in the development of British sea-power. Not so often, from then on, do we find Principal Officers hoisting their flags at sea, or hobnobbing with royal dukes of the Council and giving Lords High Admiral a piece of their minds. Few epoch-making decisions or strokes of revolutionary brilliance to change the course of history will come up from the Navy Board from this date onwards. The principles of its job are broadly laid down, thanks to Pepys, and all who work there can toil on, growing old at their desks, smoothing out, streamlining, obstructing or complicating the clerical processes. For Surveyor, Comptroller or Victualler there may be a knighthood at the end of forty or fifty years' measured plodding; but no more honours for gallantry in battle, or lucrative cruises in command of prize-hunting frigates.

After 1688, Admiralty history will mainly be made in the Admiralty itself. They are putting up a new building for it, at the top end of Whitehall, but for the time being Their Lordships have to meet in Duke Street (afterwards called Delahay Street), which runs parallel with Whitehall on its western side, in the house of Judge Jeffreys. After 1688, the Lord High Admiral comes closer to the Fleet he is administering—surveys it from a considerable eminence, but not so lofty an eminence as he used to.

The office, however, in the person of one individual, no longer exists. 'Admiralty' is the word. Councils, committees, commissions and boards—if the word 'Admiralty' occurs in their title, these are the bodies which rule the King's and Queen's Navy.

The 'quietest Invasion that ever was' brought new looks to all the Government departments, Army and Navy in particular. In Stuart days, the Navy had worked itself free of the merchant marine—had become in name and fact 'Royal Navy'. Following the arrival of the Prince of Orange it struggled to detach itself from what remained of Army control. The sea officers were manœuvred by their rulers into a separate organisation with separate rules and no more was heard of land-and-sea admirals or Army-and-Navy generals. Within Admiralty,

Navy Board and Fleet, a new kind of split appeared. The whole administration yielded up its newly-won autonomy to the politicos and, like every other office of Government, was a theatre in the Whig and Tory conflict.

William III insisted that an approximately equal number of Whigs and his Tory adherents filled his appointments. That was one reason why the office of Lord High Admiral had to go and a balanced commission of nine members replace it, acting ' to all intents and purposes as if the said Commissioners were the Lord High Admiral of England ', as the declaratory Act of 1690 put it. Across the Board, influential Tories like Arthur Herbert, who had gone over to Holland, disguised as a common seaman, to offer William the Crown, faced powerful and vociferous Whigs like William Sacheverell.

Party disputes clouded all Parliamentary and departmental debates. Down the river at the Navy Office the party system was achieving what kings and Lords Admiral had striven for in vain: watchdogs at every level. There was small chance of collusion when a Tory audited the accounts of a Whig and a Whig inspected the books of a Tory.

Government procrastination, executive corruption and clerical inefficiency were not, somehow, stamped out overnight. The age-long grouse of the sailor about his pay, victuals and clothing fell on ears as indifferent or helpless as ever. In the first two years of the reign the discount rate on pay-tickets reached a percentage hardly surpassed under the Stuarts. The Navy got its money, as before, from Their Majesties William and Mary, who had it from Parliament, who got it at a high rate of interest from the merchants of London. Votes were always in arrears, the naval accounting methods had grown more complex, logistic problems increased all the time, the transfer of cash was a grave national problem and the checking, counter-checking and witnessing of payments—to save halfpennies—had reached absurd lengths in the naval Pay and Victualling Offices.

Admiral Herbert took the Pepys-built fleet to sea for its baptism of fire in the first year of Their Majesties' reign, to intercept French squadrons escorting ex-King James to Ireland, where he hoped to find a springboard for an attempt to recover his crown. The First Commissioner got away late; ' waiting for supplies ' was his official reason—a black mark for a Navy Office as yet hardly open for business. True to the same motto, ' too little, too late ', the Ordnance Office put another spoke in the Admiral's wheel by sending him away only partly ammunitioned. There are no records of admirals dying of apoplexy, or invalided with ulcers brought on by having to hang about offshore waiting for the supply services to get to work on their demands. Admirals were made of stern stuff.

Bent on finding himself a naval hero, King William made Herbert an earl after the action in Bantry Bay and conferred knighthoods on two of his captains. (One was Cloudesley Shovel, who had begun his working life as a shoemaker's apprentice and, going to sea as a cabin boy, had found a patron in Sir John Narborough.) He also distributed rewards among the seamen, some of whom were more astonished than gratified to learn that the recent sad skirmish had been a victory.

Herbert was suspected of no great fondness for the sea, but no one could accuse him of staying chained to his quill. He led a lively social life. He arrived on board his flagship at the latest possible moment, when operations were afoot, and the sailors amended his title—Torrington—to ' Tarry-in-Town '. Reluctance to go to sea persisted as a reluctance, when at sea, to go looking for trouble. In action Herbert appeared indecisive; either he revered the book, or he dreaded being caught in some situation in which the book would not help him; or, it has been suggested, he was secure in the knowledge that, if disaster came because of the Fleet's inaction, there were those at the Admiralty more vulnerable than himself.

He played safe afloat and ashore; stuck to the letter of Navy law and custom; and when he was court-martialled for timidity in an encounter with the French off Beachy Head his peers had to acquit him because he had broken no rule. He exemplified an attitude over which Their Lordships were to shake sorrowful heads in the next century and to ask what had become of the spirit of Drake and Hawkins; an attitude which reached its climax in the tragedies of Byng and Mathews.

Whig historians have been hard on Torrington. He is said to have been totally unfitted physically or mentally for high office because from earliest youth he had been ' addicted to excesses which are ruinous to a man's nerve and energy'. Tory admirers, on the other hand, spoke of his calmness under stress —especially beautiful to watch at the Admiralty when brother Lords Commissioners were dashing round in circles.

After Beachy Head the country panicked at the rumour of invasion and the Admiralty (perhaps urged by ex-Trinitarian John Pepys) even ordered Trinity House to lift every buoy in the Thames estuary to stop the French getting up to the dock- yards and accomplish another ' Medway '. The Earl of Torring- ton smiled at the order, counselled trust in Britain's defences and coined a phrase which summed up a concept of strategy years ahead of its time: "I knew," he told the House of Commons, "that whilst we had a Fleet in Being, they would not dare to make the attempt."

The political confusions of the reign brought changes at the top in every Whitehall department. Where the Admiralty and the Navy were concerned, Their Majesties left the cliques and cabals to fight it out among themselves. William III confessed himself no sailor. He was too much fascinated by military matters to interest himself continually in the Navy.

At sea, Sir Edward Russell (afterwards Lord Orford), Sir

George Rooke and Sir Cloudesley Shovel emerged as up-and-coming admirals in the actions which, culminating in the daring assault on La Hogue, ended any hopes the former King had entertained of regaining the English and Scottish thrones. The realm was giving battle with a new offensive spirit; and taking punishment too: Admiralty papers of the time hint at sterling deeds performed by the fishermen of England, especially in the south-west, in positively Elizabethan exploits against huge foreign privateers. We hear of Their Lordships awarding a gold chain and medal and a sum of money to William Thompson of Poole, Dorset; and a gold chain, medal and the cargo of the Frenchman he has forced ashore, to Peter Joliffe of Weymouth.

But in 1693 there came a savage attack on a British convoy homeward bound from the Mediterranean, and a futile attempt to save it—futile because his intelligence was faulty—by Rooke. It was enough to set the London mob baying for Admiralty blood and to bring King William down on the side of the critics. He harangued Parliament about ‘miscarriages in our affairs at sea’ which had brought ‘so great disgrace upon the nation’. (The convoy had not been as important as all that.)

“I have resented it extremely,” his speech ended, “and, as I will take care that those who have not done their duty will be punished, so I am resolved to use my utmost endeavours that our power at sea may be *rightly managed* for the future.”

Dissolution of the Admiralty followed hard on the King’s speech. He sheltered his two favourite advisers, Rooke and Russell, from the worst of the blast and the time arrived in the winter of royal discontent, 1694 to 1695, when Sir Edward Russell cruised in the Mediterranean wearing both Lord High Admiral’s and Commander-in-Chief’s flags: signifying that all the administrative and executive power over the Royal Navy rested in the hands of one man.

Nothing short of dictatorial authority really suited the First Lord Commissioner, although he owed that title only to the accident of his name appearing first in the Letters Patent. He had already irritated his former colleagues by refusing to hand over the well-paid job of Navy Treasurer when he joined the Board, and soon he quarrelled with Rooke and demanded his dismissal. The King demurred. Russell threw up his job in protest. Invited to take over command of the Royal Navy, Lord Tankerville was heard to say he 'would rather be dragged through a horsepond'.

As Earl of Orford, Admiral Russell pursued his zigzag political career, running the Admiralty again and again, growing more despotic and petulant as he advanced in age. In 1699 the House of Commons petitioned the King to remove him who presided (says Burnet) 'with all the authority, but without the title, of Lord High Admiral'. The King returned 'a soft but general answer'—which soothed Russell least of all. Angered by His Majesty's lukewarm support, he resigned once more.

A long investigation into his private finances opened in 1703—a routine ordeal for an ex-Navy Treasurer, which invariably gave the broadsheet-hawkers plenty to shout about but was not necessarily fatal to a political sailor's career. In Orford's case it went on so long and lost his accusers so completely in its intricacies that both sides of Parliament gave up out of sheer fatigue. He was back as First Lord Commissioner in 1709—to walk out again a few weeks later in sympathy with a friend dismissed from another ministerial office. King George I on his accession in 1714 reinstated him at the Admiralty and Lord Orford resigned for the fourth and last time three years later.

Hounded by the monarch, disconcerted by resignations and dismissals, bedevilled by party quarrels and intrigues and slanders, the naval administration produced an unexpectedly respectable record for the reign. The Fleet which James left behind, and never ceased to mourn over (for was it not the Fleet he alone had created out of chaos ?—his friends in exile assured him it was), numbered about a hundred ships. In fourteen years under William and Mary the Commissioners and the Navy Board nearly doubled the total, at a cost to the Exchequer of the same half-million of money per annum which they had spent during the last years of the Stuarts. This was accomplished in spite of total non-co-operation from the Scots, in spite of constant war with France (until the Peace of Ryswick in 1697, when Louis XIV at last recognised William as King of England) and in spite of the wastage of warships and men during the long-drawn-out reconquest of Ireland. Upon the sturdy vessels of the building programme, new names were blazoned: *Greenwich*, *Royal William*, *Grafton*, *Woolwich*, *Warspight*.

Board members counted years of sea-time in their Service records, and had taken note of the signs of the times. They set to work revising and enlarging the Naval Discipline Act, providing sensibly for the particular problems of men at sea, and consolidating the Navy's standing as a distinct armed force. The Bill to Enforce Better Discipline in the Navy came before Parliament in 1694; when passed, it brought a rather alarming flood of courts martial. Justice, Their Lordships felt, must be seen to be done by as many people as possible, and under the new rules the number of officers on any Court or Board of Enquiry varied with the number of ships assembled in the neighbourhood. Around the dockyard ports you would see almost any day magnificent displays of gold lace converging on ships where the court-martial gun had been fired. Four admirals and thirty-six captains sat down in a small warship in the Downs to hear how a wretched purser had made away with a trivial quantity of stores.

The apparent crime wave was a healthy sign. More offences were being detected, not committed, and a higher standard of conduct was being imposed, perhaps a little prematurely. From a rough analysis of court-martial returns at the end of the seventeenth century, it seems that brawling and starting fires were sailors' favourite offences. A subordinate officer is tried for 'setting the gun-room ablaze'. Officers who drink the Pretender's health—usually after drinking the health of everyone else they can call to mind—or ratings who express Jacobite sentiments in mess-deck argument frequently appear in the returns. A mate is sentenced in 1697 to a flogging for saying that the Lords Commissioners of the Admiralty are 'all rogues'; and another realist—a bo'sun—for telling his captain he sees no harm in making a little on the side out of ship's stores—that everyone does it, even Their Lordships.

A notable court martial of the period is that on Captain William Dampier, for losing his ship on an Admiralty-sponsored voyage of exploration to New Guinea in 1698. He is branded 'hard and cruel . . . not a fit person to be employed as Commander of His Majesty's Ships'.

Nothing stamped the Commissioners as representatives of a new breed of admiral so clearly as their recognition of the rights and needs of underdogs—common sailors and junior officers. Suave place-grabbing and polite character-assassination was the rule among equals; but the Board of Admiralty showed an almost incongruous humanity to its errant subordinates. It was a strange interlude of understanding and enlightenment between long eras of harsh sentences barbarically carried out.

Under the new act, fines replaced corporal punishment for many offences; all fines went to swell the Chatham Chest. Sometimes one reads of the Commissioners declining to confirm brutal sentences on officers found guilty of insubordination or violence—and ordering accuser and accused to shake hands and be friends instead.

Sea officers had other reasons for gratitude to the stream of Lords who flowed through the Board of Admiralty. While Their Majesties were new to Whitehall, they had struck swiftly and got the Fleet a hundred-per-cent rise in pay. (Most of it was taken away again in 1700.) They fought hard to extend the ' unemployed pay ' principle to all ranks. The naval service, at the turn of the century, could be presented to any young man of good birth and some education as an attractive career—pay, pension, foreign travel. Britain's influence was spreading overseas and the Admiralty managed what Admiralties before it had given up in despair—to keep regular squadrons in the Americas and off the Spanish and North African coasts. New cruisers and frigates were going into service as fast as they came off the slips, and Their Lordships were beginning to rotate the fleets systematically between Home, Mediterranean and West Indies stations.

Dockyards had rarely been busier in peacetime. The Czar of Russia, working incognito, or as incognito as his height of six feet eight would allow, in Deptford dockyard under the name of Peter Michaelov, arrived at the end of a great ship-building boom, just about the time of Ryswick, when the Admiralty was told to slow down. His fellow-workers belonged to the greatest arsenal and shipbuilding port in the world, on the most congested river in the world, close to the liveliest and most energetic city in the world. Significantly, when Peter the Great came to create the Russian Navy, he placed his orders with the Dutch.

Evidence of Admiralty expansion forced itself on the notice of any traveller through southern England. Plymouth dock-yard was taking shape, Winstanley's Eddystone Light having removed the worst hazards of the approaches. (Their Lordships had been a little slow to act on this project, not being able to make up their minds between Plymouth, Dartmouth and Falmouth as a western fleet base.) The original Whitehall Admiralty was on the drawing board, and the site being prepared for it, although it would be 1725 before the building was in use and 1760 before it got its decorative Adam screen along the forecourt.

In 1694 the 'most munificent institution that has ever been seen', in contemporary phrase, came into the Admiralty's hands. King Charles II had begun to build Greenwich Hospital in the style of a palace which had previously stood on the site. Queen Mary, the story goes, determined to make the Navy a personal thank-offering from herself and her husband for the victories of Barfleur and La Hogue, fixed on a home for old and disabled seamen, to make them the Chelsea pensioners of the Navy. Sir Christopher Wren drew her attention to Greenwich and was promptly ordered to go to work ' with great magnificence and order '—and with Vanburgh and Hawksmore at his side.

Her Majesty laid the foundation stone in June 1696. When first opened, the Hospital accommodated nearly three thousand pensioners and the labour of enlarging and beautifying it went on throughout the eighteenth century. In 1873 it became the Royal Naval College, which it has been ever since: nowadays the ' Navy's University', the school for academic studies and advanced training.

Its great glory is the Painted Hall, with frescoed ceiling and perfectly-proportioned floor-to-ceiling windows, the former Hospital refectory, done by Sir James Thornhill. State visitors, potentates and honorary admirals in the British Navy have dined there, and so have most of the famous sailors, soldiers and airmen of the past two hundred years. It is the official banqueting hall of the Lords Commissioners of the Admiralty (since 1964, the Admiralty Board).

In an era remarkable for new buildings and institutions on

a stupendous scale, one strictly non-Service edifice had much to do with the growth of Admiralty and Navy Board and all the spending departments of Government. It was the Bank of England, founded to put English credit on a proper footing and enable treasurers to negotiate loans more easily and at more favourable rates. It brought the Navy's finances, among others, into line with advanced Continental practices. It brought projects which involved big capital outlay within the reach of a limited-budget office. A new vista opened before Their Lordships—buildings, dockyards, voyages of exploration—all the activities which previous administrations, because of a chronic shortage of ready money, had hesitated to embark on.

An Admiralty publication of 1700 indicates real progress in realising the dream of successive Boards to get officers of the Navy recognised as full-time professionals. Nowadays the Navy List consists of closely-printed volumes of hundreds of pages, which detail the seniorities of commissioned and branch officers, active and retired; descriptions of the officer complement of every ship and her place in the Fleet, a catalogue of all the dockyards and shore establishments controlled by the Admiralty, with the ranks and posts of their senior officials. Up to 1700—to Henry VIII and James II, to Treasurer Hawkins and Secretary Pepys—the Navy List was a simple statement of ships afloat: a pamphlet produced unofficially on behalf of, or in opposition to, someone who wanted to make a point about Britain's naval strength for political reasons.

The 1700 booklet, only a couple of pages thick, is *A List of Captains who served in the Fleet in the late War*. A companion leaflet followed it: *A List of Lieutenants who served in the Fleet in the late War*. Years were to elapse before Their Lordships got into the habit of regularly releasing information about the officers of the Navy. We can trace the development of this important work—a side of Admiralty activity which ought not to be overlooked—through the eighteenth and nineteenth centuries.

The first of a series of *Sea Officers' Lists* comes out in 1717, with seniorities attached to the captains' and lieutenants' names to enable them to calculate their half-pay entitlements. In 1732 the Admiralty publishes the *List of Surgeons with the Dates of their first Warrants*—surgeons too being by then assessed for half-pay. Fourteen years later, during Anson's time at the Admiralty, the first full *Alphabetical List of the Commissioned Officers of His Majesty's Fleet, 1746*, is brought out and next year the *List of Flag Officers*.

Twenty years more and the Court Kalendar includes a periodical supplement, *A New and Correct List of the Royal Navy of Great Britain*, with the names of all the warships, their commanding officers and their stations, and seniority dates of every officer down to the chaplain. This is followed in 1780 by the *List of Masters belonging to the Royal Navy* (the navigating officers) and in 1810 by the *List of Pursers, Gunners, Boatswains, and Carpenters*. Both were Navy Board publications because 'warrant' officers were a Navy Board concern.

Several retired admirals amused themselves by publishing their own Navy Lists. Private publishers did some too—better value, as a rule, than the official ones—which they paid retired officers to edit. 'Steel's', to personnel of the Nelson era, was what *Jane's* would one day become to their ships. From what J. A. Gardner writes in *Above and Under Hatches*, Steel was an authority in the seventeen-eighties:

'Coghlan's name was John, but someone had written to Steele [*sic*] saying his name was Timothy and it was put so on the List. Coghlan on this wrote to say it was not his name and requested Steele to alter it, but the same wag who had written before did so again, and when the List was printed his name stood as John Timothy Coghlan, and remained so, and we always

E

called him Tim.'

Policies in confusion, members at loggerheads, factions
splintering off in the two main parties, streams of resignations
pouring in—as things had gone on throughout the nineties, only
worse, the reign of William III came to a close. " Secrets are
so ill-kept," was his plaintive reiteration about the Admiralty
and Navy Board. Broadsheet printers distributed more forth-
right objections and Sir Robert Rich and his colleagues in 1702
got a particularly poor press. ' These men,' the pamphlet claimed,
' don't know a first-rate man-of-war from a herring boat, nor
the helm of a ship from a handspike.' The dual monarchy sank
convinced that its Admiralty was the most troublesome of offices.
King and Queen, unappreciative of the progress it had made
because, though solid, it was not spectacular, died pessimistic about
Britain's naval future.

Just before the end the King made a last effort to put his
Navy above party argument and get all the responsibility on
one pair of shoulders. He revived the Lord High Admiral's
office and bestowed it on Thomas Herbert, Earl of Pembroke.
The Government disapproved; everyone knew Pembroke was
no seaman, and everyone knew he would insist on going to sea.

A fine oil-painting in a private house at Hawkhurst, Kent,
portrays the eighth Earl in the ceremonial dress of a Lord High
Admiral, circa 1702, a rust-coloured velvet cloak and heavy robes
of yellow fringed with gold. Pembroke had a second brief spell
in office in 1708. He was one of those dignified old men of
the Court who can be relied on to support an office of great
ceremony and grace it, provided it does not go on too long.
He carried the sword called Curtana at four coronations, dying
greatly aged in 1733 and remembered as a nobleman of ' eminent
virtue and great learning '.

In 1702 his seals had barely cooled before Anne came to the

throne. She had a consort for whom, she decided, the office of Lord High Admiral might have been expressly designed. He was George, Prince of Denmark, and he agreed with her, as he usually did.

10　George, Prince of Denmark

'GREETING. Know Ye that I, Prince George of Denmark &c., Lord High Admiral of England, Ireland &c., And of all Her Majesty's Plantations &c., and Generalissimo of Her Majesty's Forces &c., reposing great Trust and Confidence in your Integrity, Fidelity, Prudence, Experience and Circumspection, have nominated, ordained, made, constituted and appointed, and by these Presents do nominate, ordain, make, constitute and appoint, You. . . .'

It is the Consort, not only Lord High Admiral but, as it were, Minister of Defence for the nation, gathering his council of admirals together. He chose Sir George Rooke, Sir David Mitchell, George Churchill and Richard Hill, and he made Josiah Burchett his secretary.

Once a month the Principal Officers of the Navy Board went up to Whitehall to meet them and receive directions. Sometimes only one of their number went up: the strong man of the Navy ashore, well able to hold his own with the admirals. He was Sir Richard Haddock, who had served the Navy Board through three reigns. As long as he lasted as Comptroller, Admiralty supervision of its lower house would be nominal.

The Lord High Admiral was not a man to poke restlessly into every corner of the business until he learned all about the Navy. (He was a man whom the Merry Monarch had 'tried drunk and tried sober, and found nothing '.) He declined to burden himself with detail or overtax his intellect. Sittings were called and cancelled: His Royal Highness was at Bath for his health, a sudden departure. Other times, meetings assembled and broke up without any discussion: His Royal Highness would not be present, he had gone to Newmarket for the races.

After his first year, he placed another admiral, the Honourable James Brydges, on the Board and delegated authority to any two members to take action in his absence—" As I might do," he said, " or ought to do, if I were present."

Prince George led an able team, which spent its talents on Whitehall intrigue and wasted its energy in Parliamentary tugs-of-war. Progressives condemned the organisation. It pushed the Admiralty back into courtiership, they said, and the Lord High Admiral would make changes which no one would dare scrutinise too closely, because of his supra-parliamentary status. He would allow corrupt admirals to shelter behind his name. But the admirals, like all public figures, needed more shelter than Crown or Consort could provide.

Sir George Rooke had beaten off more than one personal attack. Pressed a second time to remove him from the Admiralty at the turn of the century, King William had replied firmly: " I will not. George Rooke has defended me, and I will defend him." But soon after Rooke returned triumphant from Gibraltar the whispering campaign gained new momentum and he retired without any effort by his Prince to cushion the fall. A former ' King's Letter Boy ', Tory member for Portsmouth and afterwards Vice-Admiral of Great Britain and Lieutenant of the Admiralty, the plump, plethoric, massively-wigged hero of the Spanish wars was sacrificed for a *quid pro quo*: the Tories had driven Lord Orford out immediately after La Hogue, and the Whigs had never forgotten it.

As never before, the Royal Navy needed a strong, dedicated administration. Warship tonnage had doubled in twenty years, and so had the men. (Or so it was estimated; attempts to compile a register of seamen on the lines of the French Ministry of Marine's had failed.)   But the Navy marked time.   It was the turn of the Army, the conquering heroes in Europe, to bask in Treasury smiles.   Britain's once-renowned shipwrights and artisans patched up old ships but built few new ones.   Crafts-men, not designers, they had no incentive or opportunity to refine and modify.   They had stumbled, generations before, on a formula and, since it was a good formula for its day, they saw no reason to change it.   When crises occurred over the next fifty years they adhered to it, building ' ships by the mile and chopping them off in lots ', as a disgusted observer put it.   Mean-while the seafaring lands across the Channel were developing naval architecture as a science.

Sporadically, while in opposition, the Whig lords turned up a scandal or two to remind Queen Anne that she still had a Navy.   Members cried for the resignation of Admiral George Churchill, brother of the Master-General of the Ordnance (after-wards the ever-memorable Duke of Marlborough), for systemat-ically supporting Army against Navy while a member of the Board of Admiralty.   Fuel for their case was supplied by priva-teers from Calais and Dunkirk who harassed the south coast while the Fleet seemed deliberately to look the other way.

Patriots in Parliament begged the Queen to make sea affairs her ' first and most peculiar care '.   The result was a special commission to look into administrative misdemeanours, which was not quite what the admirals wanted.   It did not require a commission to discover that low morale and unhappiness throughout the sea Service might be traced to nervousness and uncertainty at the top—to the high rate of turnover among the senior members of Admiralty.   Their appointments depended entirely on party affiliations; with each change of Government, whether they were M.P.s or not, a new set of leaders came in and the old went out.   Just to remind retired public servants that all was not necessarily forgiven as soon as they had lost their jobs, the Commission charged old Sir Edward Seymour, Comptroller of Her Majesty's Household, with failing to keep his accounts straight while Treasurer of the Navy as far back as 1673.

Politics kept Britain's ablest commander, Sir Cloudesley Shovel, out of high office and when he lost his life in the Scilly Islands politicians pursued him beyond the grave. Promotion had never been such a gamble: it came early, late or never to brilliant and stupid alike, depending on which faction controlled the Admiralty at the critical moment. Sensational advancements by one Board could be reversed just as sensationally by their successors, within days. When the Whigs swept into office, the new First Lord instantly ordered Admiral Wishart, Commander-in-Chief Mediterranean, to haul down his flag; then settled down with his secretary to go through the rest of the list, striking out names.

Sir William Jumper, a popular hero, right-hand man of Rooke and Shovel in many a desperate encounter, conspicuous for his bravery and good sense, went no farther than Captain during his active career: but by a lucky switch of Government he was able to set off up the rest of the ladder at an advanced age. He was nominated to the Navy Board, then promoted Superintendent of the Ships at Chatham and ended in a blaze of glory as Navy Commissioner at the New Dock (Devonport).

Every time Parliament discussed defence, it attacked the Admiralty for its failure to protect British trade. Rooke had gained Gibraltar, but experts saw no future in the Rock as the answer to the country's prayer for a Mediterranean base. Port Mahon in Minorca was the Navy's aim, and this at least Prince George's administration achieved. Lord Orford brought the good news from Parliament of the passing of the Cruizers and Convoys Act, a tremendous tonic for the Fleet, for it meant that upwards of forty warships would have to be permanently stationed on the trade routes; an even better tonic was Parliament's decision to allocate the prizes those warships took to the Navy, for the 'more effectual encouragement of the Sea Service'.

While Lords Commissioners and Principal Officers dragged their cables or cut and ran in the gales and swirling tides of two-party Whitehall, one man stood firmly anchored at the Navy Office. He was Sir Richard Haddock, Comptroller of the Navy from 1688 until his death in 1714, an officer without whom, both sides of Parliament admitted, 'the Navy would stand still'. Incorruptible, a glutton for hard work and steadfast in his propaganda for a strong fleet, Haddock *was* the Navy Board, as Pepys had been before him. The Navy Treasurer, in his day, had slipped more and more into a position of aristocratic independence. Haddock filled the place he vacated, and staked a claim to that place—'first among equals'—for all the Comptrollers who came after him.

His Navy Board, without ever being called on to mobilise, store and victual for an emergency on a large scale, withstood a terrible test of its efficiency in November 1703, when the severest storm recorded in the British Isles struck the south of England, sank seventeen warships at sea and drowned fifteen hundred sailors—a tragic blow, but trivial damage when the disasters which merchant ships and foreign vessels suffered came to be analysed. The Home Fleet, part Pepys-built and part William and Mary, demonstrated that, though slow and ungainly compared with the French Navy, it had a built-in robustness all its own. The great storm's worst legacy—not properly appreciated at the time—was the hundreds of square miles of oak forest laid waste, which half destroyed in a single night and day the home-grown raw material for the warships of the future.

The Admiralty had its outstanding, all-too-permanent personality too. He was Josiah Burchett, First Secretary to the

Board—the position which Pepys created. Burchett in fact boasted the distinction of having been given the sack by Pepys when he was a junior clerk at the old Navy Board in Seething Lane. He had then gone to sea and had been lucky enough to attract the notice of the future Lord Orford—after which he never looked back.

Burchett's salary in the Lord High Admiral's time was a thousand pounds a year, plus fees on writing commissions which could amount to as much again. He took on as assistant —forerunner of the Deputy Secretary—George Clark, private secretary of the Prince of Denmark. Burchett's chief talent was in the department of tact and discretion. He could deal with loaded questions with a delicacy that offended neither party. Not without sea experience—but with not very much of it—he liked to pontificate about tactics and nautical lore from his Board Room chair, and he lectured the House of Commons on Shovel's fatal navigational blunder:

" As I cannot undertake to give the true cause of this unhappy miscarriage, I shall leave it with this common observation, that, upon approaching land after so long a run, the best Lookerout is the best Sailor, and consequently a lying-by in the nighttime and making sail in the day is the most safe, which I think this unhappy Gentleman did not do."

Burchett entered Parliament late in life as member for Sandwich borough. He wrote a *Complete History of the Sea* in five gigantic volumes, starting with the Phoenicians and Egyptians. After holding the Secretaryship of the Admiralty for forty years he swallowed the anchor with the greatest reluctance in 1742, aged eighty and nearly blind, after the Admiralty had declared him ' worn out with age and unable to attend to the business of the office ' and replaced him with Thomas Corbett.

The Union of Crowns in 1707 made little difference to the

E 2

'English' Navy. It remained ninety-nine per cent English and it was always a sore point with seamen that Scots could officially snap their fingers at the press gang. It had far-reaching political effects on the Navy's governors, however. The amalgamation of State offices tied the Barony of Scotland to the First Lordship and for a century and a half to come the chief of the Admiralty had the bestowal of patronage in Scotland in his hands.

On the coast of California the following year, a historic clique of British adventurers—Woodes Rogers, William Dampier, Alexander Selkirk (just rescued from his island) and Doctor Thomas Dover of pain-killing and anti-diarrhoea pill fame—heard from the captain of a ship they captured of the Lord High Admiral's death. They refused to believe it and continued nightly drinking his health—" which can do him no hurt if he is dead ", they agreed.

But the news was true. The Whigs, who had dismissed Pembroke from the Lord Presidency of the Council a few weeks earlier, made some amends by persuading him to take on once more the governorship of the Navy, and while he was making up his mind Queen Anne, acting through Secretary Burchett, became the country's Lady High Admiral.

Lords High Admiral, thanks partly to the Union, wielded influence and Interest as never before; in other directions their hands were tied and there was no stampede of applicants for the job. Lord Pembroke's second spell lasted hardly longer than his first. In 1709 he resigned, declaring the office ' too heavy a load ', meaning he was tired of being a Whitehall shuttlecock, lobbed from Whig to Tory court and back.

Lord Orford agreed to take it over—compromising for once in his career, insisting that responsibility be divided. The only solution—putting the office back ' in commission '—found Orford as First Lord Commissioner, with George Byng and

John Leake, both serving admirals, as his assistants.

At lower levels, rising captains and bureaucrats had come to depend on recommendations from one or other of the Churchill family. The best jobs suddenly began going to those who knew how to profit from the devastating quarrels between Anne and her lost favourite, the Duchess of Marlborough. None in the public service could stand aloof, all had to take sides.

One more year and the Harley administration was in and Orford out. Next in succession, John Leake, hesitated to expose himself on an eminence so accurately registered by invisible snipers. He devised a little constitutional fiction, representing himself as Second Lord acting in the absence of a non-existent First; and, to make matters safer, was careful to spend nearly all his time at sea. The Third Lord, Sir George Byng, therefore became in effect naval 'supremo'.

Through its leaders' anxiety to save their political reputations, the Navy lost both its interest with the Court and its representation in Parliament. Admiralty declined so rapidly in prestige that when a naval expedition to Quebec was planned (Sir Hovenden Walker's, a fiasco) no one troubled to let Their Lordships know anything about it.

Of Leake and Byng, one had his career behind him, the other in front. Leake had helped to capture Port Mahon and had followed Sir Cloudesley Shovel as Commander-in-Chief, Mediterranean. Byng, in spite of having secretly campaigned for the Prince of Orange in '88 and being an active back-bencher, member for the important constituency of Plymouth, had been discredited in the Government's eyes and had had to leave the Admiralty just before Anne died for his 'obstinacy against the ministers'.

His motto was said to have been 'Leave nothing to chance'. He bore it in mind when cultivating the Whigs, and it paid a rich dividend as soon as George I ascended the throne. Back

in command of a fleet at sea, Byng did so well against the
Spaniards that at the end of a short war he had moved into the
House of Lords (as Viscount Torrington), become Rear-Admiral
of England, a Privy Councillor and—not the least lucrative of
his honours—Treasurer of the Navy.

He had gone to sea very young and had never, it was alleged,
learned to read or write properly. He reminded people of a
devil-may-care Elizabethan skipper, but behind the tough sea-
dog's weatherbeaten scowl all the ingredients for a successful
First Lord lay hidden. Byng had to wait thirteen years for that,
until George II came to the throne. Then he proved himself
an intelligent, dignified and highly respected negotiator and
chief, for his times. He stood above the herd, but it was a
poor herd.

Naval history of the early Hanoverian period lacks outstanding personalities, active or administrative. The admirals
who made the news were the spectacular failures. Torrington's
son, the second Admiral George Byng, was one of those. In
the younger Byng's notoriety, memories of the older suffered a
total eclipse.

11   Dark Age of Admiralty

The Georges were no sailors. All four distrusted and avoided the sea. Their children had a rooted antipathy to naval service—with one exception. The House of Hanover contributed to the Royal Navy the maxim that sailoring is for the fool of the family and the principle that seamen are savages, all the better for a taste of Prussian discipline. The code which made the Service a byword for punishments of a severity hardly credible today—the keel-haulings, floggings round the fleet and the rest—came in strongly with the Georges. An offence which merited fifty lashes in the reign of Queen Anne was earning two or three hundred by the time George III arrived.

Knowing nothing about ships, King George at least had the wisdom not to interfere. The Navy continued without royal patronage. Since the growth of Party government, its leaders had slid from the inner councils, but the monarch had hitherto always found ways of keeping in touch with them. All at once the Fleet, dockyards, Navy Office and Board of Admiralty were alone in the political circus ring without a master.

Ripley's Admiralty building, pride of Whitehall, stood ready for occupation. The Lords, secretaries, clerks and messengers, drawn from holes and corners all over Westminster, crept in to inaugurate the most dismal era in administrative history. A Navy twenty-seven thousand strong had diminished between 1715 and 1720 to seven thousand—the absolute acceptable minimum of regulars, and this at a time when the Fleet was supposed to be on a war footing. Busy with their own troubles, the Lords Commissioners under Orford had given up entertaining the Principal Officers and chatting with them about the affairs of the Service. Superb new headquarters inspired a superb indifference to the pride and the claims of the lower house. Their Lordships set up an Admiralty Office, which justified the occupation of some empty rooms and may have been conceived as a liaison department, but which made a barrier and not a link between the two naval commands.

For a start the Admiralty Office took all personnel under its wing instead of commissioned officers only, then began eroding the Navy Board's ancient authority by inspecting, questioning and amending decisions about new construction, wages and dockyard material. Instead of acting, as former chiefs with all their faults had acted, as an elder brother to the Navy Office, sometimes stern and sometimes benevolent but always protective, the Board of Admiralty withdrew itself into the role of carping critic of a body which, in the strict sense, was a part of itself.

Sensibly directed, such systematic unpleasantness might have brought good results for the Navy, for the Principal Officers also had their faults and an occasional jolt had proved effective in the past. But when personal relationships were broken off and correspondence was conducted between stone-walling clerks, the Navy Office stagnated. Considering the competition for jobs among applicants dazzled by the perquisites, considering the pitfalls of public life, it is remarkable how few changes at the top occurred in about a half of the new century.

When Anson joined the Admiralty in the seventeen-forties he found the Principal Officers all frail old men; his colleagues on the Board of Admiralty either knew nothing or cared nothing about them. Comptroller Haddock, son of the monolithic Sir Richard, whose office he had succeeded to in 1733, was ripe for superannuation but a mere stripling compared with his fellows. The Surveyor, Sir Jacob Acworth, who had actually served at sea in the reign of Charles II and who claimed to remember the Great Plague with perfect clarity, could neither see nor hear and was so tottery on his legs that, as a confidential report put it with tactful understatement, he was 'unable to visit the several Yards so frequently as the Service required'. At that date the Principal Officers had increased to ten—ten mild-mannered absent-minded ancients among whom dying in harness was a tradition—and thirty-eight clerks: not a grossly over-staffed organisation for managing a fleet which covered half the globe and a much larger number of shore establishments than Pepys had known; although most of the sailors were beyond its jurisdiction, begging on the streets. Yet it took Anson to see that this was no way for a coming maritime power to run a navy.

In its own way, throughout the reigns of the first two Georges, the Admiralty was as badly served. Fortunately no major enemy threatened its chaotic operational methods— fortunately for those in office, but their successors would suffer for generations. Minor scares gave thoughtful observers an idea of what it might be like. Their Lordships panicked over rumours and lashed out wildly in all directions, usually wounding the Navy Board or an unlucky sea officer. Every decision was watered down, cancelled, re-issued, thrown out, every alternative badly hampered by political disputes within the Board and between the Board and its admirals at sea.

Timid men, taking orders from the unlikeliest of quarters, the naval chieftains of thirty years left nothing to history, except specialist period history. James, Earl of Berkeley, occupied the First Lordship through two Stanhope and one Walpole administrations: high on the list of contenders for the title of First Lord Soonest Forgotten. In Walpole's second term (1727)

Lord Torrington came to the top—a more active figure, who founded the Naval Academy at Portsmouth for forty ' sons of the Nobility and Gentry ' (a development of the ' King's Letter ' system); helped to get the world's first lightship established, at the Nore; and brought out the first printed edition of the *Naval Regulations*, which standardised the numerous local memoranda and temporary fleet or squadron orders which admirals afloat were finding it necessary to issue.

The rank of Commodore, superior to Captain, appeared the same year—1731. A term familiar but not precisely defined since the Dutch wars (it came from the Dutch and was variously spelt Commandeur, Commadore and Commandore), it had to wait seventy-five years for royal recognition. Even in Trafalgar year, ' Commodore ' had no official existence; Anson was among the first to grace the title. (Sometimes it was confused with Commander: a word in regular use, but used with different meanings. Provision was made in 1747, when the relative ranks between Army and Navy were agreed, for post-captains to serve in non-post ships as commanders; not until 1827 did the Commander appear in his modern place, as the second-in-command of a line-of-battle ship.)

A third semi-nonentity, Admiral Sir Charles Wager, became First Commissioner in 1733; the only naval man on the Board, for the first British prime minister had shuffled and reshuffled his appointments until an all-civilian Admiralty (civilians like Walpole himself, dull, prosperous, *laisser-faire* and hangers-on of the Whig nobility) had replaced an all-naval one.

As a vice-admiral, Wager had successfully shown the flag in the Baltic in his seafaring days, and had landed the Spanish garrisons at Leghorn when Don Carlos asserted his right to the dukedom of Parma. He had gone to sea with the first ' King's Letter Boys ' and, being an obedient servant of his party, he remained head of the Navy for ten years until he resigned in a huff at the age of seventy-seven on overhearing someone refer to him as an old woman. Wager bore the brunt of the 1739 tumult which rocked Ripley's building to its new foundations, when the Navy, called on in a hurry to fight for Jenkins's Ear, had to admit to a Parliament thirsty for blood that only a third of its first-line ships were fit for sea.

That short war, which merged into the more serious one of the Austrian Succession, forced a Committee of Ministers on the Admiralty, of whom the elderly Wager was one and the more elderly Sir John Norris another. Admiral Norris, a spritely octogenarian, saw himself as Wager's successor as soon as the ' old woman ' could be persuaded to go. But the job went to a creature of Carteret's, a landlubber named Finch (afterwards Earl of Winchilsea), whose only claim to naval eminence arose from his family connection with the old-time naval Nottinghams.

Thus, as ever, while a fleet hastily snatched from reserve and shockingly manned and provisioned went looking for the official enemy, the Committee of Ministers hacked and stabbed among themselves. Several times the Secretary of State (Newcastle) handled Mediterranean strategy single-handed from his own office, as though no Admiralty existed.

Troubles came by battalions in the seventeen-forties, from far away and near at hand. Learning of French preparations to support the Young Pretender's bid for the throne, the Committee of Ministers reached out for a professional administrator and, finding only Norris, sulking in his rural retreat, offered him the command of the Home Fleet together with what amounted to dictatorial powers in Home waters: he was to be a kind of floating Admiralty. But, after a month's trial, even Norris had to admit it did not seem to be working and he retired with more grace than his colleagues would have given him credit for, to facilitate the promotion of junior admirals. Among them, although he did not appear immediately, was

George Anson.

The Board of Admiralty's record in the first half of the eighteenth century was not all bad. All through its history, men of the blackest infamy or most criminal stupidity would be identified with some one redeeming contribution to progress. Wager tried hard, for example, to get a register of seamen set up, and he might have succeeded where others before him had failed, but he was howled down by professional orators. It was French, foreign, and smacked of a tyranny one could never impose on the British bluejacket; no true-blue would stand for being docketed and categorised—so Pitt thundered, a newcomer to Parliament, in ' the prettiest words and the worst language ' ever heard in the House.

The broadest enlightenment was sown in the thinnest of dark-age soil—and flowered; and that is typical of Admiralty history. Collectively, the Boards and Committees of the thirties and forties launched, almost accidentally, the one great prestige project which is still identified with Admiralty today. They began to encourage the exploration and charting of unknown coasts and the investigation of scientific phenomena in distant lands. They arranged the competition for a chronometer to solve the insoluble longitude calculation problem, and they tried to get scholars interested in the study of winds and ocean currents. Quite casually, and possibly not always with the purest of motives (as good a way as any of spiking a rival's guns was to send him on a voyage to the East Indies), the British Admiralty took a lead in a vast field of nautical enterprise which foreign Marine Ministries and Departments of Navies could scarcely ever hope to challenge. It was Charles Wager who sent Captain George Anson round the world in the *Centurion*.

Home from exotic adventures with the Fleet sailed an admiral or two not afraid to speak their minds. A curious embarrassment confronted the non-professional Admiralty in the person of a 'simple, noisy creature', Admiral Edward Vernon, 'Old Grog', hero of Portobello and declared enemy of Walpole and his Whigs.

From his seat in Parliament (he was M.P. for Penrhyn from 1727) and afterwards through leaflet raids all over London, Vernon hammered into Their Lordships' heads the Navy's needs: men of action at the top, energetic reforms at the Navy Office. In breezy nautical language (his pamphlets bore such titles as *Some Seasonable Advice from an Honest Sailor*) he damned a naval high command which had failed to protect south coast fishermen and left British ports wide open to French and Jacobite assault.

Even broadsheet authors had a code of behaviour, and Vernon infringed it by publishing extracts from confidential Admiralty letters. It gave a new First Lord (John Russell, Duke of Bedford) the excuse to suspend him from his command, just in time to save the Admiralty boroughs for the Government at the next elections.

'Old Grog' was not so old, as admirals went: only sixty-two in 1746, the year he severed his lifelong connection with the Navy. His indiscretions, fondness for playing to the gallery and contempt for deskbound officialdom kept him from an administrative job he might have been useful in. He is remembered in the Service, not so much for Portobello, as for the attempt he made to sober up the West Indies Squadron at a time when a sober sailor was 'as rare as a Black Swan'; and for the word 'grog' (Vernon got his nickname from the grosgrain boat-cloak he wore), which came to mean rum and water. Victuals in the Fleet left as much to be desired as ever, but one commodity never in short supply was rum. The sailor's daily ration consisted of the equivalent of seven double rums at midday and another seven at night—taken straight. 'Old Grog' failed to abolish the issue altogether, but he managed in the end to get the raw spirit diluted in his own squadrons, a practice afterwards adopted throughout the Navy. (It was 1824 before the Admiralty came round to Vernon's way of thinking about the 'swinish drunkenness on the lower deck', and halved the ration; 1850 before they reduced it to its present-day amount —half a gill per day—and gave teetotallers the option of taking the money instead.)

At the time he was sacked, Admiral Vernon commanded the Western Squadron, a force assembled to prevent French reinforcements from reaching the Jacobite army in Scotland. Commodore Anson, not long home from his world cruise, relieved him; Hawke went to the Admiralty as a junior Lord in Anson's place.

At Finisterre and Belleisle these two commanders, Hawke and Anson, wrecked the French Navy in the first substantial British sea victories for half a century and paved the way for the peace of Aix-la-Chapelle in 1748. At the signing of that treaty, drastic instantaneous reductions in the Fleet sent thousands of sailors to beg and bludgeon their way home—who had but recently been equally drastically conscripted. 'You will hear little news from England but robberies,' Horace Walpole told his foreign correspondent. 'The number of disbanded soldiers and sailors have all taken to the road.'

Admiralty and Navy Board dropped a few unqualified pilots. Although both departments were still to provide homes for politicians on the make, or politicians claiming payment for services rendered, the Fleet was sailing in to the rescue. A succession of popular naval heroes was coming forward, each one a natural figurehead for the Service, each reasonably independent and wary of the dustier cobwebs of politics. Anson (First Lord almost without a break from 1751 to 1762); Lord Howe (1763 to 1765); Saunders and Keppel (1765 to 1766) and Hawke (1766 to 1771)—these represented the naval element on

Boards numerically weighted in favour of the civilians, and in their time the administration regained a foothold in Government councils and the affections of the people.

12   Anson in Command

Anson came to the Admiralty to rub shoulders with anti-pathetic strangers like John Hynde Cotton, leader of the Jacobite faction in the House of Commons (who is portrayed in a cartoon as a tall, well-fed individual being forced down King George's throat by the Harrington ministers); George Grenville, scion of an influential but unscrupulous family; and George Bubb Dodington, an indefatigable place-hunter who had managed to collect the Treasurership of the Navy.

The contemporary description of the Pelham ministry—' an assemblage of unconnected units '—might have been applied to the Admiralty. A visitor to Ripley's master-building found it hard to trace coherence or communication between the offices, and left it with the impression that their staffs had all been installed there to keep each other from feeling lonely.

The slow, dragging wars at sea had spread diseases in the Navy inescapable in an organism too big and too scattered to live without co-ordination from the centre. Slackness and disobedience betrayed the Fleet's low morale, despite those ferocious punishment scales; dockyards were disorganised and their personnel ripe for mischief. A too-rigid adherence to the Admiralty Bible, the *Fighting Instructions*, provoked scandal and argument at sea, which came to a head in the Mathews and Lestock courts martial. Admirals, captains and officers, whatever they forgot of seamanship or the traditions of the Service, remembered the golden rule: the party line mattered more than the line of battle.

The future ' Father of the Modern Navy ', least of the junior
Lords, stirred the mud from the first month of his arrival,
December 1744. With his chief the Duke of Bedford he had
no quarrel. That ' indolent great noble, but honest and patriotic ' was just such a superior as a youngish admiral full of
exuberant ideas could wish for. Bedford gave him his head
and took his part against more senior Lords Commissioners;
Anson in return gave early warning of attempted wool-pulling
over ducal eyes.

An incident from his early Admiralty days illustrates the
lengths unprincipled opportunists on the Board itself could go
to in the presence of a non-professional head. Anson was
ordered to sea to convoy the East Indiamen home. Grenville,
cousin of the Board member, and ' Mad Montagu ', brother of
Lord Sandwich, another Board member, had asked for, and
got, command of two of Anson's ships. They forged an amend-
ment to the sailing orders, to advise him that they were not to
stay more than seven days with his flag. Anson was in time
to explain it to the Duke—that Grenville and Montagu were
giving themselves a free hand to cruise about and pick up prizes
—and got it erased. The Duke told the amateur privateers they
' deserved to hang '. A lecture was about as far as even a First
Lord dared go, when ministry favourites were on the carpet.

One of the problems Anson had to come to terms with
when in power was that of commanding officers on detached
service who haunted the trade routes and did everything but
hoist the Jolly Roger over His Majesty's ships in their search
for merchant prizes. Ever a realist, he persuaded the Government to offer bribes in the shape of a bounty for every captain
who attacked an enemy warship.

The convoy system creaked under strains heavy enough at
the best of times. Passages in the First Lord's excuses to Parliament suggest pictures which must be clear in the mind's eye of

twentieth-century retired naval officers: 'Nothing is more frequent than complaints from the commanders of convoys, of the obstinacy and folly of masters of merchant ships who refuse to obey their signals . . . [and] disregarding all order and government, desert their convoys from impatience of sooner getting into Port.'

While Their Lordships allowed good officer material to wear itself out in distasteful employment, socialites with influence (a seat in a marginal constituency was enough) pushed to the top. Augustus Hervey's journal gives a hint of the advantages of staying within hailing distance of the Admiralty. Hervey, afterwards Earl of Bristol, entered the Royal Navy as 'Captain's servant', aged eleven, in 1735. Ten years later, himself a captain, he describes how he wrecked a rival captain's reputation by 'showing letters at White's' which a friend had written him from abroad. In the same paragraph he jots down: 'Many of the Admiralty came on board my sloop and dined with me out of compliment to me, and returned all drunk at 2 in the morning'—a poor look-out for the libelled antagonist, thousands of miles away at sea.

Hervey rose swiftly to be a vice-admiral of the Blue and a Lord of the Admiralty (1771 to 1775) before he succeeded to his title and left the Navy. The classic instance of rapid promotion through Interest is Rodney, who became a post-captain at sixteen. Then his father died, the family lost its pull and the boy-admiral-designate had to wait another forty-four years for his next step in rank.

To rebuild morale and emphasise the Navy's own character and integrity, Anson recommended putting the officers in uniform. He was present at the daily Board session when the decision on a red and white colour scheme was taken and the Duke of Bedford came through to announce the last-minute, capricious and historic correction:

" No, the King has determined otherwise for, having seen my Duchess riding in the park in a habit of blue faced with white, the dress took the fancy of His Majesty, who has appointed it for the uniform of the Royal Navy."

The appropriate Fleet Order of 1748 is also worth quoting, as evidence that Admiralty jargon, too, preserves a certain integrity as the centuries drift by:

' Whereas we judge it necessary, in order better to distinguish the rank of Sea Officers, to establish military uniform clothing for Admirals &c., and judging it also necessary that persons acting as midshipmen should likewise have uniform clothing in order to their conveying the appearance which is necessary to distinguish the class to be in the rank of gentleman and give them better credit and figure in executing the commands of their superior officers, you are hereby required and ordered to conform yourselves to the said establishment by wearing clothes accordingly at all proper times.'

The Order was not generally well received and Their Lordships had to circularise commanders-in-chief, imploring them to discipline non-conformists and reminding them that it applied to them too: ' As example is on these occasions extremely necessary, you are to cause every captain under your command to appear in the said dress, and we do expect that you yourselves shall constantly appear in the same.'

The story of a naval officer's uniform goes on, briefly, as follows: introduced, 1748; gold stripes added (three for an admiral, two for a vice-admiral and one for a rear-admiral), 1783; design and decoration largely a matter of individual taste until the eighteen-thirties (the Duke of Clarence, says Christopher Lloyd in *The Nation and the Navy*, introduced ' every conceivable sartorial absurdity '); modern stripes, 1861.

The ' executive curl ' of gold lace on top of the stripes was extended to non-executive officers just after World War I. Epaulettes, to match the Army's, were worn first in 1795, when one on each shoulder denoted an admiral or senior captain, one on the right shoulder a junior captain and one on the left a commander.

In the year of the Uniform Regulations the Duke of Bedford left the Admiralty and John Montagu, Earl of Sandwich, became First Lord. He has had a bad press from the historians. Sandwich was a profligate with an obsessive *nostalgie pour la boue*, a preoccupation with flower-girls and market-women; a gambler whom the great gamblers of his day found it hard to keep up with, who was not above borrowing Navy money to recoup his losses at the tables; a villain who kept a string of mistresses on the profits he made by selling sea and dockyard appointments to high bidders not always suited to the work; in short, a corrupt rogue and a more dangerous enemy to Britain than the French.

Professionally he seems to have been a First Lord of average respectability who, at least during his first term of office (he came back for two more), turned temporarily virtuous and gave the administrative revolution at the Admiralty a useful shove. Sandwich could do wonders if he gave his mind to them. An impartial contemporary said of him that ' no man was such a master of business, so quick and so shrewd '.

Anson remained the sheet anchor of a wayward craft; his was the restraining hand on the gambler's sleeve. In operational and departmental matters, he was First Lord in everything but name.

Sandwich might have been among the uproarious Lords who came home drunk at two in the morning from Augustus Hervey's dinner-party, but Anson—proud, hard, ambitious and unapproachable—would have declined the invitation with perfunctory regret. He kept all his subordinates at a distance, advanced, demoted or removed them without reference to the guiding principle of the times. 'He withstood recommendations of Interest or favour more than any First Lord of the Admiralty was ever known to do,' wrote the Earl of Hardwicke in later years.

After a famous fault-finding walk-round-the-dockyards in 1749 which caught the fossilised pillars of the Navy Board on the wrong foot, Anson swept away the greybeards on his own initiative. Parliament raised a clamour for putting a civilian in charge as Comptroller (the post had become recognised as the senior office)—Parliament's traditional remedy for Service ills. But Anson, speaking for the Board, refused to entertain the idea and, although he tried five Comptrollers in two years and found them all wanting, he picked a brilliant prize at last in Captain George Cockburne, a very prince of Principal Officers.

Lord Anson's name has suffered from association with the panic building programme of the late seventeen-forties but, as Sandwich pointed out at the time, he liked building warships with green wood as little as anyone; flimsy floating coffins, however, were better than no ships at all. It was one of these dilemmas for which the 'previous administration', ever the excuse for inefficiency, really was to blame for once. But his name is also associated with reforms too numerous and varied to be set down in full. He revised the promotion rules (an intelligent revision on paper, but impossible to implement in the climate of the age); put the Fleet in uniform; reorganised the Marines (bringing them under direct Admiralty control and giving them their three divisions, Chatham, Portsmouth and Devonport; they did not become 'Royal' until 1802—the prefix was a reward for fidelity in mutinous times); experimented with the system which allows a sailor to make over part of his pay to his wife; and drew up a new method of rating

ships. A hundred years earlier, a warship was classed according
to the number of men it carried and a little later by the number
of its guns—rough and ready classifications. Anson invented a
method in which both guns and other factors had to be taken
into account; a somewhat laborious one, admittedly. (A
hundred years after his time, warships would be rated on guns
and complement again and—from 1856—on complement alone.)

The Father of the Modern Navy was laying down stiff
rules for his family even before he stepped into father's shoes.
It had been allowed to run wild, he declared; flogging was the
answer. The Army Mutiny Bill, going through Parliament
while Anson was still a junior member of the Board, looked
to him like a move in the right direction: it reinforced all the
dictatorial powers of generals and captains, and the most outrageous of Georgian-style punishments were enshrined in it.
He would, in Horace Walpole's words, 'have chained down
his tars to a like oar'—but even the Fleet was dimly aware
that there were limits beyond which Their Lordships must not
be permitted to go, and the sea officers shrieked their protests.

Provisions of a tyrannical severity went nevertheless into the
Navy Bill of 1749. Their Lordships pronounced death the
only punishment for an officer judged guilty of negligence—
not cowardice, but negligence—in the face of the enemy.
Anson tried might and main to put half-pay officers under the
same discipline as active ones. The idea was that he might
then pursue vendettas against those who had escaped his anger
by going 'unemployed', or get rid of a thorn in his flesh by
offering the half-pay officer (who might well be a member of
Parliament) a disagreeable job and court-martialling him for
refusing it.

In a pamphlet called *A Detection of the Navy Bill* the debonair
Hervey—displaying throughout his career the independence
which only ample private means sustain—exposed the motive

and, in passing, referred to Their Lordships as ' a medley of Court nobility, broken squires, and now and then a solitary nominal Sea Officer or two, who sit there and sleep for their salaries '. Applied to an Admiralty which numbered Anson among its members, the description was wide of the mark. It sounded more like the pre-1749 Navy Board.

Disgruntled officers accused Anson of favouritism. It was said in the Fleet that no representative of the ' boisterous profession ' stayed long in the waiting-room on the ground floor if he could show a recommendation from the Naval Lord upstairs, signed on board H.M.S. *Centurion* on her voyage round the world.

Certainly he was an admiral of strong likes and dislikes. He preferred, in general, officers of birth, breeding and education. Like Hawke who followed him, he set himself to raise the naval officer's standards of culture, manners and personal hygiene. The series of *Regulations and Instructions* begun by Torrington continued under Anson with:

' Linen: to be changed twice a week.
Compartments: to be adequately ventilated.
Interior decks: to be scrubbed with sand.
Officers: not to read in their bunks.
Swear-boxes: to be installed, and officers to pay a shilling a word.'

Punishments for ratings reached at the same time a new level of degradation. Blaspheming sailors wear a wooden collar; for the discontented and insubordinate there is running the gauntlet and a flogging round the fleet.

Samuel Pepys, another tireless promulgator of orders, used to complain that his words were wasted because many a captain could not, or would not, read. (A secretary's note on a letter from the tarpaulin skipper of the *Anne and Christopher*, who made illiteracy his excuse for failing to carry out an order, says: 'To be admonished from His Majesty and My Lords, by Mr Pepys, to apply himself to learning, *late as it is.*')

Anson had the same difficulty. For twenty years the Navy had had its Academy, and those superior young gentlemen the 'King's Letter Boys' had been growing up in the Service for nearly a century. But the majority of senior officers in the middle of the eighteenth century, whatever their professional qualifications, were neither gentlemen nor men of education. Tough old admirals only made things worse for themselves with pathetic submissions about it to a First Lord who hated excuses. Thomas Pye's large round schoolboy hand, borne across the ocean from a flagship on a far-off station, provoked a grimace of contempt, not a smile of pity, from Anson:

'Give me Leave my Lord to make one Observation more and I have Don—and that is When you peruse Admiral Pyes Letters you will Please not to Scrutinize too Close either to the speling or the Grammatical Part as I allow my Self to be no proficient in either. I had the Mortification to be neglected in my education, went to sea at 14 without any and a Man of War was my University.'

One would expect the First Lord to know that much about an admiral, but at that period he did not. Michael Lewis (*A Social History of the Navy*) estimates that thirty-nine out of forty eighteenth-century officers joined without anyone at the Admiralty 'passing them in'; and the great majority served and died, or retired, without any sight of or communication with Their Lordships.

Academic learning was hardly the Board's strong point in the dying years of the Pelham ministries. Members at one operational conference heard with astonishment that Cape Breton was an island, and at another half of them argued that Annapolis was a town in Greece.

' At twelve Mr Byng was shot ', as everyone knows: naval martyr, hero of many a book and play, of whom it might be said that nothing in life became him like the leaving of it. Horace Walpole had an exclusive anecdote:

' A few days before [the execution], one of his friends, standing by him, said, " Which one of us is the tallest ? "— He replied, " Why this ceremony ? I know what you mean. Let the man come and measure me for my coffin. . . . Do cowards live or die thus ? Would my Lord Hardwicke die thus, even supposing he had nothing on his conscience ? " ' (Hardwicke had signed the death-warrant.)

The long-drawn-out tragedy of the Admiral was rounded off with a retributive coda for the Admiralty. Byng was sentenced to death under Anson's fatal ' negligence ' article, which permitted no milder sentence, for merely obeying orders. The Admiralty faced their duty of confirming the sentence like a group of Pontius Pilates and passed the question to a panel of twelve judges of the civil courts. The affair was clouded by Anson's reckless boast that Byng's squadron ' could beat anything the French had '; hence the Admiral's arrest, the editing of his despatches for publication, his weary trial and—since either Byng, or the Admiralty or the Government must have been wrong—his sacrifice. Augustus Hervey, incidentally, was among the few sea officers who risked their necks by campaigning for his acquittal.

Byng has all of posterity's sympathy, and the Admiralty none, but it should be remembered that he had asked for the command of the Minorca force and had used his family's influence to get it; that Anson knew he was over-cautious and not the right man, and had appointed him under protest. " I don't know how it comes to pass," Anson had said, " that unless our commanders-in-chief have a very great superiority of the enemy, they never think themselves safe."

A wave of popular disgust swamped Anson and the Board and carried William Pitt into office on its crest. Pitt's ambitions had received a setback a year earlier, when he attacked the Court and the Government from a position of insufficient strength and was dismissed with all his supporters except the wily Dodington, who had managed to keep a foot in both camps and been rewarded with the Navy Treasurership. In 1756, with the country on the brink of war with France, the wind blew from the opposite quarter. Pitt stormed back into the ministry and made Richard Grenville, Lord Temple, his First Lord and George Grenville his Navy Treasurer—both men his brothers-in-law.

Another shift of the political breeze within the year, and all three went out. King George, unable to find anyone to form a government, decided to form one himself. After some haggling, Anson accepted the Admiralty again, with limited powers. Pitt, with no great following left, but the goodwill of the nation with him because he had never been implicated in a public scandal, was invited to ' write the instructions to the Admirals ' over the signature of three members of the Board.

Pitt had already been Paymaster-General of the Forces; then a Principal Secretary of State (there were two in the ministry) with special responsibility for Army, Navy and Foreign Affairs; and throughout his career was a student of naval matters. As Prime Minister he made the Fleet his especial concern and cherished it nobly. Sea power excited him as it was to excite Winston Churchill, whose ministerial life so closely paralleled his own. When Anson and Hawke first crushed the French in 1747 and 1748 he had urged the Government to destroy France's Navy so completely that it would never rise again—a demand the wise old Duke of Bedford had resisted on the grounds that such a course was ' against nature ' and would have ' excited all the naval powers of Europe against us '.

When carried away by a resounding naval triumph, the British tended to forget they were a small country with a population of eight millions—not much more than a third that of France, smaller than Spain, scarcely bigger than Holland.

Naval heads rolled all down the line in the year of resignations, 1756. On the illuminated scroll which hangs in the Controller's office at the Admiralty there appears against the name of Comptroller Digby Dent, in place of the customary 'Died' or 'Superannuated', the unique notation: 'Removed to a lower seat'. Board Room chairs were filled with Messrs Carker the junior, or remained empty. Anson passed a year in the wilderness, and spent most of it side-stepping moves to impeach him.

William Pitt restored the man who, though a cantankerous old martinet, personified the spirit of naval reform and had the confidence of most of the Fleet, to all his lost power and prestige. Lord Anson as First Lord took Britain's fighting ships to sea for the last time, to open a second front on the Breton coast at the King of Prussia's request. The old bogey of French invasion still disturbed a confused and hesitant Government and for once naval preparations were allowed to go ahead unhampered by non-professional interference.

A brand-new Admiralty and Navy Board infused a brand-new determination into the Fleet. Gone for ever were the worst features of an administration of which, only ten years earlier, it had been said that in corrupt Whitehall there was no department so corrupt as the Admiralty; 'when depravity spread from the top into the remotest corners of the dockyards, embezzlement was rife and peculation rampant; when the First Lord (Sandwich) divided his time between the gaming table and the political arena and supplied his own or his party's needs out of Navy funds; when every minor clerk was supposed to

F

be open to bribery and intent on making his own little fortune out of the Navy'.

Anson visualised a Navy much bigger than anything previous Admiralty Boards had dreamed of. He introduced the celebrated 'seventy-fours' and 'sixty-fours', warships of 1500 and 1200 tons, mounting guns to those numbers; then, from designs by Sir Thomas Slade, the 730-ton 'thirty-sixes', a new type of vessel built for a specific job, which he called frigates. (But captains who captured foreign men-of-war still marvelled at their neatness and seaworthiness. 'Spanish men-of-war we have taken are much superior to ours,' Rodney told his wife. British pre-eminence was beginning to show in strategy, seamanship and discipline. Individual ships could not keep up with solitary foreigners, but British squadrons, manœuvring in formation, invariably out-sailed the enemy.)

Experimental refinements, for which the First Lord had a soft spot—copper sheathing (highly successful on tropical stations), chain pumps and lightning conductors—threw dockyards into a turmoil and had shipwrights of the older school shaking uncomprehending heads.

While the cost of living remained fairly stable, warship costs had increased alarmingly in a hundred years: from five pounds ten a ton to nearly twenty pounds a ton. Timber was the Navy Board's constant headache, as it had been in Pepys's day. It took two thousand Sussex oaks to build a seventy-four and during the Seven Years War (1756 to 1763) great naked patches of countryside appeared where the forests had been.

The Navy Board, with a sailor-like readiness to tackle any job, involved itself in all the complications of the import-export business. It resolutely set its face against American timber, with which many merchant ships were being built. It looked instead to the Baltic States, as Pepys had advised—a decision which made that sea 'the Achilles heel of British strategy', although in the short term the revolt of the American colonies seemed to justify it. The envoy Blankett whom the Board sent touring in northern Europe confirmed its beliefs when he reported: 'We must owe our naval existence to Russia for . . . articles with which no other country can furnish us.'

(In 1763 Lieutenant John Blankett came to Their Lordships' notice. He was shooting at seagulls on the deck of his ship when the purser began ridiculing his marksmanship. Blankett promptly put him at thirty paces and fatally wounded him. His captain wrote to the Admiralty to beg for clemency. 'Own receipt and let him know,' says the Secretary's note on the minute, 'that His Majesty has been graciously pleased to extend His Royal Mercy.')

While Anson built the ships, Pitt provided the men. A high wastage rate, partly through desertion but mainly through disease, had long been the Navy's manning difficulty. In the Seven Years War, it was calculated, fifteen hundred sailors were killed in action and more than a hundred and thirty-three thousand lost from other causes. Naval wartime strength, up to thirty-six thousand in the Jenkins's Ear War, had doubled by the 'year of victories', 1759. (It would double again before 1815, then drop rapidly to a very low figure.) The peacetime establishment, which had touched its all-time low point at seven thousand, stood in 1763 at sixteen thousand.

Pitt is usually credited with 'scouring the gaols' to build up numbers, or rounding up vagrants or offering accused men the alternative of a sentence or a berth in a warship's forecastle. The Quota Acts, under which for the first time inland towns as well as seaports had to supply men for the Navy (London, five thousand a year, Yorkshire, a thousand), tempted local authorities to get rid of their bad characters, one imagines. But a great number of little boys from orphan homes and institutions were sent forward, and not all of them were hardened criminals.

Surprising as it seems to a twentieth-century student looking back, the Navy had a healthy intake of volunteers too. Up-to-date advertising agents would see nothing much amiss with the propaganda methods of Anson's Navy—the posters and manifestoes with which short-handed captains tempted landsmen to sign on: 'Doubloons!'—'Spanish Dollar Bag!!'—'Only strong lads who can carry a hundredweight of treasure three miles need apply!!!'

Admiralty recruiting drives took the form of parades through city streets with hauls of gold captured at sea, and brought excellent results. Generous bounty payments attracted old hands back, as well as nostalgia for a life which, with all its miseries, compared not unfavourably with some kinds of existence ashore. And the press-gang, a highly organised and dedicated body of men working a payment-by-results system, could generally be relied on to give a parting ship at least a skeleton complement. Poor Scots and Irishmen began trickling in, too; American colonists' sons joined up, having lived too far away to know what they were letting themselves in for; and most British warships carried a handful of mixed foreigners, picked up with prizes or shanghaied.

Promises of booty were not always as extravagant as they looked. Many people in the maritime counties would know, or know of, a captain who had made enough to retire on out of one single cruise. Commanders-in-chief had been known to come home after three years with a share of the prize-money earned on their station amounting to a hundred thousand pounds and more. The lucky recipients blessed the memory of Queen Anne, and of the administration which had won the prize-money for the Navy and written its entitlement into the Cruizers and Convoys Act.

The middle decades of the eighteenth century were good

years also for lawyers. Litigation in the Admiralty Court dragged on for years, especially when war scares and war operations brought out Orders in Council so fast that it bewildered the keenest legal brains to determine whether or not a certain stretch of coastline, at the time of the taking of a prize, was officially under blockade or not.

Convoy and blockade figured large on Admiralty agendas. Convoy and blockade were words every citizen was familiar with, jobs which occupied British warships throughout whole commissions. Pitt and Anson sent the Navy to patrol off the terminal ports of all the trading nations in Europe, the Americas and the Far East; the naval battle line had never been half so far-flung. The all-powerful East India Company demanded special facilities as of right, and a squadron despatched on its behalf to match the French task force in the Indian Ocean was the *raison d'être* of the East Indies station, one more interstice in the Admiralty net which was gradually spreading over the globe.

'John Company's Navy': not a few naval officers had shares or relatives in it—not a few members of Parliament and Whitehall bureaucrats breathed a heartfelt *bon voyage* to the East Indiamen. Royal Navy captains on the look-out for money or a crew did not always differentiate between enemy, allied and British merchantmen; although the Admiralty imposed a fine of up to £500 for making a mistake, it was sometimes worth it. But no sea officer in his senses tangled with John Company.

Operationally the Admiralty ran like clockwork. Hawke's despatches (we are still in the Seven Years War) show with what amazing accuracy British naval intelligence functioned, how tight it enabled commanders at sea to keep the blockade.

The hero of Quiberon Bay had his reservations when it came to the Navy Board. That branch of the administration, niggardly and faltering in its distribution of stores, immersed in the bureaucratic fiddle-faddle of its office, true to its tradition of being efficient in nothing but making excuses, lagged far behind the superior body. Captain Cockburne struggled hard, but short-term improvements were beyond the capacity of one man. Nothing, it seemed, could reform the victualling system, short of sweeping it all away and starting afresh; not a task to be undertaken in wartime.

Pursers had to buy their warrants, as of old—for about seventy pounds—and would hardly have been human if they had not tried to make the investment pay a dividend. A clumsy Navy Board expedient, which survived well into the nineteenth century, required them to keep two ' Widow's Men ' on their books for every hundred of the ship's company—the pay and allowances to go to a Widows' Fund, in theory, but an arrangement which encouraged fraud and, indeed, turned it into an accepted principle of victualling.

According to stories which helped to relieve the tedium of life in the Fleet blockading Brest, sailors were making buttons out of the cheese the Victualler supplied; and a ship's carpenter capped a damaged mast with a round cheese from the provision store, the most durable material he could find on board. Admiral Hawke whiled away monotonous months composing complaints against the dockyard storemen and working off a particular grudge against Devonport:

' I have not yet received the supplies of butter and cheese, beef, pork etc. . . .' ' I cannot help regretting the want of a commanding officer at Plymouth to see all orders executed. . . .' ' Our daily employment is condemning the beer from Plymouth. . . .' ' Give me leave therefore to repeat my entreaties for beer being sent out with the utmost despatch from the eastward.'

Within a few months his sailors were at work on their own

vegetable allotments in the French islets off Quiberon Bay. All was forgotten and forgiven, every man in the Fleet a hero, Anson and his Admiralty loaded with congratulations, the Navy Board the darlings of the nation. It was *annus mirabilis*, the year 1759, when all the bell-ropes in Britain ' wore threadbare with ringing for victories '.

13   Montagu the Unready

Speaking of 'verdicts reversed in posterity's court of appeal', Sir Geoffrey Callender and F. H. Hinsley (*The Naval Side of British History*) note how few of our greatest seamen escaped the censure of their contemporaries:

'Drake was ostracised in the year after he destroyed the Armada; Rooke a few months after he had taken Gibraltar; Raleigh was beheaded for advocating the claims of sea power, and Byng was shot to expiate the national unpreparedness for war. Torrington was dismissed the Service after his own plans had been ruined by a council of statesmen ashore; and Vernon because he insisted on bringing to light the grievances of the lower deck. Hawke was burned in effigy at the moment when he was winning the great victory of Quiberon; and Rodney was recalled home in ignominy in the hour of his greatest triumph.'

First Lords of the Admiralty, in the days when First Lords were usually sailors, were not quite so vulnerable. Unlike commanders at sea, they could always shift the blame. Yet, after Lord Anson's death, when no one could be found among the statesmen to take on the job and it was given to the admiral of the moment, he lost it again quickly; more from domestic manoeuvrings inside the ruling party than from the wrath of the mob.

Anson died in 1762. 'Very assiduous at the Admiralty,' said a not especially flowery obituary, '. . . entitled to the utmost veneration and respect.' Four gallant officers, the very cream of the fighting Navy, spread their talents over the next decade, and spread them somewhat thinly: Hawke, Howe, Saunders and Keppel. (Lord Howe received the Treasurership of the Navy when he left the Admiralty in 1765: an office of some grandeur in the eighteenth century, which we must deal with separately in another chapter.)

Pitt and Anson had had no love for each other, but both had united in a hatred of Sir Edward Hawke and deprived him of the rewards he might have expected as the nation's hardest-worked and most successful flag officer. By the time Sir Edward took the government of the Navy he was an ancient mariner, hardly fit to put back into the Service all the fire and spirit which it had lost since the wars ended.

He barely withstood a storm of abuse in 1770, when the nation burned to avenge a Spanish insult and the Fleet had to confess it was unable to oblige. The post-war rundown of ships and men had gathered a momentum Hawke found it hard to stop. The Navy Board, jerked into action by Cockburne and Keppel, had just set in motion a long-term plan for renovating the dockyards and neither Chatham, Portsmouth nor Devonport were in a suitable state for fitting out squadrons or receiving ships for repair. Upon the outbreak of hostilities, Captain Cockburne, the Navy Board's inspiration and one willing horse for twenty years, chose to die of age and worry.

To increase Their Lordships' troubles, a mysterious crop of fires burst out in the different dockyards and naval establishments. They recurred for several years, and culminated in the Great Fire of Portsmouth of December 1776.

James Hill, also called Johnny Hind and John Aitken, but known to crime-readers as Jack the Painter, was a Scot who had been to America and back and journeyed round the southern English dockyards, working or looking for work. He spent a lot of time compiling lists of ships, sketching installations and

marking the defences on maps of the coast; periodically, it was
believed, he took his information across the Channel to an
American acquaintance in Paris.

No one regarded Jack's hobby as anything but a harmless
eccentricity, it seemed, until one dark winter evening the dockyard at Portsmouth went on fire. Townsfolk gathered on the
hills behind the town to watch a blaze which flared up in the
round-house, caught the sail-loft, rope-walk and canvas store
and spread to the rest of the buildings. Hundreds of tons of
'chips' were said to have blazed to ashes, but one supposes the
Victualling Superintendent's cheeses survived intact. It was the
worst, but not the first, dockyard fire for many years.

Salvage workers shifting charred timbers more than a month
later (prompt action, by dockyard standards) came across a
'tin machine' made out of a candle-lamp stuffed with loose
hemp. 'Such,' said the Dockyard Commissioner's report,
'was the poor contrivance with which this man hoped to ruin
England.'

Jack the Painter had left behind him a trail of evidence which
even naval security experts of George III's reign could not miss.
Damp matches had prevented him from starting more fires,
and he wasted some of the time he needed to get away from
Portsmouth in going round to the shop of the woman who
sold them to him and smashing her windows. Articles found
in his lodgings—a gun, a French passport and a treatise on
fireworks—gave the authorities the idea that he might be able
to help them with their enquiries.

Having literally blazed his trail to Bristol (where he touched
off his biggest fire among the molasses barrels on the quayside)
and then to Devonport, Jack was arrested at the dockyard gates,
found guilty of treason and arson and hanged in Portsmouth
at the scene of the crime. (His skeleton, hung in chains, used
to be one of the sights of Fort Blockhouse, nowadays the head-

quarters of the Submarine Service.) In a farewell address to the mob, Jack acknowledged his guilt and treated the Navy Commissioners to a long homily, warning them to be more careful in future of the valuable lives and stores in their care.

Admiral Hawke tried to tell the Navy Board the same thing weekly, without much effect. He filled a difficult position, as post-war naval chiefs have always done: when the fever is over, the nation impatient to enjoy the fruits of victory, all the pieces to be picked up and the sailor an expensive nuisance again. Among Britain's greatest seamen and the Navy's most disappointing administrators, Hawke succumbed, tormented by illness and his political opponents' long knives.

King George III, having dismissed his Whig ministry once more, was trying to rule without one. For a time it looked certain that he would revive the office of Lord High Admiral and become the first monarch in sixty years to take an active interest in the Navy. Then he called back Sandwich, least objectionable of a list in which there was not much to choose from.

There are three portraits of Lord Sandwich in his last term of office—three guises in which he ruled the Navy without an Anson to lead him. One on top of the other, they compose a strange picture of mingled virtue and vice.

There is the drunkard and libertine who uses the Navy exchequer for his personal bank account; who undermines all the progress he has initiated by putting worthless ruffians into the jobs he has created.

There is his lackadaisical Lordship, dabbling with coloured paints to work out artistic schemes for the ships—red and blue upperworks, yellow and green sides, a red interior of course to save repainting after a battle; the dilettante chief, who thumbs through the pages of Lemprière's *Classical Dictionary* and Whitcomb's *Lives and Histories of the Heathen Gods*, picking out attractive names for the new frigates, while the frigates decay from material neglect.

And finally, and all too rarely, there are flashes of the first Montagu, Sir Edward, in his third-generation descendant, a statesman and visionary who dreams up the voyages of Captain Cook; infallibly spots the coming admiralissimos Rodney and Hood and forces them into promotion jobs; picks out a youngster too, named Charles Middleton, who will be the Navy's strong administrative personality in twenty years' time; who ruthlessly sacks an unsatisfactory Comptroller—Sir Maurice Suckling, Nelson's uncle and patron, a bold sea captain but in no other respect worth a mention; and who can put his favourites firmly in their place when they get above it, as he did Rodney: ' There is no set of men that understand these matters (Admiralty matters) so ill as sea officers; for it scarcely ever happens that, after an action, they do not call in the whole world to hear what complaints they have to make of each other, and the decision of the world is that all sides are in some degree to blame.'

Lord Sandwich made belated efforts to bring the dockyards under control. From 1773 onwards he required a weekly progress report from them—and the reports gave Parliament a convincing picture of how the money was spent. Unfortunately for the First Lord, the ships themselves lay rotting, weed-encrusted and rat-infested for all to see, and members of Parliament asked how, when no one went near them for months at a time, they managed to swallow such vast sums. Edmund Burke seized the beautifully bound volume of Navy Estimates for 1778, with its neat lists of expenditure for the previous year, called it an act of contempt against the House and flung it across the Speaker's table, knocking over a candlestick and barking the shins of the Navy Treasurer, Mr Welbore Ellis.

Smarting under the loss of the American colonies, patriotic Britons felt little disposed to make allowances for the Navy's failings. The conduct of the War of Independence on the naval side was mismanaged at home and half-heartedly undertaken on the spot. Comptroller Suckling, apathetic chief of the Navy Board, came under sharp fire; but the main responsibility rested on Lord Sandwich's shoulders, and as his last decade in office drew to a close he degenerated into a tired, sick old man no longer in touch with the realities of the naval situation.

Sea officers who knew Sandwich through gossip and the weaknesses of his Board saw only his dark side. The admirals fought him and his clique of acquiescent henchmen with every instrument they could lay hands on. A kind of anarchy ran through the Fleet. Some of the most distinguished officers refused to accept appointments, some resigned in disgust.

Students of naval affairs warned that worse than a revolt in the American colonies was to come—and Sandwich was ever ready to listen to advice, though not always inclined to take it. They had seen a comprehensive building programme getting under way in France, which made Britain's efforts look patchy and juvenile. They described Choiseul's methods of training officers and men on sea and land, and contrasted them with Whitehall's hit-or-miss system which had persisted unchanged for so long. Young commanders like Kempenfelt showed how future wars might be won and lost with signal flags and manœuvring diagrams—and told Their Lordships how much more articulate the French admiral had become at sea compared with his British opposite number, since the year of victories.

French ships, everyone who had taken the trouble to examine one agreed, were faster, better designed; their fleets better drilled, in new and dangerous tactics. What, the critics asked, was Lord Sandwich's contribution to naval ship-building and design in three terms of office spanning nearly thirty years ? —the copper bottom, which he owed to Anson, and without which half the new ships still went to sea because the Admiralty grudged the extra outlay or the dockyards could not do the work. Spoiling 'seventy-fours' for a ha'porth of tar was more than a proverb round the basins of Chatham and the slipways of Devonport.

Everyone looked to the battle England fought with France off Ushant in 1778 to see the way the balance was tilting; everyone was disappointed, because it turned out the conventional indecisive encounter. What it did reveal was the perilous fallibility of the strategic command in the western approaches, and the rottenness of relations between admirals.

After that action the Commander-in-Chief, Keppel, alleged that his rear-admiral, Sir Hugh Palliser, had disregarded signals. When an admiral accuses a rear-admiral there is normally not much doubt about the outcome, but in this case the junior had influence with the Government, besides being a Lord of the Admiralty. (He was also the Lieutenant-General of Marines, and some said this was at the root of the quarrel, because Keppel objected to his subordinate holding such a sinecure.)

Rear-Admiral Palliser, anonymously attacked in the Press, decided that 'Anon' was his late chief and brought Admiral Keppel to a court martial. The proceedings lasted five weeks, during which both flag officers featured in the latest hits of the London ballad-singers, all the nation took sides and the Admiralty was split into two hostile camps. One of the great unedifying scenes of British naval history is that of the acquitted Keppel shoulder-high in Portsmouth dockyard surrounded by jubilant supporters while, up in London, the mob smashes Palliser's windows, tries to set his house on fire, storms the parapet in front of the Admiralty building and wrenches the great gates off their hinges.

'This fatal strife,' wrote Rodney, 'which has almost ruined the Navy . . .'—but it was only beginning. Amid a general post of serving senior officers, Lord Howe and Admiral Barrington struck their flags along with Keppel and Palliser. Junior officers marched about London and the dockyard ports in open rebellion, abusing the name of Sandwich or, rather, his nickname, which was Jemmy Twitcher, after the character in *The Beggar's Opera* who sells his friend. The antagonism between the Fleet and the Admiralty made previous rows look like mere coolnesses between old friends.

When the command of the Channel Fleet fell vacant the next year, Sandwich could find only one officer of the right seniority to accept it—old Sir Charles Hardy, whom he had moved out of the governorship of Greenwich Hospital to make room for Palliser and who had not been to sea for twenty years. " My God," said Kempenfelt to Middleton, " what have you great people done by such an appointment ? "—a question which it was hardly fair to ask of the future Lord Barham who had quietly taken up his new appointment in the middle of all the bother.

' I wish the Admiralty could see what was done in former times,' Lord Hawke wrote to Admiral Geary from his little country seat in Middlesex, where he lay dying. ' It would make them act with more propriety, both for the good of officers and men.' He, at least, had cause for gratitude to the First Lord: he had received, only just in time, the peerage he had earned a generation before.

The First Lord told his successor that he feared he was handing over a Service in a rather worse condition than the Service which had been handed over to him; but pointed out that the Navy had been ' exceedingly neglected ' for ten years, between Anson's death and his own return in 1771. Another eleven years had gone by since then, but Sandwich would have liked a few more. It would have given him time to get things moving, he felt.

Not the hatred of the admirals, the decline in naval strength and morale, nor the Fleet's utter lack of confidence in its Admiralty had persuaded him and his Board to resign. The Government fell—Lord North's administration—and they went out with it.

News reached Lord Howe that he had been appointed First Lord while he himself was bringing home good news for Great Britain: he had relieved Gibraltar. Five months later, in April 1783, he stood down in favour of Keppel but kept a seat on the Board; the two, and Admiral Barrington, formed a brisk triumvirate, but the Fleet would have liked to see Rodney beside them. Hero of Martinique and the Saintes, sea-daddy of a little royal midshipman (Prince William Henry, the future Duke of Clarence, the first truly seagoing Hanover), Rodney was on bad terms with the ruling admirals. He possessed ' a bold original genius ', a reputation for ' elegant and polished behaviour ' and a seat in Parliament—for Northampton—which he spent the family fortune winning and holding. But when at last he joined the Board of Admiralty it was as a junior member among powerful personalities, and he joined it too late to make his mark.

A long spell of peace was just round the corner when Keppel's Admiralty came to office, but for the moment there seemed no end to wars and naval degradation. The exhausted Fleet failed to respond to calls for one more effort; the size of the Navy debt puzzled everyone. John Paul Jones had made laughing stocks of some of the most promising officers in the Service, reports of the French naval renaissance—across the Channel, one Ministry of Marine at least had ample funds to play with—spread despondency in Whitehall. Three months after the new Lords Commissioners' first meeting, an accident at Spithead shattered the composure of the most phlegmatic of members.

H.M.S. *Royal George*, a thirty-year-old line-of-battle ship, rolled over and sank in shallow water, at her moorings, with heavy loss of life. Down with her, never to reappear, sank ' brave Kempenfelt' who, though not such a favourite with the current Board as he had been with the last, had given the Navy its first table of signals, *A Primer of Speech for Fighting Ships*, and seemed marked out for the highest honours.

Keppel, Howe and company never disclosed their findings on the disaster. They refused to lay themselves open to charges which Navy Commissioners and Admiralty Lords of the past should have answered: charges of keeping ships at sea which had not had proper dockyard attention. They disclosed nothing, but, within the Service, they acted. Something had to be done about the Navy Board: admirals had been saying so since Hawkins was a cabin boy.

Something was done. This is the point at which, down at the Navy Office, Charles Middleton thrusts aside the actors who have forgotten or never learned their lines and takes the centre of the stage.

14   The Admiralty against Napoleon

Captain (afterwards Admiral Sir) Charles Middleton, later Lord Barham, went to Seething Lane as Comptroller of the Navy four years before the *Royal George* rolled over. Ship repairs were part of his responsibilities, and it was hardly to be expected that after such a catastrophe he would stay in his job. But he shrugged off abuse, scarcely troubling to point out that the ills of forty years could not be redressed in four. He welcomed a scandal at the Navy Office. It was just the opening he had been looking for, to set up his plan for cleaning out the dockyards. After that he would make a start on the victualling stores, the shore works generally and the Navy Office itself; perhaps, if all went well, the Admiralty too. It was remarkable how much work a Navy Commissioner could get through when he made it a full-time job. Fellow Principal Officers, just as they had done in Pepys's time, came to the Navy Office as to a weekly committee, as they might come to the weekly causerie of the Greenwich Hospital. Just as Pepys had done, Charles Middleton spent his working hours there, and took some work home. It had amused the Comptroller's department, when their new chief arrived under the delusion that he was expected to put in five days a week; before long he, and the department, were working seven.

He came into office when the Prime Minister of the day was giving it as his opinion that a navy was a luxury the nation could ill afford. Middleton met his successor, William Pitt the younger—whom he impressed—who took a different view.

Pitt made new funds available and jointly with the Comptroller saw them applied to proper uses. ' It was no uncommon thing,' wrote Admiral Sir Byam Martin, ' for Mr Pitt to visit the Navy Office to discuss matters with the Comptroller, and to see the returns made from the yards of the progress in building and repairing the ships of the line.'

With Middleton in charge and a prime-ministerial whirlwind at his service, the ' action ' side of the administration shifted back to the Navy Office. To the serving Lords Commissioners a long peace meant hasty demobilisation, a laying-up and locking-up, then relaxation and stagnation until the next emergency. Middleton saw it as the right time to declare war on the dockyards. He toured them, revising the rule-book as he went, to stamp out the unnecessary overtime habits of a century and increase their pitifully low productivity. Though he never got the riggers and shipwrights to agree with his own ideas about a day's work for a day's pay, he did manage to persuade them to work longer hours. He was fighting practices which had wormed into the industrial side of naval life in the reigns of Queen Elizabeth and James I.

The shore establishments had subsided into the comfortable stupor of the days before Lord Anson walked round. Victualling stores in confusion, sail lofts overstocked here and empty there, huge decaying quantities of non-essential stores cluttering up the jetties while frigate captains clamoured in vain for seagoing necessities, Hogarthian figures stretched in the walks and warehouses, drunk or asleep—the scenery was so familiar it had lost its power to shock. But the Comptroller was shocked, especially at the sight of the timber ponds, all empty or nearly empty.

As urgently as though—his subordinates indignantly said— there was a war on, he devised new systems for stockkeeping and a simplified method for issuing stores. (Clerks opposed it, on the grounds that the existing paperwork attached to the demand for and despatch and receipt of a marline-spike had a certain nuisance value, in that it kept ships' officers from asking too often.) He planned and built modern food stores and magazines.

Costs ran high and the results were not at first spectacular. It had ever been the Navy Commissioners' lament that they could never show much for the money they consumed. The first pat on the back Middleton received was on account of orders he managed to place, mostly in Riga and New Brunswick, which saw timber secured for the wooden walls of Britain for years to come.

Up in Whitehall the Admiralty had its own problems, apart from the sight of Mr Pitt passing by on his way to Seething Lane. From 1783 to 1788 Lord Howe belonged to a ministry pledged to economise in every department and at the same time prepare for war; indeed, if an Admiralty secretary who knew him is to be believed (Sir John Barrow), he at last resigned because he could not agree with Pitt how both pledges were to be met at the same time.

Middleton had the theory that both aims could be reconciled. A certain re-drafting and pruning of duties and personnel in the administration might do it. At the moment of greatest inconvenience—the Navy Board migration from Seething Lane to Somerset House—when his colleagues and their departments were still disarrayed by the upheaval, he revised the Principal Officers' responsibilities and bound them to regulations he framed himself. The concentration of power in the Comptroller's hands was not the end of his ambitions. He supported the view the senior body had rejected with horror, that the Navy Office should be in Whitehall, not the Strand. He envisaged a three-tier system of naval government—Admiralty, Navy Board and Victualling Board—working harmoniously in one unit. Over the years they had been growing apart physically, the two juniors trying to keep out of the senior's way; yet more and more their jobs had overlapped. Middleton, the first efficiency expert to take a look at the Navy, argued for centralisation, smaller staffs and better results for less money.

He took the chance of airing his views in the principal forum of the nation when Parliament in 1785 appointed a commission to 'consider the Fees, etc., of certain Public Offices'—of which the Navy Office was one. Middleton carried the request away and drew up his own report, which went some way beyond his terms of reference. He set down a proposal for the Government to 'keep up a line of communication between the Admiralty, the Navy and Victualling Boards' and suggested for a start that a member of the Victualling Board should join the Navy Board and a member of the Navy Board be elevated to the Admiralty. The Comptroller, naturally, would be the Navy Board's representative on the Board of Admiralty.

Lord Howe, having had for some time and with some excuse the idea that Middleton would not rest until he had him out of the First Lord's chair, killed the idea. But the Parliamentary Commission, grateful to the man who had done the donkey-work of the report for them, rewarded him by recommending that the Comptroller should govern 'the whole business' of the Navy Office. This was enough to make Middleton the tyrant of Somerset House in name and deed and to break up what he once referred to as 'the parade of nine Commissioners sitting at one table to obstruct business'. He decided to split the Board into three Committees, one for Stores, one for Accounts and one for Correspondence. Each committee was to have three members, and himself for its chairman.

The Navy Comptroller's faults were those of great admirals and statesmen: a determination to have their own way about everything, a contempt for anyone who, while not necessarily opposing, is slow to agree with them. A three-way split in the Navy Board, he felt, was neat, simple and should have been instantly acceptable. The First Lord, however, was not too keen on this either; and Parliament sat on it for so long that Middleton threw up his job in disgust. The Navy might have lost him for ever, but the signs were pointing to another war with France, the usual pre-hostilities spate of intrigues and recriminations upset the Government and in the turmoil of public affairs, as Britain entered the last decade of the eighteenth century, Pitt the younger remembered his favourite naval officer and made Middleton a personal private adviser on Admiralty affairs—a kind of shadow First Lord.

Prime Minister Pitt, his brother Lord Chatham (First Lord of the Admiralty) and Secretary of War Dundas (a future First Lord) handled the grand strategy when war began in 1793 against what Burke called 'an armed principle'—revolutionary France.

All the great admirals went to sea, to make the last series of reputations in a century of great admirals—Sir Sidney Smith, Lord Hood and above all Lord Howe, whose victory on the Glorious First of June overshadowed all the events of 1794. Awards and testimonials poured in on the ex-First Lord after that action; among the gifts was a diamond-hilted sword worth three thousand guineas. But the measure of a nation's gratitude was the announcement that the King and Queen, incredibly, had decided to visit Lord Howe on board his flagship: an unprecedented experience for the Fleet.

All at once the British public seemed to adopt a new attitude to its Navy. Hundreds of pounds were collected after the First of June in appeals for the relief of widows and wounded men; not long before, broken sailors had been a nuisance.

Throughout the nineties, the Royal Navy was news, and ever more exciting news. And once again it was 'Royal': a prince served at sea, almost the first since Stuart times; and old King George himself, once having taken the plunge, grew not averse to an occasional inshore cruise along the south coast of England.

In those years the Navy recovered from the Army the patriotic affection of the people and the gallant tar made a more romantic object for it. Sea-minded statesmen and writers brought home to every landsman, however far inland he might live, the influence of sea power on British prosperity. The country discovered with astonishment and relief that, thanks to the reforms and modernisations of men like Middleton and thanks to the hardships British sailors were inured to and the experience they had gained through a generations-old practice of keeping the seas while lesser breeds of mariner ran for shelter, the Fleet could take on the combined naval might of Europe and defeat it every time.

For half a century, in ships and men, replacements had kept pace with removals, not with increased commitments or increased expenditure. The impressive manning and new construction crusade, which Middleton and Their Lordships led in the years before the war, gave the Navy, on its outbreak, nearly three hundred seagoing ships, and forty-five thousand officers and men. Steel's List for the Napoleonic War years is a formidable work, but it is worth dipping into, to see how the naval promotion ladder for officers is being fashioned into its modern shape.

There is one Admiral of the Fleet (John Forbes to 1796, Earl Howe to 1799, Sir Peter Parker from 1799 to 1811). By right his is the supreme command of the British Fleet—but Forbes, at the time of the Glorious First of June is eighty and cannot 'turn himself in bed without assistance, being lame in both hands and feet', and in Trafalgar year, Parker is eighty-nine. For practical purposes, because Admirals of the Fleet are near their death-beds when they reach the rank, it confers a merely ceremonial dignity. The Regent angers the Navy when he puts his brother Clarence on that solitary pinnacle in 1811: no living admiral can hope to survive a man of forty-six, and the rule says there must be only one Admiral of the Fleet. But, having broken the tradition, George IV breaks the rule and promotes his 'Old Oak', Lord Saint Vincent, to the same rank. Since that unsatisfactory occasion in the seventeen-thirties (when the might of the Royal Navy was entrusted to the trembling hands of eighty-four-year-old Sir John Norris), the titular supreme commander—very often an ex-First Lord or ex-Lord Commissioner—has not been allowed to take charge in person. But he wields a wide patronage, and his pay makes the job well worth waiting for. If the scale of 1800 were applied today, Admirals of the Fleet would be getting about £60,000 a year.

There are sixty-four admirals on the old sea officers' list, ranging from Admiral of the Red to Rear-Admiral of the Blue—nine ranks. There are four hundred-odd post-captains and a hundred and sixty masters-and-commanders (a new rank) and nearly fifteen hundred lieutenants.

After them, not listed as commissioned officers, come the midshipmen, aged anything from thirteen to sixty; then the warrant officers—masters, masters' mates, pursers, gunners, boatswains, carpenters and masters-at-arms.

Hundreds of midshipmen and sometimes an outstanding master's mate (as James Cook had been) went up annually to Somerset House to pass for lieutenant's rank before a Board of Navy Commissioners which would often require of them only the answer to some single question such as "If a side of beef weighs half a hundredweight, how much do seventy-five sides weigh?" The reminiscents of that time tell many anecdotes about the ploys they had to adopt to get through. Production of their birth-certificates, to show they were over twenty-one, was the least of their worries: the hall-porter at Somerset House made them out in the corridor outside the interview room, at five shillings a time, and the Commissioners would accept them with no more than an observation that, considering the documents must be at least twenty-one years old, the ink was taking rather a long time to dry.

Interest served the young officer best, as always. Boys of sixteen, with the right recommendation, were passed on to the lieutenants' list, until it grew so congested that in spite of war and casualties many 'passed lieutenants' were awaiting their appointments ten years afterwards. It was the overcrowded state of the Admiralty waiting-room that helped to determine Their Lordships in 1804 to introduce one more new rank: sub-lieutenant; but that was not to be a substantive rank for another fifty-seven years.

Once a lieutenant, the young officer depended entirely on luck and Interest. Saint Vincent, despot of the Navy at the beginning of the nineteenth century, assured the Fleet that promotion in his time would be a matter of strict seniority and nothing else. It was another example of a naval strong man and master-mind underestimating the grip of tradition.

Successive naval administrations had loved to capitalise on the scandalous misdeeds of their predecessors, their idleness and incompetence and subservience to Government ministers and nobility. Critics had never been slow to point out how much better marine matters were ordered abroad. Much had been left undone, by both Whig and Tory Boards of Admiralty, much had been subdued to the practical necessities of politics. Yet somehow it was all coming right in the end. Somehow the general movement throughout the eighteenth century had been towards pre-eminence in sea power and fighting qualities.

Foreign observers—accustomed perhaps, as the Dutch were, to a Navy run by five separate Admiralty Boards, all working independently of each other—actually saw virtues in Britain's dual-controlled administration; and were envying Britain her Rookes and Torringtons, her Ansons, Sandwiches and Howes, while Britain envied them their Choiseuls.

That they had reason to was to be shown in the Napoleonic wars. All-conquering fleets do not arise and organise themselves of their own accord; ships do not spring fully manned and armed from the head of some hurriedly surfacing Neptune. They take centuries to grow—centuries, in Britain's case, of bitter controversy, civil war, place-hunting and string-pulling, of delays, deficiencies and disappointments. Despite them all, the broad general movement had been positive and progressive.

Britain took a lead in gunnery over foreign navies when the Admiralty adopted the carronade, a light-weight quick-firing gun of large calibre and limited range, first produced at the Carron Ironworks in Stirlingshire. It was one of a number of gunnery improvements of the seventeen-eighties—quick-firing mechanisms, block-and-tackle arrangements for moving the guns—which, thanks to the ready appreciation and swift action of a quick-firing Comptroller, gave the Fleet a distinct advantage in firepower, ship for ship, when the war broke out.

'Talk between ships' underwent a transformation scarcely credible to old sailors in the last twenty years of the century. Kempenfelt's primitive *Primer* of flag signals led to Lord Howe's signal book of 1790 and the first official Admiralty signal manual, an elaboration of Howe's code, of 1799. The following year Sir Home Popham ingeniously refined and enlarged its vocabulary, in time for Nelson to take it to Trafalgar with him.

Signal towers bristled from prominent landmarks all round the south coast of England during the wars. Signals to the uninitiated, like guided missiles today, suggested that their users lived in a surrealist technological world unattainable by ordinary mortals. Especially intriguing for landlubbers were the telegraphic structures which began to adorn church towers and hill-tops in 1796 and the swivelling discs and squares on the framework which transmitted enigmatic messages between Whitehall and the fleet anchorages. (The communication lines are described in Chapter One.)

In the previous century, Lords High Admiral and Navy Board Commissioners had given time and careful argument to such hare-brained inventors' schemes as to coat ships with cement to keep the barnacles off; to propel boats under water; to make ships go against the wind and tide and to drain silted harbours by means of certain wonderful engines. Hare-brained inventors, turned away from other government departments, have always found somebody at the Admiralty to listen to them.

The devices Lord Howe, Chatham and Charles Middleton smiled over sounded even more outlandish, but now and again an unlikely idea repaid to posterity the time and money Their Lordships spent on it: Lieutenant-General Shrapnel's explosive shell, for instance. Patented inventions offered to the Admiralty about 1780 included a wood-and-wire robot capable of playing a game of chess (to replace the First Lord, perhaps); a piece of fishing mechanism with which ' one person might operate five hundred hooks '; and an oil dispenser, for stilling the waves round storm-tossed vessels.

At the turn of the century came Fulton's ' plunging boat '— a submarine (1803), his ' carcasses and catamarans '—floating mines (1804), and Congreve's rocket-firing apparatus (1804); to all of which Their Lordships gave their best attention.

So much for officers and *matériel*. To trace the gradual improvement since Anson's day in the position of the lower-deck sailor would take us too far from our subject. But it is worth noting that Kempenfelt about 1781 first suggested to

Middleton (he seemed to prefer writing to Middleton) that ships' companies ought to be divided into as many sections as there were lieutenants on board, with a lieutenant in charge of each section and responsible for its morale, welfare, cleanliness and advancement: precisely the ' divisional system ' on which the domestic side of naval life was organised long afterwards.

British naval superiority throughout the war years must have exceeded the most reckless estimates of the wildest strategical optimist. Professor Lewis calculates that, of frigate size and upwards, Britain lost no more than ten ships by enemy action in the whole campaign—an average of under one a year (ships lost and later recaptured not counted)—while she gained, or sank, three hundred and seventy-seven of the enemy. Casualty figures were almost as startling: British losses 3,616, Enemy 35,347.

For once an outbreak of war had found the British Fleet not only ready but waiting. For once one heard nothing but praise for the former Navy Comptroller, and it was unthinkable that he should be out of a job, or sent to sea, while administrative problems extended Admiralty resources. Pitt brought him back to Whitehall as an extra ' advisory ' Lord Commissioner, with an undefined status which his protégé interpreted to suit himself. It was nothing to Middleton that his fellow admirals on the Board were senior in rank and experience; nor that he sat under a First Lord—Earl Spencer—who, though genial and courteous, expected subordinates to keep their places.

The First Lord was a civilian, leading a team of professional seamen. He considered himself more than ' first among equals ', more than a chairman of the Board. In a memorandum to his colleagues he had written that ' the responsibility (for naval operations) unquestionably rests on the First Lord. . . . Other members of the Board are always understood to concur in his measures.' When he returned from a Cabinet meeting with the news that Admiral Lord Bridport was to be ordered to haul down his flag, the naval members objected. Spencer told them plainly: "If the necessary orders to Lord Bridport are not signed, the existence of the Board of Admiralty will be ended."

This was the man to whom Middleton, without official standing on the Board or in the Government, presumed to address gratuitous advice in long, carefully-reasoned letters about the conduct of the war at sea. *A propos* the scheme for using the Fleet to block the colonial resources of France and Spain, he began: 'I think if you see Dundas it may not be amiss to urge the danger of running after distant objects while the great object lies still . . .'—excellent sense, but thrust on the Navy's political chief in a way that made him long to get rid of the busybody, as Lord Howe had often longed. Then there was Middleton's restless communication with admirals and captains afloat, which put him in possession of news before the First Lord heard it, and created an impression that he and not Spencer was running the Fleet. It drew an objection from another powerful personality of the Napoleonic era, Sir John Jervis, but it was later, while commanding the Channel Fleet, that he begged Earl Spencer to ' put an extinguisher upon the gossiping correspondence carried on between your Neptunes at the Board and the officers of every description in this squadron '. (Saint Vincent was among the very few naval officers who have never seen much use in having sailors on Boards of Admiralty. "They do nothing but confound, impede and distract," he said, after personal experience. "The only use of a seaman there is to survey men for Greenwich Hospital.")

Middleton in his turn raved to his intimates about the First Lord's aristocratic arrogance in expecting everyone to endorse his decisions and no one even to discuss, much less dispute, them; and about his poor understanding of the sailor's psychology (although Lord Spencer himself founded a distinguished naval family).

Some attention was focused on these aspects of His Lordship's character when he announced to a horrified fleet in 1796 that figureheads on ships were to be abolished: this in an age when sailors had a great partiality for decoration in their ships and their clothing and when civilians, too, taking passage by sea, would choose a vessel with a graceful figurehead—just as, later on, they would develop a semi-superstitious admiration for steamships with a certain number of funnels, regardless of other considerations.

The carved wooden figurehead of the man-of-war survived as the last fragment of that rich décor which in times gone by had encircled the ships and culminated in those huge historical tableaux or floral displays round stern and beakhead. In obedience to authority's slow pruning of unnecessary expenditure and (as science made its voice heard) the reduction of topweight, all those bright extravagances had faded away. But the warship figurehead remained, sometimes a lion's head, sometimes a mermaid or a saint, sometimes—particularly in Lord Sandwich's administration—a heavy-bosomed classical heroine.

The Fleet reacted characteristically. Ships rolled off the stocks in the dockyards without figureheads, but surprisingly sprouted them during their first foreign commissions: a tactful head of royalty or, even more tactfully, a hero of Admiralty, such as Earl Spencer. Well into the nineteenth century a figurehead led the wooden walls of Britain into action. The distinctive features of the Iron Duke were a gift to figurehead-carvers. They long survived the First Lord who said they must go: the last British warship to carry a figurehead in full undress was launched in 1901.

Figureheads were but a pinprick compared with the numerous causes of grievance among fighting sailors during Spencer's rule at the Admiralty. Seamen growing accustomed to a better cuisine cavilled at the Victualling Office's meagre imagination; they complained of lack of consideration about shore-going facilities; worst of all, they muttered about disproportionate share-outs of prize-money, which was all most ratings joined for and of which there was plenty about—but not much to find its way into the pay-packets of the common seamen who did all the hard, dirty and dangerous work for it.

Pay-rates for most categories gave perpetual ground for discontent. They had not altered since Admiral Vernon campaigned for an increase, although successive First Lords and Treasurers had promised increases as soon as the books were balanced. From an accountant viewpoint, the delay was not really defensible. It has been suggested by Sir Oswyn Murray that, if the First Lord had had Middleton at his elbow when the sailors' final demand and ultimatum arrived in Whitehall, the Nore and Spithead mutinies might not have occurred. This is doubtful. Middleton would have suggested the right approach and Spencer, out of irritation with him, would have made the wrong.

Sir Charles in any case was out of a job; the First Lord had ordered him either to knuckle under or go, and his ' advisory ' Lord was never the man to knuckle under.

Three weeks after the Portsmouth ships' companies refused their duties, Lord Spencer posted down to Hampshire with his co-members of the Board, Arden and Admiral Young, and his secretary Marsden, to hoist the banner of Admiralty on the spot and hold an enquiry. After three days the Board went back to London, satisfied that the business was in hand. With the news that Mr Pitt in Parliament had promised to ask for a rise in pay, the seamen appeared contented. There were other complaints, of course, and Lord Howe, ' the sailor's friend ', is said to have soothed the malcontents with pledges of a pardon for the mutineers and redress of all their wrongs.

The Spithead crews had not quite ceased murmuring when the serious outbreak occurred at the Nore. For a time the rebels held the mouth of England's busiest naval river, and played a winning hand. Lord Spencer and his colleagues set off once more, this time to Sheerness. But meeting the mutineers on their own ground was as far as the First Lord would go. Until they submitted unconditionally he declined to talk with them, and the coach returned to London without any progress made.

Weeks passed, the pressure on the Admiralty intensified from all quarters; but the Earl remained steady. Not diplomatic exchanges, nor interference by the Government, nor lavishly renewed promises, but shortage of water and food, backed up by signs of a fleet action against them, drove the mutineers to surrender. Then the mild-mannered and courteous First Lord, in accordance with the spirit of his times, acted promptly and savagely. "The Quota men have been at the bottom of this," said Admiral Duncan. He blamed it on the rogues and orphans whom Pitt's recruiting Act had driven into the Navy.

Earl Spencer, like his son, Lord Althorp, is remembered more for his devoted labours in the Whig interest than for his naval eminence, in spite of being the Navy's political chief for a longer-than-normal spell (1796 to 1801) at possibly the most critical period in two centuries. After he left the Admiralty he received a curious and somewhat enigmatic ' reference ' from George III:

' The uniform conduct of Earl Spencer since I have had the pleasure of having [him] in my Service, as well as the real good opinion I had of his character at all times, makes me particularly feel reluctant in consenting to his retiring from his present employment. He knows so well that it is a principle of the strongest nature, that of religious and political duty, that has alone guided the King through the present most unpleasant scene, that it is unnecessary to add more on the present occasion.'

Growing old graciously in retirement, Earl Spencer kept two irons in the naval fire, two sons as captains in the Fleet; and he saw them prosper, largely because he preserved enough Interest to get them the appointments they wanted and to pick their officers for them. He bore no grudge against the common seamen for the grey hairs they had given him. Thomas Collings, on a visit to Althorp, remembered the 'beautiful sight' of the Earl distributing his alms every Saturday morning in the kitchen:

'Precisely at nine o'clock the venerable nobleman might be seen to come in, book in hand and a benign smile on his face; he called the names in the book, and for everyone had a kind word. . . . There was constantly prepared a copper or cauldron of good wholesome soup which the cook distributed to such as should apply, and it was a positive order of the Earl's that no person in distress should ever be refused relief, more particularly if the supplicant was a sailor.'

No First Lord less like his predecessor than Admiral Earl Saint Vincent could have been picked when Addington's ministry ousted Pitt's in 1801. Spencer had stood at one end of the 'lay' spectrum; Saint Vincent was rooted at the other end of the 'professional'. Temperamentally, if the two had anything in common, it was an inclination to stubbornness when forced into a corner; but that was all.

As Sir John Jervis, the newcomer had long been a byword among the maritime nations of northern Europe for gruffness, rugged obstinacy, outspokenness and tactical expertise in battle. He was getting on in years: went to school with James Wolfe and was Saunders's first lieutenant in the assault on Quebec, nearly half a century earlier.

'Old Jarvie', an object of derision among his fellow officers

G

in his youthful days for an eccentricity he had of spending his leave periods touring foreign arsenals and dockyards, had trained himself, as it were, for an administrative climax to a dazzling sea career. In his five years as Commander-in-Chief Mediterranean, he had won the victory which gave him his earldom and title—a victory which he had approached—for it was Mutiny year—in a sombre mood, with a pronouncement that was to sound down the ages: " A victory is very essential to England at this moment."

After the battle the Mediterranean situation had continued tense and the First Lord had echoed the words to him at Lisbon in 1798: " The appearance of a British squadron in the Mediterranean is a condition on which the fate of Europe may . . . depend." And Lord Spencer was not given to alarmist talk. In that theatre, Europe had discovered, the British Navy had a tactical combination—Saint Vincent and Nelson—unequalled in the story of maritime adventures.

Sir John, as he was for most of that tour of duty, had given the administration a lot of thought during the monotonous weeks he spent in his flagship, blockading the Spanish ports. He had let himself go on paper, as he was always liable to, telling Spencer: ' The civil branch of the Navy is rotten to the core '; that ' nothing short of a radical sweep in the dockyards can cure the enormous evils and corruptions in them, and this cannot be attempted until we have peace '; and that, so far as his own command was concerned, he was appalled at the ' gimcrack and frippery ' that was creeping into the Service and the ' old women in the shape of young men ' he was burdened with.

After a short spell in command of the Channel Fleet, Earl Saint Vincent became First Lord and very soon the Navy was getting the breathing-space he had prayed for: the Peace of Amiens of 1802. Threats of French invasion vanished; but a much graver threat hung over the civil establishments of the

Navy: it was whispered that ' Old Jarvie ' would Walk Round.

" Portsmouth was bad enough, but Chatham beggars all description," he informed his Board, halfway round the circuit of the dockyards.   He inspected the Naval Academy at Portsmouth—the Navy's only school for officers—and found it (as every history book records) ' a sink of vice and abomination '. The trip taught the Service, if nothing else, that promotion to ministerial rank as the chief naval administrator had not inhibited Saint Vincent's explosive line in invective.

Where did Sir Charles Middleton stand while such tempests of abuse raged round the bowed heads of Lords Commissioners and Principal Officers ?   Had dockyard stock slumped so desperately, in such a short time ?—for, bad as the situation looked to Saint Vincent, it had been ten times worse when he was plain Captain Jervis.   The trouble was, as sometimes happens when two men of original ideas start working things out together, they could not stand the sight of each other.   The First Lord referred to the ex-Comptroller contemptuously as ' that Scotch packhorse'.   Scotsmen were among his *bêtes noires*. " You will never find an officer, native of that country, figure in supreme command," he once told his great friend Evan Nepean, the Secretary of the Admiralty.   " They are only fit for drudgery."

What Middleton thought of Saint Vincent he kept to himself.   The First Lord was not long in walking into trouble. Energetically as he probed into the shore establishments' grimy corners, he was too old and set in his ways to be an effective new broom.   The brilliant sailorly qualities of his middle and late years, when the Fleet idolised him as it idolised no one else but Nelson, when the Admiralty façade and Horse Guards Parade flared with torches and hissed with the experimental wonders of gas lamps in celebration of his sweeping victories—

these qualities were overshadowed by the deeds of his old age, in chieftainship of the Service, when the heroics of the Mediterranean conflict were obscured by the foolishness and ill-temper of a mean-spirited, conceited First Lord and the pointless vendettas he pursued on his juniors with the single-mindedness he had once shown in hunting down the enemy at sea.

Saint Vincent was strong on, and deeply involved in, party politics. Some of his worries came from having to control a predominantly Tory Board, left over from the last administration, whose members delighted in making difficulties for an out-and-out Whig.

He vented his frustration on the Navy and Victualling Boards, planting his secretary Tucker among them and thus becoming privy to their debates. What he heard determined him to ask Parliament for a commission to enquire into the goings-on at Somerset House and the abuses in the shore establishments where, as fast as he stamped out one, another blossomed next door to it.

He got his commission, but only by threatening resignation: something, it was understood, a First Lord could get away with once, but only once. While the war went on again after only a few months of *reculer pour mieux sauter*, the Lords Commissioners and Principal Officers were being harassed by interrogation, leaving Saint Vincent to organise the Fleet single-handed, which he did superbly. Pitt at the same time, in the House of Commons, signalled the opening of a campaign to bring the Government down by attacking it at its weakest point: the First Lord of the Admiralty. He returned again and again to charges of 'criminal neglect' of Britain's naval forces. The First Lord's cry for a commission, he implied, was only a blind to protect the real culprit, the First Lord himself.

And in the House of Lords, simultaneously, Saint Vincent was presenting reassuring pictures of Britain's naval dispositions to peers half-comprehending but profoundly impressed, and uttering another historic sentence: "I do not say, my Lords, that the French cannot come; I only say they cannot come by sea."

It is in politics above all that a little learning is a dangerous thing. The admiral who had time and again out-manœuvred the French and the Spaniards was a child in the war of Westminster, the defective prop in the Addington ministry, which collapsed and brought it down in 1804. Bluff, spirited, intensely patriotic, he was no match for Pitt, and he left the Admiralty, like many a fine old sea-dog before him, in disfavour with the party whose causes he had championed all his life. Outspoken as ever, he told the King, when he went to the palace to resign, that the Service was going to the dogs. In his young days, he explained, there had always been promotion for a likely lad, whatever his origin. But the Navy had been overrun by the younger branches of the nobility and the sons of members of Parliament, who had swallowed up all the patronage and blocked the promotion channels. He had tried hard, and failed utterly, to abolish Interest and give merit its due, and this was the failure that he regretted most of all.

Earl Saint Vincent is sometimes made to appear as a pompous archaism even for his own times—indeed, he must appear so in the foregoing passage. This is the impression he left, but his character had another side not visible to all. He was far from out of touch with the failings and needs of the Service; in some respects his ideas were ahead of his time. He put forward numerous schemes for improving the conditions of officers and men, and lived to see his successors get the credit for them.

He stood the Royal Naval Asylum at Paddington on its feet, with a personal gift of £1000 and a personal appeal organised throughout the Fleet. He laid down drastic new rules for cleanliness and habitability in ships (agreeing, however, that an issue of soap would be going too far). Vaccination against smallpox came in during his reign at the Admiralty, and also the provision of medicine chests for ships' surgeons, who previously had to supply their own.

Posterity is divided about his reputation as an administrator, but no one doubts the brilliance of his exploits afloat. He was the sea officer who encouraged Nelson and made Britain's fleet the terror of the seas for a generation. He lived long, and waited until the end of his life for the final accolade. It came when the Prince Regent, succeeding as George IV, bestowed on him the heavy golden baton of an Admiral of the Fleet.

15 Farewell the Principal Officers

We first looked in on the Navy Board when it sat in the Consultation Room at Tower Hill, almost a family business conducted by the Gonsons and the Hawkinses; we followed it to Seething Lane, saw it in action with Pepys, with the trembling octogenarians Haddock and Acworth and the lonely livewire Captain Cockburne; and called at Somerset House for a glance at the hurricane named Middleton.

In this chapter we visit the Principal Officers for the last time. That veteran company of the bureaucratic drama is soon to be 'abolished in ignominy'. It will go through a lively farewell performance and bow out to more catcalls than applause.

The Principal Officers—Navy Commissioners, as they are called these days—have moved around a little since we last inspected them. At the apex of the organisation the Treasurer of the Navy used to stand, brandishing the purse. But he has gained status through his hereditary association with the Lord Treasurer and other great officers of State, has removed himself from the dependence on collective Navy Board surveillance which had once been demanded of him, and has more important things to do than witness payments to dockyard officials and pursers of the Fleet.

In the time of William and Mary the Navy Treasurership, formerly a bed of laurels for a naval hero to repose on, was already a plum job for a rising politician, a launching pad to political greatness. Navy Treasurers ended up wealthy men, if nothing else. We remember how Lord Orford clung to the post, even after he had become First Lord Commissioner.

In a Cabinet List of 1711, the Navy Treasurer was actually included. (He was Robert Walpole and perhaps it was there that he discovered that every man has his price, because he lost the job the same year, avoided an investigation about missing funds, and was not heard of again for a time.) Opposition members in early Georgian Parliaments threw accusations indiscriminately at office holders, but generally managed to hit a Navy Treasurer. John Aislabie survived an assault in George I's reign, but succumbed shortly afterwards when, as Chancellor of the Exchequer, he introduced a scheme for paying off the national debt by incorporating it with South Sea stock—a scheme which burst shortly before the Bubble, luckily, pricked by the member who pointed out that Aislabie himself had invested a fortune in the Company. The ex-Navy Treasurer went to the Tower in a torchlight procession of gloating citizens.

The place traditionally kept open for the Treasurer in case he should condescend to take it—senior member of the Navy Board—passed to Charles Middleton. From 1778 to 1790 the Comptroller dominated the Board and gradually took over ship-building and repair, duties formerly associated with the Surveyor.

By the time the Napoleonic wars broke out, the Principal Officers' jobs were thoroughly mixed: Treasurer practically lost sight of, Surveyor deprived of his ancient surveying responsibilities, Comptroller in charge of all departments except the Clerk's. Middleton's dream of a three-committee Board, each committee chaired by the Comptroller, came true after he had left, in 1796. It lasted for twenty years until, after Waterloo, the Government celebrated the turn of an era by streamlining the Navy Office, dissolving the three committees and reconstituting them as departments under separate heads: the Secretary, for a correspondence department; the Accountant-

General, for the accounts department; and the Storekeeper-General, for a stores department. There was a separate Transports Committee, under a Superintendent of Transports —not a Principal Officer, but represented on the Board by the Storekeeper-General. These were the departments which, carried into the upper house of Admiralty, survived. The old-style Principal Officers strolled into oblivion.

To the end the Comptroller holds sway. After Middleton's time he is Sir Andrew Snape Hamond, Bart., appointed 1794 and superannuated 1808, after his brush with the Commission of Enquiry described below. The last Comptroller is a favourite of naval historians for the valuable reminiscences he bequeathed them at the end of a long life at sea: Admiral Sir Thomas Byam Martin. He rules the Navy Board for fifteen years, until the Whigs, returning under Earl Grey, place him on half-pay in 1831.

One year later the Navy Board itself disappears into the Admiralty, and the Comptroller is never heard of again. (He is not connected with the twentieth-century Controller.) For three years the Treasurer anachronistically survives until he is swallowed up in a corporate office of Service accountancy called Paymaster-General of the Forces. (The Duke of Wellington's finance committee of 1828 helped to bring this about, as it had helped to destroy the Navy Board: borrowing an idea from George Canning, the Duke set out to control the spending departments in Whitehall by imposing a uniform system of accounting on them; Army and Navy, the biggest drains on the Exchequer, were his first targets.)

The Surveyor of the Navy, a harmless creature without much to do except draw his salary, astonishingly escapes, and joins the upper house. In 1860 he is still going strong; that year he gets the title with the modern spelling: Controller of the Navy. From Robert Spencer Robinson (1861 to 1871)

onwards, while his brother Lords Commissioners are number-
ing themselves, he will stand apart. There will be First Naval
Lords, Second Naval Lords and Third Naval Lords: he will
be one of them, but will keep his alternative title too, of Controller of the Navy: the only member of the Board of Admiralty
whose office is linked with that whimsical creation of King
Henry VIII, the Navy Board of 1546.

Deprived of their venerable and sometimes dishonourable
authority, the last generation of Principal Officers at the beginning of the eighteenth century filled their usual wartime role
of whipping-boys for administrative blunders by Government
and Admiralty, for inefficiency and procrastination above and
below them; without a Pepys or a Middleton to set the record
straight. They might well have felt aggrieved that Saint
Vincent should spend so much time abusing them, that his
parliamentary commission should be investigating their faults.
They never claimed to perform miracles. They were supporting, with more credit than Principal Officers of the olden time
had earned, the demands of a winning fleet. The disastrous
engagements for which, when admirals dead and gone had
hastened home with their excuses, the Navy Board had
shouldered the blame, were not occurring. Yet the Government remained unsatisfied. Britain's victories at sea, it seemed,
were being won in spite of, not with the aid of, the Principal
Officers' efforts. Lord Saint Vincent had told them not to
imagine, because new units of excellent quality, captured from
the enemy, were being added weekly to the Fleet, that it con-
doned slackness in building and repairing warships in the home
dockyards.

That Admiralty and Navy Board could snipe composedly
at each other while the Grande Armée massed on the Channel
coasts of France indicated at least a mutual confidence in the

Fleet. At the height of the campaign in home waters, Their Lordships were not afraid to detach sufficient numbers of warships to protect convoys all the way from distant countries. In the darkest hours, just before Trafalgar, the First Lord was promising the East India Company's chairman a full escort for his homeward-bound flock of merchant ships. The Grande Armée, as it happened, never tackled the Grand Fleet, never set eyes on it. And it was a fleet whose ships and men were the product of a Navy Board which, the old man of the Admiralty insisted, was 'rotten to the core'.

Round Somerset House the Navy's domestic war dragged on. The Principal Officers fought, with pen and ink and their backs to the wall, a commission which was to roll on, long after its only begetter had vanished from the naval headquarters, quietly stalking its objective, steadily gathering information year after year, until it ended up something like a Board itself and started issuing annual reports. Each one, without containing much in the way of sensational revelations, became in Whig hands a powerful instrument of propaganda against a Tory Navy Board.

In Trafalgar year you could buy anywhere in London a broadsheet which took the Principal Officers to task for failing to give the Fleet naval stores and victuals, for accepting rotten timber and adulterated copper, for allowing themselves to be swindled over the purchase of trees in Sherwood Forest, for neglecting to take advantage of the cheap rate for oakum, for striking bad bargains with profiteering private shipowners, for refusing to adopt the 'shoaling' system invented by the Master Shipwright at Plymouth ('shoaling' meant organising dockyard workmen into gangs of skilled, partly-skilled and unskilled labour in definite proportions)—in short, for wrecking the Navy. A tremendous furore detained Parliament from its business of prosecuting the war while it debated the Navy Board's dreadful

crime of giving superannuated gunners jobs in the ' ordinary '
at Chatham Yard—a crime which, a member said, had turned
that great establishment into a haven for old men, cripples,
idiots and ' every vagabond who could not obtain a meal by
any other means '. (Enquiry showed that only one superannuated gunner had been entered and shortly afterwards dismissed; but by the time this was pointed out, Parliament had
switched its attack to something else.)

Putting aside Doctor Goebbels and Radio Cairo, it would
be hard to find examples of misrepresentation more persistently
sustained.

Admiralty letters of the first five years of the century drip
with the acid tones of the arch-enemy Saint Vincent and his
assistants Tucker and Admiral Troubridge. Their Lordships
' cannot refrain from expressing considerable surprise that . . .'
—' are not a little astounded that . . .'—' desire it may be unequivocally understood that . . .'—' desire to be informed of the
particular period when you *first* failed in your efforts to avoid
. . .'—and so forth. The failure of which less partial observers
might have complained, and of which Lord Melville when he
came into office instantly did complain, was in communication
between the two controlling bodies of the Royal Navy; especially of that ' frequent, full and intimate intercourse ' between
First Lord and Comptroller (Melville had been taking lessons
from Middleton) without which, he said, ' a man may as well
attempt to walk without legs, to speak without a tongue or to
write without hands '.

The Commission of Naval Enquiry probed on. To its
strictures the Navy Commissioners, having no strong voice in
Parliament, were not allowed to reply. Individual members
rebuked by name had no chance to justify their conduct or
rebut charges. When Sir Andrew Hamond was Comptroller,
he begged for the reports to be referred to the Principal Officers

to give them the Englishman's privilege of defending themselves. An interview with Saint Vincent, whose hatred of the
Navy Office in his last few weeks of office had turned patho-
logical, is recorded in Cobbett's *Debates*:

' " You intend, I suppose," said his Lordship, " to ask Mr
Addington's [Prime Minister] consent ? "—" Certainly," rejoined Sir Andrew Hamond. " Then, sir," replied his Lordship,
" be so good as to let him know at the same time that you have
not mine."—" Why, my Lord ? "—" Sir, the Commissioners of
Naval Enquiry were instituted by desire of the Admiralty.
It is for the Admiralty to direct their enquiries and, whenever
we think they have gone through all the objects judged necessary,
the Navy Board may expect to be called on for its defence."

' " I am then, my Lord," rejoined Sir Andrew, " to understand that your Lordship is determined to exclude the Navy
Board from justifying or explaining any part of their conduct
until the public mind becomes wholly prejudiced against them,
by the enumeration *en masse* of every possible error on which
the Commissioners may think proper to report. I shall not,
however, be deterred from my purpose."

' " If you persist," replied his Lordship, " in making such a
motion, I shall consider it a personal affront." '

Sir Andrew did persist, but the Prime Minister rejected his
appeal, explaining that he must support the First Lord.

Pitt replaced Addington and Dundas, Lord Melville (ex-
Secretary of War) succeeded Saint Vincent. In the new Prime
Minister the Principal Officers had an old friend. With the
aid of another old friend he planned to destroy the Commission
of Naval Enquiry. Middleton shaped the instrument: simply a
new commission, a constructive one for a change, he stressed,
with a Tory composition and a dignified title: the Parliamentary
Commission for Revising and Digesting the Civil Affairs of

His Majesty's Navy. In effect it was to be a commission on the Commission of Naval Enquiry.

Charles Middleton, former Comptroller, cousin and mentor of the new First Lord and bitter opponent of the Saint Vincent clique, made the ideal chairman for it.

The old investigators went down fighting. One of their last salvoes scored a direct hit on the First Lord himself. They published documents which showed that Lord Melville, revered as the father of a bill for ' better regulating the office of Treasurer of the Navy ' as far back as 1785—when that officer's accounts had been found to be twenty-four years in arrears—had made away with public moneys during a short spell in the same job immediately afterwards.

The Whigs howled for impeachment. Melville, innocent or guilty (he was acquitted on the main charges), could do no more than resign. At a time when it seemed certain that the position he had set his sights on would escape him in the end, Admiral Middleton became Lord Barham and First Lord of the Admiralty.

At once, with all his old enthusiasm for clean sweeps and centralisation, he revitalised the Navy Board. The Comptroller in particular received new instructions and was brought into the inner circle of Navy government. Was he not, as Barham when Comptroller had often stated, ' the person of next consequence to the First Lord ' ? " No price," he had impressed on Lord Melville, " can purchase a man fit for this extensive office: he must be in every part of it, and know everything that is going on, in and out of it."

He created one new Principal Officer, making eleven in all: the Inspector-General of Navy Works, first added to the ' outside ' staff in 1796 to superintend new buildings in the shore establishments.

He rearranged the Board of Admiralty to his favourite

triple-headed plan, with one naval Lord in charge of each section; himself the final authority in the three sections, and sole director of naval operations. Barham behaved fully as autocratically as 'Old Jarvie'. A contemporary (Sir John Barrow, then Second Secretary at the Admiralty) portrayed him as a 'placid figurehead'. It is a misleading picture, unless you see a figurehead as a serene pointer and inspiration to men sailing into battle. The genius of Barham lay in an entirely justified confidence in his own abilities, a magical grasp of strategy, courage in making a decision and sticking to it in the face of 'expert' criticism; plus the 'packhorse' temperament—solid inexhaustible stamina.

Lord Barham never led a great fleet into action. The limelight shone on the sea and his name is not even mentioned when 'Tales of the Fighting Navy' are told. To his Admiralty colleagues he was tyrant and hero. 'Colleagues' is hardly the word: he kept the naval war in his own hands, made his senior naval Lord (Gambier, his nephew) into a sort of minor chief of staff and left the other Lords to handle routine matters beneath his notice.

In the summer of 1805, from his private office, while outside in the Board Room the members muttered about not being consulted and wasting their time, but dared not leave in case the 'old man' should take it into his head to come to a meeting or send out another infuriating slip of paper for their immediate signature—from that office he engineered Britain's supreme sea victory.

His hand applied the lighted match to the Nelson touchpaper. Nelson on his last visit to England spent hours with Barham in the First Lord's office at the beginning of September 1805. 'They were superb strategists,' says Dudley Pope (*England Expects*), 'and for once war plans were being made which paid no court to fickle chance and which were not hurried halfmeasures drawn up by amateurs to placate an angry and alarmed

Parliament, nor desperate attempts to plug the breach after
some ill-digested scheme dreamed up by ineffective ministerial
placemen had inevitably gone awry.'

The Admiralty telegraph clattered a message to Portsmouth
after Nelson's first interview, to cancel the *Victory's* sailing
orders. Thereafter, for three or four days, it worked all day
distributing orders and regrouping men and ships. The story
goes that Barham handed Nelson a Navy List and invited him
to choose his own officers. Nelson handed it back. "Choose
yourself, my Lord. The same spirit actuates the whole profession. You cannot choose wrong."

Nelson then dictated his own fleet orders to Barham's
private secretary. The First Lord signed them unread and
sent them out for Gambier and the rest of the Board to add
their names. Nelson made one last brief call at the Admiralty
on Wednesday the 12th September, to remind the secretariat
that he needed several copies of Sir Home Popham's signal
code before the Fleet left Portsmouth. The last administrative
officer to see him alive was Canning the Navy Treasurer, who
went down to Portsmouth with him and spent an evening on
board the flagship.

The administration had taken its share of punishment since
the wars began—more punishment than the ships. It deflated
every critic with one redeeming triumph: having the right
man in the right place, in command when the crucial test arrived.
The right *men*, one might say—for many a less deserving First
Lord might have been chosen than Lord Barham, to get out
of bed when the courier brought his despatches two weeks
after Trafalgar and go down the corridor to announce the
annihilation of the enemy to his patient assembly in the Board
Room.

One temptation Earl Saint Vincent had never been able to

resist was meddling in Cabinet matters which little concerned him, contrary to a promise he had made the Prime Minister to stick to naval affairs. So much of contemporary life, he argued, had a bearing on naval affairs; it was on the Royal Navy that the safety and prosperity of the nation did, in the words of the quotation, chiefly depend. The First Lord had once been last in line of nine Cabinet members; more recently the very idea of a naval chief being in the Cabinet at all had been enough to raise the blood-pressure of reformist members of Parliament. But Saint Vincent acted like a number two in the Cabinet, a little step beneath the Prime Minister. The Royal Navy, one had to admit, was Britain's most important department of State, her biggest nationalised industry, employing thousands afloat and ashore. Saint Vincent could always find some naval opening in any question before the Cabinet, in which to shove his oar.

By giving Cabinet meetings priority over Board of Admiralty meetings, a First Lord could soon set himself apart from his professional colleagues and make difficulties between them. Lord Melville, while First Lord, issued operational instructions agreed at a Cabinet without troubling to consult his fellow Lords Commissioners—although they were professional seamen and he was not. (They protested and he rescinded the orders: unlike Earl Spencer before him, who would not be dictated to.) Lord Mulgrave, First Lord from 1807 to 1810 (after which he became Master-General of the Ordnance and kept his seat in the Cabinet), 'managed all the details of the Copenhagen expedition' with Wellesley Pole and one clerk, according to the *Dictionary of National Biography*, and 'sat up two or three nights copying out the orders'. Lord Gambier received the orders and carried out the attack, and the news of the action was the first his naval colleagues heard of it.

In the *Encyclopaedia Britannica* article on the Admiralty, Sir Richard Vesey Hamilton unearths another example of unilateral action from the early eighteen-hundreds, when in 1815 the Secretary of the Admiralty—who was not even a member of the Board—acted in Paris under the orders of the Foreign Secretary with all the authority of the Board and none of its concurrence.

Much less hobnobbing with politicians characterised the Barham administration. When he kissed hands on his appointment, Barham was advised by King George not to make the same mistake as Saint Vincent. He accepted the hint. It was rare to find Barham at a Cabinet meeting unless specific naval items were on the agenda.

An Admiralty Order of his time rules that no commanding officer must take time off to canvass as a Parliamentary candidate: one of the epoch-making declarations of Admiralty. Within a generation it was unusual to find a serving captain or admiral who was also a member of Parliament. Previously it had been unusual to find one who was not.

Spotting the next First Lord was a highly speculative pastime for the Fleet, when the century moved towards its teens. So many commanders in the late wars had emerged with unassailable reputations.

There would have been Nelson, had he lived—but Nelson had never served at the Admiralty and years would have had to pass before he achieved the right seniority. There was Sir Sidney Smith, one of the cleverest and best-educated of his breed—but spasmodically out of favour with authority, never a choice for high administrative post. (Fleet gossip said the Prince Regent was jealous of him because he had been a little too attentive to the future Queen Caroline.) There was Lord Duncan, victor of Camperdown, another fighting admiral, popular with the nation but not much liked at the Admiralty, who never got the jobs he asked for.

The flamboyant, wayward Cochrane wrecked his own chances. A post-captain at twenty-five, he rose no higher, in spite of the influence he commanded as M.P. for Honiton and later for the city of Westminster. Cochrane lost everything through being implicated in the stock-jobbing transactions of 1814, when premature reports of Napoleon's downfall upset the market. He was fined, ordered to stand in the pillory outside the Admiralty building (this indignity was spared him at the eleventh hour), sentenced to a long term of imprisonment, deprived of his rank and denuded of his honours and expelled from the House of Commons. Little wonder he decided to look for another job abroad. By the time the Sailor King and the Whigs restored his naval rank to him sixteen years later he had been Commander-in-Chief of the Chilean Navy and what might be described as First Lord of the Admiralty of Brazil.

Sir Edward Codrington had most of the qualifications—but also the two fatal blemishes, for a sea officer, of being a poor man and a humorist. Re-addressing the bill for the patent, registration fee and stamp duty on his Trafalgar knighthood to the First Lord was a joke Lord Barham did not appreciate. Their Lordships took care to keep Codrington well away from Whitehall, and his warm friendship with the Duke of Clarence earned him no more than the rather strange appointment, on retirement, of Lord of the Queen's Bedchamber.

Admiral Sir Thomas Troubridge was high on everyone's list of favourites in the Admiralty handicap. That ' pattern of professional excellence, of undaunted valour and patriotic worth ' had been a member of the Board under Spencer and Saint Vincent and had missed fighting at Trafalgar alongside his son because of an appointment to command the East Indies station. On arrival at Colombo he had found Sir Edward Pellew in charge, with no instructions to hand over: a common situation when mails took months to arrive, if they arrived at all, and a difficult one when, as was more likely than not, at least one of the two admirals concerned had a nasty temper. Sir Thomas had sailed for the Cape, to avoid strained relations and give Their Lordships time to sort the matter out. His flagship, the *Blenheim*, disappeared on passage and the only clue to her fate was a piece of Sussex oak sent in a parcel to the Governor of Mauritius with a note that it had been picked up at sea.

Pellew, afterwards Lord Exmouth, had acquired a name for daring and ability in ships and in politics, but would not in a purely professional navy have earned a high command. A parliamentary performance gained him the East Indies station in 1804: he put Saint Vincent under an obligation by supporting Addington in a critical debate. A parliamentary sacrifice enabled him to keep it: when the Government fell next year he traded his seat in the Commons to a nominee of William Pitt.

In the event, no sailor succeeded Barham. The Admiral who did his best to discourage naval officers from entering Parliament, who put the Navy before politics—Admiral Barham was the last naval First Lord. Before his time it was becoming increasingly apparent that the Royal Navy's role in domestic and foreign affairs needed a full-time professional politician to represent it in Parliament. After his time and up to our own times, apart from one short interlude, the First Lord of the Admiralty has been a civilian; and very often the less he has known about the Navy the better he has got on.

This is where the distinction in the Board of Admiralty between First Lord and First Sea Lord arises, to the puzzlement of laymen, until it is explained that the one is a politician and the other a sailor. It presents a puzzle to constitutionalists too, from the beginning of the nineteenth century. They begin to pose more urgently a question which has occasionally been posed before: if the Navy's political chief has no knowledge of the Navy and its naval chiefs have no knowledge of politics, who among them is responsible to Parliament and the nation ? On whose shoulders does the government of the Navy rest— the First Lord's, the First Sea Lord's, all the Sea Lords' or all the members of the Board together ?

16 The Gift of Admiralty

Travellers on the winding road of Admiralty history, nego-
tiating the ups and downs of its corruptions and inefficiencies,
its wasted funds and political entanglements, exploring the
bureaucratic ivy and parasitic growths which have mastered the
British oak nearly to the point of choking the life out of it—
travellers may well ask how, by about 1810, the Royal Navy
came to have six hundred warships in commission and more
than a hundred and thirty thousand men on its books; how all
at once it found itself competently and decisively commanding
the waves from the China seas to the Gulf of Mexico and rendering with perfect confidence, whenever two or three Lords
were gathered in one place under the Admiralty Flag, the
ceremonial tune 'Rule Britannia'.

The trend of the road for six centuries, it seems, has been
upward and forward. We have not seen the peaks for the
S-bends and the undergrowth. Bad as the surface has been
at some stages, we could always have travelled a worse by
going abroad. Perhaps corruption—since sociologists agree we
have not changed much—was no worse then than it is today,
only more blatant. That Whig and Tory conflict had its points
—collisions in Parliament, constant searchlights on some dubious
aspect of the naval control system, commissions galore to ferret
out misdemeanours, an Opposition always avid to sharpen its
claws on a Government supporter, whether First Lord or dockyard clerk. Perhaps the British sailor, like an explosive which
spends its greatest force on the toughest obstacle, flourished on

hardships and injustice and criminal negligence at the top. Perhaps they gave him his exclusively British peculiarity, inability to recognise when the fight was lost. How else does one account for sea victory after sea victory against the odds ? Of those six hundred vessels patrolling under the White Ensign, about half were built in the home dockyards and the other half snatched from the enemy.

What of the price of Admiralty?—averaged out over two centuries, about a million pounds a year; a large sum, members in every Parliament since the Rump had been heard to say, to keep the naval machine grinding on. Yet one huge item in the nation's credit balance came as a gift from Their Lordships —or, rather, as the result of a judicious investment by them.

The Duke of Bedford had put it into words in 1746, when he persuaded the Government to let him send Captain John Byron round the world: "Nothing can redound more to the honour of this nation as a maritime power, to the dignity of the Crown of Great Britain and the advancement of the trade and navigation thereof, than to make discoveries of countries hitherto unknown." That side of Admiralty—charting, exploring, empire-building and opening up new avenues for trade, was conducted almost surreptitiously and, for the most part, outside the political arena.

Elizabeth's famous navigators and colonists had formed a bright but not very big cluster in the constellation of ocean voyagers. Throughout her reign the Spanish were the acknowledged masters of navigation; they had a Pilot Major among their Admiralty officials, who supervised world-renowned schools of cosmography and navigation at Seville. England's Lord High Admiral was sometimes under pressure to make such an appointment to the Navy Board. (But not everyone was convinced of Spanish superiority. Duro quotes the passenger of 1573: ' How can a wise and omnipotent God have placed such a difficult and important art as navigation into such coarse and lubberly hands as those of these pilots ? You should see them ask one another, " How many degrees have you got ? "— One says " Sixteen ", another " About twenty " and another " Thirteen and a half ". Then they will say, " What distance do you make it to the land ? "—One answers " I make it forty leagues from land ", another " I, a hundred and fifty ", a third " I reckoned it this morning to be ninety-two leagues "—and whether it be three or three hundred, no one of them agrees with the other or with the actual fact.')

In the next century, the Dutch eclipsed the rest. Most charts and atlases of Pepys's time were copied from the Dutch. But the British had their triumphs: Sebastian Cabot first noticed compass variation, and the astronomer Halley in 1698 first put the variations on the chart—the Admiralty rewarded him by giving him the half-pay of a naval post-captain, additional to his Astronomer Royal's salary. Sir Greenville Collins issued the first *Coasting Pilot* and Sir John Narborough first surveyed the Magellan Strait and the South American coast.

From the beginning of the eighteenth century, Britain held the lead. The Admiralty of Queen Anne helped to set up a Board of Longitude (and foreign nations copied it) which offered £20,000 for a chronometer, to do away with hit-or-miss east-west reckoning. Maskeleyne the Astronomer Royal, under Admiralty persuasion, invented the complex ' lunar method ' of determining longitude and every deep-sea navigator learned it while awaiting the chronometer. Maskeleyne compiled the first *Nautical Almanac* and James Cook, Admiralty-sponsored, added more territory to the British Empire than all the military conquests had done—and incidentally immortalised some undistinguished members of the Board of Admiralty by naming tropical islands after them.

James Rennell, whom the Admiralty wanted to make

Hydrographer, head of the department it set up in 1795, founded oceanography, the science of sea-winds and currents. (Dalrymple got the job: he had been disappointed when Cook was preferred for the 1768 'transit of Venus' voyage, because Sir Edward Hawke had said he would rather cut off his right hand than sign a naval commission for a civilian.)

Parry, the Arctic explorer, conceived the world-wide series of *Sailing Directions*, which the Admiralty altruistically published. Sir Francis Beaufort, most memorable of Admiralty hydrographers, started another unique and universal series, *Notices to Mariners*, and his Scale of Wind Force is in every sailing manual of the nineteen-sixties, British or foreign.

Such great yet unobtrusive Admiralty servants and the departments they managed were completing and piecing together the marine maps of the world through the eighteenth and nineteenth centuries, until the voyage from London to New Zealand was better signposted than the voyage from London to Birmingham. They did so only incidentally for the benefit of the sailors of every nation. Primarily, they were advancing trade and colonisation; not only for the 'dignity of the Crown of Great Britain' but also for the prosperity of the venerable Muscovy Company, the hardly less-venerable East India Company and the age-old Company of Merchant Venturers of England.

In the century of naval wars, the Admiralty had given Britain's sailors their sea-legs by keeping them rolling and pitching off the coast of Brittany for months on end, administering the European blockade. In the nineteen-hundreds, Britain's sailors learned the sea on their surveying voyages in strange waters—often under oars in open boats—or in campaigns against the slave-trade on the shores and up the tropical rivers of Africa and Arabia, or on pirate-hunting expeditions in the

China seas. Incidentally they learned to contain heat-stroke, frostbite, hunger and scurvy.

Parliament outlawed slavery, but did nothing to stop it. Airy talk was heard from time to time about an international sea police force; but it was so obviously a job, all nations agreed, for which the ubiquitous British Navy was best equipped. Much of the burden fell on the West African Squadron—a task force of out-of-date sloops and frigates, far from the lime-light, from Their Lordships' notice and from the modest com-forts of Channel or Mediterranean warships. This was the station to which the bad hats, the unfortunates and those without Interest were banished, to work out their penance and sacrifice their healths and tempers and drop far behind in the betting when the promotion lists were made up.

Lord Palmerston's energetic diplomacy strengthened the Navy's hand in slave-trading zones. It was regarded as a tre-mendous victory when President Lincoln of the United States agreed to allow patrolling British warships to stop and search his country's merchantmen. The rest of the civilised world applauded the British Government's noble aims and the Royal Navy's devotion to the nastiest of duties, but offered neither to share the work, nor contribute to the cost, nor allow the squadrons the facilities they needed.

The war against slavery ran quietly on for sixty years, making no headlines but creating substantial gaps in the Navy List and the Register of Seamen. When finally won it rated no victory parade, general celebration or distribution of honours. The spoils of that war were no more than a sentence in the history books to say that civilisation was largely indebted to the British Admiralty and British Fleet for the abolition of the slave trade in African negroes.

Contemporary with the anti-slavery patrols, the Hydro-

THE GIFT OF ADMIRALTY

graphic Department of the Admiralty (it became a separate section at the time of the Graham reforms of 1832) was tracing and engraving maps of the remotest coasts and harbours of the world, and the widest oceans, from the information sent back to London by the ships of the Royal Navy's Surveying Service; another unfashionable division of the Fleet, which everyone with any hope of becoming an admiral steered clear of.

Only a handful of minor war vessels were engaged on this task—sloops and small frigates as a rule, specially built or adapted for their work and named for the great navigators of the past: there were the *Stokes*, *Fitzroy*, *Owen*, *Dalrymple*, *Kellett* and others. One day there would even be a *Dampier* but never a *Bligh*.

The department could hardly be called extensive at any period. When Dalrymple was Hydrographer, about the beginning of the nineteenth century, his staff was laid down as one assistant, one draughtsman, three engravers and a printer. Among them they produced every chart carried by a British naval or merchant navigator.

From 1829 to 1855 the Navy's best-known hydrographer was in charge: Captain (afterwards Rear-Admiral Sir) Francis Beaufort, R.N. Shortly after he arrived the department came directly under Admiralty supervision and has remained so ever since.

In 1848 he ' quietly presented ' to the First Naval Lord, who ' quietly presented ' it to the First Lord for Parliament, a plain summary of the Hydrographic Office's achievements over a generation. The known and navigable waters of the world were comprehensively covered. There was a detail and an accuracy about strait and harbour and river-mouth plans which laymen never associated with such variables as tides, sands and sea-floors.

The incredible scope and spread of work accomplished by one insignificant sub-office of Admiralty stunned Parliament and Their Lordships. It compels admiration even today. Pick up an Admiralty chart at random—the Greek islands, for example. The seas and channels are the work of some mid-nineteenth-century navigating officer of the Royal Navy. ' Surveyed by T. Hull & F. B. Christian, Masters, and F. W. Jarrard, Acting 2nd Master, R.N., under the direction of Commander A. L. Mansell, 1853-4 ' . . . ' Surveyed by Llewellyn S. Dawson, Midshipman, 1852 '—and so on, down to each tiny cove and inlet.

It is the same the world over, from Novaya Zemlya to Vancouver Island, from Brazil to Tristan da Cunha. Possibly none but local fishermen have used those soundings since Llewellyn Dawson or one of his fellow officers did their boat survey from the four-oared gig of a sailing man-of-war; perhaps no one has been near the place, except another navigator of the Royal Navy, marking corrections.

Whatever the nationality of the next visitor, he will use an Admiralty chart on which the name of an undistinguished subordinate officer of the Fleet of long ago will be unobtrusively immortalised in the bottom corner. ' Safe as an Admiralty chart ', of course, is the seaman's equivalent of ' Safe as the Bank of England '.

Charts were the Admiralty's *succès d'estime*. They are big, but not profitable, business for the modern Hydrographer, with his factory at Taunton, Somerset, his staff of hundreds of officers, ratings and Wrens and his chart-depots at naval bases round the globe. And charts are only half of the story. The other half is of those series of navigational publications which have been coming out in an uninterrupted stream since the earliest days of the Board of Admiralty. With *Sailing Directions*, *Distance Tables*, *Notices to Mariners*, *Lights Lists*, *Tide Tables* and dozens of other handbooks and periodicals, the British Admiralty helps the commodores of great shipping lines, the captains of warships, the masters of tankers, the skippers of trawlers and the single-handed adventurers in small boats, of every race and nationality, to a safe landfall wherever they may be bound. It is all part of a service so complete, well-organised and inexpensive that younger Admiralties of other lands have always made ample use of it but never ventured to emulate it.

The maritime powers paid their tribute in 1884, when they agreed to adopt the world datum meridian on the longitude of Greenwich Observatory, founded by Pepys's friend Flamsteed in 1674 and brought under Admiralty control at the beginning of the nineteenth century.

17 Regency and Reform

Naval studies after Napoleon's fall make quaint reading. Nothing much happened and nothing much mattered. It was as though the Navy, brought victoriously through twenty years of scarcely-interrupted conflict (so that even senior officers knew nothing of what warship life was like in peacetime), hardly knew what to do with itself. The grand design of the sea Service by about the time Lord Mulgrave became First Lord of the Admiralty in 1807 had been fulfilled in all its splendour; the Fleet and the administration was due, in sailors' parlance, for a make-and-mend.

Of course the day-to-day recriminations went on, the day-to-day rebukes from Cabinet to Board of Admiralty and from Board of Admiralty to Navy Board, the day-to-day siphoning off of the Navy votes in costly useless projects, the day-to-day bungling. Their Lordships bungled the run-down of the Fleet: authority's callous disregard of the heroes after the Napoleonic wars disturbed a people not easily stirred to compassion. Rehabilitation and resettlement were expressions which would not be understood for another hundred and thirty years.

They bungled the American war of 1812, with the Government's help, ordering their Commander-in-Chief on the spot to 'attack, sink, burn or otherwise destroy' all United States ships and in the same breath to 'exercise all possible forbearance' towards them. They allowed the departments and the dockyards to slide back into the easygoing ways they had known when Barham was a boy.

Small wars apart, the Admiralty busied itself making arrangements for obscure allied generals and foreign friends of the ministers to take Mediterranean cruises for their health in units of the Fleet. There are references in the diaries of the period to flagships going hundreds of miles to pick up an admiral's mistress or a box of some gastronomic delicacy.

When the Commander-in-Chief Mediterranean was told to send H.M.S. *Tagus* home to pay off, no one knew where she was. In his leisurely way (it was all done in a leisurely way) he made enquiries round the different countries and at length sent a despatch vessel off to look for her. They located the *Tagus* tucked away in a snug berth at Villefranche on the French Riviera, her sails unbent and her spars struck, bedded down for the winter. The captain calmly sent word back that his ship was not fit for a passage to England. This, however, roused the Commander-in-Chief's anger. He ordered her back to Malta, where she found the flagship Captain, three Masters from line-of-battle ships and every carpenter in the Mediterranean Fleet on the quayside waiting to survey her. They had the *Tagus* stripped and put together again and packed off within days.

The *Tagus*'s commanding officer, incidentally, was no carefree veteran passed over for promotion, but a junior-senior officer in the thick of the struggle; and he had on board a little midshipman who, potentially, was worth impressing: Adolphus Fitzclarence, illegitimate son of Admiral of the Fleet the Duke of Clarence.

Thomas Collings (*The Captain's Clerk*) remembered times when even vital scientific tasks, which Their Lordships took most seriously, had to give way to the private pleasures of senior officers. He served in the *Owen Glendower*, in which the German astronomer Tiarks was embarked 'with no end of chronometers' to determine the exact longitude of Funchal in

Madeira, an important staging-point both for warships and East Indiamen and one of the first ports since the invention of the chronometer to have its precise geographical location fixed. The *Owen Glendower* (Captain Robert Spencer, the former First Lord's son) had to sail full speed for Madeira, once Doctor Tiarks had established the longitude of her starting-point, Falmouth. He needed one day there for his observations and the ship turned again for home, but ran into contrary winds and took fifteen full days.

So long a period between observations having elapsed, it was feared the trip would have to be done again. But, says the Captain's Clerk, 'the shooting season had commenced, every day of which was precious to Captain Spencer and consequently, on our return from Madeira, the observations were pronounced to be quite satisfactory and we received orders to go round to Chatham to pay off'. Squadron gossip, perhaps, but retailed with a matter-of-factness that suggests credibility if not authenticity.

A captain, especially a captain with Interest, could take many liberties. His foot was on the ladder of automatic promotion, he had only to outlive his brother captains to end up Admiral of the Fleet. Up to the rank of captain, in a shrinking Navy, competition for the critical step ran high.

Two-thirds of the midshipmen and lieutenants who served in the Trafalgar fleets had to be got rid of over the next thirty years. It presented the Admiralty with an awesome task. Some obliged by blotting their copybooks; some went into the coastguard service and the customs, which at that time came under Admiralty supervision. For 'axed' officers with educational qualifications there were jobs at Lloyd's, which had become the centre of the world's marine insurance and which worked in close co-operation with the Admiralty in the convoy and intelligence spheres throughout the wars. Others could try their luck with that other important client of Admiralty, the East India Company. The lucky ones, after 1815, were those appointed to the South American station, where British merchants accumulated fortunes in gold in the emergent republics but could find no way of shipping them home. Naval officers did it for them, for a percentage, and a lieutenant-in-command might earn enough in one voyage to bid the sea farewell for ever.

Along with an eat-drink-and-be-merry philosophy went the *fin-de-guerre* fashion—the right, some sea officers thought it—of making what they could out of the Service before Their Lordships stranded them on the beach. It put years on Navy Board officials in dockyards abroad, when warship captains on arrival told pathetic tales of the hazards of their passage because of badly-hung rudders, short rigging and stores ' lost overboard in foul weather '—in order to draw enough supplies of timber, bolts, copper and cordage to stock a ship-chandler's emporium and sell them to the next impoverished merchant master they came across.

We have made our adieux to the Principal Officers, but they have not gone yet, and postscripts to the tales of their tribulations in the final round-up were written into the memoirs of naval officers throughout the nineteenth century.

With four home dockyards (Chatham, Portsmouth, Devonport and Sheerness) to administer and a small group of miscellaneous establishments, all in the British Isles, the Navy Commissioners had never been happy about keeping their employees on a sufficiently tight rein. By the first quarter of the nineteenth century their difficulties had multiplied. With a staff not much increased, they were looking after dockyards, stores, hospitals and barracks all over the seven seas. The larger naval bases had a Commissioner of the Navy in charge—not

H

a Principal Officer—and he was nominally under the orders of the Commander-in-Chief, but in practice he had sole charge of the Navy's repairing, storing and personnel business, often thousands of miles away from his nearest colleague and weeks distant by brig-mail from his superiors in London. Such officers and their senior staff members were officially known as naval officers; not to be confused with what in the twentieth century are called naval officers and were formerly sea officers.

In the soil of those remote outposts the corruption and double-dealing ever identified with an old-style 'naval officer' proliferated as never before. After a swoop by an unusually inquisitive—or unbribable—investigator of the eighteen-thirties, a report showed that 'the man in charge of Jamaica Victualling Yard had been drawing a steady £400 or £500 more than his official outlay for some years. . . . At Ascension Island the accounts were in a perpetual mess. . . . At Hong Kong the culprit was reputed to be the natural son of the Comptroller of Victualling, but whether or not this was so, he had powerful friends; when he very conveniently died and his friends could go into his financial affairs without causing offence, they were astounded to find that, even after the whole of his private estate had been seized by the Government, there was still a deficiency of £3000 in cash and one in stores to the amount of over £7000. . . . The worst case was at the Cape of Good Hope, where it took the Imprest Branch about ten minutes to discover a difference of £37,000 in what Mr Thomson's latest accounts showed and what they should have shown'.

The showpiece of 'foreign' dockyards, at Malta, was slow to rid itself of the semi-oriental ways of the Arabs and the Knights of Saint John. The Navy Commissioners in 1825 took the opportunity of the official introduction of British currency in place of the curious old Maltese coinage to overhaul what had been, all the Nelson era, a virtually medieval

ship-repairing service. When the casualties poured in from
Navarino the dreadful condition of the Royal Naval Hospital
(it occupied the former slave prison of the Knights) came to
the Navy Board's notice, and plans were hastily put in hand for
a new naval hospital on Bighi Bay.

' Naval officers ' of the civil branch, wrapped in the mystique
of their calling, kings of the storeyards to whom sea officers
came with cap in hand, acquired imperious manners and a
superb contempt for Jack afloat. There flourished in every port
of call where the Navy Board maintained a depot one of those
nauseatingly officious clerks whose brain, if dissected, would be
found composed of pages of the *Victualling Instructions* or *Stores
Manual*, who applied the law to the letter without fear or favour
or regard for the hardships, problems and faith in human nature
of the simple mariner. Such a one Thomas Collings became.
This is his account of a routine Fleet versus Dockyard duel at
Malta, junior stores assistant against the captain of the battleship
Napoleon had surrendered to:

' I sent (the midshipman of the ship's working party) back
with my compliments to the Commander and a message to the
effect that, as the *Bellerophon* had lost her turn, she could only
have her provisions when convenient to me. I pointed out to
the midshipman how I was engaged and moreover that, whenever the *Bellerophon* took her provisions, she must take them *all*.
I could not issue them piecemeal.

' The Ship was lying about a stone's-throw from the Wharf
and the young Gentleman went off with my message in one
of the smaller boats, leaving the larger ones, expecting I suppose
that I would be overawed by the Thunderbolt which he was
pretty sure to bring me back from Captain Leachcroft. He
came back and said, " Mr Collings, Captain Leachcroft desires
to know when you will let him have the provisions he wants."
My answer was that . . . I really did not know when the

Bellerophon could be supplied, as a time had been fixed for supplying all the other Ships, none of which had disturbed the Admiral's arrangements as the *Bellerophon* had done.

' The same Midshipman came to me a third time with this very courteous intimation—"Mr Collings, Captain Leachcroft says that if you do not immediately let him have the *Bellerophon's* provisions he will forward a complaint to the Admiral." " Go back to Captain Leachcroft," I said, " and tell him that unless he is very quick in sending his complaint mine will get to the Admiral before his." '

The victuallers and their faraway chiefs at Somerset House, too, had many an impudent customer to deal with. Independently-minded captains might give themselves twenty-four hours to think it over before they poured out their complaints on paper to the Board of Admiralty; to the Navy Commissioners they might say what they liked. The *Naval Sketch Book* of 1834 told the tale of Captain Sir John Phillimore:

' In the prodigality of its tenderness, the Navy Board used to address officers, "We are, Sir, Your affectionate Friends." Sir J., thinking such graciousness should be reciprocated, subscribed himself in the same form. This was held by the Right Honourable Commissioners to be too familiar, and a written remonstrance was conveyed, informing him that it was " unusual to say the least " for an officer to use such freedom with the dignity of the Board.

' Sir J. acknowledged it as follows: " Gentlemen, I have the honour to receive your letter of —— acquainting me that it is not according to the rules of the Service for officers to subscribe themselves in the words adopted in my last. I shall be careful to obey the intimation and meanwhile have the honour to remain, Gentlemen, *not* Your affectionate Friend, J. P." '

Not normally credited with keeping abreast of the times,

the Victualling Board in 1814 took a surprising leap into the nineteenth century by putting tinned meat on issue to the Fleet as an experiment. Thirty-three years later, corned beef supplanted salt horse on ships' menus. (How it came to be 'Fanny Adams' to the sailors, from the girl who mysteriously disappeared on the Thames waterfront about the same time, is a well-known anecdote.) In 1825 the Victualling Board was making experimental issues of fresh vegetables; they were, contrary to old salts' forecasts, an instant success.

At the time of dissolution and reform in 1832, the Board had prepared, or at least drawn plans for, three great home depots for victualling the Fleet. They were to be known, and are known today, by the names of sovereigns: the Royal William at Plymouth (where the Navy's rum is stored), the Royal Clarence at Portsmouth and the Royal Victoria at Deptford. At the beginning of the twentieth century, when Rosyth dockyard was opened, the Royal Elizabeth Victualling Yard was established just across the Forth in the West Lothian countryside.

Thus the Navy Board, in the shadows of its extinction, continued mechanically adding to its responsibilities and, at the last, ironically showed itself at its most enlightened. Meanwhile the Board of Admiralty took other departments away from it.

In the first quarter of the century Their Lordships, who had previously controlled only senior appointments, began to pay marked attention to the recruitment, training and promotion of juniors. In 1806 they rehoused the Navy's only academy for embryo officers at Portsmouth, improved its image by calling it a Royal Naval College and appointed to it the world-renowned Professor Inman (of *Inman's Tables*).

By 1815 the Admiralty was approving every midshipman's appointment, a step which cut across the ancient rights of patronage. The College opened its gates in 1829 to a big new intake. They were the Mates—non-commissioned officers, many of whom earned promotion for gallantry or passed their lieutenants' examinations in past years but who saw no hope of an appointment to lieutenants' jobs. As time went by and the Navy's governors softened towards these long-service stalwarts marooned in the lower reaches of the river of rank, the Mates became fully commissioned officers, a step below lieutenant. A new page in the Navy List was opened for them in 1861, under the title of Sub-lieutenants.

Feckless days—nothing much happened, nothing much mattered; but in them one or two significant moves towards a modern Navy were made.

Champions of bureaucratic reform looked on Admiralty as a dinosaur left struggling in its swamp while the Whitehall Noah's Ark sailed on. But nothing revealed more clearly the extent to which the administration had evolved than its cries of pain and anger when Mr Canning's seemingly capricious resolve of May 1827 put back its clock by reviving the office of Lord High Admiral and persuading William, Duke of Clarence, the Admiral of the Fleet, to accept it.

Their Lordships thereupon became the Council of Admirals —which the Government chose for Prince William. It included Vice-Admiral Sir William Hope and Vice-Admiral Sir George Cockburn—two Napoleonic sailors of Napoleonic temper; the Honourable Keith Douglas and John Denison; John Wilson Croker as First Secretary and John (afterwards Sir John) Barrow as Second Secretary. All except Barrow were members of Parliament. It was an intensely political Council. Croker in particular was notorious for 'working harder as a politician than as a secretary of the Admiralty'. He found time to edit the *Quarterly Review* (and deal Keats his mortal blow), to establish the Athenaeum and write party propaganda by the ream. Students of the Reform decade see him as an *eminence grise* of Peel Toryism, a compound—someone recently said—' of Michael Foot, A. J. P. Taylor and Malcolm Muggeridge'; a man whom Macaulay hated 'even more than cold boiled veal'.

Croker for his part soon learned to hate the Duke of Clarence, and the Lord High Admiral's arguments with his Secretary provided background noises for all the debates of the régime.

The future King William IV needed small persuasion to add chieftainship of the Navy to his nominal command of her fleets. He had gone to sea at fourteen like a typical younger son. He served under Rodney, visited America and was an outstanding success over there, at a time when relations with the 'old country' could scarcely have been worse. He had even commanded his own ship, distinguishing himself by a fondness for playing the martinet and issuing voluminous orders which not all could make head or tail of, and, paradoxically, by his distaste for awarding punishments. (On becoming Lord High Admiral he reviewed the scale of offences and restricted the 'cat' to two or three grave ones. He failed, however, to get the rule changed which said a man must have a flogging against his name on the record sheet before he could be discharged for misconduct; because of it, many worthless characters continued to draw pay and victuals.)

Clarence had met Nelson, and hero-worshipped him. He had begged Their Lordships for a command of his own again during the wars; they had declined to answer his letters.

For one brief rare spell the Royal Navy had in Clarence a Lord High Admiral who despised the Court and the politicians, whose whole heart was in the Navy and who had the time to devote himself to the Navy and nothing else. He was ready to lead the ships he loved, not only the way Barham had done, from his office in the Admiralty building, but also the way

James II had done: in person, afloat and with the gold-and-crimson flag streaming at his maintop.

For a start he put the yacht *Royal Sovereign* in commission and went cruising in the Channel with her while his Duchess, who did not care for the sea, made a parallel progress through the ducal mansions of the south coast and was ready to greet him wherever he came ashore. His Council might not have minded so much if he had stuck to the yachting. What annoyed Hope and Cockburn, the most serious of professionals, was His Royal Highness's passion for summoning the Channel Fleet and conducting it in manœuvres with all the absorption and innocence of a small boy with a flotilla of plastic boats in a paddling pool.

Throughout the Fleet the Royal Sailor enjoyed enormous popularity, especially among the officers. Rough nautical talk, a good-humoured noisy quarter-deck manner, a name for being a bit of a rake, a few illegitimate children—these were the qualities which endeared a Lord Admiral to the wardrooms of the eighteen-twenties. Senior serving officers liked to see a naval chief with a will of his own, not subservient to the minister of the day, keeping the parliamentary sailors on his Council in check. Juniors had material cause for gratitude: the Duke's arrival (though he personally had nothing to do with it) coincided with an exciting scheme for inducing half-pay officers to emigrate to Australia with a free grant of land. He personally gave new hope to the ageing, poor and uninfluential by chipping away a little more of the fortress of patronage, personally prevailed over the Lords in promoting commanders as second-in-command of big ships to open a new promotion avenue. Indeed, he promoted a few deserving cases all on his own, without waiting for Admiralty approval. After all, as he kept trying to tell Croker, he *was* the Admiralty.

He listened readily—perhaps too readily—to cranks with

novel ideas; grew enthusiastic about Steam and put the Royal Navy's first steam-vessel, the *Lightning*, into service, while his Council wagged its beards and despaired of him. He inspected the guard-ships on their stations and varied the monotony of their existence in a fashion no one had thought of since 1793, by sending them to sea for gunnery exercises.

In practically every other demonstration of his authority the Duke provoked pity, ridicule and irritation. He embarrassed the gunrooms and cockpits of the Fleet with his obsession about new clothes and decorations. Regardless of regulations he foisted gold lace and bullion on the officers and put them in scarlet and blue instead of white and blue (a piece of sacrilege which Their Lordships cancelled as soon as he had gone), until only the wealthiest and idlest could hope to keep up with the fashion. Two innovations caught on, among dozens: one was the sensible flat blue uniform cap, which replaced the medley of top hats, bowler hats and cocked hats indiscriminately worn at sea. The other was a ceremonial creation.

The Lord High Admiral appointed four admirals and six captains to his person as aides: old friends whom he liked to have about him and whom he could festoon to his heart's content with gilded knots and aiguillettes. Monarchs ever since have appointed naval aides-de-camp, generally taking them from the top of the list of captains who have missed their chances of promotion to admiral. Queen Victoria carried the habit a step farther when she created the post of Personal Naval Aide-de-Camp—a job for some naval member of the Royal family. Nowadays the Royal Marines and the Naval Reserves each supply an aide for the sovereign, but the total number is kept to about eight.

Canning's motive in reviving the post of Lord High Admiral had been to free the Government of a rather embarrassing

H 2

personage by giving him a position of dignity in which he could indulge his love of finery and ceremony and have to keep his mouth shut. The Prime Minister underestimated the Prince's self-confidence and dedication to the Service. William saw his Council as ciphers and himself as the concentration of naval power, not the other way about.

The causes of the first-class row which developed between himself and the senior Lord, Cockburn, were plain to all who had dealings in Admiralty. The Prince took all the routine on himself; he wanted his own way about everything; he could not resist making communications with his old seafaring cronies, in the name of the Lords, in terms not at all consistent with the dignity of naval government. To the imposing document which charged Admiral Codrington with his solemn duty at Navarino, the Lord High Admiral appended his own postscript: 'Go it, Ned.'

He relied more on his private secretary's advice (Captain Robert Spencer, ex-*Owen Glendower*) than on that of the Admiralty Secretary, said Croker. He stood out against the Prime Minister exercising the naval patronage, which was instrumental to governing Scotland. He tied the Government's hands with rash public utterances: the Cabinet decided to censure Codrington for his conduct at Navarino, but the Prince had expressed 'precipitate approbation' and they were obliged to make him a hero instead. After the battle, Clarence heaped insult upon indiscretion by enthusiastically distributing honours and awards, without consulting the ministry.

His failings were too numerous to count, in fact, and he added to them daily; but the worst failing of all was his inability, as brother of the King, to serve the Government as a member of the House of Lords. The humblest captain in the Navy, had he been also a member of Parliament, would have been more use as Lord High Admiral (from Mr Canning's or the

Duke of Wellington's point of view). In William's hands a powerful weapon of coercion grew rusty.

To add to disquiet, a suspicion became a certainty: that Prince William had inherited more than a touch of the excitable madness of his father George III. In Greville's memoirs the Prince's 'absurd speeches' and 'morbid official activity' were manifestations of 'a general wildness which was thought to indicate incipient insanity'.

'We have now got a Tory Government,' says Greville's entry for 12th June 1828, 'and all that remains of Canning's party are gone.' The new Prime Minister, the Duke of Wellington, seemed not so patient with royal eccentricities; and George IV was tired of rescuing his brother from procedural impasses that he, with all his faults, steered clear of. To the Lord High Admiral's last appeal for help in getting his First Lord out of the way, the King replied: 'You are in error from the beginning to the end . . . the thing is impossible . . . you must give way.' And in August he followed up the advice with a letter dismissing, not Cockburn, but William himself.

'The Lord High Admiral was turned out,' reports Greville. 'The Duke told him he must go, but that he might resign as if of his own accord. The Duke is all-powerful. . . . Many people think that Lord Grey will join the Government and that he will be First Lord of the Admiralty.'

The diarist, whose gossip was fairly accurate as a rule, goes on a few days later: 'I do not yet know the whole truth of the Lord High Admiral's resignation, but it seems that it is not yet certain. Negotiations on the subject are still going on. I believe he quarrelled with the Council, particularly Cockburn, and the Government took part with Cockburn. The Duke of Clarence wants to promote deserving officers, but they oppose it on account of the expense, and they find in everything great difficulty in keeping him in order. His resignation will be very unpopular in the Navy, for his system of promotion was more liberal and impartial than that of his predecessor. . . .'

It was certain enough. The Iron Duke contented his intimates with the short explanation that 'he behaved very rudely to Cockburn. I saw Cockburn and Croker and both agreed in stating the machine could no longer work'.

In the formal setting of the Board Room in the Admiralty building, Admiral of the Fleet the Duke of Clarence, gorgeously robed as though for installation as an emperor, laid down his office in the presence of his Council. It should have been a solemn occasion—the disappearance for ever, as most would have been aware, of the majesty and dignity of one of the ancient Great Offices of State. But William spoiled it.

He was at his red-faced, twitchy and wool-gathering worst and, after making 'a very confused speech', allowed himself to be led downstairs. Next day the Board of Admiralty became a Board again and Sir George Cockburn, no doubt with relief as well as gratification, welcomed a new First Lord Commissioner to his rightful place at the head of the table.

William, Duke of Clarence, hovers still about the Admiralty Board Room, a corpulent spectre with chops like half-filled sandbags. The wall-painting, the fine old silver inkstand—his parting gift—and other relics and associations are scattered through the Old Admiralty building like symbols of atonement for the rough handling the sailor Lords gave the last Lord High Admiral on his short, stormy passage to extinction.

18 Gales of Change

The Lord High Admiral yielded to a First Lord who, a year earlier, had yielded to him. He was Robert Dundas, second Viscount Melville, of whom Scott wrote: 'Though not a literary man, he is judicious, clairvoyant and uncommonly sound-headed, like his father'—the father being the unlucky First Lord of 1804. His first administration had lasted fifteen years, from 1812 to 1827—longer by more than half that of any other in the century. His second, from 1828, ended when the long Tory summer at last broke in 1830.

Melville acted throughout his two terms of office with caution and a respect for his professional advisers. During the second he seemed particularly careful to make none of the mistakes of his predecessor or to ruffle Admiral Cockburn. The clairvoyancy with which Scott credited him was not evident in his attitude towards Steam, if the declaration ascribed to him can be believed, that any attempt to introduce Steam into the Royal Navy must be suppressed because it would 'deal a fatal blow to British naval supremacy'.

A glance at an atlas shows where Lord Melville's talents lay: in encouraging explorations, especially on the north-western routes. There is a Melville in Saskatchewan, a Melville Bay in Greenland, Melville Island and Melville Sound in the northern territories of Canada and a Melville Land in Labrador. He also sent Captain Fitzroy round the world in H.M.S. *Beagle*, with Darwin on board.

In general, the Admiralty, like other Government departments, followed the safe peacetime policies associated with Tory governments until 1830 when, having scarcely sniffed power in their political lifetimes, the Whigs stormed in. Earl Grey turned the civil service upside down, reducing manpower and expenditure and, as reformers given their heads are apt to do, destroyed much that was good with much that was bad.

In charge of the Admiralty he placed a landowning member of Parliament from Cumberland named Sir James Graham, whom no one knew anything about. Contemporaries found him 'tall, handsome, stiff and pompous'—stiff, but not brittle. It soon appeared that his patron had dug up the perfect civil servant: a dignified character of notable industry and loyalty, with a phenomenal memory; a person who, in his rather supercilious way, heard all sides of an argument patiently and then, firmly and unequivocally, made up his mind.

He took perhaps more literally than was intended the Prime Ministers' instruction that 'some concentration' would be needed of Admiralty, Navy Board and Victualling Board. Ample scope for concentration existed. The new First Lord grasped the controls of an antiquated, creaking piece of machinery, which ran on confused precedent and inter-departmental snobbery, with hampering traditions and rituals all its own.

At the Navy Board he found eleven Principal Officers, growing old and tetchy in the service; once in, they had always been difficult to get out. They presided over thirteen separate offices distributed all over London. As their Board, though jealously guarding its own secrets, depended in a sense from the Board of Admiralty, so three more distinct Boards depended from them, the huge sprawling complex of Victualling and the tiny less-ancient offshoots called Transports and Sick and Hurt; and none missed an opportunity of demonstrating its own departmental self-sufficiency.

The clerks toiled by candle-light in cellars and attics—

nothing unusual in that, but Navy Office and Victualling Board cellars were that little bit untidier, mustier and dirtier than most. One man hardly knew what his neighbour was doing, offices side by side had no idea of each other's function, although the work of one might go hand in hand with that of the other, or even duplicate it.

Appointments to the meanest post and to the most lucrative were governed solely by Interest. There had never been an entrance examination for the Navy's civil side. No one had ever been known to get the sack, except when a change of Government brought a reshuffle of the higher offices. The clerks, earning tiny salaries but having plenty of time on their hands, ran their own small businesses and scarcely troubled to conceal the fact. Victualling assistants kept complicated sets of books on systems they alone could understand, quite unintelligible to auditors. Flagrant dishonesty had become so much the rule among seniors that the Navy Commissioners had given up issuing reproaches. Offenders never lost their jobs; the worst that could happen to them was to be ordered to pay back by easy instalments the money they had stolen.

To the great Reform session of Parliament in 1832, Sir James Graham contributed his Admiralty Bill, a comprehensive work which put the naval administration on a completely new footing. All the Boards, great and small, had to go, except the Board of Admiralty. Their Lordships would take over the Principal Officers' duties as well as their own (but one Principal Officer, as we have seen, the Surveyor of the Navy, would become a permanent member of the Board of Admiralty).

Graham's idea was not exactly original. The Duke of Wellington had already reorganised the Ordnance Office, that other byword for bureaucratic chaos, on a similar plan. Graham emphasised this point when presenting the Bill, instead of claim-

ing credit for himself. He was wise to do so. Decades later
(he probably foresaw it: he was that kind of man), whenever
the need arose to put in a good word for the Admiralty, it
would be enough to remind its critics that the great Duke of
Wellington himself had devised the system it was built on.

Without much debate and in a comparatively short time,
that 'divided control' which, in the words of Sir Oswyn
Murray, 'had maintained the Navy in the time of its greatest
achievements', was lumped into one. The name of Navy
Board, older than Admiralty in its departmental sense, vanished.
So did the name of Victualling Board, after not far short of
four hundred years. The latter, before the Admiralty swallowed
it, had swallowed Transports and Sick and Hurt in a First Lord's
preliminary concentration exercise.

Sir James helped the Navy Board into oblivion with a merci-
less exposure of its current misdeeds and a cold unfriendly survey
of the disreputable part of its past: an attack on the corpse of
one ·of Britain's most-maligned institutions which drew an
indignant protest from Mr Croker. The sight of a First Lord
and his Secretary going hammer-and-tongs in Parliament over
the epitaph for an ancient naval department was not, to Sir
John Briggs, who was there, the most edifying spectacle on
which to ring down the trianchored curtain at Somerset House.

Rulers of the King's Navy have been in turn Great Admirals
or Admirals of England; Lords High Admiral; groups of
Commissioners; and a regular Board of Admiralty, of which
the chairman has assumed increasing importance as First Commissioner or First Lord.

The Admiralty's constitution has been, like the British
Government's, unwritten and open to diverse interpretation, its
powers and activities dependent on the individual personality
of the man at the top or his ambitious aides, its way of con-

ducting its affairs related more to custom and precedent than to the few laws and Orders in Council which from time to time regulated it—which, if you came to look closely at them, were a mass of contradictions and irreconcilables.

No ruler before Sir James Graham ('Jemmy' to the Fleet) acted with more independence or more whole-hearted support from Crown or Cabinet; none is to do so again, until he himself returns to office during the Crimean War.

In the document which became the Admiralty Act, 1832, Sir James defines the duties of a British Admiralty for the first time: (1) the maintenance and expansion of the Fleet in accordance with Government policy; (2) the supply of trained personnel to the Fleet; (3) the distribution of the Fleet over the world; and (4) the preservation of the Fleet in a state of readiness and efficiency.

If Anson was the father of the modern Navy, Graham was its guardian, tutor and friend for four crucial years of office, the first First Lord to discard the remnants of old feudal trappings and appear in sober modish dress. The scheme of direction he laid down for the naval government in Whitehall was the basis for all subsequent Admiralties. The Board which he re-designed and presided over was essentially the same as that which conducted naval operations in World War II. It consisted of :

The First Lord (himself, and ever after to be a Cabinet Minister and a civilian): to represent the Navy in Parliament and to be responsible for it to the Crown and the country.

Four Naval Lords (not yet 'Sea Lords', but admirals who were sometimes called the Professional Lords to distinguish them from the civil, or Lay Lords): to run the Fleet and dockyards.

One Civil Lord: to look after finance and works ashore which involved non-naval personnel.

Two Secretaries: one for parliamentary business and one

for the Board itself.

All were to sit round the same table with an equal voice in debate, as of old. But not for another hundred years would a secretary be admitted as a full member of the Board and get a gold-embossed anchor on his blotting-pad.

Graham took the five Principal Officers of ancient lineage (Henry VIII's four plus the Victualler), abolished the Comptroller and brought in a newcomer, the Physician-General, and made them all heads of departments, responsible to one of the Naval Lords or the Civil Lord. They became the Surveyor (from whom the modern Director of Naval Construction traces his descent); the Accountant-General (ex-Navy Treasurer); the Storekeeper-General (ex-Clerk, the modern Director of Stores); the Superintendent of Victualling (now Director of Victualling); and the Physician of the Navy (these days the Medical Director-General). Some further rearrangement was to occur before long; notably the Surveyor's elevation to the Board as Controller of the Navy.

History proved the transformation, at one time considered a wild blunder, a sensible change. Arguments for an amalgamation had been overwhelming. Fears that Their Lordships would lose caste by being exposed to the familiarities of the departments they had to keep an eye on were expressed; the Fleet liked to imagine its Admiralty as a secret conclave of supermen remote from everyday affairs. Very occasionally the Admiralty was to find it needed an inner executive council—in the Crimean War and the First World War, for instance; but it always could, and did, appoint one.

Board members, Graham emphasised, must not be regarded as superior heads of departments. They must not get involved in technicalities. Their job was to ' execute the office of Lord High Admiral of the United Kingdom and territories thereunto belonging, and of the High Admiral of the colonies and dominions'—jointly and coequally. Each Lord retained his freedom of communication with another, and with the First Lord. Each member was encouraged to speak his mind about matters which did not concern departments under him, just as boldly as he spoke about those which did.

The First Lord made it clear to his colleagues that, while speech was free, decisions were his alone. The system could not work, he said, unless 'the First Lord is supreme and does constantly exercise supreme and controlling authority'. The admirals raised their eyebrows. Orders in Council later in the century (1869 and 1872) confirmed this 'sole responsibility' of the First Lord—but there were difficulties in the Act and the knotty problem remained, to be poked at by several parliamentary commissions whose findings only revealed how varied were the views of civil servants and senior officers about it. The Act allowed, for example, any two Lords to constitute a Board and legalise action in an emergency. (Afterwards it was any two Lords and the Secretary.) Such a Board once met at sea in a yacht, when it was a question of sending an urgent operational order to the Fleet.

Graham's reforms reached into the darkest crevices of old Navy Board territory. He replaced the civil commissioners of the dockyards with naval superintendents—rear-admirals, commodores and captains, according to the importance of the yard; and sea officers began to take command of the victualling yards. No tired, sprawling, dead-and-alive department of Navy, however, was revitalised with more skill and enthusiasm than the old Pay Office. The Accountant-General was John Briggs (afterwards Sir John), a bureaucratic wizard of scarcely less reforming zeal than the First Lord, with whom he came into office. He was to hold the job for twenty-two years and was able to devote nineteen of them to domestic naval accounting, after the Paymaster-General of the Forces took over the time-wasting part of the Navy Treasurer's duties in 1835.

By modern standards Briggs ran a small department (a staff of eighty-eight, compared with eight hundred in 1924 and about eight thousand in 1964), but he set Whitehall alight by insisting that his ne'er-do-well clerks and new applicants for vacancies take an entrance examination: the beginning of competition in the civil service, and strange that it should have arisen in a notoriously backward corner of bureaucracy.

Sea officers got a substantial rise in pay the year Briggs arrived, only eight years after a previous one. (The ratings had to wait until 1852 and 1862.) The first Accountant-General's historic duty was to start the new machinery for claiming and disbursing the moneys which Parliament votes the Navy annually for its upkeep: the Naval Estimates. It requires a brief explanation, because it was to become with small variations a permanent feature of the administration.

The Estimates were divided into sixteen Votes. Vote 'A' laid down the total numbers of officers and men to be borne on the Navy's books in the course of the year. The other Votes, numbered one to fifteen, categorised the Navy's probable requirements under separate broad headings—naval stores, victualling stores, medical stores and so on. They were the 'money Votes'. Every penny the Admiralty spent had to be accounted for under one of those headings. The First Lord presented the Estimates to Parliament every year, usually in March, and a committee of members went through them Vote by Vote, approving or amending each total for expenditure in the next financial year.

Once Parliament accepted the amounts, the Admiralty could spend up to each of them. Groups of Votes came under the different Lords, of course, and they were allowed to set off a surplus against a deficiency under the sub-heads within a Vote, but not to carry surpluses forward to the next year nor to transfer a saving from one Vote to another.

The preparation of Naval Estimates, in nothing like so systematic a fashion, had always been the Navy Board's job. The Principal Officers had spent the whole year on it, doing a bit at a time, and the Lord Treasurer had provided the Navy Treasurer every week with a statement—or had been supposed to—which showed him what he had drawn and how much remained. In the Graham-Briggs era, only the First Lord and the Civil Lord (Briggs's superior) signed the Estimates, although naturally the whole Board helped to make them up. Each week, as before, the Accountant-General received his statement of account from the Treasury, and the Directors of Navy Accounts were still receiving it in the twentieth century. (In 1869, Mr Hugh Childers, another maker and breaker of Board Room traditions, ordered all the Lords to sign the Estimates. This was done ever afterwards, except in 1887, when they went before Parliament without Admiral Lord Charles Beresford's name on them because he said he had not been given enough time to study them.)

The Accountant-General's crusade stood out as an example of the new spirit of Admiralty, but the effect of a clever, calculating and industrious First Lord was reflected, as we shall see over the next two or three decades, in other branches too. Not every abuse was wafted away. Some, by powerful reformers who were still, with all their far-sighted notions, prisoners of their times, were not recognised as abuses. Party affiliations still outranked professional ability, as Sir Thomas Troubridge the younger, whom Graham pulled on to the Board, pointed out when turning away an otherwise well-qualified young officer: " You were at Barham Down election, Sir, and had the largest Tory cockade of your party. . . . If we have an appointment to dispose of, and A is for us and B against us, we give it to A."

Admiral Troubridge, a dedicated Whig like his chief, came in after 1832. The Naval Lords who first assembled under 'Jemmy' Graham were less than moderately distinguished as individuals—all except one—but they were an historic quartet and deserve a pen-sketch:

Sir Thomas Hardy, First Naval Lord, with responsibility for the Surveyor: the exception. Not a political figure, not even a member of Parliament, but a man who had spent his whole life at sea, had captained the *Victory* and held the dying Nelson in his arms; was probably the most popular admiral in the Fleet. A diffident figure, conscious of his homely background and unexciting appearance. Inarticulate. Had modern ideas and was fond of introducing in his speeches the axiom that ' Britain should take the lead and keep the lead '—but in council would often submit for the sake of avoiding argument, although he knew he was in the right. He followed the elegant Cockburn, the Duke of Clarence's antagonist, to the Admiralty, and one of his early duties was to appoint Sir George to command the West Indies station. A snatch of conversation has survived: " My dear Hardy, I have come to receive your instructions, as you know I am now under your orders."—" Pray make any corrections in them you think fit, Sir."—" Oh, it is not for me, Hardy, to make corrections. I will merely offer any suggestion that may occur to me."

Admiral Dundas, Second Naval Lord, with responsibility for the Storekeeper-General: a relative of Lord Melville, the previous First Lord; the ' caretaker ' Comptroller, in the last months of Tory rule.

Sir John Pechell, Third Naval Lord and responsible for the Superintendent of Victualling: a worn-out, white-haired sea-dog, racked with gout, scarcely able to see and quite unable to get about without crutches.

Captain Berkeley, Fourth Naval Lord and responsible for the Navy's medical departments.

The Board's chief clerk has described a typical meeting of the eighteen-thirties. The Lords Commissioners were assembled in good time—about eleven a.m.—eagerly discussing with each other (they were all M.P.s except Hardy) the business of the House of Commons of the night before. Sir John Pechell had been at the opera afterwards and turned the talk on Mrs Norton, who had looked ' perfectly lovely ' and Lady Lyndhurst, whom he had never seen ' make such an infernal guy of herself '. The gossip drifted into a debate on the chances of survival of various shaky old admirals and the effect on the Navy List of their hoped-for demise. Much speculation eddied round a rumour that Admiral X was about to marry a widow with the best wine-cellar in London. At that moment Sir James Graham stalked in and all the members became extremely interested in their documents, which until that time they had not bothered to look at.

Sir James advanced to the head of the table and made a stately bow to each member in turn. He sat down and said briskly that, as there seemed to be a great many papers to get through, it would be best to proceed at once to the despatch of the business.

Not much missed his eye. He suddenly said to Pechell, " What do you think we should do in this case ? " The Third Naval Lord, rather red under his snowy locks, had to admit he had lost the place. " It is strange," said the First Lord with a laugh, " but, do you know, that is exactly what I had been thinking ? " He went on: " I must request the members of the Board to be so obliging as to minute their papers either before or after the meeting of the Board, but certainly not while the reading is going on, for it is a farce to meet for the despatch of business if the members do not attend to it."

He had an especial down on Pechell that day, the chief clerk remembers, and continually found fault with him until Hardy tried to smooth things over with: "Don't be too hard upon a man in love, Sir, you really must not."

"A man in *what* ?" (Pechell is the ancient mariner of the Board.)

"He is going to be married, Sir."

"Then," said Sir James, all benevolence and graciousness, "I beg you ten thousand pardons, Sir John. It fully accounts for a man being a little *égaré*."

With modification, it might be a directors' meeting in modern industry. Their Lordships of the eighteen-thirties took a decided turn in the direction of the present day. The Board Room atmosphere of Lord Melville's second administration had been not far removed from that of Anson's time; the Board Room atmosphere under Graham was more in line with that of McKenna's, of Geddes's or of Bridgeman's.

19 Lords of Leisure

Admiralty House went on a long lease to the House of Lords after the Graham family moved out. A procession of peers took the naval administration to the middle of the century: Earl Grey, the Earl of Auckland (twice), the Earls of Minto, Haddington and Ellenborough.

Domestically a good deal of quiet progress was made. Improvements in recruitment and training, in getting hold of good sailors and keeping them, gained momentum. Sailors of the eighteen-forties were pampered to a degree their fathers would have thought absurd. They could make allotments of pay to their dependents, for one thing; they got proper monthly payments, in advance, for another. A seaman when Victoria came to the throne could enter the Service with the option of taking up a continuous form of engagement, which ran for five years in the first instance, with regular leave periods and some choice of ships or stations. This at least was the situation on paper: Sir James had struggled hard to get it going and had paved the way with a Register of Seamen—that long-awaited blueprint for manning and mobilisation, which the French had had for about three hundred years. "And much good it did them," Hardy might have said. But not until after the Crimean War did the long-service full-time seaman come to stay.

On joining the Navy, a young man went to a training ship, H.M.S. *Illustrious* at Portsmouth, where he could learn to read and write as well as splice hawsers and run out on yards. The

Illustrious took officer cadets as well (the Admiralty applied the
word 'cadet' to its commission candidates in 1843). They
moved in from the Royal Naval College, never a highly successful institution, which Earl Grey closed in 1837 just after it had
celebrated its centenary. They moved out again to go aboard
the *Britannia*, an obsolete three-decker fitted out as a floating
schoolroom. When a nation suddenly self-conscious about
morals and welfare made up its mind that Portsmouth provided
the wrong environment for delicately-nurtured young gentlemen, the Admiralty had to send *Britannia* to Dartmouth, where
the Royal Naval College of present times was built.

The ordinary seaman, if he were scientifically minded and
lucky, might go on from the *Illustrious* to the *Excellent*, another
training ship, to become a seaman gunner. H.M.S. *Excellent*,
a hulk until 1827, had been turned into a School of Naval
Artillery by the Duke of Clarence, after suggestions made by
Sir Howard Douglas ten years earlier.

Service histories sometimes give the impression that Britain's
Navy hoisted itself painfully into the nineteenth and twentieth
centuries without the aid of its ruling body; in the teeth, in
fact, of storms of reactionary wind from hidebound admirals
on the Board whose brains had seized up shortly after the Battle
of Trafalgar. The view is coloured by gossip items of the
period, some authenticated and some not, and none of them
typical.

Sir George Cockburn, dashing Nelsonian captain, leading
fashion-plate of the London scene, maintained as long as he
remained a Lord Commissioner that where the Royal Navy
was concerned 'everything that had been done was right, what
was being done was questionable and every step in advance
was fraught with danger'. Like his fellow-Tory, Croker, a
man of persuasive oratory, he stood against progress like a rock.
It was hardly wise to mention Steam or Gunnery in his presence.

He stopped a junior officer who was trying to explain to the Board the principles of a simple sighting device for big guns with: " My young friend, it seems to me you have gone gunnery mad, for [the sights] are little more or less than damned gimcracks."

Two Lords of Earl Grey's Board, Sir John Beresford and Sir Charles Rowley, pondered the results of H.M.S. *Excellent's* gunnery trials:

Sir Charles: " Do you know, this is very strange, but I don't understand all this. Pray, Sir, what is the meaning of the word ' impact ' ? " (The Secretary explained that it meant the force of a blow.) " Then what, in the name of good fortune, is meant by ' initial velocity ' ? "

Sir John: " I'll be hanged if I know. . . . I'll tell you what I think we'd better do. We'll just go at once to Lord de Grey and get that *Excellent* paid off. The Chancellor is very anxious to get a reduction made in the Estimates."

Even experts make pronouncements which, in the light of subsequent events, they do not care to be reminded of. (One thinks of Lord Rosebery calling the old-age pension proposal ' so prodigal of expenditure as likely to undermine the whole fabric of Empire ', and Professor Hoyle as recently as 1952 stating that a moon-landing and return to earth was not to be thought of for at least a hundred years.) Viscount Melville's is often quoted—we have already quoted a bit of it: " Their Lordships feel it their bounden duty to discourage to the utmost of their ability the employment of Steam vessels, as they consider that Steam is calculated to strike a fatal blow to the naval supremacy of the Empire."

A biographer of Lord Melville denies that he ever said it. There is some doubt, too, about the statement of 1850, attributed to the First Lord, Sir Francis Baring, which Lord Fisher repeated in his memoirs: ' The Admiralty opposes the building of ironclads, because iron is heavier than wood, and will sink.'

Quite early, in fact, the Board of Admiralty opened its
eyes to Steam. It allowed Lieutenant James Hosken, R.N., to
become master of the steamship *Great Western* in 1837, and
called for reports on his numerous Atlantic crossings. It sent
Edward Chappell on an experimental cruise round the British
Isles in the *Archimedes*, the first screw-ship ever built.

Steam gave the Admiralty apparently incurable headaches in
the logistic and strategic areas, apart from bringing in a race
of technicians who fitted in badly and could not for a long time
be regarded as suitable companions for real sailors. From the
quantities of fuel which early steamships consumed before the
development of the water-tube boiler, Their Lordships foresaw
the need for coaling ports all over the world, merely to keep
the Fleet mobile; an impossible consideration during an era of
economy in public spending, when the nation, with no war in
the offing, naturally looked on the Navy as an expensive piece
of prestige advertising.

British sailing warships, ironically, were just coming to
perfection when Steam blotted out their silhouettes. At a
period when the more business-like of merchant shipping lines
were discarding masts and sails, the star pupil of the College
of Naval Architecture (founded 1808, when the realisation that
foreign warships were better designed than British had sunk in)
came of age—came into the job of Surveyor of the Navy, in
fact, which he graced from 1832 to 1848. He was Sir William
Symonds, architect of beautiful warships, and he should have
lived eighty years earlier.

Practical objections against Steam—that the paddles interfered with arcs of fire—disappeared in 1845, when the Admiralty of Lord Haddington organised the famous tug-of-war
between the paddle-steamer *Alecto* and the screw-ship *Rattler*.
Thereafter the naval building programme included increasing

numbers of screw-ships, although the Admiralty always remained
faithful to paddlers for dockyard tugs and harbour craft. Few
sights brought home more vividly the esoteric fascination of
Admiralty than the steam-tugs in action at a naval base—like
that which Turner portrays, hauling the fighting *Téméraire* up
river—when their cigarette-shaped funnels glowed cherry-red at
their bases and comet-tails of sparks flew from their tops.

Among the objects which foreign naval officers still try not
to smile at in British naval yards are the noisy, thrashing paddle-
wheelers of a not much later vintage which nose the missile
cruisers and nuclear submarines in and out of their berths.
Perhaps it was the noise of 1844, when the Admiralty already
had a temperamental steam-tug or two in its service (while
the Royal Mail Steam Packet Company and other 'iron' lines
were steaming round the world), which inspired the instruction
to the Fleet:

'As the order between "starboard" and "port" is so
much more marked than that between "starboard" and "larboard" it is Their Lordships' direction that the word "larboard" shall no longer be used.'

But for many years the Admiralty was to order commanding
officers of steam warships to use their mechanical power only
for entering and leaving difficult harbours. Life afloat was
cleanish, if not particularly healthy, but Steam produced a kind
of dirt the Navy simply could not get used to. Funnel smuts
brought exquisitely-dressed and paintwork-conscious officers to
the verge of nervous breakdowns. And it was more than a
rumour that Their Lordships measured a captain's fitness for
promotion by his skill in making one bunkering last through
a commission of three or four years.

A single 'Steam Repair Yard' at Woolwich was thought
enough in the eighteen-forties for the foreseeable needs of the
Royal Navy. Within a few years the First Lord's outlook had

altered entirely, and new machinery shops, building slips and docks were laid out in Chatham, Portsmouth and Devonport; and the old disused yard at Deptford (closed in the Napoleonic wars) was reopened.

The Admiralty kept its sailing ships until the beginning of the present century, but it was among the first of the great naval administrations to abandon sail-training for its cadets and young seamen. Steam warships remained fully-rigged until after the *Captain* disaster of 1870, of which more in a future chapter. Huge masts and canvas by the acre went aboard the big ones, for sail-power had to be suited to much heavier tonnages. 'The Admiralty said, "The engines might break down, and then where would you be?"' (Admiral Penrose Fitzgerald.)

Miracle-working admirals and politicians are too disconcerting an influence at the Admiralty to be tolerated except in time of national desperation, and through the long peace—disturbed only by the Crimean War, which was over before half the Navy knew it had begun—Their Lordships aged in mind and body, and were replaced but slowly and reluctantly. There was at least one period when every Lord Commissioner and every Commander-in-Chief, at home and abroad, was in his eighties.

Tales recounted of them, by the clerks and secretaries whom they daily shocked and amused, would fill a book—but not everyone would believe them.

In the course of a desultory conversation about gunnery, the Secretary ventured to tell Lord Auckland, "You will be surprised, my Lord, to hear that a battery established at Ryde could completely destroy the buildings in Portsmouth dockyard, three miles away."—"I am indeed surprised," said the First Lord sharply, "to hear you talk such nonsense."

The senior Naval Lord of that day, ' a gallant officer and a splendid specimen of a flag officer of the old school', was Sir Charles Adam—amiable in appearance, prone to mislay his spectacles and his papers, but perpetually irritated. He could never speak, says his clerk, without ' getting excited, talking loud, looking fierce and thumping the table. . . .' On one occasion he delivered a soliloquy for the benefit of the Board, got very angry, stood up and shouted: " I say it *is* so ! " Whereupon Lord Auckland calmly remarked, " I am not aware that anyone has contradicted you." (Sir Charles rather lamely answered, " But I thought they might.")

When Ellenborough, who had made his reputation in India and been ennobled for it, took his seat as First Lord, his professional colleagues prepared to behave themselves and keep their reminiscences of youthful adventures with Howe and Saint Vincent for a more suitable occasion. The Earl placed a chronometer on the Board Room table and said that in future he expected everyone to be in his place at one minute past eleven o'clock. He listened in silence to the discussion on matters arising from the minutes of the previous meeting until the First Naval Lord came to the item on H.M.S. *Stromboli*, which he pronounced in Navy fashion, ' Strombóli '. " For God's sake, have mercy on my Eton ears, Sir William," cried his Lordship. Somehow it led to mention of India, which was all the First Lord was waiting for and thereafter, throughout Lord Ellenborough's time, the Board meetings were devoted to helping him fight his old campaigns again, while the Secretary, Sir John Barrow, who served the Admiralty for forty-one years, administered the Navy on his own.

Lord Minto, who took his job on the understanding that he would frame the Naval Estimates on the lowest possible scale, had the satisfaction of seeing the Fleet numerically reduced to rock bottom during his administration. ' Look back upon the

year '14,' an old flag officer begged the Duke of Wellington
in a pamphlet—he meant 1814, but the situation was uncannily
similar a century later—'Look back upon the year '14 and the
Emperor Alexander with other crowned heads, sailing in and
admiring the English Fleet. Observe the contrast in '38—
England without a fleet and her ambassador, Lord Durham,
sailing in and admiring the Russian Baltic Fleet, which could
then and *may next summer* desolate England, ruin her commerce
and blockade her shores, unless England is aroused from her
stupor.'

The Paris *Journal des Débats* of November 1838 was quoted
in *The Times*: 'If we strike the "vessels unfit for sea" out of
the pompous list of the British Navy published by the British
Admiralty, we shall find that Great Britain herself cannot muster
a greater number of vessels than France.'

Lord Minto, unable to find admirals who agreed with his
parsimonious policies, surrounded himself with non-naval politicians. Serving officers whimpered about being managed by ig-
noramuses, and having to make bricks without straw; Whitehall
pretended the Fleet had never been in better heart. The naval
spokesmen, a member of Parliament complained, made such
conflicting statements that the country was becoming disgusted
with the administration and considered itself 'completely *humbugged*'. Napoleonic veterans asked what else could you expect
when a pack of civilians had been let loose on the Admiralty ?
Just across the Horse Guards Parade, at the War Office, the
military staff were soldiers every one, the Secretary-at-War a
colonel and the whole Board of Ordnance military men, with
not even a naval officer to look after naval armaments. The
First Lord, by contrast, had no seagoing experience and neither
had two of his four junior Lords. Counting the two secretaries,
the Navy was outnumbered five to two in the Grand Council
of the Navy.

Somerset House, circa *1790*

Admiralty Office, Whitehall, circa *1730*

Sir James Graham

On the executive side, a step below them, the Surveyor it was true was a naval officer; but his deputy, and the joint surveyors and Accountant-General, were all civilians, and the Director of Victualling was a major-general: you had to go to the bottom of the hierarchy to find two more sailors: the Storekeeper - General and the lowly Superintendent of Transports.

Reports of Lord Minto's speeches when introducing the Estimates ring strangely in modern ears: " The Navy does not require an increase, we have ships enough already. . . ."— " [We cannot] employ all the seamen which the country has voted." (A naval member of Parliament told him that the Flag Officer at Sheerness was being pulled round his command by Royal Marines, not being able to find enough seamen to make up a barge's crew.)

The Admiralty in the nineteenth century was responsible for running the mail-and-passenger service between England and France. Lord Minto's Political Secretary has described how he had to concoct an outrageous plan for building new battle-ships and pretend to relinquish it under bitter protest, in order to get the consolation prize of a new Dover packet. Such was the ignorance of the majority on the Board that he nearly got the battleships as well.

Lord Minto and his colleagues had no monopoly of ignorance. When Sir Charles Wood was First Lord (1855 to 1858), the Board had to consider a complaint from a father whose twelve-year-old boy had been refused entry into the Navy because he had not known the capital of Madagascar. "I'm sure I don't know, either," said Sir Charles to the First Naval Lord. "Do you ?"

He did not, nor did any member of the Board. "Mr Phinn," said Sir Charles to the Permanent Secretary, "as a first-class man, I'm sure you know ?"

I

Mr Phinn reflected and suggested they call in the Hydrographer of the Navy. When Sir Francis Beaufort arrived and the question was put to him he looked embarrassed and said he would have to make enquiries in his department. He returned even more ill at ease with the information that no one could tell him. Half an hour later a slip of paper reached the Secretary with the name ' Antananarivo ' written on it. Their Lordships unanimously agreed to admit the candidate.

Sir Charles Wood, afterwards Viscount Halifax, saw the last of the great fleet of Nelsonic three-deckers broken up or converted to coaling hulks—great by contemporary standards, insignificant enough compared with the ironclads of the coming generation.

A theory tenaciously held by Admiralty constructors stated that ships more than two hundred and fifty feet long (a quarter the length of a modern transatlantic liner) could never be a success because they would infallibly ' hog '—that is, break their backs. Old Sir Thomas Hardy ("I never knew Hardy wrong on any professional subject," Nelson had said) had always advocated during his two long spells as First Naval Lord the need for bigger ships and heavier armament and on his deathbed he told Mr Briggs: "I venture to predict that you will see vessels of five hundred feet and more, and even they will not ' hog '. . . . You will see great changes in naval architecture. Some people laugh at science, but science will alter the whole character of the Navy. Depend upon it, Steam and gunnery are in their infancy." Sir Thomas had some of the vision, but unluckily none of the eloquence, of Fisher and Churchill.

In the ' admirals' corner ' at the United Service Club in Pall Mall—the far end of the dining-room—Their Lordships got through as much business as in the Board Room of the Admiralty round the block. There, over the port, the appointments and promotions were settled, with the aid of influential old cronies retired from the Service.

Sir Charles Adam, when he was First Naval Lord, told one of them how miserable his mealtimes were made by an officer who kept pestering him for the command of a battleship. " I know the fellow," said the wise old man. " Give him one." Sir Charles appointed him to the next vacancy.

The captain-designate called on the First Naval Lord in some confusion. He explained that he was in the middle of a lawsuit and found it most inconvenient to leave England just then. . . . " But don't let it be known at the Club, Sir Charles, that I declined a battleship."

" Oh," said the First Naval Lord, who knew that the ' admirals' corner ' was already talking of nothing else, " I cannot go as far as that."

The ' admirals' corner ', all white mops of hair, blue eyes and mottled or mahogany complexions, would pass agreeable afternoons damning the Admiralty, as soon as the last Lord Commissioner had gone back to his office. In every knot of senior officers there was a percentage for whom the Board could do no right.

Someone asked which of two officers, one distinguished but elderly and the other youthful and promising, had gained the last place on the promotion list. " The old Commander, of course," he was told.

" What an infernal shame, to clog the list with a parcel of old men after that fashion ! "

The informant begged his pardon, he had made a mistake. " It's the young one they've appointed."

" The young one ? Is it not abominable that such a mere boy should be put over the head of an old, deserving officer so cruelly passed over as that ? " He would not agree that his opinions were slightly inconsistent. " What I say is, that they should have promoted them both."

Looking retrospectively over the first half of Queen Victoria's reign, a chief clerk in the Admiralty Secretariat, whose duties put him in daily contact with the Navy's political head, admitted that he found First Lords generally anxious to do the right thing; but noticed that those most in need of advice were those least inclined to accept it. In his opinion, of the dozen or so First Lords he met, the Duke of Northumberland (1852 to 1853) served the Navy least satisfactorily, because he lacked tact and ingenuity and had a genius for going about things the wrong way. The other ducal 'supremo' of the nineteenth century, on the other hand, earned everyone's admiration. He brought ironclads in (they would have come in anyway, with or without him) and he tightened up the continuous service and boys' training schemes which no one else, not even Sir James Graham, had managed to get working properly. In the Duke of Somerset's time (1859 to 1866), says the chief clerk, ships were being prepared, stored, manned, commissioned and sent to sea ' with an alacrity unknown in the days of Sir George Cockburn and Mr Croker'.

Early First Lords had taken a stand on their dignity, if on little else. But as the century wore on the staff began to mourn the decay of Admiralty ceremony and prestige and its First Lords' diminishing pomp. ' A more dignified and more courteous nobleman than the Duke of Somerset never presided at the head of the Board Room table, and yet [says the chief clerk] I have seen His Grace enter the room for the despatch of public business with no one in waiting to receive him but the Permanent Secretary and myself.' It would never have done for Graham, Ellenborough or Auckland.

20 The Specialist Revolution

In 1839 a midshipman in a warship of the Royal Navy told the Swedish officer of the watch that 'he would be damned if he would report himself properly dressed to a foreigner'. What happened to the midshipman is not recorded, but the incident resulted in the Admiralty closing the Fleet's ranks a little more firmly with an order that after 1840 foreign subjects could no longer hold commissions in the British Navy.

It was one example of numerous incidents which forced the position of officers on Their Lordships' attention; 'warrant' officers as well as commissioned ones, since the Act of 1832 had placed them all under one headquarters. Why should they not, perhaps not all at once but eventually, be placed under one deckhead as well ? Pamphleteers and parliamentarians thought the First Lord was dragging his feet about a necessary simplification in the officer structure. Many sea officers felt that Their Lordships were racing ahead much too eagerly to swing open the wardroom door and let the despised 'warrant' ranks share what commissioned officers thought of as their 'birthright'.

The rot had set in about 1802, when Masters (navigating officers) became eligible for wardroom rank. Just over half a century later the only warrant officers *not* eligible were the gunner, the boatswain and the carpenter. During those years the Admiralty accomplished the specialist revolution, a step as notable in its narrower sphere as the contemporary abolition of child labour in the mines and factories.

It brought to officer rank the several types of non-seaman members of a ship's company, or at least brought officer rank within their reach. Some the march of science was forcing on the Navy: the engineers. Others were non-combatants who had been accepted on board almost since ships first went to sea, accepted with the good-humoured contempt the sailor keeps for someone not of his own kind, who spends every night in his hammock while real seamen are keeping a watch: the clerks, doctors, chaplains and schoolmasters.

Naval doctors had always been a mixed bunch, with a high proportion of Scots and Irishmen among them. They ranged from the talented and enquiring, who thought the hardships of life afloat a small disadvantage compared with the opportunities one had in the Navy to study tropical medicine and rare diseases, to the failures, criminals and alcoholics, and those who fled to sea from some entanglement ashore.

From the sixteen-hundreds, the time when a sailor's pay had first become more than a pittance, the ship's surgeon had lived on twopence a month from each man on board, when he could get it. He had served with a warrant from the Navy Board: classed a step above the seamen, some way below the commissioned officers.

Certain celebrated naval doctors, like Sir Gilbert Blane, put medicine in its proper place in the Fleet without much encouragement from the authorities. (It was long enough before the Victualler took note of Blane's suggestion that fifty oranges or lemons were worth an extra man in the ship's company, for the illness they prevented.) Championed by Admiral Rodney, Blane became a Commissioner of Sick and Hurt in 1795, the year Their Lordships approved an issue of lemon juice to ships in warm waters.

After Trafalgar the Admiralty was gripped with what

amounted to a craze for dosing the Fleet. They distributed Peruvian Bark (quinine, for yellow fever) and ordered captains to see that it was taken; and provided 'Admiralty Pattern' medicine chests and outfits of drugs: comparatively costly items of stores which added to the surgeon's responsibilities and therefore his standing. The mortality rate in ships, it has been estimated, dropped from forty-one per hundred in Lord Sandwich's time to nine per hundred in the second Lord Melville's.

Haslar (Portsmouth), Plymouth and Chatham hospitals, built around the seventeen-sixties, were joined in the Napoleonic era by smaller hospitals at Deal, Paignton and Yarmouth; and by 1814 by 'sick quarters'—which could mean a neat cottage hospital or a filthy room above an apothecary's shop—at or near about twenty ports round the coasts of Britain and Ireland. So-called naval hospitals and sick quarters added to the Dockyard Commissioners' worries on nine foreign stations from Madras to Barbados. (Only four, at Malta, Jamaica, Bermuda and the Cape, were proper hospitals, and we have seen that the Malta wards were dungeons until the survivors of Navarino arrived home to scandalise the country with reports of their condition.)

Bigger shore establishments and bigger ships demanded better qualified surgeons. In 1843 the Admiralty gave full commissioned rank to senior doctors; the top flight were made commanders. The medical care of the Royal Navy had passed out of the somewhat palsied hands of the Sick and Hurt Commissioners and into those of specialists more closely in touch with everyday needs, when Graham in 1832 devoted a whole department to the doctors and created a Physician-General of the Navy.

An Admiralty Order of 1833 had introduced a new medical rating, the Sick Berth Attendant. But the Florence Nightingale rumpus which revolutionised Army medical care left the Navy untouched. Reforms of the nature prescribed depended on the feminine touch, it seemed. Their Lordships, however they might disagree on details, were unanimous on the main principle, that the Navy was no place for a woman.

The Chaplain, consistently neglected by the Navy's governors, boasted an honourable ancestry in the Fleet. Sir Francis Drake's father, says Camden, 'got a place among the seamen in the King's Navy, to read prayers to them'. Chaplains of Stuart and Commonwealth times drew fourpence a month from every sailor's pay, his soul being considered twice as valuable as his body; and Samuel Pepys arranged for the Bishop of London to grant chaplains a kind of 'commission' before Their Lordships thought of doing so.

In 1701 the office of Chaplain of the Fleet appeared. A century later a ship's chaplain was receiving nineteen shillings a month in pay, a little less than that of an ordinary seaman, but Lord Gambier in 1807 raised it to £150 a year—a generous figure, considering that half the chaplains afloat would have found it hard for various reasons to get any kind of job ashore. Nelson's brother William once had thoughts of offering his services as a naval chaplain, but Horatio put him off the idea, telling him it was a miserable life.

Until Lord Gambier took an interest, chaplains had no rank or position in the ship. They lived and slept where they could find a billet, and would no more have thought of approaching wardroom officers than would the average powder-monkey.

After 1812 they got their 'warrants' from the Navy Board and in 1843, the great year of Admiralty recognition of the specialists, they became fully commissioned officers but, unlike the surgeons, were forbidden to wear uniform.

It must have been Pepys again who first sent instructors, or schoolmasters, afloat—Pepys in his last period, after he had inspired the foundation of the quasi-royal mathematical schools (at Christ's Hospital in 1673 and Greenwich in 1685), which offered tuition in ' the art of navigation and the whole science of arithmetic '. But it was the Admiralty of the last year of King William III's reign, under the guidance of the Earl of Pembroke, that established the official post of schoolmaster; and pressure from within the Fleet which increased the slow flow of schoolmasters into the Navy.

For a century the ' schoolie ' was classed among the midshipmen he schooled. When the *Britannia* set sail for what was to become the naval officer's *alma mater* at Dartmouth, the schoolmaster force of the whole Navy was borne on her books; but still it had no place in the table of rank. The Navy Commissioners could never make up their minds where the schoolmaster stood: it was left to each captain, and depended on the view he took of education.

In 1836 Their Lordships put them on the same perch as surgeons and chaplains, with ' warrant ' rank. Twenty-five years later the Duke of Somerset made rules which permitted them to become commissioned officers, and which insisted on a University degree. The branch split: he who taught young officers was the Naval Instructor; his colleagues in charge of the academic training of boy seamen kept the old title of Schoolmaster.

Newest and most inconvenient of specialists, and the last to persuade the Admiralty to admit them to commissioned rank, were the engineers. Their influx into the Royal Navy, at a rate, as Steam gathered speed, that threatened to rock the whole edifice of rank, precipitated an administrative conflict which lasted for more than half a century.

The Admiralty appointed a Comptroller of Steam Machinery

I 2

in 1837. He came under the Third Naval Lord, much to that
officer's embarrassment. Shortly afterwards the man in charge
of the engines was half-heartedly welcomed in the warrant
officers' messes of the Fleet, where he ranked ' with, but after ',
the Carpenter.

In 1847 the Admiralty gave the Engineer Officer of a warship, if it were big enough and he were senior among several,
commissioned rank. The juniors were confined to the lowliest
status, and up to the eighteen-eighties Their Lordships insisted
that the second-in-command of a battleship's engine-room—
who would be a lieutenant-commander in the twentieth century
—ranked ' with, but after ' the newest and greenest sub-lieutenant
of the upper deck aristocracy. You picked out the Engineer
Officer of those days, not only by his sooty face and hands
but also by his civilian clothes and top hat, when all the other
officers and most of the ratings wore the uniform of their rank.

Once assured that Steam had come to stay, Their Lordships
made the best of it and laid careful plans for the branch. For a
long time the engineers had better educational opportunities
than their executive opposite numbers; it was understood that
they needed them more. Full-time specialist training started
quite early, in 1864, in a building close to the Science Museum
in South Kensington, London. Growing numbers forced a
move to the Hospital at Greenwich, which became a second
Royal Naval College, in 1873. Finally the engineers settled
down at the handsome pile of buildings specially built for a
Royal Naval Engineering College at Keyham, close to the naval
barracks at Devonport, and it became their permanent home.

21 Admiralty Under Attack

Equipped with at least some of the officers and men it needed to make it a civilised up-to-date force, the new-look Navy sailed on past the middle of the nineteenth century. It did what was required of it; was never extended in a grave national crisis. There were no global conflicts: the Crimean bother was substantially an Army war. There were no disasters: the Irish famine and the Indian mutiny sent no flying squadrons hastening to the nearest port, as they would have done later on. There was no heroic nautical figure to capture the nation's imagination as Cook, Hawke, Howe and Nelson had done, no romantic character at the head of affairs, no insolent Lord Sandwich, grim Saint Vincent, domineering Barham or eccentric Clarence to colour an Admiralty anecdote. The Navy was not much in the news.

In Admiralty Orders of the period the picture was pieced together of the transformation Their Lordships were bringing about, the ruthless and reckless switches (as some of the admirals thought them) from ancient to modern, in pursuit of progress, in maintaining and expanding the Fleet. Basically, it was still Nelson's fleet, but in the vast heaps of minute sheets and memoranda one detected bewildering changes. In the space of a few years wooden ships became a rarity and iron ones common; sailing-ships took on a slightly old-fashioned look and steamships no longer alarmed the timid. Screws replaced paddles. Guns went into turrets, smooth-bores were rifled, muzzle-loaders gave way to breech-loaders. (The Board of Admiralty

cautiously resisted this innovation for a while, on the grounds
that the cartridge 'might have a retrograde action and kill
the gun-crew'.)

There was the year of the monitor: enthusiasm for shallow-
draught warships of heavy armament, inspired by the curious
encounter between floating bombardment-platforms of that type
in Hampton Roads during the American Civil War. There
followed the years of the ram-bow: a craze touched off when
the Austrian flagship successfully ploughed into the Italian
flagship at the battle of Lissa.

The gunboat arrived, that 'tool of imperialist policy', born
of experience in the Crimean War, to be with the Fleet for a
long time. Torpedoes likewise—several kinds, among which
the Admiralty (after an early wrong decision which sent the
inventor elsewhere) selected Whitehead's of 1866 to develop.

Their Lordships acknowledged their dominion over the
eastern seas and up rivers far distant from the sea (an advantage
of gunboat penetration) by revising and extending the operational areas. During the Duke of Somerset's régime, in 1864,
the East Indies station became too big to handle and the China
station was split off it and given a fleet to itself.

Strategically, from about 1855 (Sir James Graham's second
administration), one could read references in the papers to a
Naval Policy. It was based on the two-power standard which
the Earl of Chatham first tentatively proposed, which had been
revived, adopted and made into a catchword for the amateurs
to bandy about in Parliament. It would keep First Lords and
successive Governments pulling towards the same goal until
they saw the nineteenth century out.

It meant that the Royal Navy must always have more ships
in commission than the next two major naval powers put together: a handsome safety margin and, whatever the French
newspapers might say, well within the capacity of the British

Admiralty and its dockyards. But a time would come when so many strange classes of ship arose that the two-power standard was awkward to apply, even as a rough rule. Then two rival powers would go in more seriously for warship building, and race each other, until Britain was hard pressed to keep ahead of them put together. And why should she, when the next biggest powers were, say, Japan and the U.S.A., whom no one could visualise combining as allies in a war ?

By the end of the century the two-power standard would begin to look artificial. For a few years it would apply to battleships only. In 1909 Great Britain would at last decline the challenges of the rearming nations; the Conservatives demanding a hundred-per-cent superiority over the next single power (Germany) and the Liberals under Mr Churchill's influence content with sixty per cent.

It remained nothing like Nelson's Navy in the correspondence rooms and clerical boot-holes of Whitehall. The heirs of the Principal Officers, as though to compensate for their lost majesty, spread their offices through the building, taking on staff and more staff to administer a reduced fleet, until a point was reached in mid-century when it became a problem to find enough work to give the clerks even the appearance of having a regular job. An anonymous captain, distributing propaganda in 1851 for a ' Standing Navy' to replace what he called ' the present Irregular Force', described from his own experience the ' immense books of forms ' which began coming aboard ships in the forties, and explained how the shore authorities achieved some pretence of justification for their ever-lengthening pay-rolls:

' If for example a bag of biscuit is opened for the day and is found to be mouldy, the Captain has to receive long written reports thereon. He must then issue warrants to the different officers, the wording of which fills sheets of foolscap, desiring

them to survey the mouldy biscuit and to report their opinion
at length in writing. The whole reports are copied and drawn
up with as much care and form as if the life or death of a fellow-
creature depended on them.

'If the smallest thing requires repair, similar forms have to
be gone through. And, to give a still more extraordinary
instance, if an extra bucket of lime were required to wash the
holds, on which the health of all on board might depend, the
number of documents, vouchers and letters that must be written
to procure the said bucket of lime at Government expense is
such that it would drive the purser and clerks mad, besides the
possibility that a correspondence might go on *for years* with the
Admiral and the Admiralty about this same bucket of lime.'

Outwardly, the old-timers of Nelson's Navy looked decidedly
outmoded. More fragments of the archaic nomenclature fell
away. If the Duke of Northumberland is remembered for
anything, it is for turning ' purser ' into ' paymaster ', in 1852.
Within a few years, the paymaster was to be distinguished by
the addition of a strip of white cloth to his gold stripe, to indicate
his branch; the surgeons, schoolmasters and engineers got
coloured stripes at the same time.

Two Navy news items of 1864 stimulated comment and
reminiscence among the ancient mariners who slewed their
quids on the foreshore walks of the south coast towns on sunny
evenings: the red, white and blue admirals were to go, and
Admirals, Vice-Admirals and Rear-Admirals to take their
places. And the Admiralty had adopted the White Ensign for
the Navy's own, bestowed the Red on the merchant service
and kept the Blue for the Naval Reserve.

Another news item, before the year was out: Mr Gladstone
dismissed the Duke of Somerset, one of the more respected
First Lords, because he was always pestering the Government

for money for the Fleet.

The Royal Naval Reserve was a recent development by which the Admiralty hoped to avoid acute shortages of trained men when any future war broke out. 'Jemmy' Graham was unable to get it established in time for the Crimean campaign, but his successor, Sir John Pakington, set up a Commission on Manning to smooth out the obstacles. Under his scheme the Admiralty invited merchant seamen to enrol in the Reserve and offered them a small annual bounty and a pension at sixty; the ratings in return to be ready for instant mobilisation in an emergency. Though slow to catch on and full of snags at first, the scheme established itself and Boards of Admiralty refined it and expanded it ever afterwards.

Until the eighteen-fifties, crews of warships were nearly always disbanded and dispersed after a three- or four-year commission afloat. A sailor's service had to total twenty-one years —which probably brought him to the age of about sixty—in order to qualify him for a pension. But the continuous service engagement, after some false starts, was under way in Pakington's time and a proportion of British bluejackets (the word comes into use in the Duke of Somerset's administration) could regard themselves as employees of a big firm, with their rights as well as their duties, working under legal contract, provided for in illness and old age and distinguished as the British soldier had been for a century and a half (this is where 'bluejacket' is coined) with a regular uniform.

In a circular signed by R. Bernal Osborne, Secretary of the Admiralty under Sir Charles Wood, the first uniform regulations for ratings were published: blue serge frock, 'blue jean' collar with rows of thin tape (the number not specified), blue cloth trousers and black silk neckerchief, straw hat or blue cloth cap. It covered most of the clothing naval ratings had been wearing since Anson's day. The Treasury was not keen to see the Navy in uniform. The old slop-chest system worked well enough in the reign of Charles II, they said, so why not now ? But the Fleet Physician strongly supported the idea. He foresaw, and he was right, a dramatic improvement in personal cleanliness.

Sir Francis Baring in 1850 gave the sailors—but not the officers—the first Fleet mail, and free postage from ships. Hitherto the sailors had had to sew pennies on to their letters. It was a more important privilege than it sounds, for about half a ship's company were capable of writing to loved ones, and postage rates from abroad were beyond the lower deck's pocket.

Hugh Childers's Admiralty in 1869 regularised the wearing of beards in a carefully-worded document; sailors tended to take an independent stand about their own persons, and had mutinied for less. But Queen Victoria had hinted that moustaches must go, unless there was a beard to keep them company, because they gave her sailors a 'too soldierly' look. It was another rule which held good for ever: in the Royal Navy of the nineteen-sixties, men either wear the 'full set' or go clean-shaven.

The last vestiges of Georgian discipline were officially removed by the Admiralties of the sixties and seventies, having been in abeyance for the most part since before the Crimean War. Heavy corporal punishments would have been done away with earlier, but this was where the admirals had resisted. Sir John Briggs recalls the case of the grizzled able seaman who, annoyed by the impudent behaviour of a fourteen-year-old lad while he was trying to do his weekly wash on the dockside, 'insulted' him with some such phrase as "Be off, you young rascal". The boy, it turned out, was a midshipman in the Service, who at once complained to his captain, and the veteran was awarded forty-eight lashes for insubordination.

The sentence went to the Admiralty for confirmation. The lay Lords were for quashing it, but the professionals—happening at that time to outnumber them four to three—insisted it must stand, 'otherwise discipline could not be maintained'.

Yet the Naval Discipline Acts of 1861 and 1866, to which Vice-Admiral Sir William Martin, the Second Naval Lord, converted the senior officers, utterly transformed the situation at sea. Their effect was summed up in Lord Charles Beresford's nutshell phrase: "Then, 'cat' and no discipline; now, discipline and no 'cat'."

First Lord Goschen signed the Order suspending flogging as a punishment in peacetime in 1871, and First Lord Smith suspended it altogether eight years later. On the subject of suspension, the last man to be hanged at a ship's yardarm had been in his grave for some time. In 1860, on the East Indies station, a Royal Marine servant was executed for attacking his officer.

Politics and personalities still swayed the fortunes of officers, and the higher you went the trickier became the ascent. In 1854, very nearly a hundred years after the Byng tragedy, another flag officer was ordered to haul down his flag 'for not disobeying orders'; to be more accurate, for doing nothing because his instructions tied his hands. He was Admiral Napier, K.C.B., as the Thackeray rhyme has it. Napier, the only flag officer of his century to suffer such a humiliation, considered his replacement in the Baltic Fleet by Admiral Dundas, Third Naval Lord, the last indignity. Being a member of Parliament as well as an admiral, he tackled Lord Palmerston about redress for 'an old officer who has served his country faithfully'.

'Had my papers been examined by your Cabinet,' he went on, 'and justice been done, instead of dismissing me you would have dismissed Sir James Graham and his Admiralty for treachery to me.' But the Prime Minister merely forwarded the letter to the First Lord, giving that all-powerful minister the excuse to ruin Napier utterly for ' disrespect to Their Lordships '.

Among the new classes of naval craft which left the slips while the Duke of Somerset was First Lord, the Admiralty yacht *Enchantress* came into a class by herself. She was a paddle-steamer with masts and sails and she justified her building costs, which Parliament cavilled at, by going on an anti-slavery patrol to West Africa and also conveying the Shah of Persia across the Channel on his state visit to Britain. ("How beautiful your weather is," the Grand Vizier said to one of the Naval Lords. "In my country it never rains like this.")

Her successor, *Enchantress II*, built in 1889, finished her life as a floating club-house for the Royal Motor Yacht Club. (Aboard her one day for an official trip to Queenstown dock-yard, the First Lord and his colleagues fell into argument about the lights and headlands, agreed that the captain was on the wrong course, assumed command and all but wrecked the yacht and drowned the Board of Admiralty on the Welsh coast.)

Enchantress III, the epitome of all the word ' yacht ' suggests, with her clean graceful lines and squat, yellow bell-mouthed funnel, was to provide a popular method of transport for more than one First Lord—not popular with their opponents in the Commons, who understood that the Admiralty yacht was meant for visiting fleets and dockyards, not for holiday cruising in the Mediterranean. (She was the size of a light cruiser and her saloon was a banqueting hall for thirty. The dinner-service, of plate collected from historic warships and the yachts of Lords High Admiral down the centuries, was said to be worth more than the main engines; but even that was put aside when a really important personage was dined on board by Their Lord-ships. Then the silver came aboard from the vaults at Greenwich, under heavy escort, and a petty officer steward carried, arranged, stood guard over, removed and personally restored to their safe the priceless Stuart salt-cellars which no one else was permitted to touch. Between 1919 and 1936 the yacht was laid up, being exceptionally costly to run.)

The fourth and last *Enchantress*, a sloop-type yacht built in 1938, was more adaptable for the serious work ahead of her. She carried four 4.7-inch guns, two of them replaceable by sponsons to make vantage-points for Their Lordships and their guests at naval reviews.

" There seems to be a feeling," said Sir John Pakington in 1861, " that any man who wants to write a pamphlet or make a speech cannot do better than attack the Admiralty."

In the time of the aristocratic First Lords and then the régimes of Graham, Wood and Pakington between 1850 and 1860, various sections of the press admitted to uneasy suspicions that the Admiralty was not keeping its end up. Doubts about the efficiency of the naval high command were too much ingrained in the national character to be discarded all at once, and the shocks of the Crimean War seemed to prove those doubts justified. The organisation founded by Sir James Graham in 1832 and refined during his second administration twenty years later, at one time acclaimed as a triumph of bureaucratic genius, had begun to be looked on, to quote Sir Oswyn Murray, as ' a very doubtful piece of machinery '.

Critics advocated remodelling it—taking a leaf out of the French Government's book by creating a Ministry of Marine, with one man at its head directly responsible to Parliament and no archaic committee of admirals to intervene between him and his departments. Sir James Elphinstone suggested it to Parliament in 1861, and claimed to be speaking for most of the forward-thinking officers in the Royal Navy.

The common man's panacea for all the ills of Government

departments—putting a business man in charge, somebody who is used to showing a profit or going under—was frequently proposed. Examples of the new-style man of affairs were springing up on all sides, and much admired in certain quarters: the sharp-practice tycoon, the piratical captain of industry, the Victorian corner-boy.

Brainy old admirals had grappled with Science—one of them was Sir Thomas Hardy, returning for a late long spell as First Naval Lord to find his young colleagues as stuck in the mud as ever—but Science had taken over without a struggle in certain walks of life. As the big businesses sprouted and astounding notions came over from America, the streamlining of traditional management techniques proceeded fast. The British Parliament, hardly a streamlined structure itself, petulantly demanded drastic simplification on big-business lines of the structures it controlled and grudged satisfying the voracious appetites of the unwieldy, complicated instruments of its power in Whitehall.

A vociferous clique in the House of Commons would have scrapped the Board of Admiralty altogether. Sidney Herbert, speaking from experience as an ex-Secretary of the Admiralty, told a committee of enquiry that the members of the Board met only three times a week and that their discussions were limited to 'formal business'. All the work was done, all the decisions taken, in the departments. They should have kept the Navy Board and done away with the Admiralty. If necessary the Navy could carry on without either, just as a well-drilled orchestra can play without a conductor.

Admiral Sidney Dacres—a future First Naval Lord, but siding with the Opposition for once—had 'seen an hour wasted at the Board on the question of whether a man was to have fourpence halfpenny or fourpence three-farthings as a pension'.

Naval writers argued that 'Boards'—naval or otherwise—were out of date. Bentham defined a Board as 'a screen for inefficiency '. During the Crimean War, it was revealed, Sir James Graham had conducted operations from his private office, for security reasons, with no one but the First Naval Lord in his confidence; and had issued orders through his Secretary, subscribed ' By Command of Their Lordships '—although Their Lordships knew nothing about them. If the Board of Admiralty could safely be ignored when the pressure was on, why not always ? What did its members do, apart from lending a certain tone to the central control ? What were they doing in return for an admiral's or senior civil servant's pay, and a handsome Admiralty allowance ?

A commission appointed in 1860 to look into the management of the royal dockyards struck a brutal blow, not by calling the dockyards inefficient—that was expected—but by adding that ' the constitution of the Board of Admiralty is the primary cause of it '. The Admiralty, its report went on, was ' a fiction not worth keeping up '. *The Scotsman* wanted to bring back the Lord High Admiral and make him, ' in the most serious sense ', *responsible*.

Their Lordships learned during that short, violent ' Abolish the Admiralty ' campaign exactly how a Principal Officer of half a century before must have felt, assaulted and forbidden to hit back. Yet Their Lordships turned out to be strangely difficult to wound in any vulnerable spot. They earned their pay by being *responsible*. But to what extent ?—and thus the argument on which many an old parliamentarian had cut his teeth came round again. Who exactly was responsible ? In the final analysis, whose was the blame for a naval scandal and whose the credit for a triumph ?

Graham in his monumental Act, carefully covering every loophole to make every member of the Board responsible for everything, had somehow, it transpired, ended up by making no one responsible for anything. And the situation had grown more acute with the development of compartments between the individual Lords. Deep chasms of non-communication could open between a First Lord who knew nothing of life at sea and his First Naval Lord who saw his political chiefs come and go without disclosing much about the kaleidoscopic manœuvrings of Cabinets. First Lords found themselves without the knowledge or the power to keep the Naval Lords in check and Naval Lords lacked the means of putting pressure on First Lords.

A particular resentment spread among the junior Lords because their professional advice was given *in camera*, at Board meetings, and carried no public weight. Besides, the First Naval Lord was beginning to rule the professional roast because, since there were never more than four Naval Lords, he had only to appoint a complaisant junior to gain parity and a moral ascendancy in discussion. In the innermost council of Admiralty there was sometimes sympathy for the factions outside which would have broken up the Board and forged a new chain of command. It was extraordinary, when one came to look into it, that the Admiralty had blundered along the right path for so long without a major upset.

The grumblings died away to a whisper, the House of Commons select committees wearied of considering what looked like the purely academic conundrum of ' individual ' or ' collective ' responsibility—and then the major upset occurred. Mr Hugh Childers, than whom no First Lord was less admired or trusted in the Navy during that century, was placed in office by Mr Gladstone in 1868. He had his own views about the relationship between First Lord and the rest of the Board: the former was responsible for the Navy, he said, and the latter merely acted as his assistants.

Mr Childers acknowledged a distinction between the First

Naval Lord and the others. He made Sir Sidney Dacres his personal aide and confidant, and heaped all the work on him, but scarcely noticed the existence of any other member of the Board. He relegated them during his two-and-a-half-year term to the status of heads of departments: precisely what Graham had insisted they must not be.

At the time of the upset—the *Captain* disaster of September 1870—the Board of Admiralty was organised in much the same fashion, allowing for the emphasis on different classes of business, as that which Barham had devised, like a trident. The First Naval Lord, with the junior Naval Lord to help him, looked after Personnel. The Second and Third Naval Lords (' Controller ') handled Matériel. And the First Secretary, with the Civil Lord, ran Finance. Above them all and remote from them all, alone in the mountain-top stronghold of his office, sat Mr Childers. His door was closed to all but the First Naval Lord. He had discontinued the daily Board meetings which Sir James Graham had instituted in the Crimean War. ' No First Lord knew as little [about the Navy] as Mr Childers,' wrote Admiral Sir Cooper Key.

H.M.S. *Captain* went down with considerable loss of life, including the lives of her designer and Mr Midshipman Childers, the First Lord's own son. She had been advertised as the warship of the future, complete with iron hull, turrets and all manner of up-to-date and futuristic devices, and the British public felt a keener humiliation than anything the Crimean War had given them; then alarm, because if it could happen to one new ship it could happen to more; then anger, that someone had blundered; then resolution, that someone must suffer.

Pundits attributed the disaster to the ' unjust and high-handed ' behaviour of the First Lord in approving the ship's design and sending her out to the Bay of Biscay on trials without regard to the warnings of officers better qualified to assess the risks. The country took the broad view—simply, that the Admiralty had done it and the Admiralty must go. Outside Whitehall, most people had a vague notion that the Admiralty was merely a collection of top admirals. They were not interested in whether the First Lord had consulted his advisers, whether those advisers had recorded their dissent, whether he had ignored their counsel or whether anyone had threatened resignation. (Resignations by members of the Board of Admiralty have been rare indeed, whatever newspaper gossip might suggest. Sir Oswyn Murray, intimately connected with the Board for most of his long life, could instance only two in more than fifty years: Lord Charles Beresford and Lord Fisher, both on personal grounds. Threats to resign, to gain a point, were not so rare; but, as Briggs put it, ' there is an immense difference between threatening to resign and actually doing so '.)

Mr Childers at least had made up his mind where the blame lay. He broke precedent, and Rule One in the Navy's code of honour, by publishing the text of a document in which he censured the Controller, Rear-Admiral Robert Robinson, for neglecting his duty while the *Captain* was building and preparing for sea. Robinson, he alleged, had gone ahead too fast, been too receptive to bright ideas—an unusual charge for a member of the Board of Admiralty to have to answer.

A key figure in the affair would have been Coles, the *Captain's* designer, but he lay at the bottom of the sea off Cape Finisterre, beyond the reach of courts of enquiry. Admiral Robinson was superannuated, his Board colleagues and various senior dockyard officials digested the First Lord's rebukes in silence, the public outcry subsided and the Fleet kept its opinions to itself. Mr Childers put it about that he meant to resign—his health was in any case not good—but the parliamentary committee which looked into the matter persuaded him to think no more about it. Its chairman, the Duke of Somerset, who knew what it was like to be a First Lord, took the opportunity of complimenting him on some of the administrative changes he had made at the Admiralty.

The compliments were not just idle courtesies, and Childers was not the anti-admiral snake in the grass naval opinion made him out to be. Those who accused him of knowing nothing about ships forgot that he had been a junior Lord in the Duke of Somerset's administration, when junior Lords had been run off their feet, relatively speaking, with Fleet reforms. Childers was a politician first, and had gone to the Admiralty as a loyal supporter of the Government, not expected to make difficulties by asking for too much money.

Before he arrived, he had announced that he would make his Board ' as little like a Board as possible '. Considering his indifference to professional advice, he ruled sensibly and his retirement scheme (the Navy List was divided into Active and Retired in his time) was afterwards held up as one of the prettiest examples of planning ever to come out of Whitehall, so basically sound that it needed little modification for many years.

The Government of his reign blocked and frustrated most of his efforts. He expected *carte blanche* from the Prime Minister and never got it. He tried to save the Navy £434 a year by revoking the commission of the Vice-Admiral of the United Kingdom—by this time a meaningless title—and combining the post with that of First Naval Lord; Childers was good at ferreting out and destroying the little medieval sinecures. But Her Majesty Queen Victoria turned the proposal down. When Parliament approved increases in the Good Service pensions awarded to elderly admirals, Childers tried again and managed to get the Vice-Admiral's £434 and the Rear-Admiral's £342 withdrawn. (The Vice-Admiral of the United Kingdom was at the time Provo Wallis, who had entered the Royal Navy in the time of Nelson and, as a centenarian and Admiral of the

Fleet, was still alive when one or two officers who are serving in 1967 joined the Service.   The Rear-Admiral of England was Admiral Hope Johnstone.)

Briggs, whose experience covered a long succession of administrations, voted Childers's the most memorable of the century—partly for the retirement scheme for officers, partly for the introduction of a seagoing training squadron for officers and men, forced on the Fleet against ridicule from those who ought to have known better.

The First Lord had an approach to strategical problems which, though enlightened, was out of tune with the reasoning of his times and led to endless acrimony.   His grand design, to consolidate and cross-connect the departments of Admiralty, was only partly translated into action.   Besides fighting continual ill-health he fought the ancient wisdom of the Navy and the entrenched self-satisfaction of the admirals.   Rows and resignations were clerks'-room gossip throughout his time, and squabbles with his Lords and between his Lords quite wore him out at the last.

Mr G. J. Goschen arrived at the Admiralty in 1871 to be First Lord for three years. He accepted the lessons which his predecessor's experiments had taught and which the *Captain* tragedy had sharply pointed: that steam warships could do without a lumbering topweight of masts and sails and that the Navy's political chief could *not* do without a circle of professional advisers.

Board meetings were called again. The Naval Lords returned to the inner policy-making council—all except the Controller, who was relegated to the standing of departmental head for Matériel, responsible directly to the First Naval Lord. (The Earl of Northbrook readmitted him a full member in 1882 and from then on, until 1917, he was almost always an admiral and very often a young progressive one. Controllers of the late Victorian and Edwardian eras included Sir John (afterwards Lord) Fisher, Sir Arthur Knyvett Wilson, V.C., and Sir John (afterwards Earl) Jellicoe.)

Some of the great names of Victorian politics are found among the First Lords of the two decades, 1870 to 1890: Goschen, Ward Hunt, W. H. Smith, Northbrook, Lord George Hamilton. From the last frayed bonds of Tudor green tape their Admiralties strained to free themselves.

Most of the important civil departments assumed a recognisably modern form. The heirs of the antique Shipwrights' Company (a fraternity which dated back to the fifteenth century) of Pett, Matthew Baker and Symonds, became the Royal Corps of Naval Constructors in 1883, with a director responsible to the Controller and, in time of war, naval ranks and uniforms for its officers.

The Controller might have temporarily lost face, but nothing slowed down the growth of his empire. Directors of dockyards replaced the old resident surveyors and resident commissioners of dockyards in 1885. At about the same time there appeared a department of considerable importance and influence in the civil works side, that of the Inspector of Dockyard Expense Accounts—not intended to curb the officers' inherent talent for manipulating their personal 'swindle sheets', but to make the complicated costing operations of ship-building and repair uniform, intelligible and economical. Last of the individual eighteenth-century titles disappeared when the Storekeeper-General in 1869 became the Director of Stores.

All these changes came about when the Controller's department was building bigger, moving faster and—to an outside observer—heading into more confusion than ever before. The British Fleet of the eighteen-seventies comprised a collection of heterogeneous craft, scarcely two ships alike and many of them purely experimental. In 1885 the horizon cleared a little and it looked as though the Controller might after all know where he was going, with the preparation of the first regular class of steam battleships, of eleven thousand tons, sixteen knots, some with sixteen-inch guns and some with thirteen-inch.

In 1877 George Ward Hunt's Admiralty attended the launching of the first British torpedo-boat, named *Lightning* like the first steam warship. Up to the end of the century Controllers watched the progress of the submersible craft which, like so many new inventions of the past, was to 'revolutionise sea warfare'. (One Controller was even persuaded to take a trip in one along the bed of Portsmouth harbour. Ten years later some of the junior Lords travelled to the bottom of Tilbury

Dock in a submersible boat and, according to Lord Charles Beresford, who was among them, it was very nearly a voyage of no return.)

The century was on the turn before Their Lordships approved the introduction into the Service of the first submarine. They could look back and note that a new kind of warship had been put into operation in the Royal Navy every ten years since the Crimean War; up to that date the rate had been roughly one per century.

But by that date—1901—additions of new types were almost at an end for the time being. The Navy's first torpedo-boat destroyers originated with the Naval Defence Act of 1889, as did the first *Royal Sovereign* battleships of fourteen thousand tons. To celebrate the new century the ' Wobbly Eight ' battleships—*King Edward VII* class—put them in the shade and were in turn eclipsed by the fabulous *Dreadnought* of 1905. Hard after the *Dreadnought* came another new type of warship, the battle-cruiser, in which the best features of battleship and cruiser were combined.

This is getting ahead of the story, but at that point the Controller will have no more peculiar, unheard-of units to produce designs for, and feel his way along with, for some years. The units of the Fleet, as most people alive in the twentieth century understand them, are complete except for the aircraft-carrier. They are battleship, battle-cruiser, cruiser, destroyer, submarine, sloop and gunboat.

During all those years it was rather hard for the layman to discover how many ships, at any one moment, the Navy had ready for war. One thing was agreed: it was never enough. Lord George Hamilton satisfied the country's appetite for more and bigger warships, temporarily, when he discovered the useful heading for the Navy List of ' Ships ordered to be Built '. It made a show brave enough to silence most critics—until the perceptive element began complaining about 'paper battleships' and 'phantom fleets'.

During economy drives, First Lords sang the old tune of the party men under orders to cut the costs. The Earl of Northbrook in 1884 told Parliament that the Royal Navy was so 'complete and efficient' that if it were voted three million pounds he would really not know what to do with it. Lord George Hamilton, following him in 1886, had plenty of ideas, however, and a powerful pro-Navy representation in the Cabinet to help him translate them into action. An ex-First Lord, Smith, was First Lord of the Treasury and another, Goschen, Chancellor of the Exchequer. Thus protected, the Naval Defence Bill surged through Parliament and the funds for new construction cascaded on the Board of Admiralty. Mr (afterwards Viscount) Goschen returned to the Admiralty himself during the Salisbury administration (1895 to 1900), the Royal Navy rode out the century on the crest of a huge wave of increased strength and renewed confidence, and the retired admirals who had pushed for space in the correspondence columns of the press to call for the blood of Northbrook and his allies contentedly sheathed their pens.

Almost within sight of the twentieth century, one knotty piece of Tudor tape bound the Admiralty. The Board of Ordnance, celebrated all those years for its 'evil pre-eminence in sloth and incapacity', had regained and retained control of naval armaments. One or two disgraceful episodes in the Crimean War had had the effect of removing the office from that powerful and unapproachable figure, the Master-General of the Ordnance. But it only went—and all the Navy's armaments went with it—to the Secretary of State for War, one step farther removed from the Admiralty.

Any gunner, in any of the nineteenth-century campaigns,

could see with half an eye (which one or two of them had, since the Navy started testing the Armstrong breech-loader) that the Army came first in the queue for ammunition. Naval armament stores were issued in their constituent items—powder in barrels, empty shell cases, empty cartridge bags and fuses boxed separately, which meant that a ship's staff needed days to prepare before they could fire a round. It was not the kind of arrangement which made for happy relations between the Services.

Naval gunnery became a matter of intense naval concern and general public interest in the seventies. During North-brook's administration, after years of cautious debate and experiment with the Armstrong gun, the Admiralty adopted the breech-loading principle. Soon afterwards it approved and purchased the Hotchkiss and Nordenfelt quick-firing guns and in 1887 (under Lord George Hamilton) applied the quick-firing principle to the main armament of heavy units of the Fleet. Their Lordships had, indeed, gone what Admiral Cockburn would have called 'gunnery mad'.

Lord George's Board, outstanding both for brain and personality, set about rectifying the scandalous situation at the Ordnance Office. They chose a roundabout way—by setting up an Ordnance department within the walls of the Admiralty building and, when the time was ripe, appointing a senior professional gunnery officer to be its director. Piece by piece the Naval Ordnance department won its ammunition back, and in the late eighties Naval Ordnance officially returned to naval control.

Every year or two a new committee or commission nagged at the Admiralty organisation, or held it up as a model for other Government departments. Certain reports were not at all complimentary; but some, like that of the Commission on Civil Establishments of 1887, declared the naval machine 'well designed . . . and on a satisfactory footing '.

"It has this advantage," Lord George Hamilton explained to a panel of M.P.s who still had their doubts about the efficiency of the curious relationship between the members of the Board, " that you have all departments represented round a table and that, if it is necessary to take quick action, you can do in a few minutes that which it would take hours to do under another system." No one could say that the Admiralty did not, in its own peculiar way, deliver the goods. Unique and unusual it might be; but it administered a unique and unusual section of the nation's affairs.

Coming on top of a historic document known as the ' Report of the Three Admirals ' (Dowell, Richards and Vesey Hamilton) on the naval manœuvres of 1888, the Hartington Commission (1889-1890) got into deep water trying to settle once and for all, for Parliament's peace of mind, the question of Admiralty responsibility. They invited Naval Lords past and present to declare themselves for ' individual ' or ' collective ' and heard very nearly as many interpretations as there were admirals.

Sir Arthur Hood said the First Lord was responsible for the Navy as a whole, but that the Naval Lords were responsible to him for the ' strength and sufficiency ' of the Fleet. Rear-Admiral Hotham believed that every member of the Board bore an equal responsibility, except where he had made it known, and had it recorded in the minutes, that he dissented from a decision. Sir George Tryon, one of the great authoritative figures of his day, disagreed with nearly everyone: he affirmed that Parliament, and not the admirals, bore the responsibility for the Navy. It was the First Lord's duty to ask his professional colleagues for advice, Tryon said, but no part of their job to offer it gratuitously.

The Commission's own conclusions reinforced the views more prominent First Lords had imposed on the Board through-

William, Duke of Clarence

Charles, Lord Barham

Earl Beatty, 1923

Lord Fisher and Mr Churchill, 1911

out the century. The First Lord was the Navy's Minister, they said, responsible to Parliament and country; the Naval Lords were responsible to him, with a ' more definite responsibility ' attaching to the office of First Naval Lord.

The British public could not be expected to excite itself over such abstruse constitutional issues. It was more interested in the two-power arguments which the ' Report of the Three Admirals ' had provoked after the 1888 manœuvres, and the Naval Defence Act which set the Navy on the road to two-power superiority. The Act had a sequel in the Spencer Programme (another Earl Spencer followed Lord George Hamilton to the Admiralty), when the Controller's and Civil Lord's departments plunged into a flurry of new works and extensions at all the royal dockyards—Portsmouth, Devonport, Chatham, Sheerness, Queenstown and Pembroke—and made provision for new bases at Portland, Dover and Simon's Bay in South Africa. In the last few years of the century the Admiralty began to move its overflowing reservoirs of men out of the hulks and into barracks at the main naval ports.

The two-power aim and all it involved—building so many ships was only part of the problem: they had to be manned, administered, repaired and distributed—was to keep Admiralty and successive governments at a perpetual tug-of-war in which, from time to time, both sides paused exhausted. An early casualty was Lord Charles Beresford, the junior Lord with ideas much above his station; but, sensational as such a resignation or dismissal—no one was quite sure which it was —appeared in 1889, it was nothing to the staggering outcome of a particularly bitter quarrel over the Estimates for 1895 between the Naval Lords and Gladstone's Cabinet.

The hard-bitten First Naval Lord, Sir Frederick Richards, who had been one of the ' Three Admirals ' and also a vocal member of the Hartington Commission, not only offered his

K

resignation but persuaded his junior Lords—Walter Kerr, John Arbuthnot Fisher and Gerard Noel—to offer theirs too. It may have been mere coincidence that the already-influential Navy League, formed ostensibly to campaign for a naval war staff but actually to fight for a stronger Navy and to goad reluctant Board members into action, had come into existence a year earlier.

During that gloomy winter, it looked as though the Admiralty, having beaten off so many attacks, might dissolve itself and its members abdicate. The civil servant of the Board, however, a remarkable Permanent Secretary, administered the Navy with Pepysian vigour. Admiralty secretaries are never much in the public eye, but to the Navy the name of Sir Evan Macgregor was sufficiently familiar. He held office from 1884 to 1907—years of the most significant changes—and he served seven First Lords: Northbrook, Hamilton, Spencer, Goschen, Selborne, Cawdor and Tweedmouth. He had guided naval administrators of the stature of Richards, Wilson and Tryon, and he was to nurse great twentieth-century leaders like Jellicoe, Beatty and Prince Louis of Battenberg. He had been lucky, before he took over the job, in undergoing a thoroughly old-fashioned training in the ways of Admiralty from Lord Brassey, the Civil Lord before 1885 and subsequently the founder of the well-known *Naval Annual*. But he considered the future more important than the past, and he gave his secretariat not only more standing in Whitehall but also a distinctly twentieth-century look.

The naval future, from inside the Board Room, looked fraught with difficulties and uncertainty. From outside, from the British public's viewpoint at home, it shone brilliantly. The Royal Navy, chief instrument of expansion, bearing the *pax Britannica* to the far corners of the earth and ensuring that the best of British institutions thrived under it, was the supreme propagandist for its Admiralty; supreme and simple denial of the scares politicians tried to whip up about feeble and extravagant 'Whitehall admirals'.

The nineties were the days when the electorate's sentimental affection for its Navy began to show; when 'Navy Cut' became a good selling slogan for tobacco; when reformers and M.P.s began to realise that, when they attacked the Admiralty, they were attacking the Navy and were on delicate ground. To every class of society there was a fine ring of power and capacity about the very word 'Admiralty' (even more so when pronounced in the vernacular, 'Admirality'). Of its ability to wage war on a grand scale, should war come, few had serious doubts. Maybe the Naval Lords could not muster a single medal ribbon between the four of them—this was the case during the nineties—but they would know what to do when the time came. The Royal Navy could not be other than in good hands.

Day-trippers to London congregated in Whitehall to gaze respectfully at the Admiralty building. When the Mall improvements were finished, 'Admiralty Arch' was the obvious name for the massive gatehouse across the top. Ask any schoolchild to name one Government department and, nine times out of ten, he would answer: "The Admiralty."

From the general run of admirals' memoirs, at least of those who had been behind the scenes, it appears that the ruling body kept its head buried in sand, raising it only to fix with a cold discouraging stare anyone reckless enough to put up a bright idea or suggest a better way of going about its business. This is nothing new: it was happening within months of Henry VIII setting up his Navy Board.

Those reckless enthusiasts, so eager to let anyone who would listen to them know just what was wrong with the naval ad-

ministration, did not always do badly for themselves. Some—
Scott and Beresford—became celebrities at large because of the
virulence and persistence of their attacks; the early twentieth-
century equivalent of first choice for a corrosive comment on
television, when the Admiralty made an obscure move. Others
—Fisher, Beatty—became Board members themselves, to be
annoyed in their turn by go-ahead youngsters and damned just
as roundly when they rejected advice. The imaginative young
commanders and captains thought they knew what *should* be
done at the Board of Admiralty; when they graduated to that
Board they discovered what *could* be done.

Naval officers with axes to grind or crusades to promote
were naturally very few. The great majority, like the great
majority of the men, saw their Admiralty, as one of them put
it, as ' a stingy but semi-benevolent fairy godmother who could
be relied on for succour and protection to the end of their lives '.
The Navy being superior to every other service and institution
in the Empire, it followed that the Admiralty must be superior
to every administrative department of state.

Vice-Admiral Humphrey Hugh Smith in his reminiscences
harped on ' the great administrative skill of the Admiralty, a
skill that cannot be equalled by all the rest of the Government
departments put together ' and, having no reason to be partial
because, like most naval officers, he had spent only a year or
two there during a career of forty-five years, he went on:

' The corner stone of the Admiralty administration is the
Golden Rule that the King's Regulations and Admiralty Instructions are a guide to the wise and a law only to the foolish.
The British Navy has abided by that Golden Rule ever since
the days of King Alfred.

' I think the Admiralty scores over other Government departments because its civilian staff is diluted with sea officers.
Whisky is good, and water is good, but whisky and water is

better than either. A sea training seems to produce a type of mind quite different from any kind of mind produced by shore training, a type of mind which, with all its many faults and grievous imperfections, will by some means or other surmount almost any difficulty.'

Most officers' relations with the Admiralty, after their initial appearance at a tender age before the Interview Board, were not much closer than they had been in the eighteenth century, when officers could enter the Navy and retire from it without knowing there *was* an Admiralty. They felt the administrative power only when explaining away extravagant claims for cab fares, or 'incurring Their Lordships' displeasure '—perhaps years after the event—for losing an item of naval stores. (Admiral Fitzgerald told *The Times* that he once mislaid an Admiralty-pattern corkscrew and the correspondence about it went on for four years.)

To the sailor, the Lords Commissioners were giants and gods in a remote Olympian citadel, who periodically gave tongue in their own lofty way and were prone to 'view with concern ' and 'observe with regret ' the little failings of mortal men.

Even captains of warships, even commanders-in-chief, before the perfection of wireless telegraphy, when a detached ship in lonely waters kept as solitary a vigil as any frigate of Hawke's day had done, could get through half a decade without any communication to or from Their Lordships, except the periodical arrival of Admiralty Fleet Orders, the printed booklet of new rules in which, as often as not, they found nothing applicable to themselves, their ships or commands.

' Ships hardly ever assembled together in harbour,' wrote an officer who knew the Far East and Pacific stations near the end of the century, 'and practically never cruised together as a squadron. British men-of-war might easily spend a year without seeing one another. The Flagship generally cruised along some coastline to be near a telegraph wire, but the rest were scattered far and wide.'

Alone and for long spells at a time a unit of the Fleet and her officers and men would be out of sight and out of mind, supervising the seal fisheries in the Bering Strait or a revolution in South America; settling a boundary dispute in the South Seas, burning a harbour full of Chinese junks, teaching a cannibal chief or an Arabian potentate a lesson. Alone they quelled mutinies in merchant ships, rescued earthquake victims and rounded up rebellious tribesmen. Their existence and nothing more was known at the Admiralty: known by a dot on the Operations Room chart which signified their position—or, to be more accurate, what their position had been days, weeks or months before. And by the time their captains' reports were being studied by the members of the Board, the officers who wrote them might have left their ships, left the Service, might even be dead.

Local orders on the big foreign stations would go something like ' Don't sail too far away, stay within a couple of hundred miles, so I shall know where to find you '. The Royal Navy had grown so fast, the unchallenged authority of the White Ensign so dominated the restless populations of a shrinking world, that warships were hard put to it to find something to do with their time. " Where can we go to-morrow, any suggestions? " was the Captain's stock question over a drink in the wardroom. A suggestion from the Admiralty, in those days, would have been for many ships as remarkable as a suggestion from Mars.

The commanding officer of H.M.S. *Impérieuse* (pronounced ' Imperoos ') grew tired of hanging round the skirts of the flagship. When he was sold a pup in the shape of an old pirate's chart, he took his ship treasure-hunting without even saying good-bye. The *Impérieuse* was away for a year, although another warship went looking for her. But the Admiralty felt this was going too far, even for the eighteen-nineties, and although Their Lordships did not exactly reprimand her captain, he was never given another job at sea.

When the Commodore on the Pacific station lost the three topmasts of his flagship in a squall off the Hawaiian Islands he put into Honolulu, so disgusted with the seamanship of his officers that he vowed he would never go to sea again; and he never did. Officers took up and relinquished their appointments, drafts of ratings came and went, and the flagship remained there until she became as permanent a fixture to visiting mariners as Diamond Head.

It was an age when eccentrics and originals could still thrive in the more secluded corners of the chart. There was the captain who wore a red cocked hat at Sunday divisions because, although Admiralty regulations about cocked hats went into minute detail about shape, size and decoration, they made no mention of the colour, which was blue; the captain who, in the era when warships on detached service carried livestock, ran short of fodder, fitted his sheep with green spectacles and fed them on wood shavings; the captain who was so disgusted with the meagre paint allowance sent to him by Their Lordships that he enquired of them which *side* of the ship they wanted him to do; the captain obsessed with a theory about the motions of the planets, which led him to spend whole days running gun-carriage wheels along the dockyard wall in Ceylon with paint-brushes attached, to trace patterns of cyclic curves; the captain who, after three requests why he had failed to demote a man for persistent drunkenness, replied to the Admiralty: 'For the simple reason that he is by a long way the finest leading signal-man in the Service and I would sooner have him as he is at sea and drunk in harbour than any milk-and-water bloody fool teetotaller.'

Even to those stations halfway round the world, in the carefree days when the fire-eating Fisher was a pushing lieutenant and the omnipotent John Jellicoe a round-jacketed midshipmite, the long arm of Admiralty, given time, would reach out and convey its reward or its retribution for deeds long forgotten by the participants. Magnanimity and a punctilious regard for justice to lesser breeds characterised the Admiralty's dealings with foreign victims of naval wrongs.

A midshipman in the Hawaiian squadron about 1870 brought back to his ship after a drunken frolic ashore a carved and gilded American eagle which he had unscrewed from the door of a humble tobacconist's shop, not knowing the tobacconist was the United States consul. Months passed, and so did a slow exchange of protest and promise across the Pacific and the Atlantic. Then, on Admiralty instructions, the offender returned to Honolulu, put on his best uniform, apologised to the consul and re-affixed the eagle above the door.

A similar incident nearer home gets half a page in the guide-books to Cornwall today. Lieutenant Goldsmith (descendant of the poet) climbed up with a party from his ship to one of the county's big rocking stones, Logan Rock, and pushed it off balance. The complaint came only from an insignificant rural council, but Their Lordships told Goldsmith to put it back, and he spent years and ran into debt trying to do so.

Such were the events, at home and abroad, which em-phasised the Admiralty's control over its scattered flocks and brought the dignity of Admiralty into the minds of sailor and civilian. Less competent societies marvelled at evidence of a discipline not less rigid because it was remote, not less firm because it was slow to act, as they marvelled at the latest news of bigger guns, longer ranges and faster and heavier ironclads.

23 'This Fatal Strife'

"Get down, gentlemen, you must get down," cried Rear-Admiral Beauchamp Seymour, rushing after the coach, "you don't know that boy, he's not safe. He'll upset you on purpose, just to say he's upset the Board of Admiralty."

The 'gentlemen' were Mr Goschen, Admiral Milne, the Earl of Camperdown and Mr Shaw-Lefevre, carrying out their annual inspection of Rear-Admiral Seymour's command at Plymouth; 'that boy', who had offered them a lift in his carriage, was the Flag Lieutenant, Lieutenant the Lord Charles Beresford.

Frustrated in his object as a junior officer, Beresford made up for it when he was a senior, and a Board member himself; more than made up for it in thirty years of service after he resigned from the Board; and ended his career as he had threatened to begin it, by 'upsetting the Board of Admiralty'.

There was perhaps never an officer who served the Royal Navy from a position of more personal advantage. Beresford, a wealthy Irishman with enormous influence in Parliament, society and Court circles, a darling of the masses and a gift to the popular press, became a junior Lord in 1886, having by then been a member of Parliament for Waterford for twelve years. (He entered the House of Commons on the same day as his lifelong friend Lord Randolph Churchill.)

While Secretary Macgregor remained out of sight at his post in the wheelhouse, as it were, of H.M.S. *President*, calmly conning the vessel past shoals of commissions and through the

K 2

flowing and ebbing tides of newspaper opinion, Beresford's was the loudest among those strident voices which shouted their conflicting orders from the bridge. He affronted the First Lord of his pre-Admiralty period, George Ward Hunt, by criticising the Board's lukewarm attitude to the Whitehead torpedo. Such admonishments in Parliament might come from a country squire from Rutland, or a miners' representative from Barnsley, but not from a mere captain in the Royal Navy. The tactless young nobleman was advised to make up his mind what he intended to be, a sailor or a politician—he could not be both, said Hunt.

Beresford reported the conversation to Disraeli, who told him to pay no attention to it. The votes of Irish M.P.s in those times commanded a high price, and Irishmen knew how to take advantage of the fact.

Disraeli helped to put Beresford on the Board of Admiralty. He was one of the youngest members for many years, and his colleagues, from the First Lord downwards, treated him generously at first; then Lord George Hamilton lost patience. ' I found him a source of considerable trouble,' he recalled, when writing his memoirs, '. . . the weak spot in my team . . . [addicted to] schoolboy expletives of the most pronounced character . . . a lovable creature, but so constituted that it was a foregone conclusion that he would make mistakes.'

Lord Charles had the Board in difficulties as early as 1887, when he set his astonishing precedent:

' A clerk came into my room with a sheaf of papers in one hand and a wet quill pen in the other. " Will you sign the Estimates ? " says he. " What ? " says I. " Will you sign the Estimates for the year ? " he repeated. " My good man," says I, " I haven't seen them." The clerk looked mildly perturbed. " The other Lords have signed them, Sir. It will be very inconvenient if you do not." " I am very sorry," says I, " I am afraid I am inconvenient in this office already. But I certainly shall not sign the Estimates."

' The clerk's countenance betrayed consternation. "I must tell the First Lord, Sir," said he as one who presents an ultimatum. "I don't care a fig who you tell," says I.' (The First Lord said it ' didn't matter ' and the Estimates went to Parliament for the first time lacking one Board member's signature.)

Still in his first year of office, Beresford had already had a big row over salary cuts, which had affected his favourite department, Naval Intelligence—a branch he had some claim to have created, from the small Foreign Intelligence Committee organised by Vice-Admiral Sir George Tryon, which up to then handled the Royal Navy's espionage and information services. The junior Lord described how a leak was plugged after he and his colleagues had been puzzled for some time to read details of their most intimate discussions in journals like the *Pall Mall Gazette*:

' Suspicion fell on the Board Room messenger and a snare was laid for him. An electric contact was made with a certain drawer in the desk of the First Sea Lord communicating with an alarm in another quarter of the building. Upon leaving his room the First Sea Lord told the messenger not to admit anyone during his absence, as he had left unlocked a drawer containing confidential documents. A little after, the alarm rang and the messenger was discovered seated at the desk making a copy of the documents in question. He was arrested, brought to trial and sentenced.'

Security operations and Admiralty ' snares ' have grown more complex since those days, but that was only one side of Naval Intelligence as Their Lordships originally conceived it. They saw in it the beginnings of a proper naval war staff, such as some military writers were advocating, such as no foreign Marine Ministry possessed. Eventually the War Staff came to stand on its own feet and the Director of Naval Intelligence absorbed minor offices, took over responsibility for Mobilising and Defence—became in effect a modern director of Plans and Operations rolled into one—and was for long periods the First Sea Lord's right-hand man, an automatic choice for membership of the policy-making committees. It took a war—the First World War—to separate the functions and confine Naval Intelligence to purely intelligence activities, under that real-life hero of spy thrillers, Admiral 'Blinker' Hall.

About the proposed pay reductions in this department, Admiral Lord Charles Beresford wrote violent minutes. His chief scrawled across the minute-sheet 'All correspondence on this subject must cease'—but his junior could not let it drop and thus, in 1889, he departed from the Board—according to Lord George's version. The reason Beresford gave for his resignation had to do with his colleagues' refusal to support his demands for seventy new ships all at once, to get on to the two-power standard, and those in the know maintained that the real cause was his anger at Lord George Hamilton's 'tyrannical authority' over the Board.

He had his admirers, even in the Board Room. The old Reader, Briggs, thought his agitations did more for the Navy than the Iron Duke's had ever done for the Army; and Briggs did not live to see the Irishman at his most agitated.

Admiral Lord Charles Beresford, for all his 'duchesses' as Fisher called them, for all his parliamentary cronies and in spite of having helped more than most to wear out the backstairs carpet at Buckingham Palace, never returned to the Admiralty; nor did he achieve the consolation prize he intrigued for to the end, the rank of Admiral of the Fleet. From the back benches and afterwards in the House of Lords, from the middle pages of the daily newspapers and at banquets, public lectures and garden fêtes—for he never lost his appeal to landsmen and the

Dictionary of National Biography calls him ' the best-known sailor of his day '—he roared and rampaged his contempt for Britain's naval administration. He died, rather predictably of an apoplectic fit, in 1919.

A fellow-admiral who missed serving on the Board of Admiralty altogether had, like Beresford, more to do with Admiralty history than several who were on it, in the critical Edwardian years. He was Percy Scott. Lord Charles and Percy Scott: in naval memory they go together, like Rooke and Russell or Keppel and Palliser.

Scott came to Their Lordships' notice as a lieutenant, when he began to bombard them with gunnery and signalling inventions, some practical and others not. As he advanced he grew more impatient and rude, and adopted an indiscreet boldness in expressing himself which was to be, not his downfall, because even the Board of Admiralty could make excuses for professional brilliance, but the barrier between himself and the highest rank. Admiralty letters ' strongly deprecated ' and ' deplored the tone of' his submissions, while approving the ideas they contained. Scott wrote to a friend, ' I pointed out to the First Lord that his Board were ignorant and did not know what they were talking about '—and wondered why he was never called back for another interview, why the big administrative jobs he was so well fitted for were slow to come his way.

Scott, to put it briefly, invented the system by which gunnery in big ships was controlled from a central position; a development which gave British weapons an immeasurable advantage over foreign ones, until other navies copied and refined the invention. After he left the Royal Navy, Scott went to work for Vickers and, since most of his subsequent ideas would, if adopted by the Admiralty, have meant huge contracts for his firm, there was naturally some resistance by Their Lordships to obliging him.

Sir John Fisher brought him as close to membership of the Board as he ever came by creating for him the appointment of Inspector of Target Practice in 1905. "Rather a peculiar wild animal to let loose on a tame Admiralty," a member of Parliament commented. But from that date, with the brilliant young Captain John Jellicoe as Director of Naval Ordnance, the gunnery of the Fleet went ahead at an impressive rate.

By far the greatest of a few great names of Edwardian Navy and Admiralty is that of John Arbuthnot Fisher, afterwards Lord Fisher of Kilverstone: Fisher the 'tornado with a nib on the end of it', the man who considered favouritism the keynote of efficiency, who subscribed himself 'Yours till Hell freezes' and quoted the Old Testament prophets, who on first arriving at the Admiralty paraded the corridors with a placard **'I HAVE NO WORK TO DO'** slung round his neck. The naval attaché in Rome expressed what Fisher meant to the Admiralty when told that he had retired from the position of First Sea Lord and gone into the country to grow roses: "They'll damned well have to grow, then."

He was Third Naval Lord (and his chief, Lord George Hamilton, forecast that he was 'too volatile . . . too assertive in self-advertisement and in his likes and dislikes to become the trusted head of a great service'. Lord George was not so far out: Fisher never did become the *trusted* head of the Navy). Then he was Second Naval Lord, and then First—First Sea Lord, the new nomenclature coming in just as he reached the summit on Trafalgar Day 1904. 'It will be *Athanasius contra mundum*,' was his often-quoted pronouncement. 'Very sorry, but Athanasius is going to win.'

Fisher picked his own team, brushing several worthy admirals aside and plunging down to the captains' list. His protégés,

Jackson, Jellicoe, Madden and Bacon all proceeded eventually to the highest ranks or posts the Service offered. In various capacities Fisher himself served the Admiralty for twenty-three years, and pushed his friends along nobly. But if ever there was a truly one-man Admiralty after Barham's time, if ever First Lords themselves bowed with good or bad grace to the leadership of a professional ' subordinate ', it was during the six years of Fisher's glorious autocracy, 1904 to 1910.

A special Order in Council, made just before Fisher became First Sea Lord, reduced the authority of the junior Lords and transferred strategy and operations *en bloc*—and that could be taken to mean practically everything—to the First Sea Lord himself. He used his powers to the full and made the perils of what had looked like a sensible centralising move very soon apparent.

Nearly all proposals and decisions at departmental level had to be referred to one man. The junior Lords were merely three more bottlenecks to decelerate the flow. The departments were stultified with delays and the old bureaucratic diseases, which had shown signs of being brought under control, broke out afresh. Of the effect on serving officers doing their time at the Admiralty, Talbot-Booth writes:

' Many excellent men, mostly of the rank of commander and upwards, entered the portals of the grim building filled with tremendous energy and love for the Service, only to find themselves confronted with a machine of such vast proportions and such slow-moving wheels that it became virtually impossible for them to achieve anything worthwhile during their period of service inside its walls.'

The First Sea Lord, paramount chief of the Royal Navy and mentor rather than adviser to the First Lord, must fall, in such circumstances, under the temptation of becoming, like his nominal political superior, a politician; and Fisher was the last man to resist such temptation. We observe him at the height of his powers and a crucial point of naval history finding time to send the Prime Minister advice he has not asked for about filling some vacant bishoprics.

His spirit was made for revelling in vast responsibilities; he was a John Gabriel Borkman whose dreams came true and who gave the 'slow-moving wheels' a spin which carried them comfortably through the World War (the date of which, ten years before it broke out, he accurately forecast). He revelled too in cutting red tape—at his own level, while it smothered his juniors. 'The first day I was First Sea Lord they brought me two feet high of papers. I said "Take 'em away—I'm going to attend to the Fleet and not to what a lot of damned old women have written. . . ."' Reminiscing about his own days as a junior Lord, he recalled that ' when I took a gigantic reform vitally affecting the Navy to a nameless First Sea Lord, he put it in his drawer and said he must first get through the papers I then saw on his table! My paper was discovered in his drawer when he was dead!'

Scarcely a month went by—a month ?—scarcely a day, without the naval Sultan issuing some new decree to alarm and nonplus the complacent and to delight the growing number of serious sailors and politicians who had been wondering how long the all-powerful British Fleet of the past fifty years would remain all-powerful after it had once been tested in battle. The movements generated by Lord Fisher—surely the highest-powered generator to have been installed in the Admiralty building since Ripley put the finishing touches to it—occupy many pages in the numerous lives of the Admiral. Here there is space only for a short catalogue of the most typical and far-reaching reforms of his time:

The so-called Selborne scheme levelling out distinctions between officers of the various branches, which incidentally was

designed to upgrade the engineer officers' status. The drastic
redistribution of the Fleet reflecting shifts in the balance of
power which Naval Lords dead and gone had never noticed.
The ruthless scrapping of units which were cluttering the dockyard ports and which, if it came to a trial, would ' neither fight
nor run away ', high on Fisher's priority list. ('I propose a
lecture on 31st October to all the C-in-C's and Admiral Superintendents,' he wrote, ' whom I am going to have at the Admiralty for an amiable and conciliatory setting-forth of their
damned stupidity, pessimism and effeteness, of which I have full
and authenticated particulars, and which I shall read out to
them and rub their noses in it. . . .')

To continue the catalogue: the building in record time of
H.M.S. *Dreadnought*, rendering every capital ship in every Navy
in the world obsolete, including a hundred and fifty-four British
units; it kept the Germans busy for nineteen months digging
out mud in the Kiel Canal to widen and deepen a channel for
their own *Dreadnoughts*. Revolutions in naval gunnery, in
steam turbines and then in oil-firing for warships' main engines,
accomplished and overthrown by new developments before
normal intelligence had time to assimilate the changes. The
infant submarine and the infant naval aircraft being nursed along.
The entry, training and promotion prospects of officers and
men continually revised (as Second Naval Lord, he had carried
through the establishment of a new college at Osborne in the
Isle of Wight) and new mobilisation schemes drawn up, in
which nuclei of trained men were kept on board ' reserve '
ships and a complement held in readiness in nearby barracks
for each unit.

Fisher suffered no argument. Subordinates either agreed
with him or found themselves out of a job. Professional jealousy
and misconceptions about the relationship between Board of
Admiralty and commanders-in-chief made Beresford, formerly

his admirer, his enemy. Sir Percy Scott, his favourite in 1905, was his adversary in 1910.

After the 'paintwork versus gunnery' quarrel at Portland and the signal controversy in the Channel Fleet—good old Navy yarns too tortuous to go into here, but to be read in the biographies of both admirals—Beresford and Scott were at loggerheads. The three most compelling naval personalities of Edwardian days had one defect in common: none would bear contradiction, each regarded anyone who disagreed with him ever so slightly as a moron and a scoundrel, and told him so.

The Fisher-Beresford undercurrent burst to the surface in April 1906, when the latter was Commander-in-Chief in the Mediterranean. Fisher addressed his new First Lord, Lord Tweedmouth: 'It is with extreme reluctance that I feel compelled, in the interests of the Navy and the maintenance of its hitherto-unquestioned discipline and loyalty, to bring before the Board the unprecedented conduct of the Commander-in-Chief, Mediterranean, in publicly reflecting on the conduct of the Admiralty and in discrediting the policy of the Board and inciting those under his command to ridicule the decisions of the Board. . . .' Beresford, at dinner with his captains, had spoken in the hearing of a Fisher spy of the 'rotters' the Admiralty was sending him in the guise of short-service seamen and had condemned the Admiralty for introducing the short-service scheme.

Next year, when Beresford was stipulating that certain changes in the Channel Fleet—the removal of Fisher spies, for one thing—must be made if he were to take command of it, Fisher warned the First Lord of the 'intended resignation of the Sea Lords if there is any truckling to Beresford'. Over the paintwork row, when Beresford thought his cruiser admiral should be ordered to haul down his flag, Fisher got in a shrewd blow by merely conveying Their Lordships' 'grave disapprobation' to Rear-Admiral Scott and leaving him in command.

It was Beresford in the end who went ashore, returned to his Conservative seat in Parliament (his party was in opposition) and dedicated the rest of his time and influence to bringing down the Admiralty Board. 'There must be no doubt allowed to exist anywhere,' Fisher forcefully reminded his political chief—for Lord Tweedmouth, in chronic poor health, was wilting noticeably under the strain—'of our unflinching determination to have Admiralty orders obeyed and Admiralty policy cordially and even enthusiastically supported.'

Fisher scored what a lesser man than Lord Charles would have recognised as the knock-out blow by getting himself promoted to Admiral of the Fleet, a rank which the Irish admiral, for all his power and popularity, saw he could never attain. Worse, it was done to prolong Fisher's reign at the Admiralty by keeping him on the active list after an ordinary admiral's retirement age, and that meant that Beresford could never be First Sea Lord either. From that moment he regularly denounced Their Lordships in Parliament in exaggerated and at times hysterical terms.

When two such figures disagreed they automatically took up diametrically opposed positions on every question; a tragedy, because Fisher and Beresford were both clever men devoted to the Service; and the nation, reading the arguments of one and then the other, felt itself, not for the first time, 'humbugged'. Both, working in harmony in Whitehall, could have made a huge contribution to the safety of the Empire and the prestige of the Royal Navy in the approaching world conflict. But Fisher's slogan on submarines as 'the *Dreadnoughts* of the future' was enough to make Beresford dismiss submarines as 'mere playthings'; and the First Sea Lord's firm belief that 'aviation will *surely* supplant cruisers' was all that Beresford needed to start proclaiming that 'aeroplanes cannot damage warships'.

(Fisher reasoned intuitively and was uncannily right as a rule; but he could be very wrong too. He disliked cruisers, seeing no need for a class of vessel between the destroyer and the battleship, and he tore up the plans for a convoy system which, had they been accepted, might have saved a million tons of shipping in 1915 and 1916.)

Sir Percy Scott cheerfully joined in the fight. He had reasons of his own for assailing the Admiralty, but would not stand by and watch it attacked by someone else, least of all Lord Charles. Speaking at a dinner in London, the gunnery admiral cautioned his audience about not believing all they read in the newspapers:

" The First Lord of the Admiralty will tell you that the Navy is all it should be and that you may sleep quietly in your beds. When you have slept comfortably you pick up a morning paper and read that the British Navy is a fraud on the public and a danger to the State and that if we went to war we should suffer a crushing defeat, that our ships have no bottoms and our admirals no brains, that our Admiralty administration is wilfully culpable and criminally wrong, that the fighting efficiency of our first line of defence is imperilled, that in our fleets there is nothing but disorganisation, demoralisation and confusion, that the very existence of our colossal Empire is in the gravest possible danger and that if the country only knew the truth there would be a panic. You read the signature underlying this gaseous bomb and again sleep comfortably in your beds.'

The signature Admiral Scott referred to was, of course, that of Lord Charles Beresford.

Fisher was not pleased when Mr Reginald McKenna succeeded Lord Tweedmouth in 1908. He had not been consulted about the appointment and on principle he preferred to have a real lord as First Lord. Failing the nobility, he would have chosen a young politician whom he had met eighteen months earlier: ' I fell desperately in love with Winston Churchill. I think he is quite the nicest fellow I have ever met. . . .'

Nor was King Edward VII pleased. Monarchs since Queen Anne had played inconspicuous parts in the naval drama, but Queen Victoria and her son both kept a shrewd eye on the action. The King suspected that McKenna had been brought in to make cuts in naval spending, and he insisted on Fisher's remaining as First Sea Lord to keep him in order. This the Admiral very readily agreed to do. The new First Lord had barely signed the inventory for the ' fittings and fixtures ' at Admiralty House when he was being put on his guard against the troublemaker:

' I think I ought to explain to you at once what the Admiralty position is, always has been and must ever remain, if discipline is to be maintained. . . . I am confident that you will give no encouragement to Lord Charles Beresford that he will receive any countenance in his disloyal and what I may even term insubordinate conduct towards the Admiralty because a new First Lord has arrived. . . .'

Except that McKenna had a bad habit of looking at both sides of a question, Fisher found little fault with him. Snipers made the most of small scandals—the Archer-Shee postal-order rumpus brought the Board into disrepute soon after the new First Lord took his seat—and Beresford in the daily press and Admiral Custance in *Blackwood's Magazine* fired poison darts at a wide range of Admiralty targets. To his detractors, a fight with Fisher became the *raison d'être* of their whole existence; he, of so much larger stature, worked off a bad temper before breakfast on his enemies (he often started work at four in the morning, before even the Admiralty charwomen had arrived) and devoted the rest of the day to a hundred naval problems and a hundred exposures of the torpor, lack of intelligence and inexperience of his colleagues. "I like you here, Lambert," he told the Civil Lord, "because you don't know anything about the Navy, but what is better still, you *know* you don't know."

What the other Sea Lords did not know, and what they sometimes hinted they should know, was sufficient about foreign policy to enable them to discuss war plans. The conduct of Edwardian diplomacy was highly confidential; exactly how far the *entente cordiale*, for example, committed Britain to assist France militarily was a secret to which even Fisher was not a party. The war plans themselves were a mystery: Fisher and the First Lord talked them over in private, rarely communicating any of their decisions to the junior members of the Board.

If the supreme council of Admiralty was in the dark, the Fleet and rival Service were thoroughly befogged. All the antagonism of the Beresford faction was suddenly focused on the dangerous and—they said—unnecessary secrecy which enshrouded the naval war plans. Beresford demanded a regular war staff, with *ex-officio* commanders-in-chief and Army generals on it, to work out a comprehensive war plan.

Something of the kind had been in the Cabinet's mind as early as 1903, when it set up the Committee of Defence (afterwards called the Committee of Imperial Defence), a triumvirate of Service heads which would often be chaired by the Prime Minister of the day and would last throughout both the World Wars to come. The first Committee had considered modernising the Army and merging the defence plans of both Services. The Navy, it had felt, needed no modernisation. Indeed, it thought that the Board of Admiralty, which had been 'founded on the proved requirements of war'—the Napoleonic War, presumably—and had 'smoothly and successfully met new demands'—a handsome tribute to a century of uneven progress —and conformed closely 'to the arrangements under which the largest private industries are conducted '—supreme compliment for a new-century institution—such a Board, the Committee had suggested, might with advantage replace the Army Council.

In 1909 Lord Charles Beresford tore off those laurels by alleging that home defences were unprepared (to some extent true) and the country not organised for a war abroad at sea (not true). The Committee of Imperial Defence appointed a sub-committee under the chairmanship of Mr Asquith himself, the Prime Minister, to have a close look at the Admiralty. The Board, says Professor Marder, was ' put on trial to defend itself against the charges of an undisciplined subordinate '. Admiral Sir Percy Scott, who was celebrating his premature retirement by stumping the country through the banqueting halls and never spoke to the toast of ' The Royal Navy ' without putting another couple of high-explosive rounds into Beresford, told the Scottish Clans Association:

' The Board of Admiralty and the officers serving on it have had to endure an existence analogous to that of the early Christians. They have not been torn to pieces by wild beasts, but the attacks upon them have been directed with a similar ferocity. Their public and private life has been attacked; odious, outrageous and abominable—and cruel—charges entirely unsupported by evidence have been written and circulated broadcast, endeavouring to undermine their authority, and scandalous imputations have been made against their honesty and capabilities as administrators.'

Mr Asquith's sub-committee found no evidence of unpreparedness. But it did feel that some commanders-in-chief—no names mentioned—might have been taken more into the Board's confidence and that a naval war staff ought to be established. A step ahead as usual, Sir John Fisher had announced the creation of the Naval War Council before the sub-committee's report was published. He put himself on it, with the Assistant Secretary of the Admiralty, the Director of Naval Intelligence and the Director of Mobilising—none of these, of course, members of the Board. At Sir Arthur Wilson's suggestion the famous War Room was built in the basement of the Admiralty building and a War Division of Admiralty set up under Captain (afterwards Admiral Sir) Sydney Fremantle.

Neither to War Council nor War Division did Fisher disclose his war plan; he condescended to inform his successor about it when he retired. His War Council has been described as a mere ' ideas department ', without influence on the naval policy or the grand strategy.

' The period [of the First Sea Lord's tenure of office] ought not to be of indefinite duration '—what Sir John's best friends hardly dared tell him was printed in a *Times'* leading article for all the world to read. That Mr McKenna had already raised the delicate question with a First Sea Lord who looked like going on for ever is clear from Fisher's letters to him:

' In recent years Sir F. Richards was $5\frac{3}{4}$ years First Sea Lord, and Sir Cooper Key 5 years and 11 months. Further back there were longer periods of 6, 7 and 8 years, but that is ancient history. However, the real limit is the period of cordial harmony between the First Sea Lord and the First Lord '.

In his sixth year of office, Fisher accepted a barony (many thought he deserved something better, but King George V had not the same admiration for him that his father had had), and departed, leaving the denizens of the so-called ' Fishpond ' temporarily floundering. At about the same date, another, though junior, Admiralty personality disappeared from Whitehall: another Scott, the Captain Robert Falcon Scott who relinquished the post of ' NA2SL ' (Naval Assistant to the Second Sea Lord) in order to take command of the 1910 Antarctic Expedition. The renowned 'A. K.' stepped into Fisher's office: Sir Arthur Wilson, an old tough sailing admiral who had won his Victoria Cross in the Egyptian campaign and who, like the able seaman's parrot, 'never said much but thought a lot'.

Within eighteen months Lord Fisher must have been wishing he had hung on, for in the summer of 1911 Reginald McKenna exchanged posts with the boy Home Secretary, thirty-seven-year-old Winston Churchill. After some preliminary skirmishing in the corridors, Fisher reached the 'Private Office', and the foremost naval officer of several generations became private eye and familiar spirit to the new First Lord, in much the same way that Lord Barham had become to Pitt a century earlier.

Wilson, he warned Churchill, loved coal and hated oil—indelible mark of the hopeless reactionary. ' You have a psalm-singing fool as Inspector of Target Practice and a very timid Director of Ordnance, and the First and Second Sea Lords have not been suckled on gunnery and don't and can't know the innermost pith and marrow of *Hitting first*.'

The new Board of Admiralty's kid-glove handling of Beresford contrasted strangely with its curmudgeonly treatment of officers from whom it had nothing to fear. Wilson, a disciplinarian before everything, signalled a laconic ' Approved ' to Vice-Admiral Cherry, a famed fellow-tyrant of earlier times, who had fallen out of the race and made his pathetic last submission to Their Lordships: ' Request I may be received into Chatham Naval Hospital for the purpose of dying '.

The day he took up his appointment, the old martinet had to send for a distinguished officer, Rear-Admiral Sir Robert Arbuthnot, in connection with some indiscreet remarks in public which had annoyed the German Emperor. He greeted him: " Captain Arbuthnot, I much regret that my first duty as First Sea Lord is to relieve you of your command. Good morning."

Regarding war plans and war staffs, Wilson agreed with
Fisher that the fewer who knew anything about them the safer
they would be. A stormy session of the Imperial Defence
Committee turned the 1903 tables on the Admiralty by recommending it should have a look at the way the Army handled
defence strategy—with a high-powered and heavily-membered
Imperial General Staff. " The present position," said Mr Asquith,
" in which everything is locked up in the brain of a single admiral
[the First Sea Lord] is both ridiculous and dangerous."

One reason for bringing Churchill to the Admiralty was to
get Sir Arthur out; he would prove, they warned the First
Lord, hard to shift. Churchill promised to do it in six months,
took three, and in November 1911 Sir Francis Bridgeman became
First Sea Lord.

Neither was he the Cabinet's idea of a professional leader
and potential inspiration to a navy fighting a war, and Mr
Churchill was soon commiserating with him on his poor health
and assuring him that there would be ' no objection ' if he
wished to resign. The First Sea Lord stoutly replied that he
had never felt better; upon which Churchill dropped an un-
mistakable hint and Admiral Bridgeman vanished.

Fisher and Churchill, Service opinion held, would have
made an impregnable combination, whether the Navy was
fighting the Germans or the Government; but Lord Fisher
had gone to the end of the queue. After Bridgeman's turn, a
figure often represented as a tragic one moves across the
Admiralty stage.

He is the German-born prince who married the old Queen's
grand-daughter Victoria: one of Her Majesty's numerous
Teutonic relations who showed almost proprietory interest in
the Royal Navy. (It personified Power in its most tangible

form, and perhaps this was part of the attraction for the Germans; as an honorary admiral in the British Fleet, Kaiser Wilhelm always took his non-existent duties more seriously than honorary officers are expected to—to the irritation of the Fleet and the Admiralty.)

Prince Louis of Battenberg made the Navy his whole career. When Fisher first joined the Admiralty in 1892, the Prince came in with him as assistant to the Director of Naval Intelligence, the new ' ideas and operations ' section of the First Naval Lord's department. Ten years later he returned as Director of the same section and ten years after that—having commanded squadrons at sea in between—he was Second Sea Lord with Bridgeman.

In 1913 Winston Churchill made Prince Louis his First Sea Lord and brought Jellicoe, whom he was grooming for the highest Fleet command, up to Second.

Legend has it that when Prince Louis was sacked after only ten months in office for the crime of not being a true-blue Englishman born and bred, the Navy lost its most proficient administrator of the twentieth century. This appears to be a somewhat romantic view of an admiral who, though experienced and talented, was no more than ' a bit above average ' in the estimation of those best qualified to judge.

Severe in appearance, gracious in manner, the Prince reminded one of some courtly old nobleman of ancient times, a relic of an age when manners were more dignified and ceremonious. It is doubtful whether the admirals and generals who came to the top in World War I would have responded to his singularly old-fashioned brand of charm; the politicians certainly would not. Prince Louis seemed more designed for a decorative post of supreme authority; a personage to grace the post of Lord High Admiral, if there had ever been a need to revive it. One could hardly see anything but difficulties

ahead in his dealings with the opportunistic political climbers,
Lloyd George and Churchill; the ethical code which governed
their actions would have been incomprehensible to him.

Prince Louis's letters and memoranda while in office make
restful reading among the blood-and-thunder Old Testament
English of the Fisher letters and the spluttering invective of the
Scotts and the Beresfords. He was celebrated for making peace
between warring admirals and heads of departments. Inevitably
he fell foul of Lord Fisher—or, rather, politely and with much
reluctance found himself in disagreement and was scurrilously
abused for it. Fisher was ever conscious of his colleagues'
failings, not always alive to their merits.

In the autumn of 1914, when the first fleet actions of the
war were beginning to take place, the Cabinet and the Navy
applauded Prince Louis faintly for the Heligoland Bight—a
victory uncomfortably close to a defeat—and rounded on him
for sending the old battleship *Canopus* to her destruction at
Coronel instead of despatching, as Fisher promptly did, the
fast modern battle-cruisers which retrieved the situation at the
battle of the Falkland Islands. (It has been suggested, however,
that Lord Fisher returned to the Admiralty just in time to scoop
the credit for the victory and leave Prince Louis with the blame
for the defeat; the conduct of both operations was principally
Churchill's—the First Lord, from the day war broke out, had
been spending far too much time in the War Room for the
Sea Lords' liking.)

'Spy at the Admiralty'—'Hun Runs our Fleet'—although
urged by some of his colleagues to stick out the campaign the
press was mounting against him, Prince Louis recognised that
there were certain jobs a born German ought not to be doing
in a war against Germany; that, moreover, he had enemies in
the Service. No one seriously believed the 'Spy' jibes, but
it was undeniable that he had maintained sentimental contacts

with his native land and naturally had corresponded with friends and relatives over there. The British nation in the first few months of the war was gripped by a manic hatred for everything Teutonic. The nation's leaders, in rabble-rousing addresses, denounced German music, literature, chemistry—the public expected it, but it was a chorus that Prince Louis could hardly be expected to join in.

Dozens of his contemporaries courted unpopularity by openly defending him, from the important Labour potentate J. H. Thomas to the former First Lord, Lord Selborne, who told *The Times*: ' I would as soon mistrust Lord Roberts as Prince Louis, and that anyone should have been found to insinuate suspicions against him is nothing less than a national humiliation.'

Prince Louis resigned, at Mr Churchill's request, at the end of October 1914, and Lord Fisher came back—at the age of seventy-two—with another and even older ex-First Sea Lord at his side, Arthur Wilson, to act as his honorary adviser and, perhaps, arbiter in the inevitable disagreements he foresaw with his First Lord.

The Royal Navy paid its debt to Prince Louis in 1921 by appointing him Admiral of the Fleet: an act of spontaneous kindness for which Viscount Lee of Fareham, the then First Lord, earned the admiration of the Service.

24   The Churchill Touch

' I can see him now, stepping impatiently along the Admiralty corridor, his short, thickset person immaculately clothed in morning coat and top hat, his little eyes screwed up with hidden purpose . . .' writes Vice-Admiral Usborne of the most wide-awake and disturbing of First Lords.   Mr Churchill's hats were giving political cartoonists their symbols, but in a Raven Hill sketch of 1913 he is portrayed for the first time with a cigar, while sprawling in a deck chair on board the *Enchantress*, some-where in the Mediterranean.   At his side the Prime Minister is going through the mail from England.

"Any home news ? " asks Churchill.

"How can there be, with you here ? " says Asquith.

For eight months of his first thirty-six as First Lord, Mr Churchill cruised in the Admiralty yacht, visited every big ship in the Fleet and met every senior officer.   Lloyd George com-plained that he had become so ' absorbed in boilers ' that he had forgotten the Liberal party.   Vignettes of his whirlwind tours and interviews survive in the recollections of naval officers of the period.

Humphrey Pakington, a flag lieutenant, went on board the *Enchantress* among the western isles of Scotland to meet the new First Lord.   To the admirals the thirty-seven-year-old Minister, half the age of his Board colleagues, looked not much more than a plump-cheeked impudent midshipman.   Over lunch he catechised them about their ammunition stowage arrangements, the expenditure of torpedo stores and other matters beneath the dignity of squadron flag officers.

'It was awkward for the admirals and awkward for us junior officers, with the admirals floundering about among the answers and the First Lord out for a kill. " Is that correct ? " said Churchill, whipping round from one admiral to another. " I haven't the slightest idea, Sir," was the reply. " But I dare say my Flag Commander will know. Shall I send for him ? " And that was the end of that little game.' The end of the admiral's promotion hopes too, one might think. But with Mr Churchill one never knew.

A junior flag officer named Beatty had refused the job of second-in-command, Atlantic Fleet, on the grounds that it would cut into the hunting season. In a conventional age it meant he would never be offered another, but Churchill said, " I would like to see this young admiral who refuses good appointments." When Beatty arrived in Whitehall he told him: " You seem very young to be an admiral." " And you seem very young to be First Lord of the Admiralty," replied Beatty. He was promptly invited to become Naval Secretary to the Board.

The Naval Secretaryship, a post for a rising rear-admiral, had grown out of Fisher's organisations at the Admiralty to become an office for helping the First Lord to wield the naval patronage and to be a personal link between the Navy and the Crown. The Secretary had no place on the Board, but he worked in a nice big room overlooking the Horse Guards Parade with a connecting door to the First Lord's apartment.

One of his duties was to draw up a rough plan of flag officers' appointments for about two years ahead, which the First Sea Lord amended and the First Lord—unless he happened to be a Churchill—usually approved with little more than a glance. The Naval Secretary pushed the sea-going admirals on, or held them back; he drew up the lists of proposed honours and decorations; he traditionally chose a plum for himself on re-linquishing his job, and that was not the least of attractions about the appointment. David Beatty's splendid future was assured by his having become Naval Secretary at a critical moment in his career.

Lord Fisher would have given the Naval Secretary much responsibility behind the scenes. He advised Lord Esher to instal a Military Secretary at the War Office and told him: " It is an ideal arrangement. The Naval Secretary has the power. He pulls the strings. He causes no jealousy. He talks to all the Lords of the Admiralty and he manipulates them all and oils the machine for the First Lord."

(One Naval Secretary's method of oiling the machine was to mark difficult papers—that is, address difficult minute sheets —to the remotest naval authority he could think of, for example the Commander-in-Chief, Australia. By the time they returned the problem had usually solved itself. Fisher had a more drastic way with fiddling bureaucratic annoyances, according to his naval assistant, Captain, afterwards Admiral of the Fleet Sir, Henry Oliver: ' Fisher got tired of a perennial discussion with the War Office over Highlanders' spats. A vast file of papers about it came round two or three times a year, and had done for years. A Highland regiment had arrived in Malta from the East and been put into quarantine. To avoid delaying the ship they had been camped on Comino Island. They had been landed on the beach by the Navy and their spats had got wet and discoloured. The War Office said the Admiralty should pay for them and the Admiralty always refused. Fisher threw the whole file of papers on the fire and told me that when the Registry asked for them I was to say he had taken the papers to his house. He knew no one dared to ask *him* for them.')

When Admiral de Chair succeeded Beatty as Naval Secretary in 1913, Churchill sent him to apprise King George V of his plan to name the latest pair of battleships *Pitt* and *Cromwell*. ' The King asked me to sit down. When I told him about the proposed names to be given, His Majesty immediately expressed disapproval. " I do not wish any ship in the Navy to bear the name of a man who was responsible for beheading the reigning sovereign and, as to a ship carrying the name of Pitt, I know enough of the lower deck to realise that the bluejackets would alter it to another word of four letters." ' De Chair reported to the First Lord, who thought the objection ' unworthy of the royal mind ', but accepted the hint. No naval craft, then or later, bore those names.

Mr Churchill's Secretary thought him clever and hard-working, but too ' impulsive, headstrong and even at times obstinate ' to be a First Lord. He could show immense courage and initiative, but saw himself as a heroic political figure and man of destiny, and was remarkably difficult when crossed over trifles—capable of vindictively wrecking officers' careers without explanation, for some momentary irritation they had caused him.

De Chair walked in one morning to find the First Lord in a passion, dictating a telegram. " Good-morning, First Lord, you seem disturbed."—" Disturbed ? I have been insulted by the Commander-in-Chief at the Nore and I am telling him to haul down his flag at sunset and give up his command." De Chair, aghast, begged him first to consult the Sea Lords. " Do you think I am going to humiliate myself before the Sea Lords ? I will not be insulted. Either his flag comes down or I go. I refuse to discuss the matter further."

Prince Louis, who was adept at handling contretemps of that kind, was unluckily out of London. Jellicoe convened the Board in minutes, however, and a mollified First Lord later looked in on his Secretary and said, " You will be glad to hear that the Sea Lords and I see eye to eye on the affair."

L

From the diaries of politicians, millionaires, newspaper pro-
prietors, come glimpses of the First Lord at sea—anecdotes too
well known and maybe too apocryphal to be told here. He
loved his yacht and he loved company. He was also far too
fond of prowling about the naval ports and dockyards on his
own, and the Sea Lords had to make him promise at least to
take a member of the Board with him.

Many an out-of-sight-and-out-of-mind admiral would receive
a summons to the Private Office, to be attacked with the question
" What is the weather like in the Channel ? "—and, on making
a stab at an intelligent answer, with another: " Will you come
out with me in the *Enchantress* today ? I would like to visit
the Fleet at Portland "—and would know, while privately
fuming at the indignity of being on trial before a youngster
who knew so little about the Navy, that a profitable and exciting
future was opening before him as long as he kept his wits
about him.

There is a glimpse of Churchill ashore from the *Enchantress*
on the Dalmatian coast, strolling with Asquith inside the massive
fortress-walls of Diocletian's palace at Split and muttering to
himself, " I should like to bombard the swine "—without making it clear who the 'swine' were, or was; of Churchill at
Naples, sending for Fisher and haranguing him and being
harangued in turn—which has the immediate result of Fisher's
re-entry into the administration, first as Chairman of a committee for organising oil-fuel supplies and later as First Sea
Lord after Prince Louis's departure; and of Churchill on the
bridge of the *Enchantress* in the Firth of Forth, watching the
Second Destroyer Flotilla enter harbour and asking in a rage
who appointed its senior officer.

The Naval Secretary had done so. 'I saw a shadow pass
over his face and he left . . . then I got a message that he
wanted to see me in his cabin.' Why had the appointment

been made without the First Lord's concurrence ? Because
First Lords did not normally concern themselves with junior
captains' appointments. They would as long as *he* was First
Lord, snapped Churchill. He had the destroyer captain to
dinner next day and put him at his ease by telling him that he
was not good enough to command a flotilla, that he would be
shifted. He reminded his Sea Lords that, argue as they might,
he knew a square peg in a round hole when he saw one. Had
he not organised Britain's Labour Exchanges ?

' Oh, dear,' writes Beatty from the Admiralty yacht, ' I
am so tired and bored with the whole thing. . . . Winston talks
about nothing but the sea and the Navy. . . . Prince Louis is of
course charming, but *not* terribly exciting. . . .'

And there is a last glimpse of the Naval Secretary himself
at the end of his Admiralty time, caught on puppet-strings of
the First Lord's patronage which, while Churchill manipulated
them, tended to become hopelessly tangled. The First Lord's
offer of an insignificant shore job was eloquently put, couched
in terms which made it sound a glittering portal to glory, but
de Chair knew his master by that time.

' I told the First Lord I was deeply disappointed. . . . I said,
" I remember, First Lord, that you have already promised me
the command of the Second Cruiser Squadron." He said,
" Oh, I didn't mean that. Well, will you accept the second-in-
command of the Second Battle Squadron ? "—I said, " You have
already promised that to Admiral Sir Robert Arbuthnot. . . ." '

These tiny sidelights on Sir Winston Churchill's Admiralty
career are only noted here because the important events and
achievements are sufficiently well known. On deeds accomplished in the face of apparently insuperable opposition his
biographers have adequately dwelt, and the Navy still remembers
them with gratitude.

In 1908, when he first entered the Cabinet, Churchill had vigorously opposed the *Dreadnought* chant of 'We want eight and we won't wait'. In 1912, as First Lord, his Estimates were the most extravagant—to use his antagonists' word—in history and they provided for new gunnery systems, oil-conversions and port installations and a new deal for sailors. *Punch's* cartoon Christmas card that year was devoted to Winston, chubby, rosy and nude, scattering largesse on the Fleet with a snatch of the old ditty: 'There's a sweet little cherub who sits up aloft, and keeps watch o'er the life of poor Jack.'

Next year his Estimates were a horrifying fifty million pounds—even the Sea Lords, accustomed to prodding First Lords into action against the Treasury, wondered if they ought not to be holding him back—and they provoked another cartoon, this in the *Daily Express*, in which a nurse pulled Winston bawling in his sailor suit away from a toyshop full of model warships. "Come away from that window, you naughty boy, you have too many toys already." Winston obtained forty-eight of his fifty millions; he generally got his own way through 1913 and 1914, sometimes at the cost of a threat to leave the Liberals and join the Conservatives.

On the outbreak of war, without awaiting Cabinet decision or royal proclamation, he ordered the Fleet to its stations and completed mobilisation. And alone, against the arguments of his Board, he thrust Jellicoe into supreme command at sea on the very day Britain's ultimatum to Germany expired.

He realised all Fisher's dreams of a one-hundred-per-cent pro-Navy First Lord; and halted Lord Charles Beresford in mid-speech merely by yawning in his face. One faintly alarming quirk, as it seemed at the time, was his determination to form the Naval Air Service—or, to be exact, expand it from four aircraft to a hundred and twenty, including fifteen airships. Churchill, egged on by Fisher, gave them a more-than-recon-

naissance role, wider duties than thoughtful strategists allowed
them. (' Aviation will *surely* supplant cruisers.') A converted
tanker, the *Hermes* (afterwards *Ark Royal*) went into service as
Britain's first seaplane-carrier; a genuine aircraft-carrier, H.M.S.
Argus, was giving Controller and Constructor Corps premature
grey hairs before Churchill left the Admiralty.

Up to the outbreak of war, the Naval Air Service had been
the province of the Second Sea Lord, Admiral Jellicoe. ' After
Churchill ceased to be First Lord,' wrote Admiral Murray
Sueter, ' certain Sea Lords commenced to smother the young
Air child, whom they subjected for some time to severe pin-
pricking.' Piecemeal the unwanted newcomer found its way
into the hands of the Royal Air Force after the war. Their
Lordships had had second thoughts by 1937, when the Fleet
Air Arm recovered its proper responsibilities and a Fifth Sea Lord
(' Air ') was appointed. But the Royal Navy entered World
War II equipped with aircraft more appropriate to 1918 than 1939.

With a few guns and searchlights, manned by a volunteer
force, the Admiralty undertook the air defence of London in
September 1914. It was Churchill's successor, Mr Balfour,
however, who had the brilliant idea of putting Admiral Sir
Percy Scott, retired, in charge; but before the little veteran
could get things moving the way he had done with the batteries
at Ladysmith, control of the anti-aircraft services passed—in
February 1916—to the War Office.

The Fisher-Churchill explosion—dealt with in the next
chapter—shook the Admiralty building to its sandy foundations.
The First Lord emerged from the wreckage with only a bruise
or two, and he bore the burden of responsibility for the Dardanelles disaster with admirable composure. But when the
Coalition Government was assembled in 1915 the price of
Conservative co-operation included the First Lord's resignation

and by November of that year he was in the trenches in France;
to the Admiralty, for the next quarter of a century, no more
than a 'Former Naval Person'.

25 The Conduct of the War

At ten minutes to six on the evening of 4th August 1914 the Admiralty warned the Fleet: 'The War Telegram will be issued at midnight, authorising hostilities to commence. Be prepared.'

Next day the King's message went out to commanders-in-chief at home and abroad for general distribution: 'At this grave moment of our national history I send to you and through you to the Officers and Men of the Fleet of which you have assumed command, the assurance of my confidence that under your direction they will revive and renew the old glories of the Royal Navy and prove once again the sure shield of Great Britain and of her Empire in the hour of trial.'

Not for more than a hundred years had the Royal Navy gone into a full-scale war, and then the communications arrangements had been rather different: from the Admiralty, post-chaise or (weather permitting) telegraph to Portsmouth; and a brig to carry the despatches across the oceans, so slowly that the instructions they contained were often meaningless by the time they arrived, former allies become enemies, the originators and addressees sometimes dead. But in 1914 the royal message could be read in the southern seas, on the China coast, in the Middle East and Brazil, within hours of its inception.

The Admiralty, in fact, in the excitement of starting a war, was a little ahead of the clock. That first night the Resident Clerk (a senior civil servant responsible for despatching signals) threw Whitehall into a flurry by telling the Fleet to ' commence

hostilities against Austria'—a country war had not yet been
declared on.

The Admiralty's world-wide wireless coverage enabled it to
order the dispositions of fleets and squadrons and often the
hour-by-hour conduct of a battle by remote control, not always
to the benefit or satisfaction of the commander on the spot.
Thus it sent Beatty's battle-cruisers from the Firth of Forth to
the Heligoland Bight, unknown to Tyrwhitt and Keyes who
had raced out with the Harwich Force to carry out a plan of
their own and had trouble in distinguishing friend from foe.

The first major action of the war involved signal trans-
missions to and from a region as distant and difficult as could
have been imagined: the far southern regions of South America.
Admiral Cradock at Coronel went to his death bemused by
streams of obscure telegrams advising him to concentrate his
squadron, to meet *Scharnhorst* and *Gneisenau*, to leave sufficient
forces to deal with *Dresden* and *Karlsruhe*, to keep the *Canopus*
and a cruiser with his flagship, to search the Magellan Strait,
to destroy German cruisers and break up German trade . . .
telegrams which crossed with messages from himself (equally
obscure ones, to Their Lordships) and which seemed to have no
bearing on the up-to-the-moment realities of the situation.
Passed through consuls-general at Valparaiso and Buenos Aires,
coded and decoded from texts which grew ever more corrupt
on telegraphic channels ever more distorted, they demanded
psychic intuition on the part of the recipients before more than
a guess could be hazarded at their meaning.

The centralising of the conduct of naval operations in the
War Room at the Admiralty was condemned after each British
reverse. It was no new phenomenon—Charles I, having laid
down the strategy to his Lord High Admiral, went on to interfere with the tactics as long as Buckingham remained within
call; but in the wireless age it was more significant, more pro-

ductive of instant catastrophe. In the *Naval Review*, Vice-Admiral K. G. B. Dewar castigated the Admiralty for Coronel:
' They could not possibly give close and continuous attention to the campaign. They bombarded the executants with signals which cramped their initiative and misdirected their efforts. They lacked the sense of urgency and personal responsibility which is only developed by direct contact with fighting forces. They made mistakes in the face of plain facts because they did not study the facts. The sequence of signals from the Admiralty shows gaps and contradictions owing to a lack of continuous attention. Earlier decisions and suggestions were lost sight of in the growing pile of telegrams and memoranda. The higher authorities only woke up to the danger of a situation when immediate disaster threatened. Then it was too late.' A brutal indictment, but the Service departments are judged more on their failures than their successes.

The Signal Division of Admiralty was opened upon the outbreak of war, the staff of the Portsmouth Signal Committee moving up to rooms in Victoria Street, London. Tales went the rounds of Whitehall soon afterwards about a mysterious compartment deep in the catacombs of the Ripley block, impossible to find, where the Scottish engineering wizard and mathematician Sir Alfred Ewing deciphered foreign signal books, secret documents captured from the enemy and wireless messages intercepted on the Admiralty monitors or bought from neutral information services. Down there, Ewing was assisted (it was quite falsely whispered) by dozens of beautiful girls, every one the daughter of an admiral.

It was Room 40 which visitors to the Admiralty who have been brought up on the fact and fiction of counter-espionage always want to see but cannot: ' Room 40 ' very soon developed into a whole series of rooms with different numbers.

Naval Intelligence, to which Room 40 belonged, had de-

generated in Sir Arthur Wilson's time to the position of a
general information office. In the first months of the war it
began to recover some of its lost responsibilities from the War
Division and came into its own again under Rear-Admiral Hall.
The story of British naval intelligence through two World
Wars and the intervening years is a fascinating success story.
The speed and accuracy which it developed in transmitting news
of enemy plans and movements—partly on account of Room
40's coup in securing and cracking the German Fleet Code—
were sometimes unbelievable; and often, unhappily, unbelieved.
Had Jellicoe shown more faith in the information the Admiralty
fed him—had the Operations Division passed on to Jellicoe all
the intercepted messages Room 40 sent up—Jutland might have
ended differently.

Activities close to home were rather less intense than Their
Lordships, in the famous war plan, had envisaged. But storm
clouds were gathering—not in near waters, but directly over-
head. The Board Room was all at once in the thick of a fight,
and it was a fight between titans, Churchill and Fisher.

For six months the pair had worked well together. Had
they not always looked forward to working together ? For
six months Churchill toiled through the night and Fisher came
in to relieve him at five in the morning. The neat way in which
their favourite working hours just overlapped not only kept
them from seeing too much of each other but also gave the
Admiralty a two-chief shift system unique in Whitehall: an
obvious advantage for those on active service at sea, though it
made life harder for Admiralty officials.

The Cabinet found its War Office high command a constant
worry, but was delighted with the naval Trinity—Churchill,
an ebullient, optimistic Father; Fisher, the elderly irritable Son,
but of vast experience; and Arthur Wilson a fairly shadowy

Spirit—not so much a Holy Spirit as a Spirit of Times Past, when discipline was discipline and duty meant obedience. Lord Fisher, composer of endless memoranda to an equally prolific First Lord, was still signing himself 'Yours till Hell freezes'. But a time was approaching when, as Churchill remarked, 'this improbable event had apparently occurred'.

In January 1915 the naval Trinity reported to Mr Asquith's War Council on a plan to force the Dardanelles. Winston with 'a happy face' supported it. Fisher and Wilson remained 'ominously silent'. Afterwards the First Lord turned all his oratory loose on them and the admirals, late at night, wearily agreed, or at least spoke of agreeing, to 'go the whole hog'.

In May the affair was turning out badly. Fisher withdrew a new battleship, the *Queen Elizabeth*, fearing further naval losses. Kitchener at a tense War Council accused him of deserting the Army in its hour of need. The First Sea Lord angrily replied that he had been against the whole adventure from the start, and that the First Lord knew it. Churchill spiritedly admonished the old admiral.

That night, smoothed with Churchillian soft soap, Lord Fisher sat down to study the new Dardanelles proposals he had agreed to and found in them more than he had previously read; the First Lord, it seemed, had been making additions without getting his colleagues' approval. Fisher entered the Admiralty building next morning, wrote out his resignation, pulled down the blinds of his room and left.

First Lord and First Sea Lord met privately for an impassioned duet, Churchill appealing with Burkian rhetoric to Fisher's responsibility to 'conscience and glory' and the scene ending with a despairing cry wrung from the Admiral's heart: "You are bent on forcing the Dardanelles. Nothing will turn you from it—nothing. I know you so well."

Lord Fisher disappeared for a few days and was run to earth in the Charing Cross Hotel, in a locked room. A letter from the Prime Minister, ordering him 'in the King's name' to return to his duty, was required to draw him from it. But he went back only to dictate impossible surrender terms: 'That Mr Winston Churchill is not in the Cabinet to be always circumventing me; that the First Lord of the Admiralty should be absolutely restricted to policy and parliamentary procedure'. The First Sea Lord wanted the kind of unique control he had exercised in the golden Edwardian era, even to dismissing or appointing Boards of Admiralty on his own initiative; in return for which, he positively guaranteed to win the war.

'I did all I could to prevent it,' wrote King George, deeply disturbed. 'I told him [Churchill] that he [Fisher] was not trusted by the Navy. I think it is a great mistake, and he is seventy-four.'

With that Lord Fisher's Admiralty career—his whole life—ended on a high note of melodrama, and the reputation he left behind—for men's memories are especially short in time of war—was that of bigot, monomaniac, saboteur of the national effort and (according to knowing ones) a naval emperor unbalanced by jealousy of a military emperor's (Kitchener's) mounting prestige.

The Dardanelles campaign failed in the end and Churchill failed with it. (King Constantine told an attaché in Athens: "I never read, I never saw, a more amateurish way of approaching a serious military enterprise than your people employed in the Dardanelles.")

Lord Fisher would not budge from his conviction that fleets could never capture peninsulas. The Sea Lords mostly agreed with him—few, it turned out, among the Admiralty's senior staff, supported the idea or the campaign. But on major problems not even the Sea Lords were consulted. Ex-First Sea

Lord Sir Arthur Wilson, respected old gentleman but no naval statesman, sat with the War Staff Group and the various exclusive off-shoots of the strategical committees, but junior Lords of the Admiralty had the greatest difficulty in getting even a sight of the minutes. Yet all, for tradition dictated it, shared the blame for the blunder. The day after Fisher's resignation they took the unusual step of drawing up a memorial for the First Lord:

' The First Sea Lord has caused us to be informed of his resignation and to be shown a copy of certain minutes which have passed from the First Lord to him and vice-versa.

' It appears from these documents that the First Sea Lord's resignation is due to two causes: (i) disagreements with the First Lord as to the conduct of operations in the Dardanelles and (ii) dissatisfaction with the procedure adopted for the executive control of the movements of the Fleet.

' As regards (i)—as we said then and now repeat, we hold that these operations most certainly jeopardise the crushing superiority of the Grand Fleet etc.

' As regards (ii)—we associate ourselves with the First Sea Lord and are of the opinion that the present method of directing the distribution of the Fleet and the conduct of the war appears to have been largely taken out of the hands of the First Sea Lord.'

Admiral Wilson stayed on under Churchill until the First Lord went, and then both Fisher and Wilson were called before the Royal Commission on the Dardanelles campaign and smartly rapped for not stating their objections at the outset in the War Council. They excused themselves by adhering to a conception of Admiralty responsibility similar to that which Sir George Tryon had expressed to the Hartington Commission in 1889: Sir Arthur understood he had been put at the Admiralty ' to help the First Lord, not oppose him '; and Lord Fisher said that every First Sea Lord had two courses of action open to him, and two only: to agree with his political chief or resign.

Mr Arthur Balfour succeeded Churchill as First Lord; Admiral Sir Henry Jackson became First Sea Lord. The latter had swum for years in the warm waters of the 'Fishpond' and the former should have been reasonably adequately briefed, for the Prime Minister had earlier noted that Churchill 'has him at the Admiralty day and night and, I am afraid, tells him a lot of things he ought to keep to himself'.

To the Royal Navy their new First Lord looked a vague and insignificant figure; following Churchill, he was bound to. Stranded at Dumfries one night on a secret mission, Mr Balfour was advised to be careful to remain incognito and disarmingly replied that he was sorry, but he had just given the lift-boy his autograph. Embarking at Gourock on another mysterious errand, his aide found him murmuring to himself instead of getting into the boat. Mr Balfour was only quoting Sir Walter Scott, because everything looked so beautiful and the blue and red lights on the water so romantic.

The first night out on a voyage to America he asked his naval assistant whether it would be all right to take his clothes off. Yes, he was assured; if the liner was torpedoed there were at least thirteen hundred women and children to be rescued before they came for him.

But Admiral de Chair, who saw a lot of him, described the First Lord of the Navy's darkest days as 'one of the great men of the old time. . . . A polished gentleman of the old school and a philosopher, Mr Balfour was always calm, never hurried. No crisis, however serious, seemed to perturb him. He was always patient and encouraging to those who worked with him. He could see through any attempt to hoodwink him. . . . Although there were many occasions which would have seriously embarrassed an ordinary man, I never saw him angry or put out and he seemed equal to any eventuality. He put everyone at their ease and always appeared interested in any subject placed before him. . . . He was the essence of kindness and consideration.'

To those on whom Churchill and Fisher had sharpened their claws, he must indeed have been an angel in morning coat and striped trousers. The Fleet would have been happier perhaps with a stronger, more ostentatious personality. The Admiralty was getting a poor press—giving itself a poor press, very often, as in the public relations blunder which represented the battle of Jutland as something perilously like a defeat. Most Service departments were learning to come to terms with the journalists. Their Lordships did so slowly and with reluctance, after ' Silent Service' had become more an expression of disgust than approbation.

Another Cabinet crisis at the end of 1916 swept both naval chiefs away and put Sir Edward (afterwards Lord) Carson and Admiral Sir John (afterwards Admiral of the Fleet Earl) Jellicoe in their places; a partial reconstruction of the Admiralty's technical and operations divisions automatically took place.

Shipping losses over the year had brought Britain closer to defeat than was generally realised. The tonnage-lost curve went more steeply up the graph as it climbed into the first months of 1917. Half a million tons sunk in January leaped to 869,000 tons in April. " Is there no solution to the problem ? " asked Admiral Sims, the distinguished American strategist in charge of the United States Naval Mission in London. " Absolutely none that we can see now," replied Jellicoe.

Of the danger the British public was ignorant, but Cabinet and Admiralty were at their wits' end. The French naval authorities, and some British ones too, urged the adoption of the convoy system by which the old fleets of Britain, Spain and Holland had brought their merchantmen home; but the Admiralty rigorously opposed convoy. Lloyd George (Prime

Minister), Beatty (Commander-in-Chief, Grand Fleet), North-cliffe of *The Times*, Sims and the Committee of Lloyd's grew hoarse advocating it. Still the Admiralty hung back.

It was Admiral Sims's promise of American destroyers which turned the scale—lack of suitable escort craft had been one Admiralty objection—but Their Lordships' change of heart dated from the day the appalling April figures were released and the Prime Minister announced that he would visit the Admiralty and hold a personal enquiry into the conduct of the anti-submarine campaign. Jellicoe met him at the door with the outline of a convoy scheme.

What inspired the Admiralty's hostility to what appeared (although not all naval experts agree, even today) the obvious way of shepherding cargo vessels safely through submarine- and raider-infested waters ? Partly shortage of escort craft; the Grand Fleet was sacrosanct, and it tied up shoals of destroyers. Then there were fears that shipping would be slowed down too much and that arrival ports would be disorganised if the labour forces had to be adjusted to cope with dozens of un-loading jobs at once, instead of two or three at a time. Thirdly, the prospect of a mass reorganisation within the Admiralty to meet the heavy responsibilities which convoying would place on it—responsibilities which, by the character of the adminis-tration, could not be shouldered by subordinates, and which the senior officers were too busy to shoulder—ruled it out. (But the alternative, which the Americans proposed, would have given Plans a much heavier and more confusing operation: nothing less than a barrage of mines from one end of the North Sea to the other.) Finally, the Admiralty pointed to its apprecia-tions, which had always come down strongly, statistically, against a convoy system.

The statistics proved wrong. After convoying was intro-duced, merchant shipping losses, imperceptibly at first and then quite dramatically, declined.

Admiralty employees throughout Jellicoe's reign spoke of a 'new offensive spirit' in the conduct of the war. From outside, it was not noticeable to Sir Percy Scott: 'We can never hope to obtain a fleet well-equipped, well-organised and well-trained until this system of evading responsibility at the Admiralty is broken, the circulation of papers is speeded up and the official who shirks responsibility is made to suffer instead of being promoted as a safe man.' Scott relied on the 'admirals' corner' at the Club for most of his information, but there was something in what he said.

Admirals in the know smelled trouble behind the happy-family façade which Carson and Jellicoe were erecting. From the Grand Fleet, Beatty wrote to his wife: 'The Admiralty again once more seem to be the target at which all and sundry are letting fly. . . . There are rumours of change, but I pity any poor devils that have to go there and work under the present régime.'

At the end of the year Jellicoe suddenly left and to a friend who sent him a note of regret on his resignation he replied:

'Thank you so much for your letter which arrived today [29th December 1917]. I should like you to know that I did not resign but was *dismissed* very curtly by the First Lord without any reason at all being given. He did not even tell me personally, but wrote me a note. I have had trouble with him, as he wishes to be an autocrat after the Winstonian lines and I refused to accept such an attitude. He had treated various flag officers badly and I took exception to that. The result you see ! ! !

'I fear Wemyss will not stick up to him. I have often told Wemyss that he must realise he is a colleague and not the First Lord's servant, but he won't realise it. I am not very happy as to the future of the Navy. The best of fortune to you. I feel the parting in the Fleet, but I can't possibly serve in any capacity as long as Geddes remains. Ever yours, J. R. Jellicoe.'

Cabinet ministers had seen the move coming. Months earlier Sir Edward Carson had noted: 'Lloyd George wants to get Jellicoe out of the Admiralty, but he will not do it while I am here. It would be a disaster if Jellicoe were to leave.'

And so the Prime Minister had taken the first opportunity to find another job for his Irish barrister and to replace him with Sir Eric Geddes, principally—as had often been seen in the past—to get rid of his professional naval adviser.

The 'new offensive spirit' died with Jellicoe's departure. Admiral Rosslyn Wemyss (afterwards Lord Wester Wemyss) gave the impression of being more interested in saving ships than pursuing glory, or watching sailors pursue it. His must have been one of the loneliest sojourns in the apartments of Admiralty since Lord Sandwich fell out with his admirals, for the junior Lords all sent him to Coventry. It had required, it was rumoured, all Carson's forensic persuasiveness to deter Admirals Oliver and Halsey from indignantly walking out at their former chief's heels.

'None of them would speak to Wemyss after his dirty work,' a contemporary writes, 'as he must have known that Jellicoe was to be dismissed when the time came and that he was to succeed him.'

Geddes tried to persuade his admirals that Balfour and Carson had had as much to do with getting rid of Jellicoe as himself. Prompted by Sir Henry Oliver, the Chief of the Naval War Staff, the junior Lords composed a missive describing it as a lie, accusing the First Lord of double dealing and inviting him either to resign or dismiss them. Geddes did neither. The quarrel died down—whatever his feelings, a serving admiral could not throw up his job, only ask to be relieved—and the Board of Admiralty saw out the war, under a minister who remained *persona* utterly *non grata* with his department.

Geddes and Wemyss, among the most misunderstood and obstructed heads the Navy had ever had, were far from being the least efficient or successful. It had happened before that unhappy associations in the Board Room had gone with useful measures, and that pleasant partnerships had resulted in administrative sloth. Wemyss proved himself a much better desk-admiral than fighting sailor; Geddes earned an occasional grudging compliment from his colleagues for the firm line he took in Parliament with the critics of the Navy. The Board of Admiralty in the summer of 1918 looked, to veteran seamen, to be composed of minor-league characters compared with the giants who had crowded the Board Room in the early days. Gazing back, they could see a succession of dangerous scuffles round the Navy's main control panel at moments when all eyes and brains ought to have been on the conduct of the war. But it had not mattered all that much in the end. The Board of Admiralty and the Fleet had come through. Overloaded, sagging, creaking and misfiring, the old machine had trundled inexorably on.

26   Traditions of the Board

The Board of Admiralty of 1918 consisted of Lords Commissioners who, differ as they might effectively and temperamentally from those of 1914, performed functions and maintained a correspondence in much the same fashion as those members whom Sir James Graham appointed in 1832, and without substantial alteration from the Lords on that first Board of Admiralty which King William and Queen Mary formed at the end of the seventeenth century when Samuel Pepys was still alive.

It had a 'modern Pepys'—various Admiralty Secretaries have been distinguished with the description, from Evan Macgregor of the eighteen-nineties to Sir John Lang of the nineteen-fifties. The wartime 'modern Pepys' was Oswyn (afterwards Sir Oswyn) Murray, who had succeeded Sir Graham Greene, an uncle of the novelist. Sir Oswyn moved up from an outstanding career in the Victualling Department, a quarter from which it was rare to pluck a Permanent Secretary, at the end of seven years in which, *The Times* once said, more victualling progress had been made in the Navy than had previously been made since Trafalgar.

As Secretary, Sir Oswyn re-introduced a formal elegance of style in correspondence which has since been emulated but not often surpassed. He perfected the cool paternal brush-off to shore-bound officers clamouring for sea appointments—and had plenty of opportunity for doing so. A typical letter went to Italy for the future Admiral of the Fleet the Earl of Cork and Orrery:

'Sir, I have laid before Their Lordships your letter . . . conveying a request from Captain Boyle, British Naval Attaché at Rome, to be relieved of his duties and I am to acquaint you that, as this officer has been informed in reply to previous applications, they desire that he should remain at his post.

'My Lords would be glad . . . if Captain Boyle could be given to understand that his repeated applications to be transferred from an appointment which, however uncongenial to himself, is the one in which Their Lordships consider his services are most required are not in accordance with the best traditions of the Service and that, if he were relieved, it would only be to go, and to remain, upon half pay. I am, etc., O. Murray.'

Sir Oswyn's hand is evident in the polished syntax of the official letters of thanks which the admirals of the First World War received at the end of it and which are to be read in most of their biographies.

At the time of Murray's death in 1936 he was engaged on a history of the Admiralty. It was never completed, but extracts appeared in the naval magazine *Mariner's Mirror*, and some of the information in this book relating to the departmental organisation in Whitehall is borrowed from them. Sir Oswyn himself enters Admiralty history in the early twenties: he was the first Permanent Secretary to be raised to the status of a full member of the Board, co-equal with the Lords.

Just before World War I, the individual responsibilities of the Lords Commissioners could be summarised as follows:

The First Lord: the Royal Navy's representative in the Cabinet; answerable to Parliament and the country for the strength and sufficiency of the Fleet. He exercised the vestiges of the Lord High Admiral's ancient patronage, bestowing awards and honours, selecting or approving all promotions, appointing the flag officers and senior captains and heads of the major civil

departments. (In practice this was normally a matter of initial-
ling lists brought to him by the First Sea Lord, for the Sea Lords
knew these officers and the First Lord did not. But at times
the First Lord was known to go it alone, as Churchill did when
he brought in Jellicoe and threw out Callaghan, and as Geddes
did when he hired Wemyss and fired Jellicoe. Naval assistants
remember lists of promotions going up to the First Lord, and
coming down with one name crossed out. No explanation was
asked or given, and the deleted name never appeared again on
any promotion list.)

The First Sea Lord: operations, distribution ot the Fleet,
fighting efficiency, promotions and removals of senior officers;
Reserves, Gunnery, Torpedo; Naval Intelligence; the Hydrographer of the Navy. In wartime he directed the naval strategy.

The Second Sea Lord: personnel, manning and mobilisation;
the appointments of junior officers; the Royal Marines.

The Controller of the Navy (Third Sea Lord): shipbuilding
and repair; all the technical instruments and apparatus; dockyards, stores, ordnance — all the big spending divisions of
Admiralty.

The Fourth Sea Lord: transport, victualling; the medical,
chaplain, schoolmaster and other specialist branches; the internal
economy of the Navy, for example uniforms, bounties and
pensions. (He was sometimes known as the junior Lord
Commissioner.)

The Civil Lord: civilian staff in naval establishments; contracts for buildings and works ashore; purchase of lands.

The Parliamentary and Financial Secretary: finance generally
and the preparation of the annual Estimates. (He had formerly
been known as the Political Secretary, and sometimes deputised
for the First Lord at Question Time in the House of Commons.)

The Permanent Secretary: the Board's mouthpiece to the
Fleet; a liaison officer between the Lords; head of the Ad-

miralty Secretariat; keeper of records and expert on precedent and procedure.

In order to make the Sea Lords' jobs more intelligible to outsiders and foreigners during the war, they were given additional explanatory titles:

The First Sea Lord: Chief of the Naval Staff.

The Second Sea Lord: Chief of Naval Personnel.

The Third Sea Lord: (kept his title of Controller of the Navy).

The Fourth Sea Lord: Chief of Naval Supplies.

Their duties were very comprehensively laid down in a document called the *Table of Distribution of Business* which had originated in the methodical days of Mr Childers. It was held by the Permanent Secretary and could be amended only by order of the First Lord.

As of old, and to some extent even more than in former times, the wartime Lords Commissioners' duties constantly overlapped. The first concept, of a Board jointly responsible for all its decisions, was preserved. Departmental questions on the higher levels were, at least in theory, laid before it. If, for example, a question arose about building a canteen at Gibraltar, the Civil Lord and Controller would outline their views before the Board, and then all their colleagues would join in. Estimates, the building programme, ship design, naval regulations and senior appointments always went before the full Board.

A vote was never taken after Board discussion, because this might have put the First Lord in a minority, or in the position of having to defend a political decision about a technical matter on which he was not qualified to pontificate.

Instead, the First Lord listened to the arguments—having perhaps consulted some of the members privately beforehand—and then announced his decision, which went forward as a decision of the full Board.

Sometimes the burdens of war augmented the Board and

sometimes they split it into curious combinations. We have mentioned the Naval War Council, where an elderly unpaid admiral doing a purely advisory job with the Board could hold forth, but where most of the Lords Commissioners for executing the office of Lord High Admiral had no voice.

At one period in 1917 there were no fewer than eight Sea Lords, plus the First Lord, three Civil Lords and a civilian Controller (Mr Alan J. Anderson). It was the only time in the history of the post, and it lasted only for a few months, that the Third Sea Lord (Admiral Lionel Halsey) was separated from his traditional office of Controller.

When the old machine was labouring the War Council gave it injections of 'organisation and methods' experiments borrowed from other Whitehall departments, and from industrial concerns. At one period the Board divided itself in two, to become an Operational Board and a Maintenance Board. But, having gradually jettisoned the topweight, it emerged in 1919 in pretty much its former state. The long-sought-after Naval Staff had evolved into a semblance of the present-day Naval Staff, and two wartime posts on the Board—Deputy Chief of the Naval Staff and Assistant Chief of the Naval Staff— were afterwards to be revived, to bring the Sea Lord strength up to six.

What would have astonished Lord Orford, Lord Anson or Lord Barham—or even Sir James Graham—if they could have inspected the old familiar Board Room and its occupants would have been to discover that none of the Sea Lords nor their Secretary had a seat in Parliament. First Lord, Civil Lord and Parliamentary Secretary were the only party men: the rest— like the rest of the Navy—were apolitical and proud of it and if they voted at an election it would only be for the party, as Fisher had recommended, 'which was doing most for the Navy'.

It would sometimes occur again that a First Sea Lord happened also to be a member of the House of Lords—like Beatty. But he would not dream of making a political speech in Parliament as long as he remained in office.

A rule laid down when an iron ship was as absurd as a cloth hammer precluded the appointment of non-serving admirals as Sea Lords; except that, very occasionally, a notable retired admiral had been invited to become a stopgap First Sea Lord. Another law of the non-existent Admiralty constitution says that no admiral shall serve for more than three years on the Board—and that is also the maximum period for which, lower down in the departments, a captain or commander expects to serve. There have been celebrated rule-breakers: Fisher, who went on for nearly six years and returned for another eighteen months, and Earl Beatty in the nineteen-twenties, with a continuous seven and a half years.

To be First Sea Lord is the culmination of a naval officer's ambitions. He can go no farther. Afterwards there can be only retirement ahead of him—except that if he is an Admiral of the Fleet he never, at least on paper, retires. Second, Third, Fourth, Fifth and Sixth Sea Lords (we are dealing with the position up to 1964, since when these titles are falling into disuse) are sometimes younger admirals for whom an appointment to the Board of Admiralty is a step to high executive command in the Fleet. Such admirals on leaving the Admiralty could perhaps pick their own next appointments, and in the days of the big fleets they could take that vital leap to the top of the tree, as a commander-in-chief or flag officer in command of battle or battle-cruiser squadrons.

All the naval members of the Board draw the pay appropriate to their rank and a London allowance of a few shillings a day. The First Lord has his Cabinet Minister's salary and his residence, for which he pays a nominal rent. The civilians on the Board receive their parliamentary or civil service pay on the established scale.

With the Sovereign's approval, the Prime Minister selects his First Lord along with the rest of his Cabinet. The First Lord chooses a First Sea Lord (with the Sovereign's and Prime Minister's approval) if he does not want to continue with the First Sea Lord in office. The First Lord and First Sea Lord together choose the rest of the Lords Commissioners. The Permanent Secretary is rarely disturbed.

It is sometimes thought odd that the nation clings to the habit of making civilians the heads of the Armed Forces. It cannot be otherwise, if the Forces are to have a voice in Parliament. Nautical Civil Lords are no better, Admiralty history has taught, than political Sea Lords. The Admiralty is not unique. No one expects the Minister of Agriculture to be a farmer, or the Minister of Health a doctor. In the Royal Navy the only ferocious complaints come from those who think the First Lord has done them down, or who have a general anti-establishment frustration to work off—Sir Percy Scott, for instance, in one of his after-dinner tirades:

'We do not believe that a gentleman can be transferred from newspaper vendor, cavalry officer, lawyer, lunatic or railway agent into a competent First Lord of the Admiralty within the time the Opposition generally allows him to hold that office. . . . There is nothing more quaint than the birth of a ruler of the King's Navee. He springs from possibly quite low down in his own profession to the head of our profession in one bound, and he has great power. Mr McKenna kicked me out of the Navy, Mr Winston Churchill kicked out Jackie Fisher and Sir Eric Geddes fired out Lord Jellicoe.'

Undoubtedly there is something incongruous in the sight of a First Lord (who has perhaps spent all his life in the Trade Union movement in inland towns) cautiously feeling his way up the gangway of a warship, or struggling through the 'Immortal Memory' at the annual Pepys dinner in Magdalene College, Cambridge. Experienced naval officers, oddly enough, would not have it otherwise. They like to have someone at the top who can look at the Fleet and the rising captains and admirals from a viewpoint beyond the Sea Lords' narrow professional angle, someone with the power to override appointments and removals made by naval officers for naval officers. The First Lord's veto has often been a just corrective of decision based on personal prejudices and jealousies, on United Service Club gossip and in prosecution of ancient private vendettas.

27 No Peace for Their Lordships

Under Mr Walter (afterwards Viscount) Long a brand-new Admiralty Board assembled with a brand-new Admiral of the Fleet, Earl Beatty, as First Sea Lord—the youngest of all time if one excepts the freak elevation of the Duke of Clarence—and listened while Mr Murray read, as custom prescribed at the first convening, the Admiralty Commission. Old Admiralty hands referred to this ceremony as the 'reading of Guinny-Binny'. The juxtaposition of two words, 'Guinny' for Guinea and 'Binny' for Benin, in the long list of territories grouped under the Royal Navy's dominion since the eighteenth century, was always good for a smile to lighten the sombre formality of the occasion.

It was 1st November 1919. A year earlier Messrs Geddes and Wemyss had presided over an Admiralty which had received the news of the Armistice and drawn up the naval surrender terms—terms which naturally fell a long way short of satisfying fighting admirals like Beatty. Wemyss had his own reasons for discontent and disillusion: his name had appeared on none of the lists of money awards and peerages conferred on the war leaders. (It was made up to him in 1919, when he retired.) On 1st November, the new Sea Lords, all drawn from the Grand Fleet which had accepted the German Fleet's capitulation, all favourites of Beatty, came (writes Admiral Chalmers) 'as a fresh breeze from the sea, and with a determination that the dust which had accumulated in a century of civil administration should neither be thrown in their eyes nor allowed to clog the wheels of progress'. Others before them had arrived with exactly the same hopeful determination.

Talk of peace for all time was much in the air. There was no peace for the Admiralty. That body's role in the twenties was that of a great administrative department on the defensive.

The admirals achieved what had long been promised: a pay-rise for seamen, who had been standing still for more than twenty years on one and sevenpence a day. (Beatty declared that they got it only just in time to avoid serious disturbances; he himself had rather rashly promised it before he left the Grand Fleet.) The Board then cast a sympathetic glance at the younger element, the non-vocal section of the Navy, brought the boy seamen and boy stokers out of the insanitary training hulks which had disfigured the harbours of Queenstown, Falmouth, Devonport, Portland, Portsmouth and Port Edgar since 1880, and prepared to add H.M.S. *Saint Vincent* at Portsmouth to the boys' training barracks at Shotley and Devonport. They closed Pembroke dockyard, which Viscount Melville had opened in 1814, when it seemed that Britain's future enemies might lie in the west.

Beatty's Board, all big-ship advocates, fought hard to keep battleships and build more, against a rising tide of expert opinion which saw no future for the large floating fortress. Post-war analyses of Jutland provoked wearisome controversies and did little to support the big-ship case. Through the medium of the correspondence columns in *The Times*, Sir Percy Scott persistently advertised for someone who could tell him what was the use of a battleship, and published the results of his enquiries: from a captain at the Admiralty—to fight other battleships; from a midshipman in the Fleet—no damned use; from a lady—' they have nice smooth decks for dancing on '.

Parliament, anxious to economise, and ministers, keen to see reductions in everyone's department except their own, welcomed the cry to ' scrap the Battleship '. Aviation enthusiasts demanded

the return of the Navy's Air Arm to the Navy, to be expanded
at battleship expense. The only people, it was alleged, in favour
of keeping big ships were those admirals who had a sentimental
attachment through having commanded them; a good number
of whom served in high places at the Admiralty.

A sub-committee of the Committee of Imperial Defence
investigated 'The Place and Future of the Capital Ship' in 1921
and recommended retaining battleships as the main fleet unit.
'Aeroplanes cannot damage battleships.' Critics asked what
else could one expect of a committee 'packed' with capital-
ship enthusiasts like Mr Long, Admiral Beatty and Mr Churchill.

Looking about them for something to slash, efficiency experts
of Government and press brought the Naval Staff under close
scrutiny. Scott, from over the horizon which his age and ill-
health were forcing him to retreat, fired a final salvo: 'The
Navy does not require a greatly expanded Naval Staff sitting
in offices at the Admiralty performing routine work. . . . The
Service requires open-eyed, well-educated, progressive, practical
seamen . . . with time to think of the needs of the future.'

But Beatty concentrated his staff, enlarged it, endowed it
with extra powers and used it in a well-meant effort to streamline
the unstreamlineable in the warrens of the departments.

Materially, Britain's two-power standard was a dream of the
past. Colonel House at Versailles must have sent statesmen of
the Viennese Congress spinning in their graves with his announcement that the United States would not " willingly submit
to Great Britain's domination of the seas any more than to
Germany's domination of the land".

" The sooner," Colonel House had gone on, " the English
recognise the fact, the better it will be for them. Furthermore,
our people, if challenged, will build a Navy and maintain an
Army greater than theirs." To this kind of Yankee bluster the
First Lord had violently reacted and Mr Lloyd George had been

impelled to declare that Great Britain would 'spend her last guinea to keep her Navy superior to that of the United States'.

But a less-than-one-power standard, parity in fact with America, was aimed at when the Admiralty prepared its plans for the Washington Conference of 1921 and 1922. Relieved at that series of meetings of the need to lay down new capital ships for ten years, and winning freedom in other directions, Beatty and his colleagues turned to the task of putting their ideas across to the home Government and the country. They submitted proposals for a big cruiser fleet and for expensive works to modernise the base at Singapore; but ran into trouble. A report from the notorious Geddes Committee of 1922 sent naval journalists and members of Parliament in full cry after disclosures of wanton waste at the Admiralty, and some of the Committee's strictures were hard to answer. Next year, to the horror of old salts everywhere, Parliament rendered all Their Lordships' ideas on strengthening the Fleet sterile by adopting the ten-year rule, based on the assumption that no major war could be expected for that period.

Lord Beatty called on the memory of Heligoland and Dogger to help him fight Naval Estimates through Parliament via First Lords who, through illness, diffidence or pressure of other interests, laid a heavy weight on his shoulders. (Mr Long gave way to Mr Arthur—afterwards Lord—Lee, who gave way to Mr L. S. Amery.) Early in 1924 the first Labour Government took office. Beatty wrote:

'Today Amery has departed and the new First Lord is Lord Chelmsford, who was the Viceroy of India and has thought fit to join Labour and the Socialists. The Parliamentary Secretary is Mr Ammon, who was in the P.O. as a clerk some years ago. The Civil Lord is Mr Frank Hodges, an out-and-out Labour man . . .'—though he could hardly expect him to be anything else. Before the Sea Lords had had time to get used to their

Red Flag comrades—whom they found surprisingly reasonable and fair-minded creatures, for Socialists, and who made agreeably short work of the Estimates—the Conservatives were back with Mr W. C. Bridgeman as First Lord.

The new Government haggled over the 1925 Estimates. Beatty had still not got the cruisers he had demanded. A stormy session at a Cabinet enquiry ended with First Lord and First Sea Lord informing the Prime Minister that they would resign unless the Admiralty figures were accepted. The popular press, having made up its minds that navies were old-fashioned and aircraft the only weapons that mattered, advised Mr Baldwin to stand firm. After several days of straight talking on both sides, in the intervals of which Beatty marched home to work on the resignation speech he intended to make in the House of Lords, both sides agreed on a compromise.

' An extremely good debater and well able to hold his own with the Chancellor of the Exchequer,' was Mr Bridgeman's last tribute to Earl Beatty; no lukewarm one, considering that Winston Churchill was the Chancellor in question. Beatty brought a regal aloofness to the job of First Sea Lord which recalled Fisher at his most superior and dictatorial, and which thoroughly cowed the First Lords and certain Cabinet ministers of the twenties. Geddes, himself a man who stood no nonsense, had earlier thought Beatty conceited, and had delighted to put him in his place—the place of Commander-in-Chief, Grand Fleet—when Beatty tried to use the same authority with the Admiralty as Haig had employed with the War Office.

Amery found him difficult and arrogant; Arthur Lee never got on to good terms with him. Beatty's relations with Bridgeman were cordial but wary. He exploited the Navy's unique strength, its popularity with the common man. Whatever Parliament and the press might say, he counted on the British

Old Admiralty Building: the Entrance Hall

Old Admiralty Building: the Board Room

Chiefs of Staff, 1939 (Sir Cyril Newall, Sir Dudley Pound, Sir Edmund Ironside)

Earl Mountbatten, 1955

public's tremendous affection for the Fleet and admiration for the dash and spirit of its professional chief—the man who blasted German battle-cruisers to bits, who steamed into action with a decanter of port at his elbow, who had stopped a taxi in Pall Mall after dining late at his club and told the driver to take him to Portsmouth, who emerged every morning from his official residence at Mall House (above the Admiralty Arch) like an ambassador on his way to present credentials, elegant in morning coat, dark striped trousers, a high collar, with black satin cravat and pearl tiepin.

"Most of 'em," said an Admiralty messenger, speaking of the Sea Lords, "'as a bit of bird-seed for lunch and don't leave the office. The Earl was different. 'E would saunter across to the Carlton Hotel and 'ave a gentleman's lunch with a nice glass of brandy, and come back all smiles, smoking a fine cigar." The rank and file, at the Admiralty and beyond, adored a touch of *panache*. It was not too common in public figures, in the humdrum twenties.

Sir Eric Geddes, an economist and perfectionist, had tightened up Board Room procedure—every hundred years or so it needed tightening up—by insisting on proper agendas, a précis of information for the Board with every item, and the systematic circulation of decisions to all the schools in the building afterwards. Beatty, too, was a stickler for the proprieties, and he contributed his own inimitable brand of battle-cruiser snap and decisiveness.

When the Imperial Defence Committee declined to include Gibraltar among the bases for which fighter-aircraft defence was to be provided, on the grounds that the levanter, the seasonal east wind, interfered too much with flying, the First Sea Lord whirled through the departments looking for substance for an argument. An assistant remembered that the Royal Navy had once kept a few flying-boats at Gibraltar under the command

M

of a Royal Marine officer. Beatty asked if the officer, Major Barnby, was still serving.

'I said I thought so,' Admiral Chalmers goes on, 'but did not know where. "Look him up in the Navy List"—I did so and found he was at Chatham. "Get him on the telephone and find out if he can produce evidence, a photograph or something."'

Barnby was playing tennis, but was ordered to 'come as he was' to the Admiralty and bring the family photograph album with him. The First Sea Lord tore out the picture which showed a flying-boat in the air and the characteristic levanter cloud covering the top of the Rock, and strode off to the Imperial Defence Committee with it—and Gibraltar got her fighter squadron.

Earl Beatty was fully into his stride when he passed the record set for the twentieth century by Fisher, of nearly six years as First Sea Lord. His were years of Service and political chopping and changing, and his colleagues rose and fell around him. He saw four prime ministers come and three go. Between 1920 and 1925 he welcomed five new First Lords, eighteen Sea Lords, seven Parliamentary Secretaries and six Civil Lords.

He was Baldwin's first choice as chairman of the Chiefs of Staff Committee—Beatty, Milne and Trenchard—which opened the era of inter-Service co-operation in 1926. In consultation with Mr Amery, he accepted for the Royal Navy the principle of independent Dominion navies, squadrons of warships built for and manned by the Canadians, Australians, New Zealanders and South Africans, 'national in spirit, national in organisation' —which Fisher and McKenna, back in 1909, had mercilessly shot down.

Earl Beatty learned what many a great sea officer before him had had to learn: that Service life at the top can be more demanding in peace than war. Contemporaries almost vener-

ated his bluff charm—or charming bluff—and the confidence
with which he trod the tortuous world of Westminster politics
—a world he entered too late in life to know everything about.
Though he always looked rather too handsome to have much
of a brain, though he often pretended to be a man of action,
a simple, direct sailorman and nothing more, he conducted the
Royal Navy through an intensely difficult phase with more
success than an intellectual First Sea Lord might have done.

His great battles over the Estimates availed nothing in the
long run. He pressed on anyone who would listen the case
for at least seventy cruisers—the Beresford syndrome—but the
number built and building during his seven years in office never
exceeded fifty, and was dwindling when he left the Admiralty.
Britain had none to scrap, when the London Naval Treaty of
1930 reduced cruiser tonnages.

He fought a lost battle over the Admiralty plan to fortify
Singapore. His skirmishes with the Royal Air Force about
naval aircraft were to spread after he had gone, but Beatty lost
the main engagement, no match for Lord Trenchard, from
whom he limped mauled in 1923. It took Duff Cooper and
Admiral Chatfield in 1937 to retrieve a portion of the Fleet
Air Arm and restore peace with the Royal Air Force, when
both sides agreed to recognise a distinction between carrier-
borne and land-based naval aircraft.

Beatty's bequest to the Board of Admiralty was the Sea
Lords' weekly meeting: no civilians allowed; not even the
Permanent Secretary to know what they plotted. He con-
sistently protected the integrity of the professionals in the Board
Room and he mastered the lay members in a way that only
Barham and Fisher had done before him.

The Navy had always assumed that another Beatty man—
feared it, because he was a dunderhead when it came to politics

—another flamboyant admiral, Sir Roger Keyes, would succeed his friend at the Admiralty in 1927. Sir Roger was not quite ready, however, to leave the Mediterranean command, and Admiral Sir Charles Madden, who had been Beatty's second-in-command in the Grand Fleet, took over temporarily. By the time Sir Roger was available, the *Royal Oak* affair of 1928 had wrecked his chances. On a trivial dispute arising between one of his junior admirals and a flag captain and a commander, Keyes ordered the admiral to haul down his flag and dismissed all three; and Parliament and public opinion were no longer as complacent as they had been a century earlier about the divine rights of commanders-in-chief.

The Admiralty wilted under the usual onslaughts for not foreseeing the trouble and for being secretive about it, and the First Lord, Mr Bridgeman, trembled on the brink of resignation. Cuts in naval spending had begun in the early post-war epoch. The trimming of naval and dockyard personnel to the bone by the First Lord's notorious 'axe' gave twenty per cent of the Service fresh and intimate reason to execrate the name of Geddes. Because of Britain's adherence to the ten-year rule, the 'axe' hung suspended over the Navy well into the thirties. When the rule was first made, the Admiralty had taken it to mean that it could prepare for war in 1933, which meant preparing at once; so much longer did it take, as First Lords were always trying to explain, to build a battleship than to build a bomber or a piece of artillery. (The two junior Services had long resented the Admiralty's favoured position in being allowed to stake out claims years ahead on industry, in creating over the decades advantageous links with the great armament firms in a manner impossible for Army or Royal Air Force.) But the Cabinet explained that the ten-year rule was renewable year by year. In 1933, when it was thrown aside, the Services were still working to an assumption that there would be no major war for ten years.

The atmosphere in the Old Admiralty building up to about 1936 little resembled that preceding World War I. No Fisher predicted with confidence the date of Armageddon, nor dominated the ministers with his personality and punch. Rather it resembled the period leading to the Crimean campaign, when First Lords boasted of their thrift and subordinates marked time. The same thing happened again. 'This country,' claimed Mr Bridgeman in 1928, 'has done more in the direction of disarmament and scrapping ships than any other nation since the armistice.' The Royal Navy had come out of the war with fifteen hundred warships in full commission; ten years later it mustered four hundred and five, and the number was diminishing.

Half the Fleet swung idly in peaceful out-of-the-way creeks, or equally peaceful dockyards, on a care and maintenance basis. The more distant royal yards, Rosyth and Pembroke, were quite abandoned. Great private shipyards on Tyne, Mersey and Clyde and great gun manufacturers who had been tied to the Navy for generations went out of business. The Admiralty did not close down. As bureaucratic organisations will, capitalising on the deepest depression, it steadily increased its numbers. A member of Parliament prophesied that 'when the [Labour Party's] dreams are almost realised and the Navy is reduced to one man, he will be found at the Admiralty '.

The Royal Navy had fewer friends than of old. Anti-capital-ship propaganda had weakened the nation's faith in warships. Sir Percy Scott and like-minded commentators had done harm they never intended. There was a piece of advice that newspapers and celebrities at school speech-days did not scruple to give, that young men of spirit ought to join the Royal Air Force, because the Royal Navy was a spent force.

The Naval Estimates for 1932—approved with a struggle,

with innuendo and insult—amounted to fifty millions, just about the 1913 figure. By the time ten millions had come off for war pensions and similar claims and the pay increases had been taken into account, Their Lordships were left with about a third of the amount Churchill and Prince Louis had had to spend. This pittance, as purple-faced admirals in the House of Lords kept pointing out, came at a time when British naval strength had reached the low point of the century, when the Fleet tally of battleships stood at less than a quarter, and of cruisers less than a half, of the 1914 numbers.

A prestige lost; a fleet jaded and vaguely depressed; promotion at a standstill—and then pay-cuts for the lower deck, applied on a more severe scale than simultaneous pay-cuts for officers. Warned by an atmosphere of discontent and some minor disturbances, the Admiralty woke up in 1932 to learn of the disciplinary breakdown in the Home Fleet at Invergordon, for which the press already had a word: mutiny.

When the trouble ended and the customary aftermath of denunciation of the Admiralty had run its course, Their Lordships adopted two interesting proposals, both designed to improve the sailor's morale.

Firstly, they discarded the top hats and tail coats in which they had been accustomed to go visiting the Fleet and the dockyards. The admirals put on their uniforms and the First Lord, Civil Lord and Parliamentary Secretary wore double-breasted dark blue suits and yachting caps with unobtrusive ' foul-anchor ' badges—the dress in which Mr Churchill, after he returned to the Admiralty in 1939, was so often pictured. Thus arrayed, the Board paid its first post-' mutiny ' visit to the Home Fleet, again at Invergordon, in 1933.

The second proposal concerned the reintroduction of sail training for young officers and men of the upper-deck branch; a plan which, on the point of being carried to Parliament for

approval, was mercifully abolished through the influence of a
new First Sea Lord who saw, apart from the disasters which
were bound to occur while seamen were adapting their brains
and limbs to the lost arts of a sailing-ship life, the incongruity
of asking Parliament for a Fleet Air Arm and half a dozen
old-fashioned schooners in the same Vote.

The First Sea Lord was Admiral of the Fleet Sir Ernle
(afterwards Lord) Chatfield, who had succeeded Sir Frederick
Field just after the ' mutiny '. In time served and still to serve,
he had, or would have, completed about eleven years at the
Admiralty through one of its unhappiest periods, until the
outbreak of the Second World War. He had been Controller
of the Navy in the last two years of Lord Beatty's reign, in
which post he had valiantly stood up to the Treasury and had
won a partial victory over the scheme foisted on Their Lordships from outside, to remove naval officers from all the dockyards and put civilians in their places.

An unhappy period—but only in poverty of achievement,
in Their Lordships' occupational necessity to run their collective
heads against a Treasury brick wall. Traditional differences
within the Admiralty, between departments immemorially at
odds with each other, sank under those which the whole administration sustained against the peacemakers in Westminster.
Professional and lay Lords had never pulled more rhythmically
together; First Lords pleaded as strongly as Sea Lords, and
usually much more ingeniously, to be allowed to restore the
Navy's waning strength. The Japanese aggressions, Abyssinian
war, Spanish troubles and German rearmament strengthened
their arguments, and before Lord Chatfield left the Admiralty
to join Mr Chamberlain's emergency Cabinet in August 1938
he had realised hopes for a big modern Fleet and big realistic
Estimates which, when he entered office six years before, had

looked utterly forlorn.

A new class of battleship was laid down: the *King George V* class, the last in British naval history. The Controller finally secured what six preceding Controllers had despaired of securing: *carte blanche* to build all the cruisers he could find slips for.

Rosyth dockyard re-opened and took on a thousand men; and a handful among them cost the Admiralty, through no fault of that department, many man-hours of explanation and embarrassment. Numerous acts of sabotage occurred in the dockyard as soon as it was back on a full Fleet repair footing. Five workmen, detected by Admiralty security officials, were dismissed; and the Fife accents of indignant members of Parliament were heard on the floor of the House of Commons, abusing the Board of Admiralty for its well-known arrogance and eighteenth-century sense of justice, in discharging men for alleged misconduct without giving them a chance to defend themselves. For fear of giving away security secrets, the Civil Lord declined to answer questions. The matter blew over, as it had blown up, in hot air, with the Navy's counter-sabotage machinery undamaged. But the Trade Unions won the right to be taken into the confidence of all the Service departments in case of future dismissals; which the Admiralty shook its head over, as a blow to dockyard discipline.

Admiral Chatfield, first as Controller (1925 to 1928) and then as First Sea Lord, and the exceptionally gifted Vice-Admiral Sir Reginald Henderson, Controller in the middle thirties, had made real efforts through the depression years to demonstrate that dockyards need not be what most sailors felt they had to be: disreputable, inefficient and unproductive. They had borrowed ideas from commercial yards and started the self-maintenance routines for warships which became an accepted part of every large vessel's domestic organisation. Instead of submitting to the Government's threat to do away with sailors in dockyards altogether, they lengthened the period which naval officers served there. Whether, when the great press of business descended on the yards towards the end of the thirties, the yards were better equipped to deal with it than they had been when they lived in terror of Sir John Fisher was debatable; but after such unheard-of novelties for an Admiralty department as clocking-in had been forced on them, the giant sloths of British naval shipbuilding and repair showed at least signs of stirring.

In the Controller's departments one would never have known the Navy was a back number. New annexes appeared in the dockyards, as important as they were untidy: the Boom Defence Depots, havens of marlinspike-fingered riggers and banes of inspecting admirals, a creation of the Naval Staff for defending the home bases against submarine attack by stretching nets across their fairways.

In another division of the Controller's empire, the Royal Corps of Naval Constructors reached an important milestone. Sir Eustace Tennyson d'Eyncourt, who designed many vessels of the First World War and did most of the work on the *Rodney* and *Nelson* battleships, retired in 1923. He was the last of the naval architects-in-chief whom the Admiralty appointed from outside. Throughout Henderson's and subsequent Controllers' times, the Navy's chief constructor was promoted from the Corps itself.

The three First Lords who so faithfully represented the Navy's case in Parliament during the thirties were Sir Bolton Eyres-Monsell, an old sailor, looking every inch a sailor in his smart new Admiralty-pattern yachting cap; Mr Duff Cooper; and, in between, for only a year, Sir Samuel Hoare (afterwards Lord Templewood). Chatfield recalls the eagerness with which Sir Samuel, who had stepped across from the India Office like many a First Lord of the past, set himself to learn all he could

M 2

in the shortest possible time about the Navy, having the First Sea Lord to dinner night after night and ' making copious notes on a block of notepaper, tearing off sheet after sheet until the carpet looked like snow '.

Sir Samuel passed an eventful year, during which he had the melancholy duty of arranging ex-King Edward VIII's passage to France in H.M.S. *Fury* on the night of his abdication. He left, if no other substantial monument, an official residence —Admiralty House—refurbished and beautified in a restoration long overdue. He found the world of Admiralty, he said, ' a world apart. The constitution of the office was peculiar to itself, the habits and methods of the sea dominated every activity, stories of the great admirals and the Fleet inspired as a religion the 250 naval officers working in it. . . . A First Lord would be extremely reluctant to override the views of the naval advisers, entrenched in so traditional a stronghold.'

There was a First Lord just off-stage, awaiting his cue, who was prepared, as he had been at the approach of the last great European conflict, to do precisely that.

Physically the Board underwent one significant change during the thirties. When Lord Chatfield arrived it consisted of the four Sea Lords, plus a Deputy Chief and an Assistant Chief of the Naval Staff; on the political side, First Lord, Civil Lord and Parliamentary Secretary; and the Permanent Secretary (Sir Oswyn Murray, a full member since 1921, died in 1936). When Chatfield left there was an extra member, whose arrival celebrated the end of a twenty-year tussle with the Air Force. He was numbered fifth among the Sea Lords and he administered the Fleet Air Arm.

When Mr Bridgeman and Earl Beatty had proposed resigning over the cruiser-building crisis, they had set new precedents for the age-old responsibility dilemma: 'individual' or 'collective'. The other Sea Lords had wondered whether they, too, should resign. But Beatty informed them that they could make their solidarity known in a statement but that their duty to carry on the naval administration outweighed other considerations. Throughout the Beatty era, mainly because of the pomp and personality which surrounded him, and his seniority in office, First Lord and First Sea Lord had walked, or appeared to walk, comfortably in step. It was not unknown for the sailor to deputise for the politician at some Commons technical committee or enquiry where the latter felt he might be out of his depth.

In the thirties, gestures were futile and the question was not asked. But Lord Chatfield, a towering figure in his quiet fashion, had ideas of his own about the relative positions of First Sea Lord and others, and he put them on paper for a guide to his successors:

'The First Sea Lord's office is largely that of making final decisions or, in certain matters, recommendations to the First Lord. In all technical matters he is the final arbiter. Not that it is necessary for the other Sea Lords to refer matters, within their separate administrative tasks, to the First Sea Lord. They are independent and, except for perhaps the D.C.N.S. and A.C.N.S., they are responsible to the First Lord alone. But the First Sea Lord is the experienced leader who stands behind them and to whom they will come in person, or to whom they will mark the paper under consideration, should they be in doubt or if the problem be of great importance. Such problems may be material ones, affecting the design and production of ships or their equipment; personal problems affecting the men of the Fleet; problems of pay, fuel or stores; or the constant ones affecting the development of naval air power.'

Long ago, the First Sea Lord was first because his name

fortuitously appeared first on the Commission and everyone agreed to let him take the chair. In the twentieth century, three First Sea Lords who served long terms—Fisher, Beatty and Chatfield—raised the pedestal of the office and enlarged its scope. The First Sea Lord of 1939 took over his post as he would have taken command of a ship. Fellow Sea Lords were his officers and the civilian Lords, if they failed to assert themselves, could end up as his passengers.

28 The First Lord Celebrates

It fell to General Sir Leslie Hollis, Royal Marines, at a Chiefs of Staff conference, to pass to the First Sea Lord news of the first major naval disaster of the Second World War: the unaccountable sinking of H.M.S. *Royal Oak* in the Fleet anchorage at Scapa Flow.

'I handed the signal to Sir Dudley Pound. He read it, turned it face down on the table without a flicker of emotion of any kind, and continued the discussion as if nothing had happened.'

Admiral Pound had gone to the Admiralty on the death of Sir Roger Backhouse in April 1939, having only a few months before been a contender with Sir Roger for the post left vacant by Chatfield. The appointment was coolly received in the Fleet: all that anyone seemed to know about Pound was that scarcely anyone knew him; that he had spent years in shore jobs, was a survivor of the discredited Beatty-Keyes clique and tended towards an autocratic manner and to surround himself with his friends.

No one expected Pound to last, especially when Mr Churchill, scourge of naval chiefs, returned to the First Lord's office. And the Admiral was, indeed, moved to offer his resignation numerous times; but only on patriotic grounds, and it was always refused. Churchill remembered how, on first being introduced, they had 'eyed each other amicably, if doubtfully'. They had reason to; what had happened the last time must have been much in both men's minds at that moment.

Yet it was the doubt that vanished, and the amicability that remained and strengthened. The mixture of seemingly ill-assorted metal, mercury and old gold, wore well, and if any leader of the Armed Forces in the twentieth century could be said to have earned and kept Churchill's admiration, and to have held his free-ranging imagination at least half in check, the leader was Sir Dudley Pound.

He was a lonely figure, an unsmiling desk admiral. Dark shadows moved over the Board Room in his time: the Narvik failure and the inexplicable loss of aircraft-carriers; the sorrow-ful episode of the actions against the French Fleet, former allies; the *Scharnhorst-Gneisenau* escape; the sinkings of the *Hood*, *Repulse* and *Prince of Wales*; the disastrous Dieppe adventure and the expensive Malta convoys; U-boat supremacy. For all these events the First Sea Lord shouldered the responsibility, for he insisted with Chatfield that ' in technical matters the First Sea Lord is the final arbiter '. They shortened his life, and Admiralty stock, chronically depressed, began to rally only just before his death.

In victory he renounced the kudos in favour of the man on the spot. He avoided publicity, explaining nothing and apolo-gising for nothing, and withstood press attacks in silence. (Those commentators who most violently campaigned for the abolition of capital ships were always the most indignant when they were sunk.) His talent for concentrated endeavour, his discretion and genius for applying the curb and the spur, his unique organisa-tional ability, were appreciated only by the inner circle of associates who saw him daily and nightly in action.

It has since been learned that Pound fought not only a war, not only his First Lord and the Service chiefs, but also a tumour on the brain. His habit of dozing off at important meetings amused his colleagues. He reminded Lord Alanbrooke of ' an old parrot asleep on its perch '. But the soldiers and airmen got him to fight their battles too, because he was the only war leader to whom Churchill as Prime Minister listened with respect. Aghast at the bee in Winston's bonnet over the proposed capture of Trondheim and weary of arguing with him that such an attempt was impossible, the field-marshals and air-marshals gave in, on condition that Pound would order the Fleet into the fiord.

'At this'—it is Sir Arthur Bryant's account—'everyone looked at the First Sea Lord who, as was often the case in long committee meetings, had begun to doze. But at the mention of the Fleet the old man, to whom the security, traditions and transmitted wisdom of his Service were life itself, awoke to full activity and shook his head vigorously. On this the Prime Minister, who had a deep respect for Pound and his judgement . . . desisted from his plan.'

He could not stop the Prime Minister from sending thirteenth-hour reinforcements to Singapore, whereby two capital ships were lost; but he firmly set his face against another pet project of Mr Churchill's, a foolhardy scheme for a naval offensive in the Baltic.

'Courageous, imperturbable and of the highest integrity, he spared himself nothing,' wrote Hollis. Pound died on Trafalgar Day 1943, having just retired through insupportable pain and exhaustion: one of the few great figures of military history who might be said to have been killed by overwork. If the Royal Navy should ever go in for a series of warships bearing the names of renowned First Sea Lords, it could well be called the *Pound* class.

Of the Navy's political chiefs during the years of crisis, Mr Duff Cooper enjoyed only a year in office before resigning over the terms of the Munich agreement. He gave every sign of 'enjoying' it. Back-benchers in the House of Commons frequently, while attacking the naval administration, objected to him taking so much time off to go cruising in the *Enchantress*. Churchill had done the same up to the outbreak of the previous World War, but some people found it hard to understand why Cooper had to take his Society friends with him. In the wrecking—as it then appeared—of a glowing political career, nothing disturbed him more than leaving what, for all the ups and downs of the inter-war years, was still a plum ministerial appointment, with outstanding perquisites. 'The First Lord has one of the finest houses in London,' he wrote, 'and a yacht in which to sail the sea. He knows also that, in any encounter he may have with his colleagues, he has the country on his side.'

Duff Cooper spent much of his Admiralty time working on the future of the Fleet Air Arm, taking advice on the subject from his friend and newly-promoted captain, Lord Louis Mountbatten, who had previously done his time in the new branch. The last battle to make the Fleet Air Arm wholly naval ended in 1941, when Admiral Pound quietly assumed joint operational control with the R.A.F. of Coastal Command.

On 3rd September 1939 the Admiralty issued in the heat of the moment an unusually human signal to every ship and establishment at home and abroad: 'Winston is back'. Thousands in the Fleet vaguely appreciated that this meant both thrills and spills, and the message probably came equally as a warning and an inspiration to the senior officers who remembered, or had read, their Admiralty history.

Mr Churchill instantly called for maximum revolutions on the Admiralty telegraph, in a steam-age manner of speaking, and the engines moved to Full Ahead—not without some protesting and throbbing of machinery.

As of old he teemed with exciting ideas, finding room in the overcrowded building for Professor Lindemann and a team of statisticians to keep his acres of maps, diagrams and tables refreshed, poking down into departments traditionally excused the attentions of senior officials and stirring up nests of somewhat somnolent hornets, loading Intelligence, Plans and Operations with frightening tasks and short-circuiting the age-old communication lines with brazen aplomb.

Far from letting memories of the Dardanelles shambles subdue him, he began by proposing naval enterprises in the Baltic and on the coasts of Norway which could have decimated the Fleet in days. Pound, without quenching the fire, directed it towards less dangerous combustibles.

'Winston is a whole Admiralty in himself,' Admiral Sir William James was writing when the war broke out, 'and will have much to say about dispositions and, probably, operations; but Pound and his *fidus Achates* Phillips start with some handicaps as, unlike most of their predecessors, they have no colourful background and that becomes of importance when setbacks are experienced. Prince Louis, Jacky Fisher, Jellicoe, Wemyss, the First Sea Lords of the last war, though men of widely different character, all had this in common—a rich, colourful past—when they came back to the Admiralty.'

The Phillips whom Admiral James refers to was Admiral Sir Tom Phillips, Pound's one-time navigating officer, an industrious administrator and excellent staff officer who had been little at sea in the previous six years and had never held a high command. Phillips had the most tragic of wars: badgered and frustrated as Vice-Chief of the Naval Staff while the Admiralty was feeling its war-legs and everything going wrong; thrust in a moment of panic into the death-or-glory atmosphere of a Far Eastern conflict dominated by the Japanese; and losing his life, along with the lives of hundreds of his officers and men, in the *Repulse* and *Prince of Wales*, before the admiral he relieved had even left for home. He had been, ironically, the supreme exponent of the big-ship school on the Chiefs of Staff's joint planning committee in the capital-ship-versus-aircraft controversy which had hampered its discussions over the pre-war planning period.

Sometimes encouraged, more often thwarted, by a firm omniscient First Sea Lord, Churchill succeeded up to May 1940 (when he became Prime Minister) in showing flashes of that reckless aggression which had sometimes won and sometimes lost startlingly imaginative naval operations. He risked ships and sacrificed men, but it was in his few months at the Admiralty that the soul-stirring events of a dreary first winter advertised to the world that the Royal Navy had got down to business: the *Graf Spee* action, the *Altmark* incident, lifting British hearts and winning back hope for pessimistic sympathisers abroad.

Mr Churchill, barred from the Admiralty for twenty-five years, newly entered with all to gain or lose, knew as well as anyone the risks he ran—knew, as he put it in *The Gathering Storm*, 'how First Lords of the Admiralty are treated when great ships are sunk and things go wrong'.

Some of his departmental correspondence has passed into Admiralty lore. His green-ink memoranda—the sight of which, a generation afterwards, still had the power to galvanise old Admiralty servants turning them up—embraced the gravest questions of the grand strategy and the most trivial of clerical problems: the distribution of battleships in the Mediterranean and of backgammon boards to the mess-decks of small craft; the removal of the magnetic-acoustic-'supersonic' mine and of colour-discrimination in patrol vessels of the Indian Navy; compensation to the Faeroese for giving up an airport, and to the Captain of the *Altmark* for losing his watch and Iron Cross; reinstatement for commodores of great ocean liners turned out of their ships and for a rating turned off his officers' course because he had the wrong accent. A naval officer of the wartime Trade Division of Admiralty remembers Churchill's first request to that department: 'Report the names of British passenger ships which, if sunk, would cause national despondency'. The Division gave the names of the *Queen Mary* and the old *Mauretania*, and those liners were shortly ordered to the United States to be kept in a place of safety until they were required for trooping duties.

From the earliest days of the war off-shoots of Admiralty were springing up. Queen Anne's Mansions, a big block of Government offices near Saint James's Park in London, started as an annexe and outgrew its parent building. The Director of Navy Accounts took over huge areas of property in Bath. Research and experimental establishments with incomprehensible names proliferated all over the Home Counties. Branches of the dozens of new divisions of Admiralty—submarine administration, weapons, minesweeping—spread over London and provincial cities, naval air stations and training establishments burst out in the countryside miles from any port. It had taken the Navy Board thirty years to make the move from Somerset House to Whitehall, and the Board was never the same again; the Admiralty of 1939 increased its staff and its responsibilities a thousand per cent, and seemed to get it done within weeks.

While Mr Churchill was First Lord he recovered for the Royal Navy the control of the Coastguard Service, which Lord Fisher had managed to transfer to the Board of Trade in order to skim something off the Estimates.

When invasion threatened Britain in 1940, plans were laid to remove Admiralty headquarters to Edinburgh, the only other city in the British Isles—it was said—with teleprinter and telephone facilities capable of handling its traffic. The

move was halted—so the Whitehall story goes—when enormous
cannon were detected travelling north through Denmark.
They were later identified as spare guns for the *Tirpitz*, but
by that time the Government had changed its mind about
moving.

One unit of Admiralty travelled much farther afield. A
miniature Controller's department arose in Australia at a later
stage of the war, to supply the Fleet Train in the Pacific.

Behind the Old Admiralty building in London, at one side
of the Horse Guards Parade, the mysterious Citadel had grown,
a squat, brown-brick monstrosity whose purpose—like that of
the Admiralty telegraph of long ago—Londoners could only
guess at. It had, in fact, a similar function. It was the iceberg
tip of the Royal Navy's 'Radio City', the underground
metropolis of the wartime communications world.

The centre of this scattered collection of buzzing hives, after
Churchill left the Admiralty, was the Labour Cabinet minister,
Mr A. V. Alexander, who had also had a previous spell as First
Lord. Unlike some of his predecessors he was not given to
letting off dazzling displays of fireworks in Parliament, or to
showing himself to the Fleet. Few of the thousands who joined
the Royal Navy to serve in World War II could, at the end
of it, have made an intelligent guess at the First Lord's name.
He conformed exactly to everything Lord Fisher would have
considered a First Lord in wartime should be—'absolutely
restricted to policy and parliamentary procedure'. The conduct
of the war at sea he had to leave to the Prime Minister and his
professional colleagues, for he was not a member of the omnipotent council, the Chiefs of Staff Committee.

Alexander's one memorable reform in the structure of the
Navy had no great news value for anyone outside the Service,
but it represented a sharp break with tradition and showed that
Their Lordships were alive to the need for striking changes at

psychological moments. Promotion to flag rank had been settled since 1718 on seniority alone. A Fleet Order of December 1940 permitted outstanding young captains to be advanced regardless, within certain limits, of their seniority on the list. It was done to reward and inspire embryo Vians and Mountbattens; a clever public relations exercise.

Mr Alexander held his job throughout the rest of the war; something that could be said of very few Cabinet Ministers. He was attacked, in the press and in Parliament—that, one might say, is what First Lords are paid for. Colleagues gave him credit for having a great deal of knowledge of the naval background and an impressive grasp of the intricacies of Admiralty. He was a twentieth-century Graham, handling an organisation immeasurably more complex than Sir James Graham could ever have envisaged. It was inevitable that someone should dub the Board of Admiralty in his time ' Alexander's Ragtime Band ', and that the name should stick.

A suffering junior once wrote in the *Political Quarterly*: ' The device carried on the Admiralty Flag is that of a foul anchor, the symbol of everything that a sailor spends his life in trying to avoid. Many officers who abandon ship and go to serve at the Admiralty also abandon hope very soon after they get there, and say, as Captain Robert Scott said of the South Pole, "Great God! This is an awful place!"'

Most serving officers at the Admiralty in the Second World War, when they were numbered in many hundreds, would have agreed with the sentiments, though a purist might have pointed out that the anchor was not really fouled; it only looked it. That was the Admiralty's position, too.

Hardly anyone left the Admiralty feeling happy, fulfilled or optimistic about the progress of the war. ' This is a far, far more difficult war for the Admiralty staff,' Admiral James explained. '. . . I saw a lot of Wemyss as First Sea Lord during the last war and I had to take my Room 40 stuff to his meetings. He would not touch minutiae and left all detail to the Deputies and Assistants, and so never worked late at night unless there was a major operation afoot, and was able to go to Paris for a couple of days when something had to be co-ordinated with the French, or take a day off when the spirit moved him. Everyone took their cue from him and there was a very healthy decentralisation in those days.

'But the high speed at which everything takes place today is reflected in all the administrative centres and I hear that the fellows at the Admiralty work unconscionably long hours. That is not good, I suppose, but it cannot be helped. I am told that the conditions of this war have reversed the 'pyramid' and that commanders leave the Admiralty at six, captains at eight, junior admirals at ten, senior admirals at midnight and C.N.S. (Chief of the Naval Staff) at two a.m.!'

Naval officers, perhaps coming in from a warship life where the day began about seven in the morning, had often looked with jaundiced eyes at their civilian colleagues who never started before ten. But the habit enabled them to continue in wartime until the early hours of the following morning, as many of them had to. The Sea Lords, when they were not touring the fleets and the battlefronts—another obligation of modern Admiralty—worked earlier and also, as Admiral James noted, later than their subordinates. The kind of curious hours which naval members of the Board put in made Earl Saint Vincent's routine (five a.m. to seven for interviews daily, and he was an old man at the time) look quite reasonable; and those same members ran the daily risk of being sent for at the end of them and detained by Churchill, who kept the strangest working hours of all.

Distinguished newcomers from civil life without prior

experience of the Admiralty ethos, who were often given senior naval rank and special departments in the style of the old-time supporters of Lord Sandwich, made things awkward for the permanent staff by trying to be super-efficient and to modernise the ancient organism. To return to the hive metaphor, it was like trying to teach a swarm of bees, who knew perfectly well what they were doing, to collect pollen and turn it into honey in a more systematic fashion. One baffled initiate, Lord Reith, whom Churchill made a captain, Royal Navy, complained:

' Anyone with experience of ordinary business administration was bound to be vexed on occasion by Admiralty procedure, or the lack of it. . . . So many departments and divisional heads . . . writing or signing incredibly pompous letters. . . . Sometimes it was shocking.'

To fit in at naval headquarters, the stranger must accept the Admiralty's old-fashioned way of doing its job, its rambling legacies of mid-Victorian bureaucracy and sailor-like improvisation; and must remember that this, with all its deficiencies in a business man's eyes, was the department of State which calmly and overnight assumed control of British shipping all over the world and arranged the routeing of every single vessel on every voyage; which—to take a few examples—instituted world-wide systems of contraband control and censorship— vast undertakings requiring the co-operation of dozens of authorities in every country of the Commonwealth; which amassed a fleet and trained and provided men and women (for the Wrens became a real force after 1939) approximately twenty times the size of the pre-war Navy; which fitted to every major war vessel, and most minor ones too, such complicated new technical weapons as the Bofors and Oerlikon guns, and equipped them with radar, asdic and various devices which the ordinary sailor had not even heard of in 1939; which dealt with the magnetic mine, the acoustic mine, the homing torpedo and the glider bomb—secret enemy weapons which had to be recovered intact, stripped and scientifically investigated, then countered by rapid new inventions and rapid protection applied to ships. Not more than any Service department should expect to be called on to do in time of modern war, perhaps; but performed with such speed, smoothness and success that observers found it difficult to support the view that the Admiralty was helplessly entangled in its own past, and Their Lordships asleep in their Board Room chairs, dreaming of three-deckers and carronades.

Admiral Cunningham (afterwards Viscount Cunningham of Hyndhope), who succeeded Pound as First Sea Lord, and who before his Mediterranean adventures had been Deputy Chief of the Naval Staff under Lord Chatfield, expressed a particular admiration for the Admiralty civil servants who, though they are after all *the* Admiralty, the guardians of its genius and continuity, have never been accustomed to receiving bouquets.

'Their knowledge and ability, their logical methods of approaching and dealing with all problems, commanded my deepest respect. I retain a feeling of gratitude for their continued tolerance and helpfulness towards one whose methods must at times have filled them with horror.'

Throughout the war the Board of Admiralty met two or three times a week; but only the two secretaries were really regular attenders. The naval Lords spent much of their week on Government, special and technical committees, and in inspecting ships and stations. The First Lord and two civil members passed long days and nights in the House of Commons and, again, in visiting establishments and taking the chair of dozens of wartime committees. Twice the Board Room was out of action, littered with broken glass. On 17th April 1941 two bombs pierced the roof above the room, shattering the panelling at each corner and bringing down the gold-and-white tracery of the ceiling, damaging the famous table and Gibbons wood-carvings and pitting the sea-pictures with rubble.

Under a roughly-plastered ceiling, surrounded by boarded-up panelling and a blank space where the historic wind-vane had once been, the full muster of the Board of Admiralty took place on VE-day, 8th May 1945.

' A day of some turmoil,' the First Sea Lord recalls. ' At the Admiralty we had a Board meeting at noon, the principal business being the drinking of a bottle of Waterloo brandy produced by the First Lord, Mr A. V. Alexander.'

29 The Road to Polaris

When presenting the Naval Estimates for 1946, Mr
Alexander gave Parliament a last resumé of the events of the
war, the final score in the shipping losses, the grand totals of
enemy vessels and aircraft destroyed; and examined the state
the King's Navy found itself in after the harshest series of all
its ordeals. He went out of his way to draw attention to the
two admirals who had chiefly contributed to the victory at sea:
Sir Dudley Pound and Sir Andrew (by that time Viscount)
Cunningham.

Alexander was soon to give up his job as First Lord. In
Mr Attlee's Government he was to be Minister of Defence,
the post which Mr Churchill throughout the war had combined
with that of Prime Minister. In October 1946 a new Ministry
of Defence was established and to a million-pound building off
Whitehall the wartime staff of the Defence Office was gradually
transferred.

Mr George (afterwards Viscount) Hall, described to the
Fleet as the arch aitch-dropper of the Labour Party, became
First Lord, and like the little boy who ran away to sea (to adapt
the American vice-presidential quip) 'was never heard of again '.
The ruler of the King's Navee lost his place in the Cabinet.
Medievally ninth in order among the Great Officers of State,
then for long periods supreme in the committees of the nation,
then for equally long periods the holder of a post which rivalled
that of the Foreign Secretary in influence and prestige, he
vanished from the inner councils. The writing had appeared

on the panelling round the restored Board Room wall.

Senior civil servants at the Admiralty spoke of a future which would hold less in the way of new building and more in the field of scientific research and development. Their forecasts were swiftly confirmed.

An Admiralty accomplishment taken for granted but a notable novelty for a department infamous in history for its brutal disregard of the men who had served it in time of need was a smooth and practically painless run-down of officers and men and a methodical laying-up of ships. The 'axe' which had mutilated the Fleet in the early twenties by an arbitrary chopping-off of a third of its long-service sailors did not fall twice. That it did not was a tribute to the scheme for demobilisation and re-shaping of the Service which Admiral Sir Algernon Willis had worked on as Second Sea Lord during the last year of the war.

But the Admiralty's old defect, poor public relations and a genius for laying itself open to criticism, brought it low in Parliament's esteem. What was the Navy doing? Impudent acts by Albania in wrecking two British destroyers, by Argentina in sending warships to assert sovereignty over the Falklands, by Guatemala in staking a claim on British territory in Honduras, were put down to the Admiralty's coy reluctance to give the world a proper idea of British naval strength and spirit. As Mr Churchill from the Opposition front benches declaimed, in an echo of a phrase which had already passed into the dictionaries of famous sayings, " Never has the Admiralty given so little fighting value for so much money and so many men, and never has such value as this is been so ill-presented to the world."

War had shown that some integration of the Armed Forces was inevitable, and all agreed that if it were to be done at all it would be as well to get it done quickly. The original proposals had been based on a central system of supreme command, abolishing the Admiralty, War Office and Air Ministry and absorbing their staffs into a single Ministry of Defence. Mr Attlee's Government adopted a modified version of the plan, leaving the three Service departments untouched at administrative level and the three Chiefs of Staff—Admiral Sir John Cunningham, Field-Marshal Viscount Montgomery and Air Marshal Lord Tedder—at their head.

The departments were intended to move together step by step, the Ministry of Defence retaining its wartime hold over them and in time gaining control of further naval and military strongholds along the corridors of Whitehall.

Cutting across this quiet revolution came the noisier and, to the country, more alarming one of naval integration in the North Atlantic Treaty Organisation. For the next five years, while the signalmen and telegraphists of the Fleet unlearned their codes and started studying NATO techniques, while engineers accustomed themselves to handling NATO-standardised fuelling equipment and electricians busied themselves converting to NATO types of circuits and instruments, First Lords were to have embarrassing moments defending the ' Americanisation' of the Royal Navy—which was what many M.P.s understood NATO was for.

Fears that the Admiralty was giving up its ancient right to rule the waves became a certainty when an American flag officer was appointed to command NATO's Atlantic Fleet. "Have we no British admirals?" thundered the Conservatives. It was nothing to the humiliation the press were able to get their teeth into when Italian servicemen and civilians—a defeated enemy—began to be preferred over Britons in the allied Mediterranean command.

There was a new Parliamentary and Financial Secretary to the Admiralty in 1951, to whom Mr Shinwell the Defence

Minister (Alexander having quitted that office and gone to the House of Lords) left most of the naval question-and-answer in Parliament. He was Mr James Callaghan and he impressed both sides as a lucid apologist for the Navy, with a thorough grasp of his subject. The Americans, he had to point out, had 850,000 sailors in their Navy, while Britain had only 150,000; our transatlantic friends must get the lion's share of the jobs.

Lord Fraser of North Cape became First Sea Lord in 1948. That year his Admiralty severed one last link with the old Navy Board, not a link that the world took much notice of. It abolished the ' warrants ' which the Principal Officers had once issued and which distinguished the Navy's inferior officers from those ' commissioned ' by Their Lordships. Naval warrant officers assumed the title of ' branch ' officers after the Admiralty had asked the Fleet for suggestions for an appropriate name, and so the gunner, bo'sun and carpenter and their modern counterparts and messmates hove, after a centuries-long march, within sight of their goal: equal status with the ' gentlemen officers '.

The Navy, said Lord Templewood, who as a former First Lord was entitled to know, ' is still almost a religion with the British people '. If so, few young men seemed keen on going to church. Recruiting figures dropped year by year—not that the Board of Admiralty was looking for a bigger Navy, but it wanted an élite force, hand-picked from a wider choice of applicants. Their Lordships had inclined away from the National Service Acts: it was axiomatic with them that two years was not enough to turn a youth into a sailor.

In October 1951, when the Conservative Government returned to power and the Korean War had temporarily reversed the shrinking trend in the Services, Mr Churchill again combined the job of Minister of Defence with that of Prime Minister. He appointed Mr J. P. L. Thomas, the future Viscount Cilcennin, to the Admiralty.

Mr Thomas, who saw six Defence Ministers in and out of office—Churchill, Lord Alexander of Tunis, Macmillan, Selwyn Lloyd, Walter Monckton and Anthony Head—also saw the Navy through the grafting operations which turned it into a fair-and-square mid-century arm of NATO and prepared it for its administrative merger with the rest of the Armed Forces. He reorganised the Royal Naval College at Dartmouth (discarding an earlier proposal to abolish Dartmouth altogether and make eighteen the age for officers to enter); put up tempting inducements for old sailors to re-engage and new ones to join, shortened periods of foreign service, promised married quarters at home and abroad, improved pay and allowances (again the Fleet was asked to contribute its suggestions); introduced the ' split list ', which divided executive officers into what naval jargon christened ' wet ' or ' dry ' categories to inform them at the middle stage of their careers whether they were booked for a future ashore or afloat; and abolished the coloured cloth (except for doctors and dentists) which for a hundred years had distinguished the seaman officer from the specialist. Not a move of earth-shaking importance, this last, but it had vital implications: it suggested that one day an engineer or an electrical officer, or even a paymaster or a schoolmaster, might command a ship or establishment, might even sit on the Board of Admiralty.

Mr Thomas had the unusual honour of being waited upon one day in his office by a delegation of five Admirals of the Fleet, three of them former First Sea Lords; probably the most awe-inspiring array of gold lace ever to beard a First Lord. They came to ask him to re-open the sad case of Admiral Dudley North, who had been peremptorily relieved of his job at Gibraltar by Pound and Alexander in 1940 for failing to take action to stop French cruisers passing the Rock, and who had ever since smarted over it.

Mr Thomas said no. Admiral North was not the first flag officer in British history to have been ordered to haul down his flag and no reason given. The Admiralty would preserve its venerable privilege of doing as it thought fit with officers of the Royal Navy. What the Admiral's parliamentary champions called ' injustice ' had little to do with it; nor did the matter concern Parliament.

The First Lord had nothing to lose politically by granting an enquiry—something to gain, in fact, because his political opponent, A. V. Alexander, who had broken Admiral North, sat in the House of Lords as Viscount Alexander of Hillsborough. But Admiralty traditions—discipline before justice; never apologise, never explain—were stronger than party ties, weightier than the combined weight of five Admirals of the Fleet.

In the upper house, Alexander was his customary tight-lipped self. Almost from the start and until the very end of the war, he had been a nebulous, unobtrusive, slightly menacing figure at the Admiralty. He had been at the centre of mysterious events which remained, and probably always would remain, only partially explained. He could speak, if he would, of enthralling debates unrecorded in the minutes. Lord Alexander's memoirs would be eagerly read by everyone who had an interest in the intrigues, betrayals, compromises, surrenders and heroisms of the ' battle of Whitehall '—if there had been the slightest chance of him writing them.

The last time Mr Thomas spoke on the Naval Estimates, in 1956, the Admiralty had two aircraft-carriers building or rebuilding; had laid down the first guided missile warship and the first gas turbine warship; had given the Fleet two kinds of the latest aircraft (the Sea Vixen and Scimitar); and had put every British battleship—there were five left—into reserve where, to the constant complaint of the advocates of thrift at any price, they still managed to cost the taxpayer three-quarters of a million pounds a year.

It was the year of Suez, with the Cyprus troubles coming to the boil; the year in which western relations with Soviet Russia touched their low point. Total Estimates for that year were exactly eight times the sensational forty-eight millions which Mr Churchill had forced on his colleagues in 1913.

Suez year brought changes at the top in Whitehall. Lord Hailsham stepped into the First Lord's shoes and quickly stepped out again in favour of the Earl of Selkirk, who was to be First Lord for the next two and a half years. The 'little admiral', Sir Rhoderick McGrigor, a pocket-sized bundle of administrative energy, having had only a few months as First Sea Lord, handed over to Earl Mountbatten.

From India Office to Admiralty had in years past been an accepted move in the ministerial game; and once again the Navy had a ruler from Delhi at its head. But Earl Mountbatten, the last Viceroy, had at first relinquished his claim to further high office by returning to active service in the Mediterranean Fleet in the rank of rear-admiral; from there he had gone briefly to the Admiralty as Fourth Sea Lord, then to be Commander-in-Chief, Mediterranean, and finally First Sea Lord. Not quite finally: the naval cadet of 1913 who, as his biographers tell, dedicated himself to wiping out the slur on the Battenberg dynasty (the removal of his father, Prince Louis) by becoming First Sea Lord himself, went one better. From 1959 to 1965 he held the super-Service-chief's appointment, Chief of the Defence Staff.

Seven Defence Ministers occupied the political equivalent of his job in that period. Mountbatten remained rock-like amid the changes—but nothing like a rock in the mobility of his departmental explorations and re-groupings. Old White-

Old Admiralty Building :
West Front on Horse
Guards Parade, 1967

Old Admiralty Building:
East Front on Whitehall,
1967

hall stalwarts likened him to Lord Trenchard for the speed and
skill with which he rushed his reforms through. In the new
Defence building they called him 'the Hound of the Batten-
bergs'. Mountbatten, a 'combined operations' expert from
the days when the expression had no universal meaning, foresaw a complete amalgamation of top organisation and Service
command, a more drastic unification of the Defence system
than Chiefs of Staff committees ventured to think about—and
went some way towards getting them.

The Five-year Plan he launched at the Admiralty in 1957
streamlined the Royal Navy and made the transformation
apparent even to outsiders. The first step—a controversial one
—was the removal of large numbers of officers and men in
obsolescent or overloaded categories—the nearest thing to an
'axe' any post-war Admiralty had applied; and Their Lordships
made sure that most of those retired were suitably compensated—
extravagantly compensated, in the opinion of some M.P.s.

Next came grievous news for sentimentalists, when the grand
roll-call and death-warrant of historic bases and commands
was read out. Harwich and Scapa were scheduled for closure,
and continuous links with Grand Fleet days were broken—in the
case of Harwich, links which went back to the Dutch wars and
Mr Commissioner Batten.

The Home Fleet—not such an old title, this, but to most
naval men alive it meant *the* Fleet—had to be split up for
NATO, and reformed in the various unrecognisable guises
of that organisation into a group of task forces to fit the fighting
structure of the alliance.

Sheerness dockyard, which Samuel Pepys himself had helped
to lay out, was to close—it did, in 1960. Portland, an old
Channel Fleet haven and repair base, round which the ghosts
of Lord Charles Beresford and Sir Percy Scott angrily whispered, was marked for closure in 1959, with that bastion of the

N

East Indies station, Trincomalee, and that of the China Fleet, at Hong Kong. Malta dockyard, associated with every great fighting admiral from Saint Vincent and Nelson to Cunningham and Mountbatten himself, passed into the hands of a commercial firm. Eleven naval air stations fell at eleven strokes of the pen.

Of England's three patriarchal naval bases, Woolwich had long been abandoned to the Army and the merchants of the river. Deptford, its two-hundred-year-old Victualling Yard reduced to a skeleton, retained only traces of its connections with the Fleet. As for Chatham, the whole of the Nore Command, citadel of the port of London and of the Narrow Seas, controlling barracks, gunnery schools, Royal Marine depots and specialist training establishments, disappeared in 1961.

The Ordnance Board remained, as detached from Admiralty as it had ever been, no more a ground for naval captains and army colonels to wrangle over. In 1967 it had an air vice-marshal for its president.

The creeks and inlets round Chatham, Harwich, the Forth and the Clyde, Devonport and Portsmouth, emptied out their jumbles of ships in reserve, and only a small percentage of the wartime and pre-war squadrons and flotillas survived a ruthless age-and-adaptability test. The battleship, as a class, was dead. The Admiralty scrapped H.M.S. *Vanguard*, the last, the greatest, the most expensive and the least employed, in 1961.

The Royal Navy that year consisted of a hundred and forty ships, one-tenth of its wartime strength. Even the Admiralty felt the pinch, and shuddered to the topmasts of the Ripley block when the severity of the cuts was brought home to civil servants by a reduction in Admiralty staff from 144,000 in 1961 to 142,000 in 1962.

Out of a chrysalis secrecy in the new scientific establishments, the new Navy emerged blinking. The Naval Estimates for 1960 touched a record £400 millions, and were to be exceeded every year as long as the Admiralty lasted. Most of the money went not on new construction, but on conversions and new weapons and equipment. It provided for the transformation of an aircraft-carrier, H.M.S. *Bulwark*, into 'commando-carrier' and the development of fantastically costly gadgets like 'Seaslug' to arm the new guided-missile destroyers. (Traditionalists objected to the term 'destroyer': they were rather bigger than some wartime cruisers.)

The Fisher mentality, which measured hitting power by weight of projectile, was still in evidence. Inside the Fleet and out, gunnery men condemned the Admiralty for stuffing ships full of instruments and leaving out the armament. But, along with the ships and the dockyards, the Navy was discarding its traditional weapons. "We have stopped doing research on guns," Lord Selkirk told an audience in 1958—a First Lord pronouncement that Fisher at his most prophetic could never have forecast.

Since Edwardian days the naval path to promotion had been by way of the gunnery school. Gunnery officers had been well represented on the Board of Admiralty for sixty years. The last generation was in office, and who was to replace them? That year an 'airman', Admiral Sir Caspar John, became First Sea Lord.

The Earl of Selkirk, just before he handed over his office to Lord Carrington in 1959, saw the keel of H.M.S. *Dreadnought* laid—the second *Dreadnought*, a nuclear-powered submarine, built in not much more time than the first, and even more a strategical pace-setter, or upsetter. H.M.S. *Valiant* followed her and the Controller's department was understood to have a whole range of ultra-surrealist underwater monsters on the drawing-boards. They would rate four to five thousand tons,

N 2

it was said—which was getting close to the size of a capital ship when the strategists of old had seen in their crystal balls ' submarines as big as battleships '.

For some years the Royal Navy had had no minister in the Cabinet. In 1960 the Parliamentary and Financial Secretary dropped off the list of junior ministers and only the First Lord remained a member of the administration. The Admiralty was sailing to the edge of its world, the end of its independent existence. Committed to fleets of small numbers and a wholly small-ship Service (the new aircraft-carriers having somehow been lost sight of), it was acting with uncharacteristic vigour, of which the submission of the highest Estimates in history— £440 millions—in 1963 was only one manifestation. When, by what the editor of *Jane's Fighting Ships* called ' a momentous decision of purely political expedience, arrived at under the aegis of a superior foreign power ', the Government presented Their Lordships with Polaris, they accepted it and developed it with an élan that might have drawn a reluctant nod of approval from Lord Fisher himself. Polaris, they recognised, provided food for more re-thinking and reorganisation than steam, or ironclads or aviation had ever done for Their Lordships of long ago.

Polaris (a nuclear weapon operated from a nuclear underwater craft) meant the creation of a big new department at the Admiralty under the direction of a rear-admiral entitled Chief Polaris Executive. The Controller proposed to build four Polaris submarines; proposal accepted *nem. con.* and put in hand with alacrity. For their refitting base the Admiralty selected Rosyth, which seemed to assure the continued existence of at least one naval dockyard as firmly as anything in the chop-and-change world of mid-sixties Admiralty could be assured. As Their Lordships once appointed an ' Air ' Sea Lord to their

Board, so they might decide one day to appoint a 'Polaris' Sea Lord. There could even be a 'First Sea Lord and Chief of Polaris', or some such dignitary.

This dignitary will not, however, preside over the professional side of the Board of Admiralty. In March 1963 Mr Peter Thorneycroft, Minister of Defence, announced a new move in the gradual overhaul of the Defence system. There was to be a single unified command under the (new title) Secretary of State for Defence. The First Lord of the Admiralty would lose his old cumbersome title and get a cumbersome new one: Minister of State for Defence (Royal Navy). Similar changes would apply to the other two Service chiefs. Instead of Admiralty, War Office and Air Ministry, there would be three 'Boards of Management'—which sounded like a concession to that school of thought which, ever since mid-Victorian days, had been advising Whitehall to take a leaf out of the book of big-business methods.

A small constitutional problem arose. (It always did, whenever someone started interfering with the worm-eaten pillars of the Admiralty.) Their Lordships would be Their Lordships no longer; they had to descend to a status resembling that of the old Principal Officers—Navy Commissioners, not Lords Commissioners. They would be entitled no longer to 'execute the office of Lord High Admiral'; and that office, going 'out of commission', must revert to the Lord High Admiral.

Her Majesty the Queen might have perpetuated some interesting ceremonial usages by conferring the title on her consort, as Queen Anne had done before her; but she followed the example Queen Anne had set at a later date, and took it herself.

Mr Thorneycroft's proposals, having been gently broken to the Service chiefs beforehand, became effective within one year, on 1st April 1964. The Admiralty, which had stepped out in its dying years from well behind to well in front of its Service rivals in the Defence parade, remained conscious enough of its ancient titles and privileges to protect them where it could. It gained one considerable victory: over the expression ' Navy Board of the Defence Council ', which matched ' Army Board ' and ' Air Board ' quite logically. One thing Their Lordships were obstinate in securing, before they lost their own titles, was the continuation of a name under which the integrity and immutability of naval ésprit had been preserved from century to century, while ships and men passed by; and, before it went into print, ' Navy Board ' became ' Admiralty Board '.

30 After 1964

The last group of Lords Commissioners assembled six months before the final dissolution of the Board of Admiralty. All but three were fairly new to their posts. The reconstituted Conservative Government (Sir Alec Douglas-Home's) included among its junior ministers a famous name as First Lord: Earl Jellicoe, son of the old Admiral of the Fleet. Sir David Luce had been First Sea Lord for two months, and continued in that office. The only members left over from the previous year were Sir Royston Wright (Second Sea Lord), Sir Michael Le Fanu (Third Sea Lord) and Sir Clifford Jarrett (Permanent Secretary).

An interesting newcomer fulfilled the expectations which the convergence of the specialist and non-specialist branches of naval officers had stimulated throughout the fifties. He was Rear-Admiral Raymond S. Hawkins, Fourth Sea Lord and Vice-Controller, an engineer officer and the first non-executive sailor ever to be appointed to the Board of Admiralty. His branch had travelled some distance since the not-so-far-off days when naval engineers pursued their troglodytic existence in a world of coal dust and lubricating oil and scarcely dared set foot on the quarter-deck, far less the bridge.

The next step, logically, would be to raise an engineer or electrical officer to the Controllership to direct shipbuilding and design. The apotheosis of technical officers was at hand. The Navy's ruling professional body, jealously reserved like the captaincy of a warship for the seaman branches—gunnery officers, signal officers, navigators and 'salt horses' (deck officers without specialist qualifications)—had to be prepared to yield to the scientists, the technologists and the mechanics.

At the same date, October 1963, the process was already gathering momentum one step beneath Board Room level. The seamen admirals in charge of the dockyards at Portsmouth and Devonport made way for engineer Admirals Superintendent; and an electrical engineer became Admiral Superintendent at the Polaris base, Rosyth. The command structure for shore establishments which Navy Board and Admiralty had erected on Tudor foundations changed too. Boards of Management took over the old tangled nets of the independent departments, in which you had had to serve a lifetime to know your way about, where the Superintending Naval Store Officer never knew what the Superintending Victualling Store Officer was doing and where ships' officers of great experience needed the advice of delegations of constructors, engineers and electricians from the different offices of the dockyards to show them which departments the repair jobs on warships came under.

The last Board of Admiralty had barely got through 'Guinny-Binny' and settled down before it surrendered its powers. (They had extended beyond the Service, incidentally: a Lord Commissioner could sign a warrant to arrest both servicemen and civilians.) On 31st March at sunset the silken red-and-golden Admiralty Flag came down from the roof above the Old Admiralty building. The massive silver verge, staff of Admiralty, went with it to Buckingham Palace. (Her Majesty kept the verge and returned the flag.) The last Admiralty Commission, a certificate in a glass box, joined the trophies in the Board Room.

Earl Jellicoe and his colleagues, after the final session of the Board of Admiralty, did not take a last look and a sentimental farewell of the Board Room. They were back next day in their usual places, for the first session of the Admiralty Board, continuing the unfinished business of the previous meeting. Only the name had changed, and that not much. It did not accelerate or hold back the slow pace of their advance towards integration.

Nor did any cataclysmic shock of dismissals and migrations disrupt the work of the departments. Their transformation had been going on for years, their staffs had accepted too many changes of nomenclature since the war to let one more change disturb them. Obedient to the process of transition, several offices had moved across the road to the War Office and the new Defence building. Army and Air Board employees penetrated into the old naval strongholds of the Ripley block, Spring Gardens and the apartments above the Arch.

The Parliamentary and Financial Secretary of the Admiralty (as though that were not enough of a mouthful) became the Parliamentary Under-Secretary of State for Defence (Royal Navy). The Secretary of the Admiralty—heir of the Clerk of the Acts, heir of the Keeper of the King's Ships—became the Second Permanent Under-Secretary of State for Defence (Royal Navy). The First and Second Sea Lords moved up to the Defence Board, and took the policy of the Fleet with them. Admiralty Board meetings took on a cosier complexion.

The fall of the British Admiralty from its high authority as a great department of State which had been so much a part of the grandeur of country and Empire brings us to 31st March 1964. Glancing past that date, over the three years following, we see that integration correctly spelt the opposite of disintegration, that the flagless veteran sailed on, full of fight though relegated to a junior squadron, with its own unique characteristics and outlook unimpaired; that it still had something to contribute to Britain's standing as a world power.

When the Labour Government returned to Westminster in October 1964, more than one politician dropping hints about office confessed that the old glory of the First Lord's post (a term many preferred to ' Minister of Defence brackets Royal Navy close the brackets') had its attractions, though the power and patronage attached to it had mostly gone. More than one confided that he would as soon be at Admiralty House as at Number Ten.

Mr Denis Healey succeeded Mr Thorneycroft as Defence Minister, and prepared to take Admiralty House for himself. Mr Christopher Mayhew replaced Earl Jellicoe—Mayhew who decided, as First Lords of recent decades had nearly always done, that in a crunch between Navy and Government his place was with the Navy. The crunch came quite soon—one of those periodic crises of Admiralty which had given Beatty, Fisher, Lord George Hamilton and others their sleepless nights in bygone days; complicated for Mayhew by the presence of a Minister of Defence between him and the Prime Minister.

Not all the big-ship men had gone to their graves with H.M.S. *Vanguard*. Most naval experts looked on aircraft-carriers as the modern capital ship, the main Fleet unit. When Mayhew learned that the aircraft-carrier programme was doomed, he asked the Defence Minister's permission to put the Admiralty case before Parliament—but was refused, until the fatal decision had been made. Then the Board Room was reopened—it had not seen a meeting for weeks—for a discussion with the Sea Lords and another fateful decision. The First Lord left the meeting to send in his resignation, and Admiral Luce, the First Sea Lord, requested permission to retire.

Across the years, in that memorable setting, under the eye of Lord Nelson at one end and royal Clarence at the other, similar threats had been heard from the Navy's chieftains, both civil and professional. Mr Mayhew and Admiral Luce were the first pair actually to carry out their threats since Gladstone's era. 'The feelings of all of us were deep,' the ex-Navy Minister wrote of that meeting, 'and I think we were glad of the Board's tradition of extreme formality, which helped us not to show them.'

Most outsiders make no attempt and Defence Ministry officials themselves no pretence at times, to understand the complexities of the triple-Service machinery in Whitehall. Ask in that area for the Admiralty today and you may get the reply Lord Chatfield once got when, on a night of celebration, he enlisted the aid of a policeman to get him to his office: "Admiralty, sir? Never heard of it."

Voters at the 1966 elections, according to opinion polls, were 'not interested in Defence'. There is a vague impression abroad that the Services have sunk their identity, that they are only recognisable now by their uniforms, and that even that distinction will soon disappear. (In Canada it has already done so.) Some of the magic went out of the Navy when sonorous old titles like 'First Lord of the Admiralty' went out of fashion. But the Navy's governing council is not finished yet.

After 1964, the unassailable personification of Admiralty remained: the Lord High Admiral, the name at the top of page one of the Navy List, represented by the Queen. Beneath it the short string of antique titles began: Vice-Admiral of the United Kingdom and Lieutenant of the Admiralty, Rear-Admiral of the United Kingdom, Vice-Admiral of the Province of Ulster. . . .

The Admiralty Board, which met but rarely in the Board Room, still consisted of eleven members. The new posts which had crept in among them had not, so far, the ring of grandeur formerly associated with the Lords Commissioners:

The Secretary of State for Defence; top of the Defence

pyramid and Chairman of each of the three Service Boards, Admiralty, Army and Air.

The Minister of State for Defence (Royal Navy): successor to the First Lord of the Admiralty, and the Vice-Chairman (who in practice usually took the chair) of the Admiralty Board.

The Parliamentary Under-Secretary of State for Defence (Royal Navy): the former Parliamentary and Financial Secretary.

The Chief of the Naval Staff and First Sea Lord: the senior sailor on the Board. His titles were reversed, and ' Sea Lord ' was another anachronism to which the Navy, for the time being, would tenaciously cling.

The Chief of Naval Personnel and Second Sea Lord: his next step was to be into the wider sphere of Defence and the tongue-twisting appellation of Chief Adviser on Personnel and Logistics (CAPL) to the Secretary of State for Defence.

The Controller of the Navy: old title ' Third Sea Lord and Controller '. Another archaism preserved.

The Vice-Chief of the Naval Staff: originally Deputy Chief.

The Deputy Chief of the Naval Staff: originally Assistant Chief.

The Chief of Naval Supplies and Transport and Vice-Controller: old title ' Fourth Sea Lord '.

The Chief Scientist, Royal Navy.

The Second Permanent Under-Secretary of State for Defence (Royal Navy): the former Permanent Secretary of the Admiralty.

Naval assistants and private secretaries, about thirty of them, congregated round the Board as before. In 1967, the Ministers of State for each of the three Services had gone, and two Ministers of Defence had entered the hierarchy in their place: one of Equipment and one for Administration. They fitted in between the Secretary of State and the Under-Secretary, were concerned with all three Services and were expected to attend the Board meetings of each, but not as full members. The Under-Secretary became Vice-Chairman of the Board and usually, like the Minister of State he had replaced, took the chair.

The divisions controlled by the Admiralty Board, dispersed through Whitehall and farther afield, flourished as Government departments do in any soil. Just before the Second World War they numbered about forty, today there are ninety-three, from the newest and most secret (Under-surface Weapons, Polaris Weapons), through the old-established (Naval Intelligence, Plans, Operations, Fuel, Movements, Trade, W.R.N.S., Fleet Maintenance, Naval Construction, Chaplain of the Fleet, Signals) to the really antiquated (Greenwich Hospital, Hydrographer of the Navy).

To the stranger it is all very confusing. To those who know their Admiralty the essential safety of the scaffolding is apparent, and its unity and strength seem to gain from the assaults that are made on it, and from the splitting and fusing and scattering of component parts.

Naval officers from the Fleet, of the rank of commander and upwards as a rule, still expect to serve at least one three-year period at the Admiralty in their careers, as director or naval assistant in one of those departments where the permanent staff is supposed to benefit from an occasional whiff of ozone.

Once inside the Old Admiralty building even today you are enveloped in the aura of its function. There is an atmosphere quite unlike the atmosphere of any other Government department. You are in the Navy's administrative world just as surely as, when stepping on board a warship, you are in the Navy's executive.

The officials who stream through its portals and flash their passes at a type-cast Admiralty messenger are soldiers, airmen, sailors and civilians. They all encounter the stony stare of

Admiral Viscount Nelson from his plinth opposite the door.

This building administers an empire—bureaucratically speaking—not much different for all the comings and goings of the years from the empire Lord Barham and Sir James Graham ruled: the Home Commands, Home Fleet, Portsmouth, Plymouth, Scotland and Northern Ireland; the commands abroad, Mediterranean, Middle East, Far East, South Atlantic and South America (two of these, however, withdrawn in 1967 and others threatened).

There are still eight royal dockyards at home and abroad; seven royal victualling yards; innumerable aircraft yards and air stations, spare parts distributing centres, machinery depots, armament depots and factories, scientific and research establishments up and down the country. The Admiralty still carries the stigma and, so they say, lives up to it, of accommodating and treating its civil servants just that little bit less comfortably than other departments of State; still keeps its pay-roll predominantly masculine.

The inner chambers and private offices, the secret rooms in which so much of the drama of Britain's story was enacted, to which entry was ever denied to all but an important few, are typing pools, filing rooms and registries today, of all three Service sub-ministries. The Admiralty has changed since the great take-over of 1964, one cannot deny that. It has changed the people who go to work there, bringing them under the influence of its ' world apart ', teaching them the mystical precepts of Pepys and Anson, Barham and Graham, Fisher and Beatty, Chatfield and Pound.

How should it be otherwise? Those whose place of duty is the Old Admiralty building, or the offices along Spring Gardens and on the Mall frontage, are surrounded all day by portrait galleries of ships and seamen and administrators of the old Navy. A curious collection of Admiralty bric-à-brac whispers to them in the corridors and ante-rooms: old globes, old chart cases, old tactical diagrams and instructions for working the telegraph. The panelling and stonework they gaze on disclose here and there a triton or trireme, a ' crown-and-anchor ' emblem or ' wooden walls ' device, worn perhaps but not easily to be effaced.

The carpeting, to many who tread it, is already ' the deck '. The very windows, on the upper floors around the Board Room, seem to rattle to a breeze from the Narrow Seas or the Western Approaches. When the clerks and typists at lunch-time on a spring day take their sandwiches out of doors, they sit in Saint James's Park, just across from the old building; and from there they watch the masts and triatic stays on the roof of the Admiralty riding across the London sky, like the rigging of a great warship on a shifting backcloth of cirrus cloud, somewhere down in Trade Wind latitudes.

A Short Bibliography

Encyclopaedia Britannica.
Dictionary of National Biography.
Annual Register.
Naval Review.
Jane's Fighting Ships.
Mariner's Mirror.
The Times.
Navy.

Abernethy, Cecil: *Mr Pepys of Seething Lane.* W. H. Allen, 1958.
Anon. (1807): *A New Key to the Proceedings of a Late Administration.*
Anon. (1839): *The Navy: Letters upon the Actual Crisis.*
Anon. (1847): *Remarks upon the Conduct of the Naval Administration.*

Beresford, Lord Charles: *Memoirs.* Methuen, 1914.
Briggs, Sir John: *Naval Administrations, 1827-1892.* Low, 1897.
Bryant, Sir Arthur: *The Turn of the Tide.* Collins, 1957.

Callender, Sir Geoffrey and F. H. Hinsley: *The Naval Side of British History.* Chatto & Windus, 1960.
Capper, H. D.: *Aft from the Hawsehole.* Faber & Gwyer, 1927.
Chalmers, W. S.: *David, Earl Beatty.* Hodder & Stoughton, 1951.
Chapman, Hester W.: *The Tragedy of Charles II.* Cape, 1964.
Chatfield, Lord: *The Navy and Defence.* Heinemann, 1947.
Churchill, W. S.: *The Gathering Storm.* Cassell, 1948.
Cooper, Duff: *Old Men Forget.* Hart-Davis, 1953.
Corbett, Julian S.: *Drake and the Tudor Navy.* Longmans, 1899.
Creswell, Admiral Sir William: *Close to the Wind.* Heinemann, 1965.
Cork and Orrery, Earl of: *My Naval Life.* Hutchinson, 1942.
Cunningham of Hyndhope, Viscount: *A Sailor's Odyssey.* Hutchinson, 1951.

de Chair, Admiral Sir Dudley: *The Sea is Strong.* Harrap, 1961.

Fremantle, Admiral Sir Sydney: *My Naval Career.* Hutchinson, 1949.

Gardner, J. A.: *Above and Under Hatches.* Batchworth Press, 1955.
Greville, Lord: *Diaries.* Longmans, 1897.

Hamilton, Lord George: *Parliamentary Reminiscences.* Murray, 1917.
Hannay, David: *A Short History of the Royal Navy, 1217-1815.* Methuen, 1898.

Hedderwick, J. B.: *The Captain's Clerk*. Hutchinson, 1957.

Hervey, John Augustus: *Journal*. Kimber, 1953.

James, Admiral Sir William: *The Portsmouth Letters*. Macmillan, 1946.

Jenkins, C. A.: *Days of a Dogsbody*. Harrap, 1946.

Kerr, Mark: *Prince Louis of Battenberg*. Longmans, 1934.

Leadam, I. S.: *The Political History of England, 1702-1760*. Longmans, 1921.

Lewis, Michael: *A Social History of the Navy, 1793-1815*. Allen & Unwin, 1960.

Lewis, Michael: *The Navy in Transition*. Hodder & Stoughton, 1965.

Lloyd, Christopher: *The Nation and the Navy*. Cresset Press, 1961.

Lowis, Geoffrey: *Fabulous Admirals*. Putnam, 1957.

Marcus, G. J.: *A Naval History of England*. Longmans, 1961.

Marder, Arthur J.: *Fear God and Dread Nought*. Cape, 1952-59.

Oppenheim, M.: *A History of the Administration of the Royal Navy, etc.*, 1509-1660. Shoestring Press (Bailey Bros.), 1896.

Padfield, Peter: *Aim Straight*. Hodder & Stoughton, 1966.

Pakington, Humphrey: *Bid Time Return*. Chatto & Windus, 1958.

Parkinson, C. Northcote: *Portsmouth Point*. Hodder & Stoughton and Liverpool University Press, 1948.

Pepys, Samuel: *Diary and Correspondence*. Cassell, 1886.

Talbot-Booth, E. C.: *The Royal Navy*. Sampson Low, 1942.

Templewood, Viscount: *Nine Troubled Years*. Collins, 1954.

Index

A